THE ORIGINS OF WOMEN'S ACTIVISM

The
Origins of
Women's
Activism

New York and Boston,
1797–1840

Anne M. Boylan

The University of North Carolina Press

Chapel Hill and London

This volume was published with the generous assistance
of the Greensboro Women's Fund of the University of
North Carolina Press. Founding Contributors: Linda
Arnold Carlisle, Sally Schindel Cone, Anne Faircloth,
Bonnie McElveen Hunter, Linda Bullard Jennings,
Janice J. Kerley (in honor of Margaret Supplee Smith),
Nancy Rouzer May, and Betty Hughes Nichols.

Library of Congress Cataloging-in-Publication Data
Boylan, Anne M., 1947–
The origins of women's activism: New York and Boston,
1797–1840 / Anne M. Boylan.
p. cm.   Includes bibliographical references and index.
ISBN 0-8078-2730-4 (cloth: alk. paper)
ISBN 0-8078-5404-2 (pbk.: alk. paper)
1. Women—United States—Societies and clubs—
History.   2. Women social reformers—United States
—History.   3. Women political activists—United
States—History.   I. Title.
HQ1904 .B69 2002   305.4'06'073—dc21   2002001556

CLOTH   06 05 04 03 02   5 4 3 2 1
PAPER   06 05 04 03 02   5 4 3 2 1

For Peter
and for Michael and David

CONTENTS

ACKNOWLEDGMENTS

BECAUSE THIS BOOK HAS been a long time on its journey from idea to reality, it is a special pleasure to be able to thank all the people and institutions who helped it on its way. I am especially indebted to the librarians and archivists who provided access to research materials, answered questions, and took the time to find sources for me. In the course of my research, I spent many happy hours at four great research institutions: the New York Public Library, the Boston Public Library, the New-York Historical Society, and the Schlesinger Library at Radcliffe College. The staffs at all four were most helpful and welcoming. I want particularly to single out the Milstein Division of Local History and Genealogy at the New York Public Library; without its rich resources, my search for obscure obituaries, marriage records, genealogies, and genealogical indexes would have been impossible. In addition, I thank the staffs of the following institutions: the New York Public Library Rare Books and Manuscripts Division; the New York Weill Cornell Medical Center Archives; the Columbia University Library Rare Books and Manuscripts Division; the Brooklyn Historical Society; the University of Delaware Library, Interlibrary Loan Department, and Archives; the Presbyterian Historical Society, Philadelphia; the Massachusetts State Library, Boston; the University of Massachusetts–Boston Library Manuscripts Division; the Massachusetts Historical Society; the Congregational Library, Boston; and the Boston Public Library Rare Books and Manuscripts Room. I am also grateful to the staffs at the New York City Mission Society, Inwood House in New York City, and the Boston Widows' Society, who made room in crowded quarters for a researcher interested in their organizational records.

Among the many efficient and interested librarians who assisted me, I want especially to thank Scott Taylor at the Georgetown University Library and Elizabeth Moger at the Haviland Records Room of the New York Friends Yearly Meeting. Other archivists, librarians, and historians answered queries or checked local records for me. They include Robert S. Cox of the William L. Clements Library, University of Michigan; the staff at the New York City Municipal Archives; Johanna Herring, archivist of Wabash College, Crawfordsville, Indiana; David Arthur, College of Arts and Sciences, Aurora University, Aurora, Illinois; the University Archives staff at Furman University; Mary J. Oates of the History Department at Regis College; Robert Johnson-Lally of the Archives of the Archdiocese of Boston; Rhona Neuwirth of Graham-Windham Services, New York City; John Van Horne, Philip Lapsansky, and the staff at the Library Company of Philadelphia; William Asadorian of the Queens Borough Public Library; Judith Metz, S.C., editor of the Elizabeth Bayley Seton Papers; Jewell Anderson Dalrymple of the Georgia Historical Society; Jay P. Dolan of Notre Dame University; Chris Kauffman, editor of *U.S. Catholic Historian*; J. Charles Swift; and Lori Beth Finkelstein.

Many colleagues and friends have actively supported my efforts over a long span of time. From the beginning, Ronald Walters and Anne Firor Scott had faith in the project, a faith that sustained me more often than they know. So, too, did conversations with Nancy Hewitt, Lori Ginzberg, Darlene Clark Hine, Leslie Friedman Goldstein, Susan Porter, Lynn Weiner, Susan Porter Benson, the late Winifred Wandersee, Joanne Meyerowitz, Jeanne Boydston, Nancy Cott, Kathryn Kish Sklar, Maris Vinovskis, Leslie Maria Harris, J. William Frost, Deborah Van Broekhoven, Lisa Norling, Catherine E. Kelly, Erica Armstrong, James Brophy, Gail Murray, and Joseph Hawes. Susan Porter, Debra Gold Hansen, Lee Chambers-Schiller, and Shirley Yee generously shared research notes, sources, and biographical materials with me; with each of them, I was also able to share the less tangible experience of conversing about long-dead women in the present tense. At one point, Evelyn Brooks Higginbotham and Sharon Harley gave me a valuable lesson about sources for African American women's history; I have tried not to forget it.

I have benefited greatly from comments on papers and public talks. The following individuals and groups have my warm appreciation for taking the time to read and respond to parts of this project: Anne Firor Scott; Carroll Smith-Rosenberg; Jean Fagan Yellin; Robert Gross; Darlene Clark Hine; Susan

Porter Benson; Barbara J. Berg; the late Annette K. Baxter; Tamara Hareven and the Family Research Group at the University of Delaware; Sandra Harding, Marian Palley, and the women's studies faculty at the University of Delaware; Joanne Meyerowitz and the Cincinnati Seminar on the City; Joan Cadden and her colleagues at the Kenyon College History Department; Janice Radway; Gerda Lerner; Guy Alchon; and Steven Buechler. My colleague Christine Heyrman, through her thoughtful reading of two chapters, not only gave me helpful advice but also boosted my confidence most graciously. At a conference in Hanover, Germany, entitled "Women's Associations in Bourgeois Societies," Rita Huber-Sperl and Manuela Thurner welcomed me warmly and facilitated a series of discussions from which I benefited greatly.

Over the years, members of my monthly seminar have read several of these chapters; for their comments, questions, and suggestions, I thank Adrienne Berney, Marguerite Connolly, Janet Davidson, Marie Laberge, Tina Manko, Jalynn Olsen Padilla, Sandra Pryor, Nina de Angeli Walls, and Regina Blaszczyk.

Lori Ginzberg and another reader provided thoughtful and appreciative evaluations of the entire manuscript. I am deeply grateful for the time and care they gave to the task and for helpful suggestions that improved the final version.

For financial assistance that enabled me to travel to archives or have time for writing, I thank the National Endowment for the Humanities for a summer fellowship; the University of Delaware for a General University Research grant and three semester-long sabbaticals; the Radcliffe Research Scholars Fund; and the American Historical Association's Beveridge Fund. Parts of some chapters appeared in very different form in the *Journal of American History*, *American Quarterly*, and *Journal of the Early Republic*. I am grateful to those journals for permission to reprint that material.

My friends have been hearing about this book forever and cheering me on. I appreciate the interest and unflagging support of Leslie Goldstein, Phil Goldstein, Carole Marks, René Marks, Kathy Steen, Drew Faust, Charles Rosenberg, Joanne Meyerowitz, Howard Johnson, and the late, much-missed Howard Rabinowitz.

It has been a delight to work once again with Chuck Grench, this time at the University of North Carolina Press. His confidence in my work and the ease with which he guided the manuscript through the press's deliberative process have been soul-warming indeed.

My family buoyed me in ways large and small. At a crucial moment, my brother John Felix Boylan assumed domestic and filial tasks so that I could get the first draft finished. My sisters Mary and Bridget Boylan sought out informational tidbits, supplied endless streams of encouragement, and, just when I needed them, came for helpful visits. My mother-in-law, Kate Kolchin, was unfailingly interested and supportive, providing wonderful meals and good conversation as I made her home my base for yet another trip to the New York Public Library. My mother, Brigid Boylan, was always willing to be proud and to ask how it was going. Peter Kolchin has lived with this project from its inception, enduring research trips and authorial misery and reading endless article and chapter drafts. All the while, his encouragement pushed me to reach beyond my grasp; I hope the final product validates his faith in my abilities as a historian. Michael and David have lived with this project their entire lives; now that they are grown and it is done, it's time to celebrate!

THE ORIGINS OF WOMEN'S ACTIVISM

The Female Asylum; the Orphan Asylum Society; the Society for the Relief of Respectable, Aged, Indigent Females; the Widows' Society; the Roman Catholic Asylum for the Children of Widows and Widowers; the Afric-American Female Intelligence Society; the Association for the Benefit of Colored Orphans; the Abyssinian Benevolent Daughters of Esther Association . . . These evocatively named organizations, and dozens of others like them, were the projects of New York and Boston women who, in the era spanning the 1790s through the 1830s, threw time, energy, skill, resources, and talents into what modern Americans would term volunteer work. As women's associations launched a variety of religious, benevolent, charitable, mutual aid, and reform projects, their founders and leaders set out together on new seas of opportunity and activism, collecting individual women almsgivers into entire fleets of charitable laborers. Some groups set a focused course concentrating on raising money for a single purpose—such as supporting Protestant missionaries—but others encompassed as much activity as a modern United Way agency: running institutions such as orphanages, hiring employees, placing neglected children in foster homes, and lobbying for municipal funding. Whether substantial or slight, each vessel that women organizers built had its own distinctive shape and appearance; the arrival of first a few, then many such vessels altered once and for all the forms of women's charitable labor. Simply by banding together, women leaders and their supporters acquired a way to pursue individual and group interests—of class, gender, religion, race, ethnicity, or some combination thereof—and validated collective female action. In turn, women's associations shaped urban histories in ways large and small.

To historians of women, the extent of women's organizing during the era of nation-formation is hardly news. Ever since pioneering researchers such as Mary Beard, Mary Bosworth Treudley, and Eleanor Flexner identified women's organizations as crucial mechanisms by which historical change occurred, historians have produced a large and significant body of work on women's organizing, establishing the import of women's associations, both for the history of women and for the development of communities, states, and the nation.[1] Although considerable attention has gone to the large national groups that emerged after the Civil War (the Young Women's Christian Association [YWCA], the Woman's Christian Temperance Union [WCTU], federations of women's clubs, suffrage associations, Protestant foreign missionary organizations), and we now have an impressive array of works establishing the crucial importance of women's collective activism to the creation of the modern welfare state, the local groups that emerged in virtually every urban locale in the antebellum years have also received a goodly share of scholarly attention.[2]

For a long time, that attention produced an interpretive image drawn in clear, bold strokes. Until well into the 1970s, historians depicted a scene of linear progress, from the timid early efforts of missionary support groups to the full-blown reformist campaigns of the 1830s that aimed to eradicate slavery and other ills from American society. Scholars assumed that women gradually built upon each other's experiences, escalating their group activities from small- to large-scale, and from benevolence to reform. They also traced a direct developmental line from those early nineteenth-century societies to women's rights activism, suggesting that an individual's participation in women's associations provided the necessary preconditions for developing a feminist consciousness. The sketch was appealing: one could imagine solid matrons throwing down their missionary society subscription lists in order to pick up abolitionist petition forms, or serious-minded young women letting charitable sewing fall from their laps as they stood to grasp women's rights banners. But it proved untenable.[3]

Challenges to the sketch redrew its outlines, filled in its details, and reworked its overall pattern. If members of the very earliest women's missionary societies, formed around 1800, met in members' homes and confined themselves to sending small sums of money to male-run organizations, their counterparts in forming benevolent associations often met publicly, acquired charters of incorporation, petitioned successfully for public monies, and undertook ambitious aid programs. Temporal change did not bring convergence either. In the 1830s, as some women suffered intense public wrath because their organizations attacked slavery, prostitution, and male drunkenness, others met quietly in each other's homes to form yet more missionary fund-raising groups. Throughout the antebellum years, women founded both small-scale single-focus associations, and ambitious multi-purpose ones. Moreover, while some societies began small and gradually expanded, others contracted over time. The new portrait was substantially more complicated, detailed, multi-dimensional, and complex than the old.[4]

Historians also decisively dispelled the assumption that the path from joining organizations to attending women's rights conventions was straight and swiftly traversed. Studying white women's church groups in New England, for instance, Nancy Cott pointed to their dual potential—"to encourage women's independence and self-definition within a supportive community, or to accommodate them to a limited, clerically defined role"—and suggested that involvement in some groups might actually have prevented women from disputing their subordinate status within the existing gender system by fortifying their sense of value and self-worth. Suzanne Lebsock's study of Petersburg, Virginia, confirmed Cott's intuition: southern white urban women participated in a full panoply of charitable organizations without ever developing a feminist consciousness or questioning the social institutions—most notably, slavery—that defined their lives. Looking at the issue through the lives of white feminist-abolitionists, Blanche Glassman Hersh found no correlation between their activism and previous participation in benevolent groups. Women in organized benevolence, she concluded, were "in no way defying tradition or questioning male authority"; feminist-abolitionists came to their activism by other routes. Nancy Hewitt's detailed study of women activists in Rochester, New York, provided a clear explanation for Hersh's conclusion: members of different women's organizations formed separate social networks and often had little in common with each other. Even as "ultraist" reformers in the 1830s began their attacks on slavery and sexual immorality, for example, benevolent society organizers continued to labor in missionary and educational fields; few crossed the divide to join radically reformist causes. Whereas women's work in charitable societies constituted "an indicator of, rather than a challenge to, female and familial status," Hewitt noted, the activism of reformers made them "both agents and objects of social change, . . . reproducers and reshapers of social order and social value." For benevolent or reformist women, organizational involvement expressed values, views, and commitments; it seldom changed them.[5]

Increasingly, too, it became clear that one pattern would not suffice to describe all women's early-republic and antebellum organizational activities. As long as historians relied upon the most available and abundant sources for women's associational history, they could portray some endeavors with a richly colorful palette, but supply only faint pencil marks to depict others. Entire canvases labeled "the history of women's organizations" could be filled with white, native-born, privileged, Protestant women. It was their organizations that kept and preserved records, guaranteed the permanence of their work, and built monuments to their labors. And despite the early reclamation work of historians such as Dorothy Porter Wesley, Dorothy Sterling, and Gerda Lerner, the less tangibly documented associations founded by African American and working-class white women were excluded from the frame or relegated to its margins.[6] If the more prominent nineteenth-century women activists and writers had pictured a unitary "woman" drawn in their own image, and assumed that all women shared common concerns as women, historians instead had to avoid confusing representation with reality and find ways to convey the unity and multiplicity, focus and diffusion, clarity and shadows, centrality and marginality that characterized the history of women's organizing.

Scholars have done so with excellent, focused studies of individual organizations, the variety of groups in some localities, and broad patterns of association evident across geography in the early nineteenth century. Studies of African American and working-class white women, for example, have uncovered the significance of mutual benefit and church-based assistance societies as supplements and alternatives to middle-class white benevolence. Local histories have extended our understanding of the range of activities in which women engaged, while also focusing our attention on the interaction between middle-class white women's charities and their working-class clients. The local approach has been particularly fruitful for underscoring the range and variety of organizing along class, racial, ethnic, and religious lines, while also highlighting the radicalism of groups, especially antislavery societies, that, however tentatively and incompletely, sought to bridge class and racial boundaries. Recent work has immeasurably enhanced historical understanding of rank-and-file African American and white abolitionists and their tension-fraught common labor in the Female Anti-Slavery Societies. Similarly, local studies, such as Mary P. Ryan's pioneering interpretation of women's associations and class formation in Utica, New York, have deepened scholars' understanding of the process whereby women came together to form associations. Most notably, Lori Ginzberg's broad-ranging analysis of "the work of benevolence" across a broad swath of time has taught scholars to look at the role of white Protestant women's associations in class formation and class definition, and to analyze the ways in which some women used rhetoric that claimed to encompass all women.[7]

Clearly, in taking up the subject of women's organizational labor, this book rests on a broad and sturdy platform. It builds on existing work but also departs from it, most notably by broadening the angle of vision to include the entire spectrum of women's associations in two cities while also concentrating on the very earliest decades of women's collective labor. Rather than treat each group separately, it analyzes together organizations that are African American and white, Catholic and Protestant, working class and middle class. By considering New York and Boston, two places where women's organizations first emerged and in which they thrived, it focuses attention on the process of organizing, the timing of organizational evolution (as later generations sailed into waters first charted in the 1790s and 1800s), and the importance of locality to process and timing. And by studying both the organizations women founded and led, and women leaders themselves, it seeks to connect the history of women's organizing to the larger stories of the era, especially the economic and political changes that accompanied nation-formation, but also the emergence of a new gender system with new ideals and realities of family life. Organizational records, whether in the form of lovingly preserved complete sets of minutes or scattered references in African American newspapers, become richer and more revealing when paired with biographical information on the women who sat in the meetings, kept the minutes, reported on their labors, and initiated and carried out decisions. Surviving materials from over seventy groups (45 in New York and 32 in Boston), combined with life histories of their founders and leaders (722 in New York and 420 in Boston) have enabled me to analyze both women's associations and association women, in order to understand how individuals fit their voluntary labor into their lives, and how collections of individuals used voluntary societies to achieve both personal and group goals.

In a key sense, this book is not so much about the historical questions "what happened and why," as the more specific question: "how." It asks how the ideologies and practices of postrevolutionary womanhood turned into the ideologies and practices of antebellum northern womanhood. To be more precise, it asks how the nineteenth-century gender system came into being. Along the way, it considers how that gender system came particularly to be characterized by an ideology stressing feminine and masculine spheres and distinguishing sharply between the "public" and the "private." And it suggests that the best way to answer these questions is to study women's organizations and women leaders.

Women first built associations with enduring foundations immediately after the American Revolution, in the two decades between 1795 and 1815. The 1820s and 1830s witnessed a proliferation and diversification in type and scope, so that by 1840 a startling array of woman-run organizations could be found in both cities. A crucial era of nation building, the period between the 1790s and the 1830s was one of rapid economic and political change, religious upheaval, and intense conflict over gender relations. What some historians term "the market revolution" or "the transition to capitalism," an economic transformation in which capitalist market relations increasingly came to pervade most aspects of daily life, occurred during those years, notably in the North. So, too, did the first great democratization of politics, in which increasing numbers of free white men gained access to full suffrage. The religious revivals of the Second Great Awakening energized older Protestant sects while also fueling the explosive growth of Methodist and Baptist churches, especially in the South and in the backcountry. Despite its roots in the colonies, in terms of sheer numbers, Roman Catholicism really arrived during those years. And a new, more democratically structured patriarchal family replaced the hierarchical one of old. Men would still exercise power over women, especially over wives, but fathers would no longer rule sons, and women's continuing subordination within families would be ideologically reconstructed through a discourse of equal-but-separate "spheres." Historians have described the transition to the new nineteenth-century gender system in various ways, most often by invoking two incommensurate images: the 1790s' "republican mother" and the 1830s' "true woman." What has been left unexplained is the path that women traveled —individually or collectively—from republican motherhood to nineteenth-century domesticity. The study of women's organizations and organization women, I believe, offers some crucial answers to the question of how the transition occurred.[8]

In Linda Kerber's powerful formulation, the concept of republican motherhood enabled historians to understand how, in the postrevolutionary years, Americans accommodated republican ideology to the maintenance of sex hierarchy. As Kerber explained, republican motherhood "merged the domestic domain . . . with the new public ideology of individual responsibility and civic virtue." Still, it was a "deeply ambivalent" ideology, with both progressive and conservative tendencies, requiring as it did that "egalitarian society [would rest] on . . . deference among a class of people—women—who would devote their efforts to service," especially to their families. That aspect of republican gender ideology received particular grounding in church publications, ministers' musings, and evangelical women's narratives. Struggling with their own and their churches' place in a democratic republic in which no sect would enjoy political pride of place, and seeking legitimacy for their endeavors, evangelical clergymen in upstart groups such as the Separate Baptists moved to exclude individual women from praying, exhorting, or voting in religious meetings. At the same moment, their counterparts in more established denominations, struck by the growth of women's collective activity in prayer groups and mission causes, sought to employ womanpower in the cause of denominational ascendancy while avoiding potential conflicts with individually ambitious women. Evangelical women themselves, drawn to republican motherhood by its affirmations of female virtue, indeed its "conflation of the virtuous with the feminine" (as Ruth Bloch put it), effectively blended republican and evangelical representations into a broadened compass of womanhood that permitted both individual and collective means of civic action. By 1815 or 1820, the experience of twenty (or more) years had shown evangelical women how to "merge the domestic domain with . . . the new ideology . . . of civic virtue," not alone as wives, mothers, and daughters, but also together, as members of women's organizations. A close examination of women's associations and their evolution, as well as scrutiny of the lives of their leaders, explains how the shift occurred.[9]

This approach can also offer historians answers to questions about women's responses to the changing experience of womanhood in the postrevolutionary era and to new evangelical constructions of womanhood. Historian Susan Juster, for example, chronicling the "suppression of women's voices" in New England's Separate Baptist churches as a result of the Revolution, found no evidence that Baptist women resisted their exclusion from church governance. Moreover, Juster considered puzzling the restoration of both speaking and voting rights by 1830. But surely the extraordinary proliferation of women's associations—both within and outside of the church—gave energetic women a place to exercise both voice and decision-making power at the turn of the century and afterwards. In forming female-based organizations, women reenacted in church work the supposedly parallel world of their familial roles; they saw themselves as partners with their ministers and husbands, adopted a complementary rather than equal model of gender relations, and readily embraced a separate arena of action in collective association. Although I agree with Kerber, Juster, and others that the complementary model remained predicated on male supremacy and the denigration of women who did not fit the "domestic ideal," I would still answer historian Elaine Crane's question "What could a republican mother do that a colonial mother could not?" by pointing to the new arenas for collective action that some women opened up for themselves—and others—in the 1790s. Individual women may have lost access to some forms of public action, but through their associations they gained access to others.[10]

In the pages that follow, I use the histories of New York and Boston organizations and the life-stories of their organizers to chronicle how the republican version of womanhood disappeared into an evangelical construction, largely as the result of evangelical efforts to capture and define republicanism—and the nation's future direction. The evangelicals' success, in turn, rested upon the strong appeal that their principles held for many postrevolutionary urban Americans, particularly the belief that social discipline stemmed from self-discipline, and the conviction that true personal freedom originated in voluntary submission to God's authority. Because evangelicalism connected personal liberty with religious principles, and self-discipline with public virtue, it had broad appeal to individuals struggling to balance the liberating effects of the eighteenth-century political revolution and early nineteenth-century economic revolution with the need for social and political order. Moreover, evangelicalism's particular appeal to women reflected its offer of both personal fulfillment and new social roles, an offer redeemed through organizational participation that provided structured opportunities for social usefulness and self-mastery, opportunities eventually available at all stages as a woman moved through her life course.[11]

In explaining how the marriage of evangelicalism and republicanism worked, I focus on the simultaneous emergence of women's organizations and new domestic ideals, and the "turn" that many groups took toward evangelical goals during the crucial years between 1810 and 1820. Examining the relationship between domesticity and organizational participation in individuals' lives, I trace how certain women oriented their organizational careers around their family roles, or pursued voluntary labor in ways that never let it *appear to* conflict with family needs. As they did, they helped create and entrench a new gender system based on masculine superiority and feminine subordination. By no means did all women participate in the merger; by no means did all benefit equally from its consummation. Indeed, nineteenth-century domestic ideology, by creating unitary and oppositional versions of "woman" and "man," suppressed evident differences among women, especially those of race and class, and permitted only some women access to the qualities of "true" womanhood. Well-off and politically powerful women's associations completed the process by making some women's power dependent on their control of other women. Moreover, the radical potential of a republican femininity based on equality instead of subordination never fully disappeared, and by the 1830s it had reemerged in both secular and religious guises. Insofar as women's rights advocates such as Frances Wright and Sarah Grimké invoked the republican heritage, one in the language of Thomas Paine, the other in the language of the Bible, they sought to tap the progressive strain in republican ideology. By the 1830s, the evangelical consensus on womanhood no longer held; how that consensus splintered can also be traced through the story of women's organizations and women organizers.

In this book, I also seek to explain how—despite a restrictive political and legal climate that closely limited individual women's (especially wives') exercise of direct political and economic power—women's associations acquired and deployed influence in both arenas. By analyzing organizations' practices as they courted (or refused) publicity for themselves, learned to approach politicians for favors, absorbed some state welfare functions, and sought to influence public policies, I sketch out how some women leaders meshed their organizations' interests with those of city fathers. At the same time, I chronicle the process whereby, in the contentious political climate of the 1830s, those organizational leaders' dependence on feminine influence pushed them to the sidelines of politics. Yet other leaders, who adopted a politics of mass mobilization in pursuit of specific political goals, ended up agonizing over the proper balance between their duties and their rights. As they did, evangelical religion often became the weight that tipped the scale toward duties. Moreover, organizations were economic as well as political actors. By following their money trails—examining how they raised, invested, and spent funds—I show how the economic decisions and economic practices of women's associations both reflected and shaped antebellum urban market relations. The contradictions between members' individual lives as unpaid volunteers and their collective activities as employers, investors, and purchasers become more visible in the process. Women themselves certainly viewed their religiously inspired and self-sacrificing donations of time and money as alternatives to self-interest; nevertheless, their organizations pursued (and often could not avoid) economic policies that promoted the interests of the powerful at the expense of the weak, and even bolstered the structures that turned poor women and children into supplicants in the first place.

Just as this book looks at both women's organizations and organization women, it is also a tale of two cities. In studying both New York and Boston, I seek to understand shared historical conditions in northern antebellum urban areas and conditions peculiar to specific localities. Although Boston and New York were both port cities, their economic, religious, and demographic histories followed separate paths during the first four decades of the nineteenth century. Whereas Manhattan's economy diversified rapidly, and by 1840 rested on pillars driven into solid manufacturing, commercial, and financial bedrock, Boston's economy was anchored to shipping, finance, and mercantile pursuits; most of the significant industrial employment in New England was located in rural areas and new industrial towns such as Lowell and Pawtucket. During this period, as New York became the new nation's largest city, outstripping Philadelphia, its population reflected an enormous diversity of accents and colors. Although Boston became a major destination for Irish famine immigrants in the 1840s and 1850s, before 1825 its white population was ethnically homogeneous and mostly native born. Its black population, though deep-rooted in its life, was proportionately smaller than New York's or Philadelphia's.

Religiously, too, the cities were different enough in the antebellum years to offer fruitful comparison. Although both cities had Protestant majorities, each possessed its own distinct theological and ethnic colorings. As the cradle of Puritanism, Boston remained a center of orthodox Calvinism; in the postrevolutionary era, most Calvinists were Congregationalists and Baptists, but Presbyterian polity made some inroads into Congregationalist practices. More important, the ascendancy of newer "liberal" Protestant sects, such as the Unitarians and Universalists, challenged Calvinist orthodoxy, and by 1807 Unitarian churches increasingly attracted Boston's elite. By contrast, New York, long the home of a religiously and ethnically varied population, sheltered no Unitarian congregation until the 1830s, but supported a thriving Quaker community (few Friends tarried long in Boston). New York's Calvinists were mostly Presbyterians and Reformed Dutch. Among the former, the Scots and Scots-Irish burr echoed from the Sunday pulpit; among the latter, Dutch language and theological influence remained significant throughout the antebellum years. Boston's African Americans worshiped in the largest numbers at the African Baptist Church in Belknap Street; in New York by the 1820s, African Americans could be found at a wide range of Protestant churches, including their own African Methodist Episcopal, African Methodist Episcopal Zion, Abyssinian Baptist, and St. Philip's Episcopal. Among some of the upstart new sects of the era, most notably the Methodists, Manhattan's environs proved fertile soil in which to plant and propagate churches. Methodism came somewhat later to Boston, but found adherents along the city's docks and in the working-class districts of East Boston.[12]

Both New York and Boston were home to small Catholic and Jewish populations, with subtle differences shaping each. New York's Temple Shearith Israel was its only synagogue, serving a tiny population of Sephardim (of both Dutch and English descent) until an influx of German Ashkenazim in the 1820s. Between 1822 and 1840, however, the city's Jewish population increased twelvefold. Until the 1830s, no one European ethnic group dominated among Catholics in either locality, but European-born priests ministered to the growing numbers of communicants. In 1815, for example, two French-born priests served Boston's 1,500 Catholics (5 percent of the city's population); by 1845, when Catholics accounted for one-fourth of Bostonians, fifteen priests, ten of them Irish-born, staffed the city's nine parishes. Indeed, until 1845, European Catholic churches treated Boston as a missionary field, sending regular donations to the bishop. In 1815, New York's 14,000 Catholics supported two polyglot parishes that included African-descended Caribbean migrants, some of them enslaved, along with groups of Irish, French, Spanish, and German residents. By 1845, ten parishes spread across Manhattan, including two ethnic congregations—German and French. But it was the arrival of large numbers of Catholic Irish in the 1830s that transformed each city; more important, the Protestant response ended an era of casual toleration and occasional cooperation, one in which "Irish" did not necessarily mean "Catholic" or "poor." By 1840, and certainly by 1850 as the famine Irish disembarked in droves in each city's harbor, the term "Irish Catholic" had become almost one word, with other words—"vicious" "criminal" "dissipated"—trailing close behind.[13]

Both the differences and the similarities in racial, ethnic, religious, and economic characteristics make the study of the two cities together interesting and revealing. Most striking, perhaps, is the repetition of common patterns in both localities; here is an example of a comparison that reveals convergence more than variation. Women's organizations in both cities looked similar to each other, and women leaders behaved in markedly similar ways. To be sure, members of Boston women's reform associations exhibited sharply different behavior from their New York counterparts during the 1830s, as some Bostonians embraced a far more radical interracial abolitionism and women's rights agenda than New Yorkers. But in most other respects, New York and Boston organizations and leaders were surprisingly alike. When the organizational behavior of women in two separate locations falls into rhythm, historians can be fairly confident that they are seeing large historical processes at work. In the case of these two cities, the rapid growth of the antebellum northern economy produced common urban experiences of social class and race; those, in turn, shaped the context within which local women's groups came into being, funded their activities, sought political access, and defined their economic interests.

These findings have implications for our understanding of how women in the new nation helped construct, elaborate, and refine the gender, class, and racial systems that characterized northern cities; how their religious commitments facilitated or limited their social activism; how some women gained and used political influence; and how, through their associations, women bolstered (and only rarely challenged) an economic system that systematically devalued women's labor. Crucial to the creation of these systems was the elaboration of a set of new public/private distinctions. As feminist theorists and historians have made abundantly clear, those distinctions, although presented in nineteenth-century writings as natural and absolute, were in fact continually under construction, and constantly shifting. Used both to explain women's subordination and to construct it, distinctions between "private" and "public" activities powerfully shaped the material experiences of nineteenth-century women, even as women's own actions helped draw and redraw the lines. Because collective activity through associations was the first and most enduring way in which women helped define what constituted both public and private life, studying both women's groups and women in groups renders the boundary-making process visible, and gives it historical specificity. And because individuals entered women's groups as members of households, exhibiting and building family status and reputation, and imagining their voluntary labor as extensions of familial concerns, an analysis of how women interlaced their domestic and organizational concerns highlights the crucial process whereby individuals pursuing ostensibly "private" concerns as wives, mothers and daughters took family interests into the nominally "public" arenas of politics and the economy. As long as women in groups behaved as members of families or social classes, rather than in the interests of women as a group, they encountered little opposition to their involvement in public labor. Indeed, for most of the era covered by this book, the work that women did for their organizations resided rhetorically in the "private" arena, even when it involved highly visible political and economic activity.[14]

In addition, because the early national and antebellum years were particularly noteworthy for the emergence of what is often termed "civil society" in the United States—that arena of action and discussion lying between the subject and the state on which Alexis de Tocqueville commented admiringly—the study of women's associations underscores the strongly masculine cast of public life and the marginal place of women within "civil society."[15] Women's organizations, no matter how well funded and well led, were never as significant, visible, audible, or powerful as men's. Still, as a locally based study that combines organizational histories with the life histories of their leaders, this book makes it possible to scrutinize closely how women's voluntary associations worked. Its findings should give pause to social theorists who look to the nineteenth century for models of civic engagement for contemporary Americans—or for citizens of newly democratic states. To be sure, readers will find in these pages plenty of examples of how Americans formed associations to achieve goals unattainable by individuals; they will also discover a rich and inventive tradition of influence-seeking by political subjects—women—who were not yet fully citizens. But rather than offering a blueprint for using associationalism and volunteerism to deliver public services, solve social problems, or encourage citizens' involvement with each other, this study demonstrates the extent to which voluntary associations have served and extended the interests of the powerful, often at the expense of the powerless. Women's associations, especially the most visible and well-funded, produced and reproduced the political and economic inequality that marked the nineteenth century, entrenched the power of their class and racial groups, and defended their interests when that power was contested. And why should they not? Women's identities as women are and were simultaneous with and usually inseparable from their ethnic, racial, class or other identities. What is perhaps surprising is that in the 1830s small groups of radical reformers imagined that it could be otherwise.[16]

There are also discussion points here, and more than a few cautionary tales, for readers interested in how voluntary associations work to promote individual empowerment and self-help. Some of the organizations discussed in the following pages took the form of mutual aid associations founded by working-class women to protect themselves and their families from the battering winds of economic change; others were church-, parish-, or synagogue-based societies through which comfortably situated women helped their poorer neighbors. Whether founded by African American or white women, mutual assistance and parish charitable societies quietly challenged the hegemony of wealthy white Protestant women's associations, and offered an approach to benevolence that stressed care for one's ethnic, racial, or religious "own." In the brutally competitive world of the market, such cooperative community projects could feed and clothe children, visit the sick, and bury the dead. Whatever challenge they offered to large and well-funded benevolent societies, however, was muted indeed. Restricted by exceedingly limited financial and human resources, women's mutual aid societies met only a tiny fraction of the need, and usually only for members who could afford to pay dues. The lesson that such organizations learned is that power matters—especially economic power—and that self-help seldom generates the resources to change the condition of the most disadvantaged.

This book begins at the moment when women first came together to form permanent associations. As it chronicles the wide range of organizations that New York and Boston women formed during the initial decades of collective female activism and scrutinizes the lives of the women who made them run, it assesses the significance and impact of that activism. Organizations certainly changed both women and cities. But the story is no simple one of female unity; nor is it a story of unequivocal progress or decline. Instead, it is a complicated account of how groups of women sought to express their social concerns and social visions in institutional form, to greater or lesser degrees of success. Moreover, it is a record of both unity and division, as the social experiences of race, religion, and class brought women together in pursuit of common goals, or drove them apart.

CHAPTER ONE

Patterns of Organization

omen's voluntary societies proliferated in the postrevolutionary years. As much as did men, American women helped create "the age of benevolent institutions" so striking to Noah Worcester in 1816, and so impressive to Alexis de Tocqueville in 1832.[1] Some were little more than fundraising agencies dedicated to a particular purpose—such as sending missionaries to convert nonbelievers—while others conducted far-flung charitable businesses that raised money, ran institutions such as orphanages or old age homes, lobbied politicians, and found foster homes for needy children. Still others devoted their energies to mutual aid and self-help, or to the eradication of specific social practices, such as prostitution. Many had nothing in common with others but the sex of their founders.

Paralleling the emergence and spread of these groups were important changes in women's social experiences and in ideologies about womanhood. The same decades that witnessed the development of the first permanent women's societies saw a major refiguring of the colonial gender system to accommodate the economic, political, and religious upheavals that accompanied and followed the American Revolution. The coincidence among these developments was not a mere temporal accident. After all, the earliest groups emerged in urban areas among Protestant women whose personal experience and social location provided both the motivation and the means to remake the traditional almsgiving woman into the modern organized benefactor. Moreover, the existence of collectively organized, publicly visible female benevolence quickly came to symbolize the new womanhood of the nineteenth century, and an individual's participation in associational endeavors came to be accepted and admired as evidence of her claims to "true womanhood." Only in the 1830s did some organized women—notably abolitionists—come under attack for their labors, and then only for their methods and goals, not for organizational activity per se.[2]

In both laboring and justifying their labors, the founders of women's organizations helped create and reproduce a gender system to fit the times. Although it remained hierarchical by sex, the new gender system incorporated democratic ideals, largely by defining women's secondary status within society as separate from and complementary to men's. Just as the primacy and political independence of the free male citizen would rest upon his control of property and dependents (wife, children, servants, or slaves), the authority of the democratic patriarch would devolve from his ability solely to represent the interests of the entire family unit in the public arenas of politics and law.[3] By founding organizations and incorporating organizational work into new definitions of femininity, some women helped shape the new gender system and define the feminine sphere. At the same time, by setting limits on appropriately feminine activities, their labors created new distinctions among women themselves and new hierarchies of acceptable female behavior.[4]

Nineteenth-century gender ideology obscured these hierarchies by considering masculine and feminine "spheres" as equal, and by stressing women's common experiences as women. The concept of a unitary female nature rooted in biology served many useful functions in nineteenth-century society, including "contribut[ing] to many women's sense of power and autonomy . . . [and] to a process of middle-class self-definition." In embracing that notion, women activists shaped the new gender ideology while also justifying the extraordinary proliferation of woman-run organizations. New female social experiences, gender ideologies, and women's associations took root and blossomed together, their vines inextricably intertwined. In the process, the republican mother of the 1790s became the "true woman" and Christian mother of the 1830s, as femininity and religiosity came to be closely associated.[5] The contradictory consequences that ensued from these new definitions of femininity can be seen in the differing experiences of women in different associations (as well as of their clients). For some, social experience and ideology blended seamlessly, offering personal validation and collective power. For others, especially those women whose racial, class, or religious identities made them ineligible for membership in the best-known and most prestigious organizations, ideology and experience could be confusingly at odds. Although they all gazed into the same ideological mirror, looking for the unitary "woman" of nineteenth-century lore, often the image became a fun-house reality fractured by the deep divisions of nineteenth-century urban life.

Examining the patterns of organization evident among various groups of women in New York and Boston over the decades from the 1790s to the 1840s enables us to see how the dominant antebellum gender ideology evolved and to connect it to new practices in class relations. For as historians have frequently noted, in the nineteenth century, gender ideology and class definition were closely linked, and both found expression in the associations people joined.[6] When we look at how different types of women's organizations came into being, created conditions for additional groups to form, institutionalized opportunities for organizational activity, formed networks or snapped linkages, and in general rooted associational activity deeply into women's "sphere," we can better understand both gender ideology and class formation in antebellum New York and Boston.

The First Wave, 1797–1806

Several patterns recurred independently in the two cities. The first pattern was temporal. Both cities witnessed an initial wave of organizing at the turn of the nineteenth century, followed by a cascade of activity during and after the War of 1812, then an ebb in the 1820s, followed by a new surge in the late 1820s and 1830s. (See Appendix 1 for a list of organizations.) The latter surge contained within it smaller waves that broke separately, creating a succession of three organizational types: benevolent associations, which arrived first and remained the most numerous and ubiquitous throughout the era; mutual benefit or mutual aid societies, which arose in each city during the 1820s; and reform associations, which arrived in the 1830s.

Women in each city established the tradition of organized female benevolence in the 1790s; by 1840, both had an array of such groups. Devoted to improving the temporal and spiritual welfare of clients ranging from widows and orphans to ministerial students and prostitutes, such endeavors responded to concrete economic changes, especially in the conditions facing poor urban women and children. These efforts also reflected parallel alterations in well-off women's lives. Both "subjective necessity" and objective reality transformed individual charity into organized benevolence.[7] Like their charitable forebears, members of benevolent associations assumed a vertical relationship between benefactor and client; unlike them, they employed a "rhetoric of female benevolence" that presupposed a uniform experience of womanhood. New York's Society for the Relief of Poor Widows with Small Children, initiated in 1797 with a singularly descriptive title, fit the genre, as did an offshoot for orphaned clients, the Orphan Asylum Society (1806), and the Female Association (1798), a Quaker group providing "donations to the Poor" and then opening a school for children "whose parents . . . are evidently unable to defray the expenses of their education." So, too, did Boston's Female Asylum (1800), whose organizers created a refuge for young female orphans, and its Female Missionary Society (1800), which raised "an annual collection for the express purpose of aiding" Congregationalist and Baptist missions.[8]

In creating formal associations with written constitutions, elected officers, fund-raising mechanisms, printed reports, and (sometimes) incorporated legal status, the founders of these societies cast conventional female charity into a new mold. Existing men's societies provided an accessible model, on which women drew freely, but the sources of their formalizing instincts were more numerous and diverse. One was certainly the revolutionary experience, when American women had first organized independently to pursue a collective public goal. Another was the Quaker tradition of women's meetings, which provided the proximate model for New York's Female Association. Still another was the long history of organized women's prayer meetings, which were well entrenched in evangelical practice by the 1790s. Yet a fourth was the experience of aiding men's groups; Isabella Graham had labored actively for the London and New York Missionary Societies, "gathering intelligence and endeavoring to collect money," before helping initiate the Society for the Relief of Poor Widows with Small Children, and the Orphan Asylum Society. But such specific precedents were less important than key alterations in northern urban women's experiences between the 1760s and the 1790s, including improved access to formal schooling, increased exposure to a new world of printed books and magazines, practical immersion in the rapidly changing commercial economy of the late eighteenth-century city, broader exposure to nonfamilial and noncongregational forms of religious proselytizing, and a new consciousness of gender as a way of organizing social experience.[9]

In various ways, changed female experience led separate groups of women to create these pioneering organizations. Within the ranks of their founders were women who embodied some or all of the elements of that changed experience. New York's Female Association, made up largely of young unmarried Quaker women, owed its existence not only to the long Friends' tradition of benevolence but also to the founders' superior educations, their awareness that literacy provided through formal schooling was becoming valuable currency in the new commercial world of the nineteenth century, and their temporary freedom from direct family responsibilities. The older, wealthier married women who founded Boston's Female Asylum drew upon a different experiential base, but stressed the same need to teach orphaned girls "to read, write, sew and do all kinds of domestic business." As treasurer, fifty-seven-year-old Elizabeth Peck Perkins could marshal thirty years' experience as a shopkeeper and businesswoman; undoubtedly it was her advice that led the founders to decide at their very first monthly meeting to invest donated funds in stock and use the interest for operating expenses. When Perkins died in 1807, her place was taken by Eleanor Peirce Davis, born in 1750, who had wide experience managing her late husband's property and running a sugar refinery. New Yorker Mary Weygand Chrystie, a china and glass merchant, contributed similar worldly financial expertise to the Society for the Relief of Poor Widows with Small Children, as did Isabella Graham, owner and principal of female academies in Scotland and then New York since 1776.

With extensive literary and epistolary contacts on both sides of the Atlantic, Graham represented yet another strain in the founders' experience. Like many of them, she regularly read English and Scottish publications; she also sent examples of American publications to her correspondents. But more than most, she was immersed in an evangelical religious world, one that fostered affiliation and outreach and worked against narrow sectarian parochialism. In this she resembled Bostonian Mary Webb, the twenty-one-year-old founder of the Female Missionary Society who by 1817 was corresponding with women in ninety-seven similar organizations. Whether evangelical or not, the founding generation inhabited a mental world increasingly constructed through printed materials circulating through national and transatlantic arteries. They also shared an understanding of gender—the experience of womanhood or manhood—that stressed common feminine experiences and common values. Members of the Boston Female Asylum might phrase their mission in terms of women's collective sympathy for "those of their own sex, when unprotected by Parents or Friends," while members of the Female Missionary Society voiced their plans in specifically evangelical appeals to "females professing godliness," but the effect was similar. In uniting as women (albeit as white, Protestant, and privileged women), both evangelical and nonevangelical founders harnessed new understandings of womanhood and new beliefs in the importance of shared feminine experience. As they did, they "conflat[ed] . . . the virtuous with the feminine" and justified creating pockets of authority for themselves through associations.[10]

The authority they sought was to be exercised primarily over other women and over children. The same economic and social changes that altered the founders' lives, opening new possibilities to them, simultaneously rendered many poorer women's lives more precarious and changed their relationship with their social "betters." The poor widow and her orphaned children, cast unprotected onto a cutthroat labor market, figured centrally in the founders' plans as the embodiments of an alternate fate. When the women of New York's Orphan Asylum Society invoked the "divine compassion" that "has marked the *fatherless*" as "peculiar subjects" of concern, they did so without irony. Motherlessness was a sad fate; fatherlessness could be devastating. Without a protector, an inheritance, or a remunerative skill, the widow and her children were thrust into a situation where women's work commanded the lowest wages, and children were liabilities. References by members of the Boston Female Asylum to girls lacking "patronage" or being left "unprotected by Parents or Friends" reflected stark realities. But if, in an earlier time, individual charity and almsgiving had sufficed to enable the fortunate giver to assist her poorer counterpart, by the turn of the century "protection" or "patronage" seemed best furnished collectively.[11]

These early associations facilitated the formation of subsequent organizational waves by creating precedents and clearing paths that remained open for all successor groups. Leaders of both the New York Society for the Relief of Poor Widows with Small Children and the Boston Female Asylum, as pioneers in their cities, faced down criticisms that quickly evaporated. Seven years after helping found the New York group, Isabella Graham marveled at the change she had witnessed: initial "ridicule" and "opposition" had turned to approbation and fame. Whereas at first "the men could not allow our sex the steadiness and perseverance necessary to establish such an undertaking," she told the young women who operated the society's school, by 1804 God's "seal upon it" was evident in its prosperity. Almost as she spoke, members of the Boston Female Asylum could read letters in a local paper challenging the group's plans. "The direction of property requires masculine exertions," wrote their critic; it was "unnatural" for "frail feeble *woman*, to thwart the design of her creation," as asylum leaders proposed, by organizing formally. "The indelicacy, the indecency of the thing is manifest," he concluded. Although asylum founder Hannah Morgan Stillman had (anonymously) used the public press to propose such an endeavor, fearing "objections and delay . . . [and] unmerited censure from some," she had held the first meeting in a private house.[12] Like Graham's group, hers prevailed, not only in organizing but in acquiring legal standing through incorporation. Later societies might sometimes face severe obloquy, but whatever criticism came their way focused on their particular programs or activities, not their right to formal existence. Once settled, that question remained settled.[13]

So too did issues surrounding organizations' legal status and financing techniques. Once the Society for the Relief of Poor Widows with Small Children had acquired corporate status under New York State law in 1802 and Boston's Female Asylum had done the same under Massachusetts law in 1803, future groups' right to incorporate was not challenged. Not all women's organizations sought acts of incorporation, but those that did had the process smoothed and simplified by their predecessors. Legislatures in both states quickly got used to treating women's associations exactly as they treated other petitioners for incorporation — churches, men's voluntary societies, joint stock companies — and granted most requests automatically. This occurred despite the ironic reality that, as several historians have underscored, corporate status granted the collective female body a range of legal rights that none of the wives within it could claim individually, including the right to own property, bring legal suits, indenture minor children, invest funds, and control wages. Whether incorporated or not, early societies drafted constitutions and by-laws and composed annual reports to supporters; when they published some or all such documents, they established their right of access to the public media. (See Figures 1.1 and 1.2.) Later societies (such as moral reform groups) might be roundly disparaged for the content of their publications or the purposes of their asylums, but the critique of a specific group never turned into an attack on all of organized womanhood.[14]

In developing fund-raising and financing techniques, too, early organizations smoothed the route for others. Women's first efforts to collect funds for public purposes dated to the Revolutionary War, when Philadelphian Esther De Berdt Reed instigated a campaign to provide monetary bonuses to soldiers in the Continental Army. The permanent organizations that followed the Revolution elaborated on techniques employed by Reed and her associates, including door-to-door solicitations and annual or lifetime membership subscriptions. The anniversary sermon delivered by a sympathetic and admiring clergyman was another existing technique; adapted from men's organizations, it proved a mainstay of women's fund-raising for generations. And selling clients' products or access to their labor power was a popular practice derived from revolutionary-era poor-relief projects. In 1805, for example, the Society

THE

ANNUAL REPORT

OF THE

FEMALE ASSOCIATION,

IN THE

CITY OF NEW-YORK.

━━◈◈◈◈◈◈━━

New=York:

PRINTED BY MAHLON DAY,

NO. 372, PEARL-STREET.

. . . .

1824.

FIGURES 1.1 AND 1.2. Title pages of the New York Female Association's 1824 *Annual Report* and the Boston Seamen's Aid Society's 1843 *Annual Report*. The Seamen's Aid Society's report is inscribed by the secretary, Mary F. Quincy, to Mrs. Rufus Choate, a subscriber. Published reports and circulars ranged from simple four- or eight-page pamphlets to larger productions with illustrations. (Courtesy of the Library Company of Philadelphia)

TENTH

ANNUAL REPORT

OF THE

SEAMEN'S AID SOCIETY,

OF THE

CITY OF BOSTON.

EASTBURN'S PRESS,

No. 18 State Street.

1843.

for the Relief of Poor Widows with Small Children sold client-made shirts at its store, while girls in the Boston Female Asylum labored on cash-producing sewing projects solicited from local families. Urban residents quickly got used to the sight of women soliciting donations in cash or in kind; when such solicitations proliferated or supported controversial activities, they might be annoyed or withhold contributions, but they would not challenge the womanliness of fund-raising. Even the parish and antislavery fairs of the 1830s, which represented a new form of fund-raising because organization members sold the fruits of their own labor, along with donated goods, to the general public, nevertheless occupied, not terra nova, but a new section of older ground. Similarly, insuring an organization's permanence by financing it through a combination of annual fund-raising and judicious investment in income-producing bank stocks or United States treasury bonds reinforced the acceptability of woman-run institutions.[15]

The Second Wave, 1812–1820

Societies founded during the second organizational wave drew upon and developed these precedents, sometimes quite directly, as individuals brought their experience to new organizational involvements. The continuities between the first and second surge were especially evident, however, in their concern for women and children. Situated at significant international and regional trade and commercial crossroads, both New York and Boston witnessed rapid accumulations of sheer human misery during the Jeffersonian embargoes and the War of 1812. As in the 1790s, charitable women in the 1810s acted upon their concern through associations. Between 1812 and 1820, women in both cities formed at least ten such groups. In each city, an organization arose to provide work to women whose jobs had evaporated during the economic crisis: in New York, the House of Industry (1814), and in Boston, the Society for Employing the Female Poor (1820). Each was also home to new societies assisting older women, widows, and orphans. The title of New York's Association for the Relief of Respectable, Aged, Indigent Females (1813) clearly specified the targets of its beneficence: elderly single women and widows "who once lived respectably." Boston's Widows' Society (1816) aided "destitute infirm widows and aged single women, of good character," and its Fatherless and Widows Society (1817) relieved widows and their children. Boston's Fragment Society (1812) provided clothing to destitute children and mothers, New York's Hebrew Female Benevolent Society (1820) quietly raised funds for impoverished Jewish women and children, and the Female Assistance Society (1813) did the same for Methodists. The Ladies Association Auxiliary to the Roman Catholic Orphan Asylum (1817) supported the religious Sisters of Charity in their effort to rescue Catholic orphans both from the city streets and from Protestant clutches.[16]

But change as well as continuity marked the second tide. Most striking was the surge in specifically religious societies run by Protestant women. Between 1814 and 1816, a Female Bible Society, Female Society for the Promotion of Christianity among the Jews, and Female Tract Society appeared on the Boston landscape. Reflecting the struggle between orthodoxy and Unitarianism for Bostonians' souls and Boston's churches, all three organizations adopted orthodox Congregationalism as their guiding star. In one year alone, 1816, New York's evangelical women created a Female Union Society for the Promotion of Sabbath Schools, Female Auxiliary Bible Society, and Female Missionary Society. In both cities, women formed congregation-based maternal associations and tract societies; New York women then collected these into citywide organizations in 1818 and 1822 respectively. Boston's orthodox women employed their sewing and fund-raising skills in the Corban Society (1811) and the Graham Society (1817), both supporting "indigent pious youth" studying for the Congregationalist ministry. Regardless of the initial concentration or eventual shape of these societies, their founders shared the conviction that endeavoring to fulfill "the *temporal* wants of the indigent and to mitigate the miseries of this life" was insufficient. The "best happiness of mankind" was promoted only "by the diffusion of the knowledge and influence of the Gospel of Jesus Christ," whether through gathering Sunday schools, distributing tracts or bibles, educating ministers, or hiring missionaries.[17] (See Table A.1.)

Paralleling this development came a noticeable shift toward evangelical themes in the rhetoric and work of existing charitable societies. In 1816, for example, the officers of the Society for the Relief of Poor Widows with Small Children agreed, after nineteen years without such a practice, to open each meeting with a reading from the Bible. Thereafter, the minutes recorded chapter and verse. At the 1820 annual meeting, First Directress Hannah Ker Van Wyck Caldwell carefully outlined the society's charitable work, then recounted a visit to a "decent" widow who needed the society's aid because she and her children were "destitute of all religious concern," not because they lacked worldly goods. By 1823, clients were required, on pain of losing benefits, to place their children in Sunday school and see to it that they attended regularly. Whereas in 1810 the officers of the Orphan Asylum Society defined their task as training "useful artisans and faithful servants" while perhaps "gathering many a wandering Lamb into the Fold of Heaven," in 1818, Asylum Secretary

Isabella Ogden reversed the emphasis, suggesting that the primary "incitement" for members should be the prospect of "rescu[ing] these little immortals from the danger of ruin, and . . . rear[ing] them for a brighter inheritance." Even Boston's Female Missionary Society, which had begun as a solidly evangelical endeavor, underwent a metamorphosis during the decade. In 1817, under Mary Webb's continuing leadership, the ladies turned their attention to the religious needs of their impoverished neighbors, hiring two missionaries, proposing a refuge for repentant prostitutes, and buying Bibles and religious books for distribution in "destitute places," all designed to deploy the "counteracting influence of the gospel" against "ignorance and vice."[18]

New charitable groups stressed similar themes. Almost a year into their work, the managers of New York's Association for the Relief of Respectable, Aged, Indigent Females determined to open all their meetings with scripture readings. Three years into their work, the women of Boston's Fragment Society carefully noted that they provided "relief temporal and spiritual" and labored "to reform the morals of the poor" by distributing Bibles obtained from the Female Auxiliary Bible Society. Indeed, soliciting or accepting gifts of religious materials for circulation among charities' clients (not only Bibles but also evangelical books and tracts) became commonplace in the 1810s, within both old and new associations, as the number and visibility of Bible, tract and publication societies grew. On occasion, such gifts applied the pressure needed to propel an organization in a more evangelical direction. Sending an unsolicited donation of twenty tracts in 1814, the men of New York's Protestant Episcopal Tract Society lectured the women of the Society for the Relief of Poor Widows with Small Children about the need to "unite with temporal relief the consoling hope of a blessed immortality." Seemingly taken aback, the women replied that they had always combined charity with "an attention to the Spiritual Interest of [our] poor" designed to "lead them into the paths of truth." Perhaps they had, but after 1814 their minutes and reports emphasized the combination much more explicitly.[19]

To note this evangelical turn is not to suggest that all societies took it, or that those taking it had theretofore displayed no interest in evangelical religion. The two existing nonevangelical associations—New York's Quaker Female Association and Boston's increasingly Unitarian Female Asylum—continued along their accustomed paths. However gratefully received, a gift of twenty-four Bibles to the Female Association's school from the New York Bible Society would hardly turn Quakers into evangelicals. (Besides, prominent Quaker philanthropists such as Thomas Eddy, whose daughters helped run the Female Association, were active promoters of Bible societies.) The two new work-providing endeavors—New York's House of Industry and Boston's Society for Employing the Female Poor—made no attempt to attach religious goals to their programs. In 1810 the officers of the Boston Female Asylum crisply (and unanimously) rejected an effort by the asylum's newly hired superintendent to abandon the institution's accustomed pew at the liberal New South Church and escort the children instead to Edward Dorr Griffin's strictly orthodox Park Street Church. Unmoved by Susanna Bacon's complaint that "morality alone [does not] constitute a christian," and that "the Gospel" could not be preached except by a minister who "believe[d] in regeneration, election, and decrees," the asylum officers simply suggested that she attend Griffin's church on her own. The superintendent remained in her position for another twelve years, until fired by a different (and more heavily Unitarian) set of officers.[20] Within the other first-wave organizations, religion in general and evangelical religion in particular had provided powerful motivation for individual actions. One need only read the spiritual writings of Isabella Graham or Mary Webb to recognize the strength of their evangelical convictions in the 1790s—convictions they shared with male activists. What was different in the 1810s was the increasingly tight package in which womanhood and evangelical associationalism came wrapped. The republican mother was becoming the true woman.[21]

This evangelical turn in women's organizational behavior was part of a larger trend through which evangelical sects labored to enhance their cultural power. For men as well as women, this was the era of the Bible, tract, Sunday school, and missionary society. Indeed, several of the new women's organizations were "auxiliaries" to men's local or national groups, such as the New York Religious Tract Society (1812), the American Board of Commissioners for Foreign Missions (1810), or the American Bible Society (1816). Although the direction of the affiliation could vary—Boston women's Bible Society predated the American Bible Society by almost two years, while New York women's Bible Society was "auxiliary" from the start—women's groups were significant partners in creating, building and sustaining local and national Bible and missionary societies.[22] These collective endeavors were crucial players in subtly shifting the balance of religious power in both cities. In New York, evangelicals used their associations to speak with growing authority on public issues, giving those discussions an evangelical accent to replace the more secular republican intonations of the 1790s. They were particularly successful in shaping the terms of public debate over poor relief and welfare provision, largely by creating institutions designed to put their ideas into practice and supported by a combination of public monies and organizational fund-raising.[23] Boston's evangelicals did the same, but with somewhat less success. In part, their experience reflected the city's smaller population and more homogeneous character. But in part, too, their experience testified to the ongoing contest between orthodoxy and liberalism, in which religious liberals held the balance of economic and cultural power. As Unitarians gained control of significant symbolic institutions such as the Harvard Divinity School, evangelicalism came to be seen as the religion of the emerging middle class. Thus, the lines of demarcation between the elite and the middle class in Boston were much more sharply religious than they were in New York.[24]

In practical terms, these developments had concrete ramifications for Protestant women in both cities in the 1810s. Joining overtly evangelical organizations became a significant means whereby they signaled their religious commitments. In a way not possible in the 1790s, when republican and evangelical representations of womanhood were still separable, evangelical women in the 1810s combined religion and social action in collective, rather than individual ways. Affiliating with a missionary, Bible, or Sunday school society thus became an accepted and admired way to express one's faith, and root one's conversion experience in solid ground. In turn, associations enlarged the terrain of individual influence. When the young Philadelphia Baptist Lydia Morris Shields experienced her "new birth" in 1818, the logical expression of her newfound commitment, after baptism, was organizational involvement. She became, in succession, a visitor to the poor, a manager of the Philadelphia Female Bible Society and of the Baptist Female Education Society, as well as superintendent of a Sunday school for black children. After her marriage to Baptist minister Howard Malcom in 1820 and subsequent move to Boston, Lydia took over the girls' department of his new church's Sunday school, formed a sewing circle to raise money for the school, headed up the church maternal association, and joined the Boston Female Auxiliary Bible Society. When the organizers of the Boston Infant School Society asked her to join them, she agreed, eventually serving as first directress. Although few organized women could count as many involvements as Lydia Malcom, her story was repeated endlessly in the experience of each individual whose conversion led her to volunteer as a Sunday school teacher, tract distributor, Bible-seller, or missionary collector, or to join a maternal association, orphanage committee, or prayer society.[25]

Moreover, such opportunities multiplied rapidly during the 1810s and 1820s. Not only did men's groups create or recruit women's auxiliaries, especially for fund-raising purposes, but women in both cities formed their own adjuvants. Five years after its founding, New York's Female Tract Society began sponsoring auxiliaries within local churches, to collect money and distribute tracts.

Boston's Female Bible Society, which predated the American Bible Society but added "Auxiliary" to its title by affiliating with it in 1816, sponsored an auxiliary Distributing Bible Association eight years later. Maternal Associations did most of their work through auxiliaries, as mothers organized themselves through their churches and met in each other's homes "to pray for the salvation of their children, and . . . converse about the best means for their religious instruction and government." Sewing societies were a particularly common type of auxiliary, employed to provide cash or sewn goods, for example, to Boston's Widows' Society, and the Fatherless and Widows Society, and to New York's Association for the Relief of Respectable, Aged, Indigent Females and the Female Tract Society.

Beyond collecting contributions, making clothing, or distributing tracts, subsidiary organizations served the important function of training and recruiting potential new members. Most were peopled with young women, often the single daughters of parent society leaders. Just as the pastor of New York's South Dutch (Reformed) Church prompted a group of teenage girls to collect themselves into a Juvenile Female Tract Society in 1814, the women of the Female Auxiliary Bible Society encouraged their single young adult daughters to form a Female Juvenile Bible Association in 1818. Formally organized with constitutions, lists of officers, and (sometimes) published annual reports, "juvenile" auxiliaries effectively propagated the ideals and practices of evangelical womanhood. (See Figure 1.3.) Less formal practices, such as encouraging girls' and young women's charitable donations, had a comparable effect. No doubt when "the young ladies of Mrs. Byron's school" saw listed in a benevolent society report their gift of $43 and "19 pr. of stockings . . . of their own knitting," and when "Miss Catherine Robinson, six years old" saw the "bed quilt of her own making" similarly highlighted, they received a nudge toward self-definitions that incorporated evangelical volunteer labor. Indeed, when Catherine was twenty-eight, she joined her mother, Frances Duer Robinson, as a manager of the Society for the Relief of Poor Widows with Small Children.[26]

As such definitions acquired shape and mass, and were disseminated through women's organizations, they revised and displaced nonevangelical republican ideals of womanhood. Hannah Morgan Stillman, founder of the Boston Female Asylum and wife of a prominent Baptist minister, invoked a republican ideal in an 1800 appeal for monetary and moral support, asking rhetorically: "Can *Virtue*, can *Talents*, can *Wealth* be employed in a more laudable way?" Her appeal produced a donation and commendatory letter, so admired by the managers that they entered it into their permanent record. In it, Mercy Otis Warren requested more information about the society. Some years earlier,

FIFTH

ANNUAL REPORT

OF THE

NEW-YORK

FEMALE AUXILIARY

BIBLE SOCIETY,

AND THE

THIRD ANNUAL REPORT

OF THE

NEW-YORK FEMALE

JUVENILE BIBLE ASSOCIATION,

TOGETHER WITH THE NAMES OF THEIR

SUBSCRIBERS AND DONORS,

AND THE

ADDRESS OF THE REV. DR. MILNOR.

———————

NEW-YORK:

PRINTED BY DANIEL FANSHAW,

NO. 20 SLOTE-LANE.

1821.

FIGURE 1.3. Title page of the New-York Female Auxiliary Bible Society's 1821 *Annual Report*. Formally organized "juvenile" societies encouraged adolescents and young adult women to practice evangelical virtues. This association changed its name to the Young Ladies' Bible Society in 1826. (Courtesy of the Library Company of Philadelphia)

Warren herself had helped define republican motherhood, allowing that while women's primary responsibilities were domestic, they could find time, by "an acquired habit of continual industry" to engage (as she did) "in the pursuit of knowledge." Now, she expanded her calculus of feminine virtue to include collective, nondomestic enterprises such as the asylum. Evangelicals went further, wedding religious conversion to organizational participation, and grafting religious meanings onto the newly feminized concept of "virtue."[27]

One result was that as evangelical women began to place themselves historically, they subtly distanced their organizations from that republican heritage, preferring instead a religious or domestic origin. In their 1815 annual report, for example, the officers of the Society for the Relief of Poor Widows with Small Children took pride in describing the association as "the First Charitable incorporated institution in the United States conducted by Ladies." They went on to claim for "those who first instituted" it "the Honor, by their example, of enlarging the sphere of female benevolence, and usefulness." Their words encapsulated the female past in a domestic "sphere" that had only begun to "enlarge" with the formation of women's associations. Absent from their version was the practical, public life that founders such as Isabella Graham had lived. Over the years, this version of women's collective history became commonplace in organizational accounts. Writing the early history of the Boston Female Asylum in the early 1840s, the group's secretary remade her experienced and capable predecessors into timid souls, "high-minded and kind hearted women" who left "what had usually been considered their prescribed sphere" to start the orphanage. "The Asylum was," she argued, "after their own homes the next object of interest and effort." In actuality, the women she described had included merchants and businesswomen, individuals whose homes were businesses, and who had only rarely used a language of "spheres." That term itself evolved alongside groups like the Female Asylum. By the time these chroniclers summed up their organizations' past, the historical figures to whom they looked for models were less often the classical Roman matrons or Old Testament warrior women from whom many in the revolutionary generation had drawn inspiration. More frequently, they were the women of the scriptures; evangelical British writers such as Hannah More, whose publishing careers constituted "happy examples" of "silent preaching"; and the "eminently pious" American women whose memoirs increasingly crowded evangelical publishers' shelves. As Bostonian Mary Webb wrote in 1815: "Miriam and Deborah and Priscilla and Phebe have led the way; it cannot be dangerous for succeeding professors [of religious conversion] to follow them." In fact, Webb herself had "led the way," and was still doing so. But now it had become commonplace to employ evangelical femininity both to justify a collective public role for women and to redefine collective action as an extension of domesticity.[28]

The Third Wave, 1823–1840

The third organizational wave coincided with significant changes in the religious and economic topography of each city. Especially in New York, evangelical revivals associated with the growth of Methodism and the preaching of the Presbyterian Charles Grandison Finney (who first came to New York City in 1827) transformed the features of evangelicalism and sparked new concern about social problems. In turn, these changes led to the formation of new women's associations. In Boston, evangelicals renewed their counterattack against Unitarianism, as Lyman Beecher took over the Hanover Street Church in 1826 and installed his son Edward at Park Street Church a year later. Finney himself preached from the Park Street pulpit for eight months in 1831 and 1832. Concurrently, evangelizing Unitarians sought to change both their church and their city, using some of the same mechanisms associated with orthodox Congregationalism, including city missions and voluntary societies. As in New York, these endeavors stimulated attention to social problems and interest in associational solutions. The breathtaking pace of economic change in each city, evident in the growth of manufacturing, the accumulation of capital and its investment in real estate and in projects such as canals and railroads, the creation of new forms of inheritable wealth, and the explosion of urban areas, shaped the revivals themselves, the participants' experiences, and their perceptions of urban society. In response to new urban circumstances, women's organizational endeavors grew rapidly in number and variety.[29]

Third-wave benevolence included new missionary enterprises such as those supplying tracts to sailors or sponsoring schools in Liberia, but most benevolent endeavors continued to highlight the problems of women and children. African American orphans received unwonted attention with the formation of two new societies: New York's Association for the Benefit of Colored Orphans (1836), run by white women, and Boston's Samaritan Asylum (1838), a project of the integrated Boston Female Anti-Slavery Society. In general, though, the orphan and the widow moved to the periphery as the focus shifted subtly to young children and working women. White women in both cities, for example, founded white and black "infant schools" designed to provide religious instruction and basic literacy to "children of the laboring poor" aged eighteen months to six years. Both the New York and Boston Infant School Societies enjoyed significant popular support, with the New York society garnering public funds as well as the use of existing school facilities. As sources of child care, they were also popular with working mothers. Whether candidates for infant schools or not, the children of the working poor attracted new interest and became potential clients of the New York Roman Catholic Asylum for the Children of Widows and Widowers (1829), the Boston Children's Friend Society (1834), and the New York Protestant Half-Orphan Asylum (1835). Each in its own way, these groups took over familial prerogatives, housing children who would otherwise be "deprived of the necessaries of life but also of the benefits of moral instruction," requiring a parent to pay a weekly fee toward the child's keep, training girls in domestic work and boys in trades, and indenturing them to families until they would reach adulthood.[30]

If the poor widow had been a figure of particular poignancy to members of first- and second-wave organizations, the working woman assumed that symbolic role in the 1820s and 1830s. In a rapidly changing economy characterized by large-scale migration of young women to new manufacturing jobs or servant positions, the white working woman seemed particularly vulnerable and in need of protection. Although her potential rescuers saw infant schools and children's asylums as indirect sources of succor, they made little effort to renew the work programs launched with such high hopes during the second wave. Indeed, both New York's House of Industry and Boston's Society for Employing the Female Poor were defunct by the time of the 1837 panic, and no comparable projects were attempted during the depression that followed it. Aside from labor unions, such as New York's United Tailoresses' Society (1831), among third-wave endeavors only Boston's Seamen's Aid Society (1833) directly pressed for pocketbook protections for working women, through wage supports and work guarantees. Much more typical of 1820s and 1830s benevolence were schemes to guard their virtue. New York's Asylum for Lying-In Women (1823) promised "respectable destitute" white married women a place to give birth in privacy and comfort, while avoiding contact with "*degraded, unmarried* mothers" in the almshouse. Two prostitution reform efforts—the Penitent Females Refuge Ladies' Auxiliary in Boston (1825) and the Female Benevolent Society in New York (1832)—sought religious and temporal redemption for young women, preferably "those whose departure from virtue has been the least aggravated, either in character or duration," that is, those not yet "hardened in vice." Both encouraged evangelical conversion as clear evidence of penitence; both offered domestic service as an alternative occupation.[31]

Working women themselves had a different view of protection, as was suggested by the emergence of women's unions and mutual aid organizations during the same decades. Although the type was not novel—men's mutual benefit groups had a long history and both African American and working-class white women in other cities had formed them earlier—groups such as the New York African Dorcas Association (1828), the Boston Afric-American Female Intelligence Society (1833), and the Martha Washington and Lady Howard Temperance Societies (1841) nevertheless were new to the two cities and addressed the immediate needs of women and children quite differently from benevolent societies. Dues paid regularly into the organization's treasury translated into benefits paid out in sickness or death. By one estimate, Manhattan and Brooklyn had "at least 58 female mutual benefit societies" in the early 1840s. To the extent that their funds permitted, some mutual aid associations undertook charitable activities as well, particularly when their members shared religious or ethnic bonds. New York's Female Branch of Zion, constituted by members of the African Methodist Episcopal Zion Church, provided death benefits to members and cared for their orphaned children while also raising money for the church and aiding "the sick and distressed." Catholic laywomen's parish organizations, Jewish women's synagogue societies, and immigrant women's ethnic clubs often exhibited the same mixed-purpose character. In New York, the Martha Washington Societies underwent something of a metamorphosis when the members abandoned their early emphasis on benevolence and moral inspiration in favor of strict mutual benefit activity.[32]

The initiators of these endeavors were responding to the same economic and social conditions that were simultaneously shaping middle-class women's benevolence. Designed as forms of self-protection and self-insurance, mutual aid societies sought to allay some of the deepest fears of urban working women: the fear that illness would destroy their earning capacities, that burial in a potter's field would obliterate their very existence, that their motherless children would face a desolate, friendless future. In an economy in which the demand for female workers was high yet women's labor commanded extremely low wages, only those with some margin of disposable income could sequester the odd twenty-five or fifty cents against some future calamity. Still, the emergence of such organizations was an important indicator that working women were well aware of how vulnerable and unprotected the economies of the two cities rendered them. Their approach to protection was simply very different from that of middle-class women.

The growth of these societies also testified to changes in working-class women's consciousness of gender. Whereas existing mutual benefit groups offered assistance to women on the basis of their connection to men, in the form of widows' or survivors' benefits, their presumption of feminine dependence on a male breadwinner was increasingly at odds with the realities of urban existence. In forming their own societies, women exhibited an awareness that they faced different problems from the men of their class, and expressed their belief in the power of collective womanhood to address those problems. The particular popularity of such groups among free African American women, not only in Boston, where slavery had ended in 1783, but also in New York, where it remained a reality until 1827, reflected their lack of access to conventional notions of female dependency and male providership.[33]

Commanding few resources, yet responding to desperate need in free black neighborhoods, black women's associations often blended mutual aid activities not only with benevolence but also with self-improvement, community service, and social reform. The African Dorcas Association, which held Wednesday sewing meetings at leaders' homes, and accounted carefully for all garments distributed, dispensed its bounty toward members' neighbors and friends and toward their children's schoolmates. Benevolence and mutual assistance shaded into each other as the women plied their needles. As one of the group's managers in 1828, Maria Van Surley De Grasse undoubtedly could afford to clothe her fifteen-year-old son Isaiah and thirteen-year-old daughter Maria for classes at the African Free School. With her husband George owning his own provisioning business and other property, the family qualified as members of New York's tiny free African American elite. (Despite the facts of George's birth in Calcutta, India, and his naturalization as a citizen in 1804, the family adopted Maria's identity as a free black person.) But Maria never knew what the future held for her younger daughters Theodosia and Serena or her three-year-old son John; even running a business or owning property did not always offer protection from a volatile economy and virulent racial discrimination. Education was no guarantee of occupational success, and hard-won economic prosperity could be wiped out overnight, as it was in 1834 when white mobs descended upon African American neighborhoods, making property holders particular targets of their fury.[34]

During the 1830s, self-help increasingly encompassed activities directed at ending slavery and aiding fugitive slaves. Women in church and literary societies added abolitionism to their lists, reasoning that by counteracting negative stereotypes of free blacks, they aided the cause of emancipation and promoted the welfare of all African Americans. In addition to buying books for a library and engaging lecturers to address them, the women of the Boston Afric-American Female Intelligence Society made provisions to aid members experiencing "any unforeseen and afflictive event" by agreeing to visit them when sick and furnish monetary assistance ("one dollar a week out of the funds of the Society as long as consistent with the means of the institution"). Members of New

York's Colored Ladies Literary Society, while seeking to "acquir[e] literary and scientific knowledge" for individual and collective advancement, used their resources to raise funds for the New York Vigilance Committee, a men's group that assisted runaway slaves. At the 1837 Anti-Slavery Convention of American Women, the society pledged five dollars to a petition campaign aimed at ending slavery in the nation's capital. By the late 1830s, even church fund-raising groups connected their efforts to the attack on slavery by carefully advertising that all items sold at church fairs would be "the product of FREE LABOR."[35]

It was just such reform activity by white women that sparked major controversy in the 1830s, as new, reform-oriented societies emerged in both cities. Their members' commitment to destroying important social institutions and practices such as slavery, prostitution, and liquor-dealing differentiated the Boston Female Anti-Slavery Society (1833), the New York Female Moral Reform Society (1834), and the like, from existing organizations. By abandoning or downplaying an emphasis on individual reformation, such groups instead stressed the need for radical changes in society. Antislavery societies in particular, with their demands for an immediate end to slavery, their commitment to racial equality (in principle if not always in practice), their integrated memberships, their claims of sisterly bonds with enslaved women, their adoption of highly visible political tactics, and their championing of white women's right to speak to mixed audiences, appeared so different from women's missionary or orphan societies that opponents reviled participants as "unsexed" or "amazons." Female Moral Reform Societies melded agitation against prostitution with rescue work for prostitutes. Their approach differed radically, however, from benevolently oriented groups such as Boston's Penitent Females' Refuge Ladies' Auxiliary, not only in their willingness to discuss "this vice" openly but also their championing of women's right to speak publicly on it. Whereas members of the Ladies' Auxiliary seldom published annual reports and only very delicately made their work known to the public, warning that they could not discuss prostitution in print "without great danger of communicating defilement and pollution as well as information," moral reformers courted publicity by starting their own newspapers and lobbying for laws to punish male seducers.[36]

Using evangelical ideals of femininity, which two decades earlier had been instrumental in validating collective action, white women reformers challenged restrictions on the particular forms their actions took. Speaking in the language of evangelical femininity, the editor of the *Advocate of Moral Reform* reiterated the existing belief that women "have an important part to act in the renovation of a sin-ruined world," then went on to champion their right to advocate "the cause of moral reform" as well as that of Bible and tract distribution. Pointing to precedents—"women have organized associations, held meetings, published reports, appointed solicitors, . . . resolved themselves into committees, [and] even ascended the editorial chair"—she claimed the same privileges for female moral reformers. "If our sphere of action is limited to private life exclusively," she noted in 1837, "then we have long since left our own province and entered that of the other sex." The right to take "a personal responsibility in *all* that concerns the amelioration of the condition of man, and the good of society" was conferred "by God himself." Antislavery activists, too, claimed the mantle of divine sanction and pointed to the approbation that generally greeted "'woman, stepping gracefully to the relief of infancy and suffering age,'" through benevolent associations.[37]

Yet it was the very lack of such approbation for their work that elicited abolitionists' and moral reformers' comments. Even when they combined public agitation with stereotypically feminine fund-raising and charitable activity, they found the same religious ideals that energized them used against them. (Members of the Boston Female Anti-Slavery Society, for example, not only petitioned Congress for an end to slavery and sponsored public lectures by Angelina Grimké but also ran the Samaritan orphanage for black children and conducted fairs at which they sold their needlework and fancy imported trinkets.) This fracturing of religious and, specifically, evangelical ideals into warring concepts of womanhood reworked the gender ideology of the era by delineating acceptable from unacceptable female activism. Whereas in the 1810s, associational activity by itself marked the "true woman," in the 1830s women were judged worthy or unworthy according to membership in specific groups.

Organizational Networks, 1806–1840

By 1840, the third wave of organizational formation was over. The controversies swirling around abolitionist and moral reform organizations during the 1830s had precipitated another important reworking of gender ideology, largely by forcing benevolent women to define and specify the precise limits of womanly public action. Although couched almost exclusively in religious language, the debate over women's "sphere" in the 1830s also helped define social class boundaries. Just as the evangelical turn during the second wave had bound womanhood and religion together, the 1830s controversies over reform organizations cemented and entrenched the existing close connection between organizational participation and social class standing. As organizations multiplied and organizational types diffused during the third wave, individual societies and organizational networks functioned both to reflect and perpetuate important fissures in urban society, particularly those of social class, denominational religion, and race.

Organizational networks took several forms, including spinoff and auxiliary groups, and overlapping leaderships. Experience in one organization sometimes led members to discover a new issue that appeared to require their attention, and to embolden them to tackle it. Members of New York's Society for the Relief of Poor Widows with Small Children founded the Orphan Asylum Society in 1806 because when clients died, their children were usually consigned to the city almshouse. Some of the same women led the effort to establish the House of Industry in 1814. In 1820s Boston, the men who ran a Penitent Females' Refuge recruited a group of women from the Female Society for Missionary Purposes to create a Ladies' Auxiliary.[38]

Overlapping societal leaderships, though, created the most significant networks in both cities. Indeed, the lines of coalescence and separation were remarkably similar in the two localities. At once expansive and exclusionary, such networks had the potential to make a profound impact—on individuals, on organizations, and on localities. Overlapping leaderships enabled one society to learn from another, build upon existing programs, share resources and knowledge, and garner new recruits. New societies typically tapped individuals with organizational experience to lead them, counting on their possession of practical knowledge, political contacts, access to donors, and fund-raising techniques. Joanna Graham Bethune and Ann Amory McLean Lee were much in demand to preside over new societies, no doubt for those very reasons. On occasion, individuals' contacts in other cities sparked additional sharing of knowledge and interests; Boston's Female Auxiliary Bible Society, for example, traced its origins to a letter circulated by the Philadelphia Female Bible Society. And women moving from one city to another could provide the basis for forming new organizations. When Theodosia Steele Post moved from New York to Chicago in 1836, she took with her two years' experience as manager of the New York Female Moral Reform Society and a new position as vice-president.[39]

But the same networks that empowered some women excluded others, bore witness to existing divisions, and reinforced the hierarchies (of religion, race, or social class) underlying those divisions. If some leadership networks bespoke their members' relative power and permitted participants to have a voice in city politics or to shape some aspects of public welfare provision, others testified primarily to their participants' powerlessness. Elizabeth Jackson Riley, an African

American nurse in Boston, undoubtedly brought the skills she had developed as president of the Afric-American Female Intelligence Society to her work as head of the Colored Female Union Society at the Belknap Street Baptist Church. Yet Riley herself had to rely on sister members for other skills; as late as 1849 she was signing legal documents with a mark, not a signature. Circles of inclusion and exclusion thus reflected and entrenched separate experiences of womanhood.[40]

Those circles grew in complexity over time. In 1800, when permanent women's associations were new to both cities, their numbers were few and leadership connections between them nonexistent. Although drawn from the same broad spectrum of middle- and upper-middle-class white Protestant women, the New Yorkers who led the Society for the Relief of Poor Widows with Small Children shared no personnel with those who headed up the Female Association. The same was true of Boston's Female Missionary Society and the Female Asylum. By 1840, when New York had almost four dozen women's organizations and Boston over two dozen, there were clearly evident leadership overlaps, some of them substantial, among groups. Between 1806 and 1840, for example, fourteen women, or 32.5 percent of New York's Orphan Asylum Society officers, also labored for the Society for the Relief of Poor Widows with Small Children. (The fourteen women represented 11.5 percent of the Poor Widows' Society's leadership.) With the founding of the Female Bible Society, many of the same women joined it, too. Almost 36 percent of Bible Society leaders also led the Society for the Relief of Poor Widows at some point between 1816 and 1840. Yet another leadership network connected Bible Society women with the Female Tract Society, and the Female Union for the Promotion of Sabbath Schools. (See Table A.2.) In Boston during the 1810s and 1820s, similar webs encompassed officers of the Widows' Society, Fragment Society, Female Auxiliary Bible Society, and Society for the Promotion of Christianity among the Jews. And during the 1830s, reformist organizations in both cities formed their own separate networks. Sixteen leaders of the New York Female Moral Reform Society (30.1 percent), for example, were either officers in the Ladies' New York City Anti-Slavery Society or delegates to the Anti-Slavery Conventions of American Women, or both. None served concurrently in any existing benevolent organization. In Protestant religious and benevolent circles, then, entwined organization leaderships created dense thickets of connection among women with similar social characteristics and conferred status and power upon their associations. An increase in the number of associations did not necessarily translate into corresponding increases in the number of women leaders or participants. The circle of leadership could remain relatively small as some women simply increased their workloads by taking on new positions, while simultaneously adding to a new organization's clout.[41]

Over the course of a lifetime, a particularly energetic individual might bring the benefits of her experience and her connections to a number of societies. New Yorker Sarah Beach Hall, born in 1786 and married at the John Street Methodist Church in 1806, had a long record of service both to pan-Protestant groups and those of her own denomination. She was manager and then vice-president of the Female Union Society for the Promotion of Sabbath Schools from 1817 until 1825; held parallel offices in the Methodist Female Assistance Society from 1818 to the 1840s and was president of the Methodist Ladies Home Mission Society; and was an officer of the Asylum for Lying-In Women, 1824–28, the Female Religious Tract Society, 1838–40, the Association for the Benefit of Colored Orphans, 1836–38, and the Female Benevolent Society in the 1840s. When she died suddenly in 1846 while on holiday with her husband, Francis, owner of the New York *Commercial Advertiser*, Sarah Hall was widely mourned by Methodist and non-Methodist alike. Bostonian Mary Webb had a similar record as founder and officer of the Female Society for Missionary Purposes (1800), the Corban Society (1811), the Penitent Females' Refuge Ladies' Auxiliary (1825), and the Children's Friend Society (1833), and an officer of the Female Cent Society (1804) and Charles St. Church Sunday school (1816). When a woman such as Sarah Hall or Mary Webb affiliated herself with a new group, it gained much from her experience and connections.[42]

At any one point in time, busy women such as Hall or Webb might be working for several associations. In 1836, for example, Lydia Howland Coit, wife of the New York merchant and broker Levi Coit, was first directress of the Society for the Relief of Poor Widows with Small Children (which she had served since 1811), manager of the Female Auxiliary Bible Society (she had helped found it in 1816) and the Female Religious Tract Society (she had been present since its creation in 1822), and manager of the Protestant Half-Orphan Asylum. Similarly, in 1837, when Bostonian Ann Eliza Bigelow Safford (whose blacksmith husband Daniel became wealthy enough in the iron business to endow Mount Holyoke College) stepped out onto Beacon Street from her home at Number 3, she might be on her way to work for any of her societies: the Corban Society, the Society for Promoting Christianity among the Jews, the Fatherless and Widows Society, the Penitent Females' Refuge, or the Children's Friend Society. Of the ninety-five other Bostonians who led more than one association, four-fifths (80 percent) did so simultaneously. But some individuals did things differently, giving time first to one association, then to another. Of the 177 New York women who helped lead more than one organization, over one third (38 percent) did so serially rather than concurrently. (See Table A.3.) Whether leaders served concurrently or sequentially, the entangling of organizational ties concentrated societies' economic and political clout.[43]

Information on mutual aid society officers is much more difficult to come by, especially for African Americans, but here, too, individual biographies provide examples of networks created by overlapping leaderships. New Yorker Henrietta Green Regulus served as secretary of the African Dorcas Association in 1828; a few years later, as Henrietta Regulus Ray, she presided over the Colored Ladies Literary Society. In a similar fashion, Bostonians Lavinia Ames Hilton and Jane Clark Putnam led both a black women's temperance society in 1833 and the Garrison Juvenile Society in 1837. Perhaps most notably, by the late 1830s in Boston, a few tentative strands had begun to connect black and white networks: Margaret Scarlett, a vice-president of the temperance society, was serving as an officer of the Boston Female Anti-Slavery Society, as was Lavinia Hilton's sister, Eunice R. Ames Davis.[44]

These circles of inclusion and exclusion rippled across the surface of the antebellum city, stopping at invisible dikes formed by race, religion, social class, and ideology. Concealed by the singular "woman" of nineteenth-century usage, a multifaceted reality took shape in individual and collective lives, raising effective barriers that separated benevolent from reform groups, Catholic benevolent from Protestant benevolent groups, and white from African American groups. If some barriers seem of small consequence—orthodox Calvinist missionary groups such as the Boston Female Missionary Society, comprised of Congregationalists and Baptists, neither attracted nor accepted Unitarians or Quakers—others were of substantial significance because they both reinforced and masked existing hierarchies of social power. Protestant women routinely described as "nonsectarian" groups that in actuality embraced only a segment of the Protestant spectrum and that accepted only Protestant clients. Likewise, they described clients as receiving "religious instruction" through "attendance at Christian worship" even as they refused to include Catholic churches in their calculations. White women could advertise societies as being open to "every person" or "every female" paying an annual fee and that, in reality, accepted no black members or included no working-class members. Despite particular examples of Protestant benevolence toward Catholics, especially before the great immigration waves of the 1820s and 1830s, or of white benevolence toward African Americans, the common use of inclusive terms such as "nonsectarian" or "women" by exclusionary organizations obscured the specific class or racial interests their work embodied.[45]

Organizational leaderships never crossed the great divide separating Protestants from Catholics and Jews, who created their own associations. Catholic laywomen generally conceded to nuns the social tasks (forming schools, running orphanages) undertaken by Protestant women's voluntary organizations, and devoted their charitable energies to parish needs. Two exceptions to that concession underscore the rule. The New York Ladies' Association of the Roman Catholic Orphan Asylum (1817) and the Roman Catholic Asylum for the Children of Widows and Widowers (1829) were citywide fund-raising concerns founded by laywomen. (Catholic women in Boston, at the urging of their bishop, formed the Roman Catholic Female Charitable Society.) While members helped out at both asylums, their position vis-à-vis the religious orders that ran them was distinctly subordinate and represented a significant reversal of prevailing practice in Protestant women's orphanages. Jewish women formed congregational organizations to aid the ill, indigent, or orphaned among their co-religionists, but their labor remained unknown to outsiders. Indeed, when the Hebrew Female Benevolent Society of New York's congregation Shearith Israel held a public dinner in 1847, the women, who had been providing aid to poor Jewish women and their families since 1820, were severely rebuked for making their work public.[46]

The dearth of laywomen's benevolent groups beyond the parish or synagogue and the absence of even upper-class Catholic or Jewish women from Protestant groups requires some explanation. After all, Philadelphia Jews took pride in Rebecca Gratz's career as a leader in both interdenominational and Jewish charitable and educational work, and Catholic men in both New York and Boston participated with Protestants in ethnic charitable and mutual aid organizations. Their religion did not bar successful Catholic merchants or professionals from joining the Friendly Sons of St. Patrick, the Hibernian Provident Society, or the German Society (even though it did keep them from running for public office in New York until 1806). Cornelius Heeney, whose mercantile wealth underwrote many Catholic buildings and charities in early nineteenth-century New York, including the Roman Catholic Orphan Asylum, devoted time and resources to Irish causes, serving on both the council and the charitable committee of the Friendly Sons of St. Patrick. In such instances, ethnic affiliation and economic achievement triumphed over religious divisions and provided a basis for cross-denominational association. Catholic women, on the other hand, although eligible for assistance from ethnic associations, experienced ethnic identification through their ties to men, not to other women, and so had little basis for making common cause with Protestants. For them, gender awareness was inseparable from religious affiliation; they could not claim the falsely universal term "woman," which Protestant women routinely employed for themselves. For that reason, it is significant that the occasional affluent Catholic laywoman found in the ranks of a Protestant organization was invariably a convert. New Yorker Catherine Mann Dupleix, for example, remained active in the Society for the Relief of Poor Widows with Small Children for a couple of years after her conversion in 1812, and participated with her co-workers in running the New York House of Industry between 1814 and 1819. By the latter date, however, she had severed her ties with both societies. Ten years later, in 1829, drawing on her earlier experience, she presided over the formation of the Roman Catholic Asylum for the Children of Widows and Widowers.[47]

The relatively greater worldly engagement experienced by American nuns, as compared to their European counterparts, also played a role in shaping the associative behavior of laywomen such as Dupleix. In France, where many American religious orders of this era originated, members commonly lived in cloistered or semicloistered conditions and relied for income on dowries or donations. In the United States, however, both financial necessity and a differing legal and social climate brought nuns much more into worldly society. To finance their schools and orphanages they charged tuition, solicited state or city funds, did domestic or farm labor (or, in the South, sold the products of their slaves' labor), and established laywomen's auxiliaries, as well as accepting donations from wealthy supporters. They established their legal existence through charters of incorporation (a practice virtually unheard of in France) and worried their supervising bishops by traveling in secular dress. Whereas the cloistered situation of French nuns and the numerical dominance of nominal Catholics in the French population nurtured laywomen's charities for poor women and children, such as La Societé de Charité Maternelle de Paris, circumstances in the United States bolstered laywomen's role as parish almoners or nuns' auxiliaries. In this way, both Protestant hostility and Catholic circumstance combined with peculiarly American conditions to reinforce the religious divide.[48]

Racial differences formed another chasm that organizational labor did not cross. White women's groups occasionally provided benevolent assistance to African Americans—through small handouts, gifts of Bibles or tracts, and Sunday or infant school—but such aid functioned to sustain existing racial hierarchies. Black and white women might unlatch the same door onto a city street or even share a genealogy, and black women's labor might free white women's time for meetings, but they belonged to entirely separate collectivities. (Did Silvie de Grasse Depau, wealthy French-born benefactor of New York's Catholic orphanages, know anything about the work Maria Van Surley De Grasse did for the African Dorcas Association? Family legend had it that Maria's husband George was Silvie's adopted brother.) It was not until female antislavery societies emerged in the 1830s that white women helped found organizations that were, in theory at least, colorblind. When African American women began to organize in both New York and Boston in the 1820s, their groups attracted no white members, or to be more precise, their groups were invisible to whites. African American groups thus constituted a separate network, often located within black churches. At least five women's organizations met at New York's African Methodist Episcopal Zion Church during the 1830s: the Female Branch of Zion, the Female Mite Society, the United Daughters of Conference (and its offshoot for young members, the Juvenile Daughters of Rush), and the Female Assistant Benefit Society.[49]

The racial fissures that kept white and African American women from joining the same organizations also played a role in separating white Protestant benevolent from reform organizations. Despite the long tradition of women's organizational activity in both cities by the 1830s, only an occasional woman (seven in New York, one in Boston) with experience serving in a benevolent organization became active in the new reform groups that emerged in that decade. When she did, she invariably dropped her former affiliations.

The stories of Harriet Cornelia Ely Green and Abby Ann Newbold Cox provide striking cases in point. Born in Connecticut in 1804, Cornelia Ely arrived in New York City in 1826, upon her marriage to William Green, Jr., a successful thirty-year-old merchant and widower with two-year-old twin daughters. An older brother, Ezra Stiles Ely, the Presbyterian minister, had preceded her to the city, serving for a time as chaplain in the city jails, but by the 1820s had moved on to pastor the Third Presbyterian Church in Philadelphia. As members of Samuel Hanson Cox's Laight Street Presbyterian Church, the Greens strongly supported the liberalization of church practice in two areas: use of Charles G. Finney's controversial "new measures," and eliminating pew rents in "free" chapels affiliated with a new Third Presbytery. Along with Arthur and Lewis Tappan, William provided financial support to the Presbytery and to the Second Free Presbyterian Church (the Chatham Street Chapel), where Finney was installed as pastor in 1832; Cornelia and William named their fourth child, born in 1835, after Finney.

With its mission of outreach to the urban poor, and its policy of welcoming black members (but confining them to the gallery), the Chatham Street Chapel soon became a center of secular as well as religious controversy. The founding of the New York City Anti-Slavery Society there in October 1833 signaled the members' commitment to abolitionism and their rejection of colonization. Soon, a key group of the men, including William Green, comprised the executive committee of the new American Anti-Slavery Society. At the same time, Finney's presence made the Chapel a focus for the growing split between New School and Old School Presbyterians. The Greens devoted themselves both to Finney and to abolition.

Amid all these changes, Cornelia Green's organizational involvements shifted rapidly. In 1829, with three children to mother and a fourth on the way, she became an officer of the Asylum for Lying-In Women, a group of middle-class wives providing maternity care to poor married women. An older sister, Julia Ely Hyde, who had been active in the asylum since its founding in 1823, undoubtedly recruited her. Two years later, she ended that involvement and served briefly with another agency, the Female Religious Tract Society, also with her sister. Both groups represented uncontroversial forms of female benevolence; both brought them into some contact with poor urban women. By 1834, however, Cornelia Green's organizational interests had taken a radical turn: she was now president of the Chatham Street Chapel Female Anti-Slavery Society, and after briefly serving with the Female Benevolent Society, an anti-prostitution organization, had joined with other New School women, including Finney's wife Lydia, in seceding and forming the New York Female Moral Reform Society. Considerably more confrontational than the Female Benevolent Society, more willing to take up public preventive campaigns against prostitution, and more devoted to championing the charismatic missionary John McDowall, the Female Moral Reform Society soon undertook an energetic program that involved publishing its own newspaper, the *Advocate of Moral Reform* (which Cornelia edited for a time), hiring women agents to promote the cause, opening an employment office, and operating a prostitutes' refuge. Identifying predatory male sexual behavior as a central cause of prostitution, the *Advocate* took strong stands on public issues, including opposition to slavery and advocacy of expanded rights for women. For over four years, first as vice-president, then as president, Cornelia Green was "a prime architect of the Society's policies." But in 1838, Cornelia's and William's religious views took yet another controversial turn, as they converted to perfectionism, a doctrine that held out the possibility of "entire sanctification" (or holiness) in human time. Viewed as having "fallen into the snare of the devil" because she espoused a "dangerous and seductive heresy" that supposedly encouraged adherents to dispense with "personal obedience to the moral law" and thus abrogate conventional marital and filial obligations, Cornelia was branded a "Fanny Wright" and expelled from the Female Moral Reform Society. Leaving New York for New Jersey, the Greens cut their organizational attachments.[50]

Abby Ann Newbold Cox's associational history came to no comparably dramatic conclusion, yet it exhibited similar themes. Born in Philadelphia in 1801, she was twenty-four when she married Abraham Liddon Cox, a New York City physician of Quaker background. After first associating with the Society of Friends, the Coxes soon switched allegiance to the Laight Street Presbyterian Church, perhaps because Abraham's brother Samuel was its pastor, perhaps because of the Hicksite schism within New York Quakerism. Like the Greens, whose membership in the Laight Street Church coincided with theirs, the Coxes became active abolitionists in the 1830s, with Abraham Cox serving alongside William Green as an official of the American Anti-Slavery Society. While bearing the first four of the couple's seven children, Abby Ann served as an officer of the New York Female Auxiliary Bible Society, a position that re-quired monthly proselytizing and collecting visits to an assigned district in the city. It is likely that her sister-in-law, Abia Cleveland Cox, introduced her to the group, for she was already an officer when Abby Ann arrived in New York City. But in 1834, just when the Bible Society discontinued its missionary visits and restricted its activities to fund-raising, Abby Ann Cox resigned her position. The following year, she became a key officer of the newly formed Ladies' New York City Anti-Slavery Society, an affiliation she maintained even while bear-ing her fifth and sixth infants in 1836 and 1839. When the first Anti-Slavery Convention of American Women met in New York in 1837, Abby Ann served as a vice-president.[51]

The same affiliational pattern repeated itself in the cases of two other New York reformers, Abby Welles Ludlow and Sally Stanton Willcox. The wife of the Presbyterian minister and abolitionist Henry G. Ludlow, Abby Welles (or Wills) Ludlow served a brief term with the Female Religious Tract Society be-fore becoming an officer of the Ladies' New York City Anti-Slavery Society. It was with the Ludlows that Angelina and Sarah Grimké resided during the win-ter of 1836–37, while confronting "the prejudice here against women speaking in public," and the fear that if Angelina addressed the Ladies' New York City Anti-Slavery Society, "it would be called a Fanny Wright meeting." Sally Will-cox, married to Oliver Willcox, treasurer of the Presbyterian Education Soci-ety, was briefly affiliated with the Female Missionary Society in 1818, and with the Female Benevolent Society in 1834, but abandoned the latter in favor of service with the Ladies' Anti-Slavery Society, of which her daughter Henrietta was secretary, and the Anti-Slavery Convention of American Women, which she and Henrietta attended together.[52] In Boston, the separation of organiza-tional networks was virtually complete. Only one officer in a reformist organ-ization, Eliza Jackson Meriam, who became treasurer of the Boston Female Anti-Slavery Society in 1840 and served as a delegate to the 1837 Anti-Slavery

Convention of American women, had any background in a benevolent organization. Before her marriage to Charles Meriam in 1836, Eliza had briefly assisted the Fragment Society.[53]

After 1840, when the political winds blew so stiffly as to permanently rearrange abolitionists' loyalties, some members of the Boston Female Anti-Slavery Society found shelter in traditional benevolence, or retreated to the somewhat less exposed position of moral reformer. "At least fifteen" white former officers and members, notes Debra Gold Hansen, repudiated abolitionism entirely in 1841 and instead "helped constitute the Baptist Sewing and Social Circle of . . . [the] First Baptist Church," giving their energies to Sunday-school and orphanage fund-raising, as well as sewing garments for theological students. Others remained committed to both antislavery and moral reform, but devoted their energies to the latter. The faithful stood firm against the currents gusting about them and stuck to their advocacy of both racial and gender equality. The close association between abolitionism and moral reform, so evident in significant leadership overlaps between antislavery and moral reform societies in both cities in the 1830s, wafted away. As it did, the clear-cut lines of demarcation between benevolence and reform blurred considerably. But until the whirlwind over women's position within abolitionism began to rage, the absence of reformers from benevolent groups was virtually complete.[54]

Organizational Profiles

In order to understand the connecting filaments and the isolating divides characteristic of women's organizations in the antebellum city, we need to pay attention to the ways in which organizational involvements reflected the social-class, denominational, and racial identities of their founders and leaders. Each organization acquired a particular profile shaped by its officers' racial, class and occupational backgrounds, membership in particular denominations and, in some instances, location at a specific life-cycle stage. Each society also created its own organizational culture, which it perpetuated through recruitment of new members and entrenchment of their concerns.[55]

In both cities, early white benevolent groups drew their founders and officers from families of upper-middle and middle-class merchants, shippers, professionals, and the ministers of the churches they attended. (See Table A.4.) Economic and social standing based on merchant capital and its attendant professions, including government service, provided these women with the means to act. The Boston Female Asylum (1800), for example, numbered among its officers in the early years not only Hannah Morgan Stillman and

Elizabeth Peck Perkins, but also Perkins's daughter-in-law Sarah Paine Perkins, Sarah Bowdoin (whose husband James had a distinguished career in state politics before becoming Jefferson's minister to Spain), Mary Lynde Smith (married to physician Nathaniel Smith), and Mary Vans Mason (widow of businessman and revolutionary patriot Jonathan Mason, Sr., and stepmother to United States Senator Jonathan Mason, Jr).[56]

New York's Orphan Asylum Society had a board comparably well filled with women from the city's mercantile and professional families, real estate investors, and commercial traders. It included Joanna Graham Bethune, the group's founder and long time president, whose husband was partner in a prosperous shipping concern and a successful investor in New York's booming real estate market; Elizabeth Schuyler Hamilton, widow of Alexander Hamilton; Sarah Ogden Hoffman, widow of the auctioneer Nicholas Hoffman, and her niece Isabella W. Ogden, daughter of Colonel Samuel Ogden and Euphemia Morris Ogden, prosperous New Jersey landowners; and Sarah Clarke Startin, widow of the wealthy merchant Charles Startin and sister-in-law of the painter John Singleton Copley. Few wives or daughters of artisans or shopkeepers found their way into societies such as these; the occasional woman who worked to support herself was inevitably an older widow whose experience at self-support was more in the tradition of the eighteenth-century republican woman than the emerging nineteenth-century ideal of invisible female family labor.[57]

Societies with less elite profiles nevertheless remained solidly middle-class. Women's missionary and religious associations were more likely than the Female Asylum or Orphan Asylum Society to include in their leaderships the wives and daughters of ministers, shopkeepers, and prosperous artisans, as well as merchants. Jane Inglish Parke, president of Boston's Female Missionary Society in 1816, was married to a grocer. Her associates that year included Mary Webb, the Society's founder, whose late father had been a bookbinder and whose mother taught school. Webb herself, unable to walk or stand due to a disabling childhood illness, contributed to her own support in later years by taking paying positions with benevolent societies. Still, 50 percent of the Female Missionary Society's 1816 leadership roster sprang from mercantile and professional families such as those of Heman Lincoln, a wharf owner (his wife, Sarah Cushing Lincoln, was a vice-president), John Phillips, Boston's mayor (his sister, Margaret Phillips Cooper, married to lawyer and judge Samuel Cooper, was another vice-president), and William Clouston, a city surveyor whose sister Lois Clouston was one of the society's secretaries.[58] In New York, two denominational societies providing relief to needy women and children (and occasionally to men), the Quaker Female Association and the Methodist Female Assistance Society for Relief of the Sick Poor, had comparable profiles.

Women who created reformist organizations during the 1830s often shared similar class backgrounds with officers of benevolent societies, but enough of them did not to give their associations notably different class profiles. The most obvious example is the Boston Female Anti-Slavery Society, led in the 1830s by such diverse women as Maria Weston Chapman, the wealthy and aristocratic wife of merchant Henry Chapman; Lucy and Martha Ball, sisters and school-teachers; Mary Parker, whose boardinghouse at 5 Hayward Place was a haven for traveling abolitionists; and Margaret Scarlett, founder of the African American women's temperance society and wife of used-clothing dealer John E. Scarlett.[59] A similar mixing of classes (if not races) was evident in the New York Female Moral Reform Society, whose officers derived not only from mercantile families but also from the families of physicians and small shopkeepers and included self-supporting women. The mixed-class character of the New York Female Moral Reform Society offered a striking contrast to its parent group, the New-York Female Benevolent Society, whose leadership had regrouped when Cornelia Green and others seceded in order to create the Moral Reform Society. Although both groups focused on the problem of prostitution, the Female Benevolent Society, which, as its name indicated, offered benevolence toward repentant prostitutes and attempted to convert them to evangelical Protestantism, was run by the wives of merchants and ministers. By contrast, the New York Female Moral Reform Society, with its more reformist approach, including public exposure of prostitutes' clients, use of female missionaries for fund-raising and publicity work (the Female Benevolent Society hired only men), and efforts to change state laws regarding seduction, exhibited a more heterogeneous officer pool.[60]

The same contrast was evident in Boston, where two-thirds of the managers of the Penitent Females' Refuge Ladies Auxiliary hailed from mercantile, manufacturing, or professional families, as compared to one-quarter of the Boston Female Moral Reform Society's managers. Like its New York counterpart, the Boston Female Moral Reform Society pursued vigorous public campaigns against prostitutes' clients and sought to protect young rural migrants to the city. By contrast, the Penitent Females' Refuge Ladies Auxiliary shrank from anything resembling a limelight, even refusing to publish regular reports for fear of "communicating defilement and pollution as well as information."[61]

Within Protestant groups, denominational variations added another dimension to each organization's profile, although the overall mix among the societies was shaped by each city's particular religious makeup. In New York, for example, where Unitarianism had little foothold, Unitarian officers were rare, but in Boston, where Unitarianism was strong, several societies had large Unitarian contingents. Similarly, the dominance of Presbyterians and Reformed Dutch on New York's religious scene helps explain the heavy involvement of women from those two groups in benevolent and reform causes. Boston had few Quakers or Presbyterians but many Congregationalists and Baptists; hence, Congregationalist and Baptist women showed up frequently in Boston's organizations. In both cities Episcopalians played small but significant roles and the rapidly growing Methodists organized denominational associations while also participating actively in pan-Protestant groups. Episcopalian women made up a substantial leadership contingent of New York's Orphan Asylum Society; the city's Methodist women sustained their own Female Assistance Society while also joining the Female Union for the Promotion of Sabbath Schools, and the Asylum for Lying-In Women.[62] (See Table A.1.)

Within each city's overall sectarian framework, too, members of reform-oriented societies founded in the 1830s displayed different theological orientations from those of women in benevolent groups. Although often belonging to the same denominations (whether Congregationalist, Presbyterian, or Unitarian) as their benevolent predecessors and contemporaries, they usually did not belong to the same churches. White women abolitionists and moral reformers were likely to attend churches that charged no pew rents or to those mission chapels that catered to poorer city residents and accepted African American members. Black women belonged either to integrated free churches or, more commonly, to black Protestant groups. Presbyterian moral reformers and abolitionists in New York, such as Cornelia Green and Abby Ann Cox, joined the Chatham Street Chapel, the First or Second Free Presbyterian Churches, or, later, the Broadway Tabernacle—all enterprises associated with Finney's revivals. Their Boston counterparts attended the Marlboro Chapel, the First Free Congregational Church, the African Baptist Church, liberal Unitarian and Baptist congregations, or Universalist churches.[63]

Religious differences were most significant in shaping an organization's profile, of course, when the founders were Roman Catholic. In terms of social class, members of New York's Asylum for the Children of Widows and Widowers and Ladies' Association of the Roman Catholic Orphan Asylum were an eclectic group, ranging from artisans' wives to women from well-off mercantile families to the occasional French aristocrat. Helping to run the Ladies' Association during its first decade, for example, were Charlotte Crone Lasala (who died in 1820) and Ann Louisa Lametti Lasala, the first and second wives of

John B. Lasala, a Front Street merchant; Ann Louisa's sister, Maria Theresa Mooney, wife of local ward official Thomas Mooney; Mary Lloyd, who ran her own dry goods store on the Bowery; Mrs. Adam Duncan, a stonecutter's wife; and Anna Paul Cooper, whose husband Francis was a coppersmith, real estate investor, and New York state legislator.[64] The city's Catholics planted the roots of their small middle class in the same economic soil that nurtured their Protestant counterparts—commerce, land, and skilled labor—and cultivated class standing through charitable associations. But religion rather than social class was the dominant feature of their organizations' profiles. Silvie de Grasse Depau's wealth and aristocratic French pedigree provided entrée into New York's elite social circles; two of her daughters married Protestants (one of them a New York Livingston), but as a Catholic, she directed her benevolence toward her own church.[65]

Once created by the founding generation, an organization's profile usually remained intact. Although a particular group's activities might change over time, the defining characteristics of its profile produced an organizational culture that each generation of leaders then reproduced as they recruited coworkers and successors. The secession of Cornelia Green and her associates from the New York Female Benevolent Society and the 1840 split in the Boston Female Anti-Slavery Society offer dramatic evidence of what happened when some members developed concerns or interests at odds with the group's culture. In both instances, a struggle for control of organizational goals produced a new group whose culture better matched the dissenters' collective characteristics (the New York Female Moral Reform Society and the Massachusetts Female Emancipation Society). More commonly, individuals joined organizations whose profiles and cultures were compatible with their own personal characteristics, or quit when a lack of compatibility (for whatever reasons) became evident.

Conclusion

The recurrence of similar organizational patterns in two different cities during the same era helps explain the rapid dissemination of the new ideology of gender "spheres" and its power as both a descriptive and a prescriptive model. In New York as well as Boston, the quick acceptance of women's organizational work in the first decade of the nineteenth century, followed in the second decade by the pairing of organizational participation and female religiosity, created female collectivities that largely replaced the individual charitable lady of the eighteenth century and provided a venue—church and voluntary society networks—through which women in one locality could contact and learn from each other. If the founding of early organizations depended upon some shared female experience, the proliferation of successor groups multiplied the number of possible locations for that experience. Similarly, the turn toward evangelicalism provided a stimulus and a rationale for individuals to join associations. Once joining a maternal association or Sunday school society became a means of signifying a woman's religiosity, an almost unlimited arena for women's collective labors came into being. Associational experience in one location could quickly be replicated in another, as individuals carried their organizational skills through space and time. And the existence of parallel men's groups helped reinforce a belief in the equality of male and female "spheres."[66]

Over time, new societies built upon the precedents established in the early decades of the century. As the first women's organization to lay claim to national status, the American Female Guardian Society, which "boasted four hundred forty-five local auxiliaries in 1839," owed its "prodigious scale" to those precedents. Undoubtedly familiar with men's associations that layered local, state, and regional groups into national societies with extensive reach (such as the American Bible Society), the women of the Female Guardian Society did not need to reinvent the organizational wheel. But existing patterns could stifle as well as facilitate, as the women discovered when their collective labors were measured against standards of both religiosity and womanliness—and found wanting. In this way, the activities of specific organizations became yardsticks by which to measure both the extent and the limits of "woman's sphere."[67]

CHAPTER TWO

Domesticity and
Organizational Work

T oday is my Asylum meeting," Catherine Hickling Prescott told
her daughter-in-law in 1845; "I feel as if I had got the seven
Churches on my shoulders." She clarified that somewhat por-
tentous reference to the Book of Revelations by outlining her
day's work: "children to put out, children to take in, arrange the
expenditure of the Appleton fund, [and] decide what is best to be done with
poor Theresa who is very unhappy at the Alms House." At seventy-eight,
Catherine continued to run her own household while remaining deeply involved in helping manage the Boston Female Asylum, whose board she had
joined thirty-two years earlier, in 1813. The similarity between her household
tasks and those required by the asylum "family"—managing children, accounts,
and servants—might suggest that organizational leadership simply lengthened
a woman's domestic lines, extending her daily routines into another realm.
After all, Catherine had joined the Female Asylum's managerial board at age
forty-six, just as her family nest was emptying. At the moment of assuming this
leadership post, Catherine had been married to Judge William Prescott for

twenty years, survived seven pregnancies, endured the heartache of four infant deaths, and watched her three living children reach the age when they no longer needed her full attention (Edward, her youngest, was nine). Her new vocation as organizational leader, which proved by turns rewarding and exasperating, might be interpreted simply as another phase in a life devoted to domesticity.[1]

Such an interpretation would, however, miss a crucial element evident in the life histories of nineteenth-century women leaders: their simultaneous engagement with domestic and organizational labors. As we saw in the preceding chapter, participating in women's organizations permitted individuals to cement their religious commitments and signify their class locations and racial identities. But it also facilitated their endorsement and elaboration of an emerging ideology of domesticity that, as Nancy Cott has put it, "made woman's household occupation her vocation." During the first decades of the nineteenth century, organizations and domesticity grew and flourished together, subtly yet securely entwined. Women performing organizational labor attributed their motivation to their sex's special capacity for religion or nurturance; domestic advisers applauded the extension of feminine caring into collective enterprises. With rare exceptions, they encircled home, motherhood, and organized charity in wreaths of laudatory prose. Individual women could lay down advice manuals or sermon texts on their parlor tables, leave hearth and home, and walk city streets transacting organizational business without worrying that their actions violated the "central convention" of domestic ideology: "the contrast between the home and the world." Indeed, the reciprocal relationship between organizational activity and the ideology of domesticity seldom came under close scrutiny.[2]

And reciprocal the relationship was. The same women who pursued organizational careers also devoted themselves to family concerns, blending domesticity and vocation in ways that might seem to challenge the separation of "home" from "world." That few contemporary observers perceived any contradictions in their behavior (at least not before the 1830s) suggests that women leading organizations found ways to balance family life with active involvement in collective endeavors without attracting criticism. Their balancing act is most visible in the behavior of bourgeois white Protestant women, such as Catherine Prescott, whose experience illuminates the parallel emergence of voluntary organizations and the new domestic ideology. Their strategy was to create conjunctions between family and organization, but never permit the demands of volunteer work to compete with family labor. Instead, white middle-class female leaders oriented their volunteer work around key personal events, shaping their involvements to fit life-course events that loomed large in their lives: marriage, childbearing, child-rearing, widowhood, and remarriage. Although African American and white working-class women often pursued paid labor alongside organizational work, they were never the models on which domestic ideologues drew. Only when reform-minded abolitionists and antiprostitution crusaders sought to separate the carefully entwined strands that bound organizational work to the feminine life-course, by claiming the right to pursue public activity as individuals, did the contradictory claims of domesticity and benevolence become fully visible.[3]

Leadership and Marital Status

Most members of women's voluntary societies in New York and Boston did little more than send in their yearly donations. Organizations' work fell to the chosen leadership, and most women leaders were married or widowed. Despite the large pool of available single women in both cities who had (one presumes) more time than their married sisters to devote to volunteerism, single (that is, never-married) women filled few positions as directors, managers, trustees, or officers. Typically, married women constituted between three-quarters and nine-tenths of leadership lists, and in some cases, *all* of a society's officers were married or widowed. (See Table A.5.)[4] Only in three of thirty-seven groups analyzed in the two cities did single women constitute a majority of the officer corps, and in two of those, the preponderance was slight. It seems clear that organized women of widely varying backgrounds shared common assumptions about qualifications for leadership: that marriage was superior to singleness, that it was desirable to have leaders whose lives were anchored in the daily experience of domesticity, and that tasks should be allocated according to marital status.

Arrayed along a spectrum, from groups with no single officers to those with a substantial number, New York and Boston organizations provide evidence for those shared assumptions. The three white Protestant women's societies that were led entirely by wives, mothers, and widows engaged in activities that either required marriage (in Maternal Associations, mothers shared child-rearing tips and prayed for their children's conversion to evangelical Christianity) or assumed knowledge appropriate only to married women. New York's Asylum for Lying-In Women provided medical care for poor married women during childbirth, while Boston's Penitent Females' Refuge Ladies Auxiliary helped supervise a prostitutes' reformatory. Clearly, these two groups' founders and their successors believed that pregnancy and prostitution were subjects to which single women's eyes, ears, and mouths should be shut.[5]

Closely matching the outlines drawn by these societies were three other prostitution-reform organizations selecting primarily married women as leaders. Although differing broadly from each other on crucial matters regarding the causes and remedies for "this vice," members of both the New York and Boston Female Moral Reform Societies and the New York Female Benevolent Society chose leaders with surprisingly similar marital profiles. Like Boston's Penitent Females' Refuge Ladies Auxiliary, the Female Benevolent Society emphasized the rescue of "abandoned females" through restriction, reeducation, and religion; for their part, the two Female Moral Reform Societies concentrated on prevention, publicity, and piety. In seceding from the Benevolent Society in order to challenge accepted social practices by means of moral reform, women such as Cornelia Ely Green clearly understood that they also challenged existing social roles. At their 1838 meeting, when her Boston counterparts affirmed the "duty" and *"privilege"* of *"un*married ladies . . . to labor perseveringly to promote the cause of moral reform," they expressly repudiated the silencing of single women within existing antiprostitution efforts and the superior status accorded to wives. Yet when it came to choosing officers, *"un*married ladies" were almost as scarce within moral reform societies as they were within less radical endeavors.[6]

At the other end of the marital spectrum, each city was home to a few organizations with significant proportions of single leaders. A little over half the leadership cadres of Boston's Widows' Society and Female Anti-Slavery Society were single women, as were about two-fifths in the Fragment Society and the Society for the Promotion of Christianity among the Jews. In New York, only the Quaker Female Association, founded in 1798 to dispense charity and education, was clearly a project of single women; only one-quarter of the group's leaders are known to have been married. Only one other organization, the Female Union Society for the Promotion of Sabbath Schools, had a noteworthy proportion (about 42 percent) of single women among its managers.[7]

The similar marital makeup of these groups reflected both the social experiences of single women and beliefs about their appropriate work. The Society for the Promotion of Christianity among the Jews gathered money for missions, assigning especially the role of "collector" to young single women. (In some comparable societies, single women collected dues and annual subscriptions but had no official titles.) New York's Female Association and Female Union Society for the Promotion of Sabbath Schools coordinated day and Sunday schools, enlisting in particular single women for the cause. And Boston's Fragment Society, emulating Jesus's example of "gather[ing] up the fragments" after "feeding the multitudes," made and bought clothing and bedding for poor infants, children, and mothers. Sewing was work generally assigned to spinsters, especially when the garments were to be worn by children and women. The Fragment Society's Roman Catholic counterpart, the Female Clothing Society, explicitly suggested that members meeting monthly to sew for local Catholic schoolchildren would be "young women"; New York abolitionist Henrietta Willcox Norton viewed sewing as something that required "young eyes." By contrast, when members of another society met to sew clothing for orthodox Calvinist ministerial students, their circle held three times as many wives as single women. Young unmarried women, concluded a correspondent from Amherst, were "less willing and less able . . . to mend the apparel of young men" than married women. Only the Boston Female Anti-Slavery Society, with an officer corps that was 47.6 percent married, 45.2 percent single (and 7.1 percent undetermined), fits no obvious marital pattern. As an abolitionist group with an active, energetic membership, the Female Anti-Slavery Society was structured differently from most other contemporary women's organizations, which were run almost exclusively by their officers. Moreover, as radical social critics, female abolitionists formed tightly knit circles both for activism and for mutual support. In their desire to challenge hierarchies beyond those of race and thralldom, including the hierarchy of marital status, they were very unusual.[8]

The bulk of both cities' organizational leaderships fell between the two poles, clustering around the wedded standard. Wives and widows made up between 70 and 90 percent of their directors. Throughout the three waves of organizational formation that occurred in both cities during the first four decades of the nineteenth century, women organizers clearly preferred leaders who could write "Mrs." instead of "Miss" before their names. Whether a leader was a wife or a widow seems to have been of little consequence.[9]

When individuals addressed as "Miss" did serve in leadership roles, they were almost never chosen president or first directress (the title varied from group to group), or even vice-president or second directress. Indeed, of all the groups analyzed here, only two ever placed unmarried women in the presidential chair: Margaret E. Dominick served as first directress of the New York Association for the Relief of Respectable, Aged, Indigent Females from 1829 until her death in 1831 at the age of fifty-seven; and Mary Grew and then Mary S. Parker presided over the Boston Female Anti-Slavery Society from 1834 until the group suffered a divisive crisis in 1840.[10]

More commonly, single women kept a group's books or minutes, or collected its funds. Although common law constraints on married women's control of property often dictated that a society's treasurer be a spinster or a widow, and Massachusetts incorporation statutes specifically required it, no such requirement applied to the post of secretary. And either of those positions could be more laborious than that of president. As secretary of New York's Orphan Asylum Society from 1814 until her death in 1820, Isabella Ogden recorded the meeting minutes and wrote the organization's annual reports, while also being responsible for all of its correspondence, including that delegated by sister officers. Bostonian Betsey Lane, as treasurer of the Fragment Society for over fifteen years, kept track of every penny spent for materials and every item of clothing loaned or given out, down to the last diaper. So demanding were both jobs that in some societies two individuals filled them. Whereas the Boston Female Anti-Slavery Society, reflecting its extensive correspondence with other abolitionist organizations, divided the secretary's position into "domestic" and "foreign" scribes, the New York Female Bible Society for a time split its record-keeping between a "recording" and a "corresponding" secretary. In 1814, the founding members of Boston's Female Auxiliary Bible Society, deciding that they would need both a treasurer and an assistant treasurer, chose two single women for the work.[11]

In making these choices about who would lead and in what capacities, single and married (or widowed) women shared common assumptions about the necessity of having a married leadership. The woman who bore the title of "president" or "first directress" not only presided over meetings and directed group activities, but assumed a higher public profile than any other officer and represented the society in the larger world. Never-married women were, by virtue of their singleness, seldom considered for such responsibilities, although they were welcome to fill other positions. Of course, being an organization's secretary could provide a significant kind of visibility, as the secretary's name often appeared on written and published documents, but it was a different kind of visibility from that experienced by the presiding officer. The extent to which assumptions about the superiority of the married state shaped these decisions is most starkly revealed in the behavior of single founders who, almost to a woman, deferred to their married colleagues. In Boston, Mary Webb founded several organizations—including the Female Society for Missionary Purposes (1800), the Penitent Females' Refuge Ladies Auxiliary (1825), and the Children's Friend Society (1834)—yet headed none. In each case, she recruited a married friend to wield the gavel and relegated herself to holding the secretary's pen or, in the case of the Penitent Females' Refuge, removed herself from the governing sorority entirely. New Yorkers Anna and Mary Shotwell, Quaker sisters who founded the Association for the Benefit of Colored Orphans in 1836, seated themselves in less conspicuous spots while asking a well-known and well-married leader with over twenty years' experience managing charitable societies, Martha Livingston Codwise, to take the first chair.[12]

The effacement of single women reflected an underlying theme in both republican and antebellum domestic ideologies, both of which assumed women's dependence upon men but championed the wife and mother's "control and influence" over the domestic realm. Both matrons and spinsters endorsed the notion that visible leadership within organizations belonged to the married, and that the appropriate role of the single woman was to follow. Moreover, hard economic realities could make the choice of single leaders risky business. Regardless of the legal advantages spinsters enjoyed over wives, unmarried women's common law independence did not necessarily go hand-in-hand with economic freedom. Even well-off single adults lived as sisters or daughters in married-couple households and faced both constant demands on their time and the expectation that they would behave as dependent daughters. A wife's legal dependence on her husband for support made her a surer and more likely source of economic security for women's organizations than her never-married sister. Through a wife, too, the group often had access to her husband's advice and expertise. A widow was an even better bet, provided that her husband had left her more than a bare competence. To be sure, some wives suffered the humiliation of having to ask for every coin they spent. But nineteenth-century gender ideology still gave them a moral and emotional lien on family funds that their unmarried sisters could not impose.[13]

Even women who worked for their own support encountered these realities. Take the example of two self-supporting writers—one single, one married— who assumed different leadership roles within their Boston organizations. Hannah Adams, the "famous authoress" whose works included *A History of the Jews*, occupied the post of corresponding secretary in the Society for the Promotion of Christianity Among the Jews from its founding in 1816 until her death in 1831. But a second famous writer, Susanna Haswell Rowson, author of *Charlotte Temple*, appeared more suited to the presidency of the Fatherless and Widows Society. Perhaps the divergence in the two writers' official status simply reflected contrasts in the two women's personalities (Adams's memoirist considered her notably diffident); still, it is hard to avoid the conclusion that Adams's coworkers preferred not to be led by a single woman, however helpful her fame might be to their endeavors. Perhaps, too, like other single women, Adams believed herself unsuited for preeminence in this area of her life. Whatever the reason, as the organization's secretary she served its presiding officer, transcribing more than dictating, following more than leading.[14]

How single women such as Adams, Webb, and the Shotwell sisters felt about this privileging of the married state is difficult to know. Such women seldom spoke about the deference expected of them, preferring instead to buff their self-effacing personae to a high luster. Throughout her busy, productive, and visible career (which included a public contest with Jedidiah Morse over access to the history textbook market), Hannah Adams insisted upon her personal timidity and reluctant authorship, and claimed that "want of bodily and mental firmness" made her authorial life a constant struggle.[15] One individual did comment, intriguingly if indirectly, on that persona. Hannah Murray, who along with her sister Mary devoted a lifetime to New York Protestantism's benevolent causes, including stints as secretary of the Society for the Relief of Poor Widows with Small Children and treasurer of the Female Bible and Infant School societies, was the subject of a posthumous memoir written by her pastor, the husband of a close friend. In burnishing the selfless patina of Murray's life, Gardiner Spring's prose contrasted strangely with her diary's dream narratives. In them, Murray envisioned herself preaching powerfully from the pulpits of prominent churches, and effecting "much [spiritual] good." Asleep, she indulged ambitions unacknowledged in her waking life. We can only wonder how many other single women, quietly taking minutes and becoming skilled at reticence, shared Hannah Murray's somnolent visions.[16]

The widespread consensus among women of separate religious and racial backgrounds that most organization leaders should be married might suggest that such women shared common beliefs about and experiences of domesticity. They did not. Roman Catholics are a particularly interesting case in point because they elevated celibacy above marriage as a qualification for religious leadership, and because celibate women—that is, nuns—took on many of the tasks for which Protestant women founded organizations. Whether caring for orphans, the elderly or the sick, or educating the young, nuns and Protestant matrons engaged in very similar enterprises. Yet nuns' chosen singleness was anathema to many Protestants, in large part because embracing celibacy rather than acquiescing in it as a blessed, but decidedly secondary, fate was so much at odds with the gender ideology of nineteenth-century America. Although Protestants at times favorably compared nuns' useful and seemingly autonomous lives with the restrictive social codes under which other single women lived, or even held nuns up as models of self-sacrifice, the most common popular images were exceedingly negative.[17] Indeed, a characteristic literary expression of antebellum anti-Catholicism, the convent exposé, inverted nuns' celibacy into rapacious sexuality. Lurid depictions of convents as brothels and of nuns as prostitutes or madams, as well as the use of religious terms to describe whores and brothel-keepers, expressed the anxieties of antebellum northerners about a group of women who seemed to reject the feminine fates of marriage and motherhood, and to undermine the patriarchal order by living independently of the control of particular men. Convents' "alternative femininities" seemed to embody "perverse domesticities" that could appeal to Protestant daughters and threaten Protestant marriage. Fears that smoldered in the pages of literary exposés occasionally produced actual conflagrations, most famously with the burning of Boston's Charlestown convent in 1834.[18]

In the face of such hostility and the denigration of cherished practices, Catholic writers sought, as Joseph Mannard has noted, to compose "a feminine ideal that in most essentials was virtually indistinguishable from that of mainstream Protestantism" and to define nuns as mother figures practicing "maternity of the spirit."[19] As they did so, they displaced some attributes associated with wifehood and motherhood onto single, celibate women. Corporeal mothers thus had to share mothering and domesticity with spiritual mothers, in ways not experienced by Protestant wives. Perhaps for this reason, as well as the increasingly desperate poverty of the Catholic masses, Catholic laywomen's organizations remained small in number during the era before 1840 and focused their activities primarily at the parish level. Even so, like Protestants, Catholic laywomen preferred that organization leaders be married. Until 1838, no unmarried laywoman served on the board of the New York Roman Catholic Orphan Asylum's Ladies Association, and parish organizations, such as the Transfiguration Church Ladies' Society for Clothing the Poor and St. Mary's parish Ladies Charitable Society, had married presidents. Four of the five women trustees of Boston's St. Vincent de Paul Society were wives or widows. While all Catholics deferred to the cultural authority and leadership conferred on celibate priests and nuns, within the lay world, marriage enjoyed privileged status over singleness.[20]

Catholic laywomen thus experienced two hierarchies of singleness and marriage, both of which they enacted in their organizational behavior. In one hierarchy, clerical status commanded greater esteem than lay status; within it, nuns served as the primary charitable and educational workers and laywomen as their adjuvants. The other hierarchy, which prized married over single status among laypersons, led laywomen to confer leadership roles on married women. In combination, these hierarchies created an organizational pattern in which laywomen formed parish-based charitable organizations or ladies' auxiliaries to Catholic urban institutions. It was no accident that Catholic laywomen in New York, unlike Protestant women, initiated on their own only one citywide project during this era, the New York Roman Catholic Asylum for the Children of Widows and Widowers, or that its founder and first directress, Catherine Mann Dupleix, was a convert. In her former life, Dupleix, a ship captain's wife, had helped lead the Society for the Relief of Poor Widows with Small Children, and the House of Industry. Other citywide laywomen's societies, such as New York's Roman Catholic Orphan Asylum Ladies Association and Boston's Roman Catholic Female Charitable Society, owed their existence to the prompting of a bishop or the request of a group of nuns. Catholic benevolence, like Catholic devotionalism, was parish-based and parish-focused.[21]

To free African American women as well, the choice of married women for leadership roles had particular meanings. Because women outnumbered men within the adult free population, and because in New York slavery remained a legal reality until 1827, gaining access to the married state was never simple or uncomplicated. Moreover, the marginal economic position of all free African Americans, including separations dictated by job demands, often required heroic efforts at family support. Men employed as sailors and women as domestics might spend long stretches of time apart from their spouses or children; few jobs available to free blacks permitted one individual to support others comfortably. Contributing to the "fragility [of] black life and particularly the black family" were impossibly crowded living conditions and accompanying high death rates, widespread co-residence by whites and blacks (that is, blacks living in white-owned residences), and frequent white interference in black family arrangements. All these conditions rendered men's economic power over women negligible and made patriarchal family relations, let alone private family life, almost unattainable. As in Petersburg, Virginia, during the same era, "there was less inequality between the sexes than there was among whites," in large part because New York's and Boston's free African American women and men had so little to divide.[22]

Under such conditions, the married state carried with it symbolic weight and cultural authority within African American communities, because it was so hard-won. Moreover, married women's wage-earning activities provided them with a tangible source of power within their families and communities that many white counterparts lacked. When free African American women chose wives or widows to head their organizations, they had both similar and different reasons from whites for doing so. By virtue of being married, the four women chosen in 1828 to head the African Dorcas Association could muster more economic resources than single women. They also enjoyed more autonomy from whites. The husbands of two owned small businesses—an oyster-house and a shoemaking shop—a third was married to an African Free Methodist minister, and the fourth to a whitewasher. Yet in the teeming Five Points area of Manhattan where the women's sewing circle gathered, the stability that a married leadership promised could be fleeting. Within twelve years of the association's formation, three of the four were dead, one at age twenty-eight, another at thirty-three, and the enterprise itself was defunct.[23]

Leadership, Age, and Life-Course Stage

The roles of married women, widows, and spinsters within organizations were inevitably connected with age as well as marital status. After all, most single women were young and would eventually marry. Susan Mansfield Huntington conflated singleness and youth when she answered her own query to a friend in 1815: "Do you find as much leisure for public charities, as you used to before your marriage? Young ladies should consider the talent which is entrusted to them of time, disencumbered of domestic cares, as a precious deposit, and devote it faithfully to the service of Christ." Acknowledging that "they may not have so much influence . . . as married ladies" although "it is far from being always so," the twenty-four-year-old Huntington, who had married at age eighteen, suggested that young single women commanded instead "time and opportunity for action." Despite her own relative youth, Huntington understood that marriage conferred authority while singleness kept it out of reach. Abigail Frothingham conveyed the same understanding in terming herself "a young and timid girl," who as the new secretary of the Boston Female Asylum "almost wondered at finding herself associated with venerable widows and dignified matrons" (including her recently married sister). Aged twenty and single, Abigail was still "in the days of my girlhood."[24]

Although no married woman was a "girl," wives and widows could be in their teens or their sixties. Age and marital status overlapped in organizational leaderships, producing various combinations of the two categories. Leaders of New York's Female Association were mostly young and single; those of Boston's Penitent Females' Refuge Ladies Auxiliary and Children's Friend Society were married and over forty. But within both cities' Female Moral Reform Societies, young married women predominated, as they did in Boston's Infant School Society and New York's Female Anti-Slavery Society. In no society, however, were the members predominantly single and over forty. As a woman aged, singleness became increasingly disadvantageous, marriage increasingly advantageous, not only within society at large but often within women's organizations as well. Roman Catholic laywomen encountered this combined hierarchy of age and marital status as much as did Protestants. Once above their mid-twenties they were usually ineligible to enter a religious sisterhood "without a particular dispensation grounded on their great merit and character," although widowed women without minor children were eligible. Convent entrants were generally young; a laywoman who reached her thirties as neither a wife nor a nun was at a disadvantage in relationship to women who could be called "Mrs.," "Sister," "Mother," or in rare instances, "Madam." By the time she was in her fifties, the wealthy French Catholic aristocrat, Silvie de Grasse Depau, daughter of Admiral Count Francois Joseph Paul de Grasse and wife of the New York importer Francis Depau, merited the honorific title by virtue of both marital and class status.[25]

Wives' and widows' preponderance on organization boards, then, was not merely youth's deferential curtsy to age. To be sure, age distinctions themselves were considerably less specific in the antebellum era than they later became, and "the degree to which age pervaded culture and institutions . . . was far less significant" than in recent times. Nevertheless, nineteenth-century Americans made rough associations between age and life-stage and, especially for women, between life-stage and social role. More than men, women used gender-specific rituals to note and mark transitions between stages of the life course, and associated certain activities with particular segments of their lives. Because marriage and childbearing shaped a woman's life with such transformative power, they also directed her organizational involvements. For the reciprocal relationship between domesticity and organized benevolence to work, individuals needed to merge the trek through the life-course with the path to organizational leadership. Most managed it by accepting the social roles assigned them at different stages in their lives—wife, mother, daughter—and then stepping on and off the leadership route, taking detours, or sacrificing leadership status as the via domestica required. Only a few, in rejecting the primacy of socially structured feminine roles, attempted to make their chosen work primary, or one among many identities in their lives. As we will see below, those few were generally radical social reformers.[26]

The process is best seen in the varying age structures that organizational boards exhibited. (See Table A.6.) Such variations provided opportunities for women at different life-cycle stages to take leadership roles. Some boards were composed of women from a broad age spectrum, others from a narrower age range. The early meetings of New York's Female Bible Society, for example, where women ranging in age from 25 to 67 gathered to manage group business, would have presented to the eye a different impression from comparable meetings of the Female Missionary Society, where virtually every member walking through the door was in her 30s.[27] When Mary Webb, at age 54, called the first meeting of the Boston Children's Friend Society in 1833, the other women in the room, whose median age was 45, were closer in age to her and to 59-year-old President Ann Amory McLean Lee than to the youngest manager, 34-year-old Lucy Pico Bird. If by chance Lucy Bird, on her way to a Children's Friend Society board meeting, had mistakenly stopped in at one of the first Female Anti-Slavery Society meetings, where the median age of those running things was 25, she would have been among the oldest, not the youngest, in the room.

Moreover, when members moved, quit, or died, age structures often retained the broad or narrow imprint set by the founding generation, particularly in benevolent, nonreform oriented organizations. As if stamped with matching forms, new members settled into departing members' grooves, leaving the overall age structure intact. When Boston Female Asylum treasurer Harriet Otis died, for example, her sister Mary took her place. Mary was 31; Harriet had been 38 when she joined the board. Similarly, three women leaving the board of New York's Asylum for Lying-In Women in 1826, who had been 28, 28, and 32 upon joining, were replaced by women aged 26, 30, and 40.[28] When a group's age makeup did shift, the striations sometimes inched upwards, but might just as well move downwards. As a group, the leaders of Boston's Fragment Society and New York's Female Sunday School Union got slightly older over time, but those of the New York Female Tract Society, Boston Female Asylum, and Corban Society got younger. (See Table A.7.) What was true of particular organizations was true of them collectively; in neither city was there a clear-cut, linear progression from age to youth or from youth to age. Societies in which younger women were heavily represented, such as New York's Female Association and Boston's Fragment Society or Female Anti-Slavery Society, were present both early and late, as were endeavors tilted toward older officials. And organizations that brought together members from a broad age spectrum, especially ones with strongly evangelical interests such as raising money for Bible or missionary work, retained their mixed-age character over time.

Except in the very early years of the century, when the number of organizations was still small, individuals could readily find a group or groups that fit their particular characteristics at any point in time—as long their interests ran to charity and benevolence rather than social reform. The existence and persistence of these marital and age lineaments suggests that, in keeping with other factors (such as religion or race), family role and life-course stage were key considerations in determining benevolent women's choice of organization and especially the timing and extent of their labors. Unlike reformers in the 1830s, they thought of themselves first as daughters, sisters, wives, or mothers;

for them, social role much more than individuality defined the behaviors they expected of themselves—and of others. Hence the close correlation between age and task within benevolent and charitable enterprises. Groups that drew a sizable proportion of their members from among women under forty years of age (such as school and sewing societies) often undertook labors particularly associated with young and unmarried women. Societies run primarily by older and married women were often called to provide refuge, in an extension of the maternal role, for orphaned and impoverished children, or, before 1830, to prostitutes. By definition maternal associations were comprised of young mothers; almost nine-tenths of New York's group were under forty when they joined.[29]

But because individuals defined the connection between life-course stage and organizational involvement, particular linkages could vary across time and space. About four-fifths of the women in Boston's Infant School Society were in their twenties and thirties when they joined; 70 percent were married. Their work, providing day care for young impoverished children aged eighteen months to six years, must have seemed very appealing to women like Elizabeth Carter Reynolds, a thirty-one-year-old wife and mother of three young children, who joined in 1829. Elizabeth, who had been married to businessman William Reynolds for eight years, sustained her interest in the endeavor while bearing and rearing three additional infants of her own.[30] But the three founders of New York's Infant School Society were in their fifties. One was a widow and grandmother, the other two were single, and all three had long experience in benevolence.[31]

Links between volunteer calling and life phase also varied from person to person, enabling individuals to orient their volunteer labor around family needs, much as other women did with paid labor. Boston's Amory sisters, who entered and left organizations as their home responsibilities permitted or dictated, provide concrete examples of how life-course events intertwined with religion and class (and historical time) to form each woman's organizational history. Ann Amory McLean was twenty-six and had been married for four years when she briefly became secretary of the newly formed Boston Female Asylum in 1800; she then settled into the post of manager until 1806. Despite a rapid numerical increase in the number of women's groups after 1810, she remained absent from any society for eighteen years, except for a brief stint with the Female Bible Society. Suddenly, within a year of John McLean's death, the wealthy and childless Ann burst onto the city's benevolent stage, quickly becoming president of both the Widows Society and the Fatherless and Widows Society, assuming the role of vice-president of the Penitent Females' Refuge

Ladies Auxiliary and returning to the board of the Female Bible Society. Re-married to William Lee in 1830, she continued her work uninterrupted, then added the presidency of the Children's Friend Society upon its formation in 1834. Widowhood freed Ann McLean to pursue a career in benevolence, and remarriage did not alter her commitments; her orthodox Calvinism dictated which organizations would have the benefit of her labors, and her wealth made her an especially attractive choice for organizational presidencies or vice-presidencies.

Her two sisters, Catherine Amory Codman and Rebecca Amory Lowell, ex-hibited a different life-course pattern. Unlike the childless Ann, each began bearing children immediately after marriage during the 1790s, when organized benevolence was still in the future; as John Codman's second wife, the twenty-one-year-old Catherine began mothering his children as soon as she had re-peated her wedding vows. Both she and Rebecca then waited until she had finished bearing children before undertaking benevolence work. Catherine, whose sixth and last child arrived in 1802, joined her sister Ann in the Boston Female Asylum, which she helped manage from 1803 to 1812, leaving when the group's Unitarian tilt became too pronounced. Soon, the Female Bible Soci-ety became her life work. She served as manager until her death in 1831. Re-becca, age forty-three, joined her sisters in the newly formed Female Bible So-ciety in 1814, when her youngest child was four; unlike them, she served only four years. Like many of their contemporaries, Catherine and Rebecca com-bined benevolence with family labor: directing a servant, attending a meeting, praying with a child, consulting with a sister, advising a client, making a finan-cial decision, and visiting a neighbor were all in a day's work.

In the next generation, two of Catherine's three daughters, but neither of Rebecca's two surviving girls, followed in the family tradition, but at different points in the life-course. As they came of age, an increasing number of organ-izations meant expanded opportunities for service; their religious devotion dic-tated that they serve groups with orthodox leanings, and their family ties gave them entrée into particular circles. In 1812, nineteen-year-old Catherine M. Codman attended the founding meeting of the Fragment Society, then be-came an officer of that new sewing society; two years later, at age twenty-one, Catherine, along with her forty-four-year-old mother and aunts Ann McLean (aged forty) and Rebecca Lowell (aged forty-three) helped organize the Fe-male Bible Society, becoming its first Recording Secretary. Her sister Mary Ann, nine years younger than Catherine, joined her first organization, the Widows Society, at age twenty-two, adding the Fragment Society two years later and the Infant School Society in 1831 when she was twenty-nine. Marriage ended the sisters' Boston involvements when Catherine moved to New York and Mary Ann to Salem. As young single women, Catherine and Mary Ann would have had many peers in the Fragment and Widows Societies; as daughters and nieces, they would have helped give the Bible Society its mixed-generation quality.[32]

Catherine's organizational behavior after marriage illustrates yet another way in which life-course experience shaped the ways women did volunteer work: when single women married, they typically resigned their official positions (although they often continued their financial support). Upon her marriage to John R. Hurd in 1815, Catherine disappeared from the ranks of her Boston organizations, moved to New York, and spent almost eight years in retirement as a young wife and mother (John Codman Hurd was born in 1816). When she returned to benevolent labor in 1823 at age thirty, she chose the New York Female Tract Society, a mixed-age evangelical organization to which she devoted many years of service. Despite the births of four more children in 1826, 1829, 1832, and 1836, Catherine also devoted shorter periods of time to leading the Female Sunday School Union and the Asylum for Lying-In Women. Clearly, being married or having children did not curtail Catherine's volunteer career (or that of the many other wives and mothers in her organizations). Instead, it was the transition to marriage and motherhood that proved limiting. Once that transitional period was over, she comfortably accommodated family labor and benevolent work.

Catherine was not alone in her decisions. Only a very small fraction of benevolently inclined brides remained active on association boards after the wedding day. Most seem to have found it very difficult to combine volunteer work with making the life-course transition from maiden to wife. Of twelve single women who helped lead the New York Female Association between 1799 and 1810, for example, six are known to have married; one moved to Philadelphia, but none of the others remained active in the association (although one returned to the group after her husband's death). To be sure, changing a location as well as a name left a woman little choice but to quit, and some brides packed their organizational plans with their trousseaus, then took them out as soon as they went to housekeeping. But the experience of another Boston newlywed who moved to New York, Augusta Temple Winthrop Rogers, confirms that a wider pattern was at work. Upon her marriage to New York physician J. Smyth Rogers in 1820, the twenty-seven-year-old Augusta took three years off from organizational work, during which she bore two children and looked longingly toward Boston. When she returned to benevolence work in 1823, this "beloved & respected . . . pious, active lady" became corresponding secretary of the Orphan Asylum Society, a group that perhaps better fit her new maternal role than her old haunts, Boston's Female Bible Society and the Society for Promoting Christianity among the Jews.[33]

The occasional young newlywed who did stay active was more likely to be found in Boston than in New York, perhaps because of the city's smaller size, but even for this handful of women the transition to marriage often brought changes in organizational work; the transition to motherhood usually interrupted or ended it. Harriet Moore was not quite as youthful as her Boston Female Bible Society coworker, Augusta Winthrop, when she became the second wife of Congregationalist minister Richard Storrs in 1819. But at thirty-five, she was still a newlywed. Committed to four endeavors before her marriage, she dropped three of them, remaining only with the Corban Society, a sewing group. Even then, "a change of name required a change of office, too," as a colleague later commented. Harriet Moore had been the society's treasurer; Harriet Moore Storrs joined the ranks of its managers. Moving soon thereafter to Braintree, she took up the work of a minister's wife full time.[34] Sophia Thompson Cross was a twenty-seven-year-old widow when she took on one board membership in 1826. Remarriage to Willard Badger in 1830 did not lead her to resign from the Boston Female Asylum, but the birth of two children within three years did. Sophia sent regrets that "her domestic cares [were] such as to prevent her giving that attention to the duties of the office which is desirable." One of Sophia's predecessors, Louisa May Greele, had come to a similar conclusion when her first child arrived; her three years with the asylum included transitions to both marriage and motherhood, but it was the second that precipitated her retirement.[35]

Indeed, the number of women who weathered these two life-course transitions successfully enough to create uninterrupted careers as benevolent leaders was surprisingly small. Most exhibited the back-and-forth and organization-shifting behavior evident in the lives of Catherine Codman and Augusta Winthrop. The few who began as single women and continued through marriage and/or motherhood resembled Bostonians Abigail Frothingham Wales and Betsey Lane Jackson, who were forty-five and fifty-one, respectively, when they married for the first time, and had been economically self-supporting for years. By the time they made the leap from singleness to the married state (and in the case of Abby Wales, to first motherhood at age forty-eight), these women had undoubtedly figured out how to juggle the demands of two kinds of work. More typical were those whose inability to balance both jobs at key transitional moments led them to shift priorities and to focus (sometimes only temporarily) on family demands, then return to activism when family needs relented. Time was the scarce commodity; most continued their financial contributions, but declined requests for their leadership talents.[36]

Once a woman had borne a child or two and taken up or returned to organizational work, however, the arrival of additional children was often of less consequence. Few matched the record of New Yorker Judith Hone Anthon, who began serving as a manager of the Orphan Asylum Society when the ninth of her fourteen children was just starting to crawl, then continued to serve (with one interruption) until she was a great-grandmother. But many individuals in both cities ran to meetings or completed organizational responsibilities while expecting, nursing, weaning, toilet-training, disciplining, and mourning children. During nearly a decade of service to New York's Asylum for Lying-In Women, Julia Ely Hyde, a mother of five at the outset, entered her own lying-in room three times and put on a mother's mourning garb twice. When she quit the asylum's board, Julia pleaded the pressure of other associational work, not familial needs. Indeed, childless wives, who might be expected to dominate the ranks of those who served on several volunteer boards, were no more prominent among women with multiple affiliations than were mothers of six or eight children. Of the 192 New York wives whose childbearing histories are known, the twenty-two (11.4 percent) who bore no children averaged two leadership positions apiece, about the same number as mothers of eight. Among Bostonians, the 140 wives with known child-bearing histories included eighteen (12.8 percent) with no children, who averaged two affiliations apiece. Mothers of six, however, averaged 2.2 affiliations. (See Table A.8.)[37]

As these examples demonstrate, married leaders found it easiest to combine family responsibilities and volunteer labor after experiencing major life-course transitions, not while particular shifts were occurring. Even at that, family needs—or as one individual put it "the numerous cares of a large family"—might require other interruptions in one's benevolent career. Mary Robertson Wyckoff gave a year to the Society for the Relief of Poor Widows with Small Children between her 1799 marriage and the 1804 birth of her first child. Retired from leadership for over a quarter-century, she returned to the board when her third and last child was thirteen years old, resigning only when her husband's final illness once again shifted the demands placed on her. Mary's interrupted service to one endeavor was somewhat unusual; more often, when a woman quit an organization in order to devote time to family labor, her return to organizational activity entailed a new undertaking. Mary's sister Elizabeth Robertson, for example, replaced her on the board of the Society for the Relief of Poor Widows and served until her marriage to James Walsh in 1806 at age twenty-five. (An older sister, Helen Rodgers, worked continuously on the board from 1800 until her death in 1818.) When Elizabeth Robertson Walsh re- turned to organizational leadership in 1828, it was the Orphan Asylum Soci- ety's board she joined, not the Widows' Society, though by then she herself was a widow. A variety of factors shaped decisions like Elizabeth's; in her case reli- gion was crucial (she was a devout Presbyterian), as was her friendship with Orphan Asylum Society president Joanna Graham Bethune, and the organi- zation's religious, racial, and class "profile," which fit her comfortably. But age, marital status, and life-course stage were significant elements fostering that sense of comfort, as the orphanage management included a number of women like herself: over forty (Elizabeth was forty-eight), widowed, finished bearing children, and ready to begin mothering the motherless.[38]

Like the Robertson sisters, and like countless wives who worked for pay, in- dividuals oriented their organizational careers around life-course phases, re- signing when family responsibilities took precedence, then recommitting or choosing new avenues of service as family needs permitted. If some changes, such as marriage or first childbirth, usually forced them to choose between fam- ily and organization, others, such as ending childbearing or being widowed, could seem expressly liberating. Lydia Butler Griffin undoubtedly thought she had completed her childbearing years when she joined the New York Female Bible Society's leadership in 1822. Thirty-nine-year-old Lydia had been married for twenty-one years and had borne seven children, the last two in 1814 and then 1820. But an eighth pregnancy leading to the birth of Ellen in 1826 seems to have given her pause; she quit the organization and did not return, perhaps because Ellen, who died at age five, needed her full attention.[39]

Regardless of the catalyst, when married women leaders interrupted or ended their careers in benevolence, they were refusing to permit vocation to compete with family. By subordinating their volunteer careers to their family labor, and matching volunteer work with particular phases of their marital and repro- ductive lives, these leaders enacted and reproduced a gender ideology based on feminine self-sacrifice and subordination. Rather than assume women's right to individualism, they embraced the duty of selflessness. In this fashion, they shaped domesticity and benevolence into reciprocal, mutually reinforcing experiences, reconciled organizational work with the ideology of domesticity, and did both jobs while always appearing to give primacy to domestic needs. To be sure, some expressed deep ambivalence about their priorities, and ac- knowledged the inherent tensions between the demands of two forms of labor. Susan Huntington, a minister's wife and mother of three, found her conduct scrutinized, first by an observer who asked "with a tone and manner which gave peculiar emphasis" to the inquiry, how she could "'go out so much . . .

and be engaged in so many charitable societies, without neglecting [her] family,'" and then by a critic who "censured" her "for doing so little in a public way, and confining myself so much to my family." Facing these contradictory pressures, Huntington first decided that a wife "can exert greater influence in her own family than any where else," but then concluded, with all the deceptive self-confidence of a modern "superwoman," that "industrious women" could "redeem much time from their families for more public duties." Few other women leaders were so explicit about the conflicts inherent in their dual roles; they performed both but gave priority to one.[40]

At the same time, by managing to balance family and work, married women leaders validated volunteer labor and created opportunities for others to use it differently. Women interested in radical social reform seized those opportunities during the third wave of organizational formation in the 1830s. In attempting to sever femininity from dependence and wed it to gender equality, these leaders challenged dominant assumptions about how age and life-course stage should mold an individual's public activism. They did so, however, within a specific, and still limiting, racial and class-defined context.

White abolitionists and moral reformers represented perhaps the starkest example of that difference. Not only did they expect members to do an organization's work, thus repudiating the distinction between inactive members and active officers so commonplace in other societies; they chose officials whose age and marital characteristics challenged the notion that women were to think of themselves (and be thought of) primarily as wives, daughters, and mothers. Two of the Boston Female Anti-Slavery Society's first three presidents were single women, and one of the two, Mary Grew, who served briefly before moving to Philadelphia, was twenty-one. Her successor, Mary Parker, who became president in 1835 and remained in that office until the organization split, was thirty-three, single, and self-supporting. After 1836, the group generally adopted Quaker practice and refused to indicate, by the use of titles such as "Miss" or "Mrs.," whether members were married or single. Distinctions based on marital status were to be irrelevant. Moreover, although the group's membership included women of varying ages, younger women were especially visible as officers. Youth could take the foreground, rather than to defer to age when it came to leadership opportunities. Sarah Southwick was nineteen when she became the group's recording secretary in 1840, Harriet Jackson a mere sixteen when named treasurer in 1841.[41]

Officials of the Boston Female Moral Reform Society, over 70 percent of whom were also active abolitionists, questioned some dominant tenets regarding marital status and age, but acceded to others. On the one hand, they affirmed that "*un*married ladies, members of this Society, feel it our duty and our *privilege*, and appropriate to our standing and class as *young* ladies . . . to labor perseveringly to promote the cause." On the other hand, they retained the use of marital titles and chose very few single women for leadership positions. As abolitionists, it seems, they could question the significance attached to marital status, but as moral reformers they deemed it important to be able to affix "Mrs." to one's name. A woman who spoke out publicly on sexual matters had better be wrapped in the protective covering of marriage, lest she find herself accused of harlotry; hence the varying tactics of white women abolitionists when charged with seeking racial "amalgamation." Unlike their bolder Boston sisters, members of New York's Ladies' Anti-Slavery Society chose an all-white, heavily married leadership who carefully used titles in public documents. When individuals attending the 1837 Anti-Slavery Convention of American Women were given a choice of whether to list themselves by titles, eleven of the nineteen New York officers in attendance (58 percent) opted for a title, while two of the seven Boston officials (29 percent) did.[42]

However tortuous the route that moral reformers and abolitionists took when reaching these decisions, it was a path formed (or more precisely, deformed) by the dominant racial ideology of their day. It was their respectability as white women that they were required to defend, and any association with African American women, of whatever class status, endangered the defense. Few had the steeliness of will, let alone the personal resources, to resist all elements in the dominant code of femininity. It was difficult enough to challenge its commandments on whether married—let alone single—women could properly discuss the double standard of sexual morality, or to indicate some knowledge of African American women's daily vulnerability to sexual assault. Perhaps for that reason, white women who agonized about how to find their way through the whitewashed maze of respectable femininity seem not to have considered looking to their African American coworkers for guidance.[43]

Yet blending family life with public work was something that African American women organizers well understood. Unlike those of most white activists, their daily rounds included paid labor alongside familial and associational endeavors. The experiences of Bostonian Elizabeth Jackson Riley—nurse, wife, mother of five, and president of both the Afric-American Female Intelligence Society and the Colored Female Union Society—incorporated all these elements. As she entered people's homes to care for the sick and dying, Riley acquired intimate knowledge of their circumstances, knowledge that underlay the Colored Female Union Society's assistance to widows and orphans. In turn, her wages, along with William Riley's income, buttressed the mutual aid principle on which the society rested. And because the hands that could cool a fever or conduct a meeting were unpracticed at something so simple as writing her name, Elizabeth Riley sought self-improvement and group uplift in the Afric-American Female Intelligence Society. Its public lectures and insurance program promoted "the welfare of our friends" and "the diffusion of knowledge" for "women of color of the Commonwealth of Massachusetts." Even while managing these two societies and nurturing her two youngest babies, Elizabeth joined the Boston Female Anti-Slavery Society, along with her two older daughters. When she died in 1855, Frederick Douglass captured the protean quality of Elizabeth Riley's life in a warm eulogy recounting her intertwined labors as "the good Samaritan of Boston," "a nursing mother in Israel," and "one of the most intelligent workers for the elevation and improvement of our afflicted people."[44]

In meeting the demands of remunerative, familial, and associational work simultaneously, Elizabeth Riley exemplified a model of female activism that her black coworkers would have found familiar. Yet white associates in the Boston Female Anti-Slavery Society drew no inspiration from her ability to be at once a wife, mother, worker, and community activist. Immersed in the racial and class conventions of their day, they were unlikely to model themselves on the Elizabeth Rileys who sat in their midst.[45]

At the same time, white abolitionists were aware that their work required different priorities from those observed by most white women of their class. While New York's Abby Ann Cox sought to reassure supporters that abolitionist work could be pursued "without calling them from their own firesides [and] identifying them with the scenes of political strife," Boston's Maria Weston Chapman insisted that membership in "the human family" imposed duties on women that took precedence over "any popular notions of feminine propriety." Divergent ideas about how to meet both familial and organizational demands reflected differences over whether individuals should define themselves primarily in terms of family roles and created tensions for some abolitionists and moral reformers. Some, especially the Garrisonian abolitionists of the Boston Female Anti-Slavery Society, refused to choose between being mothers or reformers, women or individuals. The confluence between family and reform that historians of abolitionism have often noted, with whole families devoting themselves to the cause, made that refusal somewhat easier.[46]

Others, especially moral reformers, had hopes of both accepting and transforming existing ideas about white women's proper roles as sisters, daughters, wives, and mothers—ideas prevalent among their contemporaries in benevolent associations. The strong presence in moral reform ranks of self-supporting working women (most of them single or widowed) undoubtedly facilitated the process. Fifteen percent of the New York society's leadership earned their own bread. Moreover, moral reformers consciously rejected existing distinctions between board members and employees, and refused to ask agents, missionaries, or magazine editors to walk behind unpaid officials within the organization. Unlike Mary Webb, whose singleness and employee status rendered her ineligible to lead an organization she had founded (the Penitent Females' Refuge Ladies Auxiliary), Abigail Bartlett Ordway joined the Boston Female Moral Reform Society's executive committee as a self-employed milliner, and continued to serve while embarking upon a second career as a paid antislavery, moral reform, and educational society agent. New Yorkers Margaret Allen Prior, Sarah Ingraham, Mary Irena Treadwell, and Sarah Towne Smith served in key positions on the Female Moral Reform Society's board while also drawing salaries for their missionary or editing labors.[47]

As both paid and volunteer laborers in the work of sexual reform, but especially as single women, Treadwell and Smith lived lives very different from those of other prostitution reformers in New York and Boston. Whereas all officials of the Boston Penitent Females' Refuge were married and almost 60 percent were over the age of forty when they took up their posts, Mary Irena Treadwell was twenty-five and Sarah Towne Smith was thirty-two when each became an official of the New York Female Moral Reform Society. Both subsequently married, but continued to work through various life-course transitions, which for Smith involved becoming stepmother to her dead sister's babies (Smith married her brother-in-law Job Martyn in 1841), and bearing four of her own. Both served at some point as editor of the *Advocate of Moral Reform*, and although Sarah Towne Smith Martyn left the Female Moral Reform Society in 1845 and evinced increasing exasperation with the limits of "moral suasion" as a reform method, she maintained a lifelong commitment to social change, including, by 1854, woman suffrage. Treadwell remained a moral reformer, convinced that feminine influence, not political involvement, would bring about true social transformation. Yet her 1838 marriage to Joel Hubbard caused no interruption in her chosen work.[48]

In the end, although many moral reformers created careers that blended life and work, and rejected the subordination of organizational needs to family requirements that other workers endorsed, their experience with political strife in the 1830s led those who remained with the cause to develop a compromise between the position of benevolent officials and that of abolitionists: they made sure that their vocations never *appeared to* compete with their domestic duties. That compromise is especially evident in the ways moral reformers tamed the early radicalism of their enterprise in later accounts. In 1843, for example, Sarah Ingraham posthumously swept her coworker, Margaret Prior, back into the kitchen, even though Prior had lived as a paid missionary, walking New York's streets visiting prisoners, prostitutes, and almshouse inmates. Her "interest for others," Ingraham assured readers, never led Prior "to neglect the duties of *home*." Both a biological and an adoptive mother, Prior emerged from the pages of Ingraham's memoir as maternal and domestic, in public as well as in private life.[49] Some of Boston's abolitionists replicated the story in their rejection of women's rights activism. When the Boston Female Anti-Slavery Society split along ideological, class, religious, and racial lines in 1839–40, those who "withdrew from organized abolitionism . . . in favor of moral reform and missionary causes," notes historian Debra Gold Hansen, were those who "courted images of female piety, morality, and domesticity."[50]

Family and Organization, Home and Work

In their aggressively domestic imagery, these later accounts obscured the frankly public character of women leaders' chosen work. Even though leaders of different organizations enacted different versions of domesticity, accounts of white women such as Prior homogenized them into one, home-based blend. Yet in their own renditions, particularly in the carefully kept minute books and published annual reports that have survived, organizational leaders made little reference to their domestic existences. Apart from the occasional notation that "the duties of the new relation into which she had entered," namely remarriage, required an individual to stop working, or that a prospective officer declined to serve because "her Familial avocations would not permit her constant attendance" on associational concerns, minute books and published reports seldom acknowledged that members had personal lives. Although the routine demands and crises of individuals' family lives surely affected on occasion their ability to attend a meeting or complete a task, organizational records made scant mention of them. Minutes and reports can provide lush detail about clients' family lives, but for the historian seeking a word about members' experiences of birth, death, marriage, remarriage, or widowhood, organizational records are a desert. Without comment, the scratch of a secretary's pen transformed the remarried Mrs. John McLean into Mrs. William Lee, or dropped the newly married Catherine Codman Hurd from the leadership list. Without self-contradiction, the ladies of New York's Asylum for Lying-In Women, such as Julia Ely Hyde, maintained close tabs on clients' experiences of pregnancy and parturition, but kept silent on their own.[51]

Even obituary or memorial notices dried out the bloom of individual lives. When Helen Robertson Rodgers died in 1818, her colleagues lauded her "zeal, fidelity & ability," "knowledge of human life," "firmness & decision," and devotion to "established christian principles." Twenty years later, the deaths of two other leaders of the same organization brought a tribute to them as "bright ornaments among the intelligent and the well-informed" who "turned their grateful hearers minds to thoughts of Jesus and heaven." No personal details breathed life into the almost interchangeable descriptions. In both cities, secretaries' inscriptions praised deceased coworkers in the same impersonal adjectives: faithful, wise, charitable, punctual, amiable, firm, cheerful, kind, sincere. Perhaps most notably, unpublished minutes included none of the congratulatory comments, birthday observances, sympathetic condolences, or other rituals that marked women's associational and work culture in the late nineteenth and twentieth centuries. Except within Maternal Associations, where the labor performed (praying for one's children and improving one's mothering skills) was family labor, unpublished minutes eclipsed comments on members' private lives. Only the occasional fleeting nebula making visible a woman's "numerous and multiplied cares" or "health and domestic concerns" hinted at an entire universe of familial experience. Just as most women leaders kept their organizational commitments to all appearances secondary to familial needs, they kept their individual lives as mothers, wives, or daughters largely invisible in organizational contexts. By keeping their meetings free of the trappings of their individual domestic lives and, over time, shifting their gathering places from members' homes to church vestry rooms or women's institutions, they created, in effect, a distinction between individuals' familial roles and the social roles (whether of fatherhood or motherhood) that some organizations enacted.[52]

Yet women leaders regularly interlaced domesticity and organizational concerns. On the yellowing secretary's page and off, there is abundant evidence for the ways in which they blended family and organization. Familial terms and terminology, for example, were the most common ways in which women described their collective endeavors. Associational names identified clients as infants, orphans, half-orphans, widows, or fatherless children; published reports employed parental and sororal metaphors to convey organizational goals and concerns, including mending fractured family relationships. Moreover, some replicated what they saw as ideal family arrangements within their organizations by establishing family-based hierarchies or enacting familial roles in relationships with clients, and within asylum walls. In some instances, the intertwining of family and organization was quite literal, as women used their organizations to serve family needs, and enlisted their families for the benefit of their organizations.

The contrast between these women's reticence about their personal lives, in organizational contexts, and their free use of familial language and family practices in those same contexts highlights the simultaneous and related emergence of domesticity and women's organizations. In the early nineteenth century, in both their families and their organizations, women leaders formalized processes that had been informal and formulated new rules and boundaries in both areas. Women's associations rejected earlier practices of individual almsgiving in favor of collective social provision, and established specific rules and procedures for clients. At the same time, middle-class urbanites began separating family life from social life, especially through the two-address strategy: one for "home" or reproductive household, the other for "work" or economic production. In the process, they emptied their households of people (apprentices, clerks) and things (artisans' tools, merchants' goods) with nondomestic associations, and created new lines between "private" and "public" activities, and between women's and men's "spheres." As leaders of women's organizations worked out the relationship between their own work and home lives, they developed the understanding that women's realm contained both a "private" and a social dimension. Women's organized activities, in other words, were neither fully private nor fully public, neither wholly integrated with nor fully separate from their domestic lives. Over time, their ideas about the social space that volunteer work occupied became more distinct, and the space itself acquired clearer definition.[53]

One way to observe the definitional process is to pay attention to the language women leaders used about families, because familial images suffused the language they employed to describe their work. From the beginning, they cited the biblical injunction to "visit the fatherless and widows in their affliction" as justification for associational activity, and they referred to clients in parental, but especially paternal, terms. In 1803, for example, the organizers of Boston's Female Asylum created a seal to represent their work visually; it depicted a woman welcoming a girl at the door of a house and bore an inscription from the Book of Esther: "for she had neither father nor mother." In 1811, children ensconced at New York's Orphan Asylum Society were a "little fatherless group," and in 1817 a newly founded Boston association chose to designate itself the Fatherless and Widows Society. When the New York Female Moral Reform Society opened an employment bureau in 1837, the officers specifically singled out "respectable unprotected females, especially the fatherless and the orphan" for assistance. By the 1820s, reports of benevolent societies routinely constituted clients as "the family" and compared orphanages or refuges to "a well-regulated family of brothers and sisters" or "well regulated Christian famil[ies]" where "family worship" was daily practiced. A New York asylum opened in 1837 served as a "home" for "our aged children" (respectable, indigent women over age 60), many of them former servants in their patrons' families; the opening of a contemporaneous children's refuge in Boston created a "family" under the care of "wise and affectionate parents."[54]

In describing their charities as substitute fathers or husbands, or imagining their asylums as families, charitable women intended no irony. Their use of paternal and familial language simply stated what was, to them, the obvious reality that children without fathers were orphans, and that fatherless families lacked adequate security. (In actuality, plenty of children in their orphanages had one living parent, usually a mother.) When asylum managers emphasized the difficulties of fatherlessness, they invoked seemingly natural hierarchies, including those of both gender and social class. Clients "deprived of their natural Guardians," having lost or "outlived their natural protectors" needed surrogates for the absent male provider and protector. Such familial language reflected organizational leaders' deep intellectual and experiential roots in hierarchical concepts of domesticity and gender relations. In an earlier era, the surrogate for the lost protector would have been found in another family, through indenture, apprenticeship, or domestic service. In the new urban economies of New York and Boston, anyone attempting to aid less fortunate women and children would still need to provide a substitute for the male breadwinner, and replicate patriarchal family relations; indenture would continue to have a place in the process. But to those informal practices, charitable women added their collective willingness to assume the masculine social role. They could not be fathers, but their organizations could fulfill a role assigned to fatherhood.[55]

Because motherhood did not encompass providership, maternal imagery was neither as strong nor as ubiquitous as paternal imagery. When invoked, it conveyed notions of sympathy and a protection that was moral rather than economic. Herself a survivor of fourteen pregnancies, Hannah Stillman signed herself "A Mother" in 1799, calling upon the women of Boston to hire a "capable, discreet woman" who would house and teach "female orphans suffer-[ing] for want of early patronage." Ten years later, New York's Orphan Asylum Society managers offered to provide needy children the "fostering care of those who can feel as mothers." Such maternal language generally referred to the women hired to run orphanages or asylums, or to counsel clients, not the women or the organizations sponsoring them. In 1832, for example, the women sponsoring New York's Roman Catholic Asylum for the Children of Widows and Widowers termed the nuns whom they recruited to run the asylum "mothers to the afflicted orphan [and] . . . parents of the fatherless and motherless." A counterpart, the matron at the Asylum for Lying-In Women provided "motherly kindness and attention"; another gave "maternal care" to "motherless" girls who had become repentant prostitutes. The relative scarcity of maternal imagery indicates the extent to which asylum founders or managers conceptualized their institutions as fulfilling the masculine social roles of provider and economic protector.[56]

Only in the 1820s and 1830s did some groups, by designating coworkers or clients as "sisters," employ familial language that evoked more egalitarian ideals. African American women most often used the word, addressing each other as "sisters" while also agonizing over "the sufferings of our enslaved sisters." Among white women, only mutual aid society members used the language of sisterhood for themselves; moral reform and antislavery women were more likely to employ it for coworkers in other localities and for clients. While the Boston Female Moral Reform Society embraced their New York coworkers as "our sisters," the New Yorkers themselves extended the language of sisterhood to "our suffering colored sisters," publishing articles on the sexual abuse suffered by both free black women in the North and enslaved women in the South. "They are our sisters," wrote Sarah Towne Smith, asking readers to sympathize with slave women and to condemn white women who "tacitly connive" in the "unblushing profligacy" of slaveowning men. Abolitionists simultaneously addressed coworkers and described slaves as "sisters."[57]

Such egalitarian ideals, which gave the horizontal notion of sisterhood primacy over the vertical concept of parenthood, and introduced the concept of mutual assistance as an alternative to masculine providership, remained the exception rather than the rule. Only radical abolitionists continued to use egalitarian language throughout the 1840s and 1850s. Indeed, one way in which conservative abolitionists and moral reformers (many of whom were the same people) responded to criticisms of their public visibility in the late 1830s was to wrap themselves in the familial language of wifehood and motherhood and cast off the familial language of sisterhood. Meeting in Utica, New York, in 1839, members of the newly formed American Female Moral Reform Society reassured supporters that "every wife and mother" in attendance was as "prepared to discharge her relative duties" when the meeting ended "as she would have been, if conscientious scruples had kept her at home." Moreover, the delegates agreed that through efficiency and plain living, "our sex might meet the claims of the various benevolent associations of the day, without neglecting our domestic duties." Ten years later, the group described itself as providing "friendless or destitute girls" with "strictly *parental*" discipline that replicated "the order and decorum of a well-regulated Christian family."[58] By reverting to concepts that emphasized gender hierarchy and conflated women's individual positions as wives or mothers with the narrowly defined social expectations of wife- and motherhood, the delegates backed away from the radicalism inherent in notions of sisterhood.

The terminology and assumptions surrounding the "well-regulated" family evolved subtly, too. Both early and late, women leaders envisioned their job as substituting orderly families for disorderly ones. The notion that placement within a proper family setting could be the means of reclaiming "neglected," troubled, or unprotected individuals was widely shared, as was the idea that in-denturing older children could help poor families reorder themselves. In its early years, the New York Society for the Relief of Poor Widows with Small Children made the indenturing of youngsters over ten years of age a condition for assistance. Both Protestant and Catholic women imagined orphanages as family-like protective spaces within which young children (usually those over three years of age) could receive education and training, until they were old enough to be indentured or go directly into the workforce. Both Protestant and Catholic women ordinarily required parents to relinquish legal custody of their children to the orphanage trustees; both attempted to place youngsters (at around twelve or fourteen years of age) in same-faith families. Similarly, mag-dalen refuges in both cities sought to place repentant prostitutes as domestics in "christian families," but at least one, Boston's Penitent Females' Refuge, re-quired an initial institutional stay within "the family" of at least a year, during which the young women were to learn the "habits of regularity and industry" that their own families had failed to inculcate. Once retrained by the institu-tional family, they could (in theory) join a private family's household.[59]

Definitions of orderly families were rather inchoate at first, with many early organizations specifying only that good families were "virtuous" or "respect-able." At the turn of the nineteenth century, households and families were still expansive institutions that accommodated individuals beyond blood kin; many of the merchant and artisan households from which organizational leaders set out every day sheltered blood relatives beyond their nuclear families, or housed apprentices. Most relied on servants to bear the heavy burden of regu-lar household tasks; indeed, without their servants, wives and mothers could never have participated in organizational activities. And household labor still encompassed a wide-ranging variety of tasks, both productive and reproductive.

Only gradually did organization leaders refine their understanding of orderly families, a process clearly seen in the ways they sharpened, lengthened, and made more specific institutional rules. Orphanage and asylum managers, for example, formalized and clarified fuzzy and informal practices, revealing alterations in their own thoughts about what constituted proper family arrangements. From the outset, New York's Orphan Asylum Society required that a couple head its orphanage "family," that children presented for admittance be legitimate, and that surviving relatives waive all legal claim to them. Boston's Female Asylum similarly took only legally surrendered children whose parents had been married. The institution constituted its own "family," with legitimately born clients cared for by a hired couple or matron. Both groups soon found that, regardless of the rules, many orphans had truculent relatives who interfered with institutional order by taking them for unplanned excursions, plying them with sweets, and returning them with nasty stomachaches (to institutional siblings jealous of the outing and the sweets). Increasingly strict control of visits followed. "The unruly conduct of many disorderly mothers and relations" led the Female Asylum's managers in 1803 to insist that families apply formally for permission to see their girls; by 1815 most outings were banned, replaced instead by a monthly visiting day, with family time limited to a half hour. The New York Orphan Asylum Society's lengthening list of rules, which, by 1844, ran to several pages and included a monthly visiting hour and a prohibition on taking children from the building, testified to the managers' continuing efforts to separate an orderly institutional family from disorderly blood relatives, and to define good families as ones that kept schedules and maintained boundaries between themselves and outsiders. Whether at magdalen asylums or orphanages, benevolent women insisted upon regular schedules, both to maintain institutional order and to offer an example of correct "family government" to inmates, their families, and the world at large. "It is unhappily the case, in many poor families," sighed Bostonian Mary Webb in 1835, "that many have no *regular* meals, and therefore think that their children must be feeding the greater part of the day"; in "poor families," giving a child food only at three scheduled mealtimes was tantamount to starving her. In Webb's view, of course, by scheduling three meals the Children's Friend Society taught a discipline of rules and routine.

In placing children as apprentices or servants, too, women's organizations added a logic of privacy and strict gender-role division to that of orderly government. The New York Orphan Asylum's initial 1806 regulations specified simply that boys be bound out "to farmers or mechanics; the girls to respectable families." The 1844 wording introduced a subtle change; girls were now to serve in "respectable private families." Moreover, boys could now apprentice in mercantile or "other respectable business[es]," and only those "married or keeping house" and regularly attending "a Protestant place of worship" should bother applying for a youngster. These alterations reflected the women's evolving notion that "respectable families" were "private," and that privacy required the presence of women who separated their home and work lives, an understanding they embodied in their personal organizational behavior. Indeed, the very term "private" came into use only after the term "retired," which benevolent women used initially to describe their own familial roles. In 1812, Boston Baptist and Congregationalist women raising money for missions saw women as "destined . . . to fill more retired stations in life than our brethren"; two years later, a group of New Yorkers setting up a job-furnishing workroom described themselves as "females in the retired walks of life" who on this occasion would "come forward into public view" in order to pursue the project. Women's prayers, suggested New Yorker Hannah Caldwell in 1825, emanated from the "retirement of the domestic circle"; and an 1832 newspaper article described nuns as "retiring females" who "emerged from . . . obscurity" to become "mothers to . . . afflicted orphans . . . [and] parents to the fatherless and motherless." The rhetorical move from "retired" to "private" was complete by 1844, when the New York Orphan Asylum Society compiled its lengthened list of rules, and the Boston Female Asylum opened its new orphanage building. "The Asylum house has not so much the appearance of a public building as to lose its domestic character," noted the secretary in the minutes; "and yet [it] may be easily recognized as belonging to a larger, than any private family."[60] Not a "private family" house, the building was nevertheless "domestic" in appearance; hence, it could be distinguished from "public" edifices.

Through such alterations in language, women leaders expressed their understanding that associational work belonged outside an arena they called "public" but also outside the "retired" or "secluded" space in which "private" family life took place. Henrietta Willcox Norton reflected this understanding in letters to her sister in 1847 and 1848, almost ten years after a move from New York City had ended her organizational commitments. Now living as a farm spouse in rural Illinois with her Presbyterian missionary husband, and nursing her fourth baby, Henrietta was lonely, tired, overworked, and missing the "opportunity for usefulness" she had enjoyed in Manhattan. There, in addition to serving on the board of the Colored Orphan Asylum, she had been both manager and secretary of the Ladies New York City Anti-Slavery Society, a member and delegate to the 1837 and 1838 Anti-Slavery Conventions of American Women, and a moral reformer. It was not her marriage to Oliver Norton in

November 1838 nor her first pregnancy that had interrupted these labors, but "moving from the city" to Oliver's new pastoral assignment. In her letters, Henrietta inquired often about both abolition and moral reform, lamenting her difficulties in getting copies of the *Advocate of Moral Reform*, the "very valuable paper" for which another sister, Augusta Willcox Marvin, wrote "lucubrations." Henrietta confessed that she envied Augusta's "time to visit the poor and do a great deal of good." By contrast, she observed, "I am so secluded from the world, seldom going beyond the precincts of my own domicile and all my energies absorbed in ministering to the wants of my own little flock [that] . . . I often feel that I am living to no purpose." To Henrietta, her labor in caring for her four young children took place within the "secluded" arena of her "domicile"; were she to have an "opportunity for usefulness" through organizational activity, she would go out into "the world." Moreover, Henrietta was very clear about what kept her from that sort of "usefulness": the lack of domestic help. "If I could afford the expense of getting a young girl here from the city," she suggested, "I would have one of those from the M[oral] R[eform] Society very quick." But "as long as the Lord does not send me any person to whom I can entrust [my children], home is the place for me." Henrietta understood families as private in the sense of seclusion, and she viewed associational work as taking place outside of that realm, in the world beyond the home.[61]

Given these assumptions, it is not hard to understand why, in placing clients, women leaders sought out families that fit their notions of privacy and respectability. When sending older children out to indentures, or into foster or adoptive families, women's groups showed a marked preference for married couples. Over nine-tenths (92 percent) of the families permitted to take servant girls from the Boston Female Asylum fit that description. Asylum leaders also preferred families of solid middle-class status, with father-providers earning their livings as professional men, proprietors of shops, or town officials. Almost two-thirds of the girls went to such families. Yet placements within female-headed households were not unheard of, and the asylum managers displayed some flexibility, accepting widows and single women, including their hired governesses, as constituting appropriate families. Similarly, at New York's Roman Catholic Orphan Asylum, a few selected older girls filled out their indentures as servants; some eventually took the veil themselves. (A few of the boys moved on to seminary training in Rome.) And when two sister-schoolteachers from Providence, Rhode Island, wrote to the Boston Children's Friend Society in 1838, asking for two young girls whom they could adopt, the society accommodated them. Having tried out and, in turn, rejected two of the girls sent to them, the teachers eventually took a third, changed her name, and raised her. In the actual management of institutions such as orphanages, feminine leadership was the norm. Sisterly groups of religious women headed Roman Catholic orphanages, and Protestant "homes" for children routinely had mothers, not fathers, as leaders (the New York Orphan Asylum being an exception).[62]

As charitable women clarified these notions of privacy and respectability, they also reworked the mechanisms by which they intertwined institutional business with the concerns of their own families, or those of their financial supporters. In the early years, the interlacing of domestic and organizational concerns was sometimes quite literal, as a president's or manager's own door opened to accept a client completing her refuge stay. For four of the original thirteen girls (30 percent) taken into the Boston Female Asylum in 1800, the route out of it led to a manager's service entrance; after spending a few years in the institution, each joined an officer's household. Nabby Lang, indentured to Mary Chapman Gray in 1806, was one of them. Although Nabby might have had a different version of it, Gray's son John later recalled that he "was brought up with the Asylum children," including Nabby, who was married from the Gray house after she completed her indenture. During those years, too, a number of the asylum's donors took advantage of their right to first claim on a girl going out to indenture, thereby securing household help. Indeed, officers and donors' informal family, kin, and acquaintance networks were important resources to be tapped when institutions wished to place clients. Between 1816 and 1822, for instance, thirteen girls from the Boston Female Asylum found their way to Nantucket through Eliza Frothingham Lincoln's family connections; although Eliza had gone off the asylum board in 1811, her sisters Priscilla and Abby undoubtedly played the go-between role.[63]

Very quickly, however, it became much more commonplace for women to use their organizational ties in the opposite way: to send destitute neighbors (or their children) to a refuge, asylum, or relief-granting organization. In this way, women's organizations helped create, maintain, or protect their managers' evolving concept of family privacy. By requiring that prospective clients apply in person to an officer, for example, New York's Society for the Relief of Poor Widows with Small Children insulated middle-class families from giving handouts to needy supplicants. A referral to an officer of the society did away (in theory at least) with personal discomfort or guilt; the referral process specialized charitable provision. Whether the society's designers intended to have that effect, a group of them were explicit about their objectives in promoting a subsequent project, the House of Industry. It would "free [individuals] from the importunities of that class of females who beg because they cannot get work." Helping poor women to secure paid employment, in order to "do away with the necessity of begging" at kitchen doors or townhouse steps seemed a worthy goal for a women's organization.[64]

A similar concern about separating the private dwellings of respectable urban dwellers from the problems of wage-earning women could be found in any number of charitable proposals. At least one initial goal of New York's Association for the Relief of Respectable, Aged, Indigent Females and of Boston's Widows' Society seems to have been to provide for the founders' retired servants and elderly relatives. An occasional oblique comment about client histories hinted at that goal; for example, the elderly New Yorker Margaret Gillespie "was sent to the Almshouse . . . by the Bayard Family, from whom she received $50 Annualy." The close correspondence between managers' and clients' religious affiliations provides another hint, as does the correspondence between their surnames. Between 1814 and 1832, a majority of both clients and managers of the New York association were Presbyterian or Episcopalian, although nineteen Catholic women, or about 7 percent of the 269 whose religion is known, did qualify for assistance. Moreover, both organizations repeatedly described clients as women "who once enjoyed a good deal of affluence, but [were] now reduced to poverty" and evinced a strong desire to save them from a humiliating reliance on public welfare. By providing them with annuities, visiting them in their "dwellings of misery," or collecting them into an old-age home, the organizations found solutions that salved members' consciences while not requiring that elderly women be sheltered in private households. The women of New York's Asylum for Lying-In Women wrote into their constitution a provision that a membership subscription bought the right to recommend patients to the asylum. "We cannot receive them into our houses, or afford them suitable aid and comfort in their wretched tenements," the women noted in their first report; but when confronted with "respectable married women" needing medical care during childbirth, "the ladies" could now recommend the "public asylum" to which they contributed.[65]

In other words, although there is clear evidence that women used their associations to help them find household help (Henrietta Norton's hope for a "girl . . . from the M[oral] R[eform] Society" testified to a longstanding practice) and household members, what is striking is how infrequently they did so, especially after 1815 or 1820. Much more commonly, they referred or recommended individuals to their institutions. The early minutes of the Boston Female Asylum are filled with notations such as: "Mrs. Matthew Park presented Betsey Durrill for admission"; "Mrs. Mason proposed admitting" a fatherless child; "Mrs. Park presented Eliza Gray for Admission"; Hannah Whitten

Smith "reported that" Mary B. Edes was living "in a miserable upper apartment" with a dying mother and overworked grandmother and needed shelter; or a mother appeared at a manager's friend's doorstep asking for charity, and then left her child. Nabby Lang herself had arrived at the asylum in 1801 through the good graces of founder Hannah Stillman, who knew the family well enough so that when Nabby's father returned from Newfoundland and, in violation of his surrender agreement, made contact with Nabby, she agreed to "call on" him to "forbid his interference, or noticing his Child on the Sabbath at Meeting." When Catherine and Brissenta Hearn's uncle asked Abigail May to take his nieces under her wing, Abigail's position as manager and then second directress of the Boston Female Asylum enabled her to put them in the asylum. With eleven children of her own, the youngest aged eight in 1803, Abigail may have preferred not to take on more mothering. Besides, the girls' status was unusual in that their uncle's "liberality and affection" paid their expenses at the asylum. In 1811, however, when the girls had already been permitted to stay beyond the usual age of indenture, Abigail agreed to "take them into her own family" in order to "give them such further opportunities as would qualify them for the station to which they were destined." Unlike Nabby Lang, who had joined Mary Chapman Gray's family a few years earlier, the Hearn girls became Abigail May's foster daughters. Still, the Hearn girls' case was unusual in its outcome—foster care—not its origin. In all these instances, women leaders were formalizing an older system of informal charitable assistance, and using their new institution to create and manage a zone of privacy in their own households, a zone they increasingly defined as essential to middle-class family status.[66]

New institutions and organizations enabled them to sharpen the boundaries that separated household members from nonmembers, and to decide who belonged under their roofs. The process paralleled (and was contemporaneous with) the mechanisms whereby upwardly mobile city-dwellers separated their workplaces from their living spaces, acquired separate addresses for their residences, and abdicated any responsibility for supervising the nonwork lives of young male apprentices and clerks. By no means did these women seek to empty their houses of nonnuclear kin; servants, relatives, and boarders continued to be significant actors in the drama of middle-class life for generations to come. By separating women's labor from men's, however, and leaving women's labor within the household, they drew one sort of boundary between households and other arenas; by seeking to control who came into the household, they drew another. And their associations facilitated the second project by furnishing a collective, feminine means for handling the problems of needy neighbors, friends, and strangers, while also providing a way to screen potential hired household helpers. At New York's Asylum for Lying-In Women, for example, individual officers occasionally sent servants or former servants to give birth; the asylum offered "comfortable accommodation" and the "sympathy" of "those of her own sex." Within five years of opening, however, the Lying-In Asylum's managers found that individuals knocking on the matron's door were not just the "respectable and virtuous married" women for whom the spot was intended because they would shrink from "the mortification of being sent to the common receptacle of paupers," the almshouse. Some inquiries came from members of "our wealthier classes," new mothers who were "unable to nourish [their] own offspring." The institution could meet their need, not merely for wet-nurses, but for certified, reliable ones, whose "character . . . tempers and dispositions" were known quantities. Between March 1827 and March 1828, for example, twenty-three of the fifty postpartum clients leaving the asylum (46 percent) took jobs as wet-nurses; between 1829 and 1843, the proportion varied from nineteen to forty-eight percent. Although the managers themselves rarely hired clients, by formalizing institutional procedures, establishing an application process, and requesting that prospective employers offer a donation to the asylum (a finder's fee, if you will), they facilitated middle-class families' ability to sift and winnow the members of their households.[67]

As middle-class white women leaders separated their own personal lives from their organizational labor, drew boundaries between their home lives and their work lives, and used familial imagery to describe their labors and work out definitions of "order" and "privacy" in family composition, they produced the experience of middle-class domesticity and the gender roles that went with it. As they ordered the spaces they inhabited, deciding who could cross the threshold into their houses, then stepping across the threshold themselves in order to complete organizational tasks at quasi-public sites, they participated in the larger social labor of defining class by defining gender, and establishing the private middle-class household as a place apart. Even their increasing willingness to create formal male advisory boards can be seen as part of this process. (See Table A.9.) Historians have interpreted this phenomenon, especially evident during the 1840s and 1850s, as evidence for previously independent women's increased subservience to masculine authority, a subservience reflected, too, in wives' increased use of marital titles and names in print. No doubt the move toward formal advisory boards helped women leaders resolve the dilemma of how to conceptualize men's role in their organizations, a dilemma forced upon them by the creation of mixed-sex antislavery groups and by changes in wives' legal status. Yet by devolving upon male advisers the responsibility for overseeing organizational finances, women leaders also reworked familial ideals to meet group needs. Such arrangements formalized the informal consultations with husbands, fathers, sons, or brothers that organization treasurers had always relied upon for keeping proper books and investing funds lucratively. They had a dual, contradictory effect: inserting masculine authority into feminine realms and devaluing women's money management skills; and separating women leaders' vocational work more fully from their home duties. When women created advisory "committees of gentlemen," they clearly subordinated their authority over financial and legal matters to the committees; when the gentlemen advisers came calling at meetings, they received a deferential reception. At the same time, however, by formalizing the relation, women leaders took an additional step away from associational arrangements that mimicked domestic ones, and a step further in the direction of separating "home" from "work."[68] In this instance, as in others, they made it possible for middle-class women's domestic and organizational labors, which had been twinned from birth, to have separate existences.

In chronicling how some women drew new lines of division between arenas that they labeled private and public, while also separating their familial from their organizational labor, it is important to acknowledge that other women's interests limited and structured the process. Whether needing or resisting the services that women's organizations offered, poor families adapted their coping strategies to accommodate their wealthier neighbors' evolving philanthropies. Indeed, on one level, the records of women's charitable organizations can be read as a complex dance in which the directresses, secretaries, and managers called the tune but the poor widows with small children, the orphans' parents, and the respectable aged females kept trying to change the steps. The ink was barely dry on the Boston Female Asylum's list of rules, for example, when the ladies voted to admit Abby Wilder, whose situation as a "half-orphan" (her mother was living but unable to care for her) should have made her ineligible. Three months later they took in the first of many girls who had two living parents. Indeed, during the asylum's first four decades, only 17 percent of its clients were dictionary-definition orphans. And given the rapidly shifting urban economy of the early nineteenth century, and poor families' resourcefulness in finding ways to cope, middle-class organizers learned a lot of new steps. Clients' own family needs and strategies forced changes in organizational practices.[69]

Moreover, during these same decades, for working-class white and middle-class African American women, membership in a mutual aid society, not a benevolent organization, was likely. Such memberships flowed from and structured women's familial roles, but in different ways from the patterns outlined above. Based not on a paternal model of providing "fathers to the fatherless" but on a sororal strategy of mutual assistance, such organizations responded to the new economic realities of the nineteenth century through members' co-operative labor and the exclusion of non–wage earners. For the women who belonged to such organizations, the connection between domesticity and or-ganization, home and work, was certainly reciprocal; but often it was organi-zational membership that supported domesticity, rather than the converse. No doubt New Yorker Susannah Peterson, a washerwoman caring for three chil-dren under the age of ten, as well as the five-year-old "daughter of a deceased friend," spent some of her 1833 earnings on a membership in the Female Branch of Zion as a hedge against family destruction. Coping with the tragic drowning of a son, as well as her husband's illness, Susannah had reason to think about the ten-dollar funeral benefit or the weekly sick payment that her membership bought. However diligently she worked for her employer, a physi-cian in Park Place, even to the point of staying up all night, she had little access to the model of domesticity that her employer's wife could emulate. And if her employer was Dr. Ansel W. Ives, 3 Park Place, Susannah's "decent" and "re-spectable" home would not have induced Ives's wife, Lucia Jones Ives, to spon-sor her at the Asylum for Lying-In Women, where Lucia served as a manager. However decently and respectably married she may have been, as an African American woman, Susannah had no entrée. Whereas Lucia structured her do-mestic existence around intensively mothering her four children, hiring house-hold help, and spending time at benevolent society meetings, Susannah's ideals of domesticity included extensive mothering, paid labor, and pennies set aside for mutual aid society dues.[70]

Conclusion

"The work of benevolence, like that of the household is never done," wrote Sarah Josepha Hale in 1839. Her comment, enclosing domesticity and benev-olence within the same field of action, reflected common usage, common conceptualization. Not until later in the nineteenth century would women's labor in organized charities acquire a materially separate reality from their labor in households, particularly as single women found full-time occupations in settlement houses, child-saving, and missionary rescue work, as married women built centrally located public buildings (such as Young Women's Christian Associations [YWCAS] and Phillis Wheatley Homes) to house and dis-play their benevolent activities, and as the management of charitable institu-tions passed into the hands of professional social workers. Then, activist women reconfigured public spaces to create woman-friendly enclaves, sometimes "literally transferr[ing] their private lives into public institutions" such as colleges and hospitals. Access to spaces, buildings, and rooms of their own enabled later groups of women to claim identities as individuals separate from families, and to challenge the masculine orientation of downtown business districts in ways unimagined in the antebellum era.[71] (See Figures 2.1 and 2.2.)

Still, during their formative years, women's benevolent, mutual aid, and reform associations did more than simply make collective feminine activism an extension of individual women's family responsibilities. Between the 1790s, when women's collective activism was new, and the 1830s, when it had become commonplace, women of varying social backgrounds worked out their notions about what their family roles should be while simultaneously constructing associations. Some would manage organizations, paid labor, and families all together. Others—in fact, most—women would serve both their families and their organizations, but in cases of conflict, always defer to family needs. By figuring out how to do associational work while also completing family labor, they opened up an arena of feminine action that was neither strictly familial nor wholly public; it was "private" but not "retired." And within that essentially social arena, the availability of a growing number of organizations provided a wide range of roles for different sorts of women, so much so that when Henrietta Willcox Norton found herself isolated in the rural Midwest, "seldom going beyond the precincts of my own domicile and all my energies absorbed in ministering to the wants of my own little flock," she lamented her lost "opportunity for usefulness" compared to her active associational life in New York. "I often feel," she reflected, "that I am living to no purpose." Henrietta Norton's plaintive comment, written in 1848, that her "secluded" family life might compare unfavorably with a life that permitted both family and organizational labor suggests how much had changed in her lifetime (she was born in 1814). Although married and raising children, she connected her own "usefulness" with both familial and quasi-public labor.[72]

In 1848, when Henrietta penned her wistful letter, most women doing the "work of benevolence" still did so as members of families, social classes, or racial and ethnic groups. A few, however, had begun to organize as women in the interests of women. Not only had moral reformers begun to champion individual women's right to independent lives as single adults, but abolitionists had begun to delineate other rights denied to women as a group. For these reform-minded, "ultraist" women, family bonds were not the restricting sort that limited associational labor, but the elastic sort that sustained their public work. Whole families labored together in the abolitionist cause, attended antislavery

STATE OF NEW YORK. 420286

CERTIFICATE OF DEATH,
IN THE CITY OF NEW YORK.

1. Full Name of Deceased, Sarah R. I. Bennett
2. Age, 75 years, 7 months, days. Color White
3. Single, Married, Widow or Widower. 4. Occupation, Recording Secretary
5. Birthplace, New York State
6. How long Resident in this City, 50 years
7. Father's Name and Birthplace, Unknown
8. Mother's Name and Birthplace, Unknown
9. Place of Death, No. Home for the Friendless
   No. 32 East 30th St.
10. If a Dwelling, by how many families, living separately, occupied.

11. I Hereby Certify, that I attended deceased from Jan 1882 to Apl 24 1882
that I last saw her alive on the 24th day of April 188 2, that she died on the 24th day of
April 188 2, about 6 o'clock, A.M. or P.M.

Cause of her death was as hereunder written:

Chief and Determining: Angina Pectoris
Consecutive and Contributing: Apoplexy of Lungs

Witness my hand this day of April 1882

Burial, Woodlawn Cemetery April 27th 1882

Undertaker Charles R. Calyer No. 142 East 50th St.

DIED,

On the 12th inst. Mrs. Catharine Duplex.
    In the death of this amiable and accomplished woman, society has
met a severe, and her disconsolate husband, an irreparable loss. Benevolent, humane, and charitable; and though fondly attached to her
own faith, and the doctrines of her Church, she obeyed to its fullest
extent, the divine precept of her Redeemer in loving her brethren,
of all religious denominations. She long suffered under ill health,
but submitted to her affliction with fortitude and Christian resignation, and when the grim conqueror of all assailed her, she hailed her
entrance on a new existence with that hope and trust which never
faileth the just and the upright. She was a native of Cork, daughter
to the late, and sister of the present Doctor Mann of that place.

> Dearest sister, thou art gone
> To a fond, eternal home;
> Freed from the toilsome load of life,
> From this vain world's toil and strife,
> Thy sainted spirit's now at rest,
> And in your Saviour's bosom blest.

FIGURES 2.1 AND 2.2. Death certificate for Sarah R. Ingraham Bennett, 1882, and obituary for Catherine Mann Duplex [Dupleix], from *The Truth Teller*, February 20, 1836. Note that at her death in 1882, Sarah Bennett's occupation was "Recording Secretary" and her home address was the American Female Guardian Society's Home for the Friendless, 32 East 30th Street, New York. (Courtesy of the New York City Municipal Archives and Georgetown University Library Special Collections)

and women's rights conventions, and attempted to practice as well as preach principles of radical egalitarianism. They would remake families and gender roles within them as well as gender-based divisions of labor in churches and reform associations. Unlike most of their contemporaries in women's organizations, whose associational activities bolstered and strengthened nineteenth-century gender roles and familial gender hierarchies, "ultraist" women, both white and black, championed alternative familial practices, including flexible domestic roles and even role reversals. By organizing their families so that they could pursue public lives, they highlighted the ever-shifting nature of seemingly fixed lines between "public" and "private," family and organization, home and work.[73]

CHAPTER THREE

Portraits of Women Organizers

M uch of the history of nineteenth-century women's organizations can be told through the life stories of the women who
founded and ran them. While the preceding chapter sum-
marized biographical data on several hundred such individuals from the two cities, covering an extensive canvas
with broad strokes, this one seeks, through intensive consideration of a few individuals, to limn the broader story in finer detail. In the experiences of these
women, one can discern the themes found in other chapters, particularly the
shaping force of religion, race, social location, marital and life-course stage,
and generation.

Their energetic and lifelong activism and their positions as stalwarts within
several societies make these women notable, but typical only of the committed
minority. Among organization leaders, some gave a year or more to the management of a group; but those most involved often spent significant portions of
their adult lives in such leadership positions. Of the 722 New York women
leaders covered in Chapter 2, for instance, 177 (or about one-quarter) gave
their talents to leading more than one group; in Boston, the proportion was
very similar. On a spectrum of organizational involvement, then, from those

who helped lead one organization for a year or two, to those who fashioned lifelong career in volunteerism, the women portrayed here define the activist end.

The energy, commitment, labor, devotion, and resources of these women—and of their coworkers—made women's organizations possible, but could not guarantee their success or permanence. Some of these women were able to watch their organizational seedlings grow, thrive, blossom, spawn offshoots, and mature into sturdy plants. Others nurtured blooms that faded, withered, and died, or survived only in small, obscure corners. Something similar could be said of their nurturers. For some of the women profiled here, organizational activity provided all the rewards, challenges, and triumphs associated with professional careers. In their societies, they found useful work, compatible associates, wider worldly vistas, and satisfying achievements. As the reward of their labors, some experienced the warm embrace of public acclaim. A few became saints to later generations, their life stories retold, their letters and journals preserved in libraries or published, their organizational successors eager to honor their names, and their descendants able to claim the halo of the family legacy. Such women are relatively accessible to the historian. Other women, no less energetic or devoted to their work, remain as invisible to historians as they were to most contemporaries, their lives reconstructable only through scattered traces in surviving records. Accordingly, although this chapter aims to depict a variety of representative activists, some portraits of necessity are more richly textured and fully detailed than others.

Isabella Marshall Graham, Joanna Graham Bethune, and Elizabeth Bayley Seton

Among the first generation of white organizational activists, few did as much to chart the roads that others followed as Isabella Marshall Graham, her daughter Joanna Graham Bethune, and their co-worker Elizabeth Bayley Seton.[1] When they came together in 1797 to found the New York Society for the Relief of Poor Widows with Small Children, they brought to their work personal experiences, religious beliefs, educational skills, and financial resources that shaped the institution's contours and its fate. In their later organizational activities they built on what they had learned as founders and managers of the society.

In 1797, Isabella Graham was a fifty-five-year-old widow and the mother of two grown children (three others having died), while Joanna Bethune and Elizabeth Seton, aged twenty-seven and twenty-three, were both recently married and the mothers of young children. In other ways, too, they were very much alike and, more important, were typical of the kinds of women who pioneered as benevolent society founders in the 1790s: religiously motivated, well-educated, well-connected. Graham and Bethune were Presbyterians and Seton was an Episcopalian, but they shared an intensely introspective approach to religion, and a reliance on religious beliefs and spiritual counselors as sources of everyday guidance. Impressively educated at a time when only about half of white women could read and write, they were individuals who had the ability and the time to write letters, keep journals, read newspapers, and develop opinions on the issues of their day. Although Graham and Bethune were not as wealthy as Seton, all three women had experienced the benefits that comfortable economic circumstances allowed, including not only schooling but also the service of paid, indentured, or enslaved laborers and the leisure and time that that service created.[2] Moreover, they possessed close connections to significant centers of social, economic, and political power within New York City, and beyond it, too. Their letters crossed the Atlantic on a regular basis, reaching correspondents in England, Scotland, France, Italy, the West Indies, and India; as they watched ships returning to New York's harbor, they could anticipate receiving penned replies, new magazines, freshly printed books, as well as religious tracts and devotional works.

In all this, they resembled several hundred women of their rank and station. Still, they represented the core of the group who imagined, created, and successfully breathed life into organizations like the Society for the Relief of Poor Widows with Small Children. Some of the details of their individual biographies provide clues to their motivations.

Despite her upbringing in a Scottish gentry family, Isabella Graham could claim to know something about the experiences of poor widows with small children. Married at age twenty-three to John Graham, a British Army physician, she left Scotland in 1766 in order to accompany him to an assignment in Canada. Her two stepsons (Dr. Graham was a widower when they married) and an infant boy (who soon died) remained behind with her parents pending the Marshall family's emigration to North America. Posted to Antigua in 1772, Dr. Graham was making plans to sell his Army commission and settle, with his in-laws, on the Mohawk River near Schenectady when he died. His death in 1773 left Isabella in Antigua, aged thirty-one and pregnant with her fifth child.

Returning home after the birth of her son John, she found dramatic changes in the family she had last seen eight years earlier. Her highly religious mother had preceded her beloved husband to the grave by a few months. A bad investment had led her widowed father to lose the family's land, and he was living on a small farm while working as an estate manager. He soon lost that position. Graham herself was a changed person: more religious, less "self-willed," less worldly. After supporting the family for two years on her widow's pension and the proceeds of her butter sales, she began a girls' school, first in Paisley and then in Edinburgh. Her own boarding-school background and her school's evangelically oriented curriculum, along with the patronage of "persons of distinction and piety," facilitated the Edinburgh venture's success. By combining traditional instruction in "those accomplishments which were to qualify [young women] for acting a distinguished part in the world" with prayer and religious devotions, and by charging ministers' daughters half-price, Graham found a large clientele among evangelical families.[3]

Despite substantial advantages—a pension, marketable skills, breeding, helpful friends, influential sponsors—that enabled her to weather serious economic reversals, Graham interpreted the two years that preceded her school's founding as ones of great hardship. In her own mind she became "a widow, helpless and poor, neglected and forgotten," reduced to "earn[ing] my porridge, potatoes, and salt," "totally neglected by some who once thought themselves honored by my acquaintance," and "brought so low as to be obliged to part with [my] last servant and do [my] own housework." Yet if Graham was hardly the stereotypical helpless widow, the image seemed so true that she incorporated it into her life story. This interpretation of her experience, along with her belief that only God, the "Father of the fatherless, Husband of the widow" could soothe life's troubled waters, shaped her compassion for "poor widows with small children" and her views on how to help them.[4]

Graham's decision to emigrate to New York in 1789 was not precipitous. It was well planned and well timed. Her earlier six-year residence in Canada and New York and her engagement with extensive transatlantic network of Scottish evangelicals brought Graham a number of American friends. They included the Scots-born Presbyterian clergyman John Witherspoon, president of Princeton College, signer of the Declaration of Independence, member of the Confederation Congress, New Jersey state legislator, and moderator of the first Presbyterian General Assembly gathered in the United States. It was Witherspoon who had overseen Isabella Marshall's public profession of faith at a Paisley church in 1759, and who, on a visit home in 1785, persuaded Isabella Graham that the new American nation needed her. As a key figure in the postrevolutionary struggle to "make the American people Christian," Witherspoon labored assiduously to recruit people and promote institutions that would achieve the goal. Graham became a recruit. Convinced "that America was the country where the Church of Christ would pre-eminently flourish," and offered "assurances of patronage and support" by "many respectable characters" in New York City, she determined to take her school and her three daughters to the capital of the new republic.[5]

Graham's timing was superb. In 1789, New York City, second only to Philadelphia in population, was poised to become the most important commercial and cultural center in the country. With its port facilities providing access to European and West Indian trade, the city surpassed Philadelphia in registered tonnage in 1797, and by 1810 had become the nation's largest city. Although it lost its political preeminence when the national capital moved to Philadelphia in 1790 and the state capital moved to Albany in 1797, New York nevertheless continued to produce leaders with influential voices in state and national politics. Religiously dominated by the Anglican church during the colonial era, the city in 1789 was home to an energetic group of Presbyterians, many of them with close ties to British evangelicals, who were determined to capture the city and the nation for God. They included John Mason, a Scots-born minister who became the Graham family's pastor at the Scotch Presbyterian Church, and his son and successor John Mitchell Mason. The outbreak of the French Revolution and its subsequent association with deism and irreligion only redoubled their determination. They became significant architects of an American Presbyterianism that emphasized private devotion and family worship over the communal, ritualized religion of Scotland.[6] Isabella Graham's arrival in New York City thus added yet another apprentice builder and gave her immediate access to a network of local religious and political leaders.

Graham opened her planned school within a month of her September landing. With her daughters Joanna and Isabella serving as assistant teachers, the school quickly grew from five to fifty pupils, with a clientele that included Martha Washington's granddaughter Nelly Custis. Offering a standard curriculum covering English grammar, writing, arithmetic, and geography, along with sewing, art, music, dancing, and French, Graham transplanted her school from Edinburgh to New York. But she differentiated it from other girls' academies that sprang up in the aftermath of the American Revolution by emphasizing both "the practice of virtue" and "the principles of religion." In this fashion, she promulgated her political and social vision to New York's elite daughters. Holding a deep aversion both to the French Revolution (which she viewed as irreligious) and to the deism associated with Thomas Paine, she worried that if such principles gained the ascendancy in the new nation, they would fundamentally undermine the government of "our dear country." Socially, her views reflected those of British evangelicals such as Hannah More. Like More and her American devotees, Graham was critical of "worldly" amusements and fashionable habits, preferred piety to gentility, expressed the conviction that private family life best nurtured pious members, and equated "female virtue with chastity, modest dress, . . . useful knowledge . . . [and] moral instruct[ion]" (as Ruth Bloch has phrased it). In her vision of republican womanhood, properly educated and evangelically oriented daughters, sisters, wives, and mothers could shape the country's future destiny. That her curriculum did not include oratory, a subject taught at the Young Ladies' Academy of Philadelphia and at Susanna Rowson's Boston seminary, and practiced at their annual exhibitions, suggested that women's shaping role would be exercised indirectly, through influence, not directly, through politics.[7]

As her school prospered, Graham immersed herself in the religious life of New York's evangelicals. Corresponding regularly with like-minded friends, keeping up a round of personal evangelizing activities, working to promote missions, helping to establish the New York Missionary Society in 1796, and laboring for her own spiritual growth, Graham improved her leisure hours. Her "prodigal son" John's "captivity to Satan, the world, and self-will" remained a serious personal trial; when he died without spiritual rebirth in a French war prison in 1794, her submissive attitude to God's ways was sorely tried. Yet her faith enabled her to accept his death and that of her beloved eldest daughter Jessie in 1795 with humility and resignation. Jessie's marriage to Hay Stevenson in 1791 and Joanna's to the Scots-born importer Divie Bethune in 1795 provided additional ties to that group of New Yorkers who combined secular success in the world of international commerce with spiritual labor in the Lord's vineyards. Indeed, Divie Bethune quickly became her spiritual comrade and confidante, as well as a close adviser and friend.[8]

Viewed against this background, Graham's role in founding the Society for the Relief of Poor Widows in 1797 acquires sharper definition. Fully acquainted with both Scottish and American evangelical organizational techniques, engaged in correspondence with leading British evangelicals, and securely located within a network of evangelical activists, Graham had wide knowledge and resources on which to draw. Also available were those "respectable characters" who had supported her school, and the girls she had taught over a period of eight years, along with their parents, brothers, and, in some cases, husbands. They were undoubtedly the targets of the "circular letters" that announced the society's formation. Secure sources of economic support, her own house, and at least two household servants gave her time to pursue her concerns. Within a year of the group's founding, Graham had given up teaching to devote herself fully to religious and charitable causes. Personal experience had given her a deep concern for the temporal problems that widows faced; she was also familiar with the traditional means of meliorating widows' conditions, including almsgiving, mutual aid insurance schemes, and work programs. Although not inevitable, the decision to actualize through collective means her intense sympathy for women left destitute by the death of a breadwinner was hardly serendipitous.[9]

The idea for the Society for the Relief of Poor Widows was not Graham's. It came initially from her daughter Joanna Bethune, who shared her mother's religious views and some of her worldly experience. Aware that charitable practices differed in key ways between Scotland and New York, Bethune had begun collecting small sums to distribute to individuals not entitled to mutual aid and charity from the St. Andrew's Society, because they were not of Scots or Scots-Irish descent. Because all the existing charitable agencies provided aid on the basis of religious or ethnic affiliation, many needy women had no recourse but the city almshouse. The heterogeneity of New York's population, the instability of its economy, the depredations of several yellow fever epidemics in the 1790s, and the low wage rates that women's work commanded guaranteed that there would be large numbers of poor widows with children whose lack of access to charitable agencies made them candidates for the almshouse. These were the women whose situations elicited Bethune's concern, and who became the organization's clients. Although they were not the most destitute of New York City's women (poor free black widows, for example, had no place on client lists), they suffered from "reduced circumstances," and needed help getting through the winter months, finding work, or, in the case of refugees from the revolutions in St. Domingue and France, adjusting to new circumstances. In their way, many clients bore the imprint of Isabella Graham's widowhood: they had seen better days and were struggling to "eat their own bread, hardly earned."[10]

IF JOANNA BETHUNE shared much with her mother—religious beliefs, energy, education, worldly experience, resources, connections—she nevertheless came to the society with a different personal history. She and Elizabeth Seton represented the younger founders and leaders of the organization, the women in their twenties and thirties who constituted a significant contingent on the board of managers. Both Bethune and Seton were still quite young; neither was yet a widow. What they had in common were experiences and connections that made their involvement in the Society for the Relief of Poor Widows logical and powerfully influenced the society's blueprint.

Joanna Bethune had been born in Canada in 1770, Elizabeth Seton in New York four years later. Like Bethune, Seton was the second of three girls born to her parents and the daughter of a physician. Both undoubtedly had memories of a similar early trauma—the death of a parent—for Joanna had been almost four when John Graham died, and Elizabeth was three at the time of her mother's death. Although raised an ocean apart, the two women had similar educational experiences. Seton left New York City at age eight to live for four years with Bayley relatives in New Rochelle and attend a girls' academy, where "Mama Pompelion" taught piano, French, and the accoutrements of gentility. Bethune's education took place first at her mother's knee in Antigua and Scotland, then through the sponsorship of Isabella Graham's patron Lady Glenorchy (Williamina Campbell), with whom Joanna lived for almost a year and who paid the fourteen-year-old girl's tuition at Madame Marc's school in Rotterdam "in order to fit me for being an assistant teacher to my Mother."[11]

Although "Jacky" Graham Bethune's expectation of undertaking paid labor and her teaching experience in Edinburgh and New York set her teenage years off from those of Elizabeth Seton, the two women had corresponding memories of stormy adolescent years. In their religious autobiographies, both described themselves as pleasure-loving, worldly young women whose excessive attraction to "the company of gay thoughtless people . . . flitting in the dance to the sounds of viol," led them to neglect their religious training. Bethune remembered yearning to "come out from the world entirely" while Seton longed for a place "where people could be shut up from the world and pray and be good always."[12] Seton's adolescent misery was compounded by her educational exile in New Rochelle and her father's extended absence in England. She found solace in religion, referring in her diary to God as "my Father, my all." However commonplace in nineteenth-century women's religious narratives, the conflicted terms in which Bethune and Seton described their experiences —as a clash between worldliness and spirituality, willfulness and self-control— nevertheless reflected their self-understanding. A battle story in which selflessness triumphed over self presented both an explanation and a continuing life challenge. Although all evangelicals believed that the good Christian learned to deny his or her impulses in the name of spiritual growth, women faced the double burden of submission both to God and to men. To be female, regardless of one's social rank, was to occupy a subordinate place in the family, church, and society. Small wonder, then, that two religiously inclined girls living in New York City in the 1790s and experiencing brief periods of personal autonomy would describe adolescence in terms of conflict and eventual submission.[13]

For both women, resolution of these conflicts coincided with marriage, and with attachment to a spiritual mentor. Marriage in 1794 to William Magee Seton, a New York City businessman six years her senior, brought nineteen-year-old Elizabeth Bayley Seton an intimate companion and enveloped her in the familial cocoon for which she longed. She and William had a great deal in common, including religion (like the Bayleys, the Setons were Episcopalians), politics (both families had been loyalists during the American Revolution), social standing, and personal experience (William had also lost a mother and gained a stepmother and new siblings). The births of five children—Anna Maria in 1795, William in 1796, Richard in 1798, Catherine in 1800, and Rebecca in 1802—cemented their devotion to each other. They lived for a time at William's family home, where Elizabeth found her "soul's sister" in William's half sister Rebecca; in recognition of the bond, the Setons named their youngest child for her. After briefly dabbling in Rousseau's secular ideas, Elizabeth found a spiritual brother in John Henry Hobart, appointed assistant minister of Trinity Church in 1801, whose blend of High-Church Episcopal theology and evangelical fervor she found hugely appealing. Coming at a time of temporal trials, including the bankruptcy of William Seton's firm and the deaths of her father-in-law and father, Elizabeth's attachment to Hobart proved comforting.[14]

Joanna Graham Bethune's experience paralleled that of Elizabeth Seton, but with the additional dimension of a classic evangelical conversion experience. In an account composed three weeks after her mother's death in 1814, Bethune recalled years of internal ambivalence, as she tried "to serve God & mammon" but only ended up "miserable." Despite a "sincere" confession of faith upon taking communion in 1791, she "attained to assurance" of conversion only after a "longer season of darkness and doubt," culminating in physical illness and spiritual "rapture." Through it all, her suitor Divie Bethune served as "helpmeet" and "dear Friend." She had rejected his initial marriage proposal because he appeared to have "no prospect of supporting me," thus angering her mother "who loved him dearly . . . and said I refused him because he was religious." As her spiritual crisis deepened, their personal attachment grew; in her view, his constancy (he once walked nine miles to her sickbed) and her mother's prayers saved her soul. Their marriage in 1795 symbolized Joanna's acceptance of her mother's world and brought Isabella Graham a son to replace the prodigal who had died the year before. Thereafter, the three of them formed a team. Isabella Graham came to live with the Bethunes and their baby daughter Jessie when she retired in 1798, dividing her time between them and the family of her youngest daughter, Isabella Smith. After 1803, when the Smiths left the city, the three lived together full time, pooling their resources in the cause of Christian evangelization, attending the same church, and drawing solace from the ministry of the same pastor, John Mitchell Mason, who had succeeded his father at the Scotch Presbyterian Church in

1792. John M. Mason, who was her own age, furnished the kind of fraternal spiritual mentorship that Elizabeth Seton found in John H. Hobart.[15]

THE SUCCESS AND PERMANENCE of the Society for the Relief of Poor Widows with Small Children were made possible by the resources that women like Graham, Bethune, and Seton brought to the enterprise. All three were highly educated; Graham and Bethune were skilled teachers and managers; all had access to the sources of labor, influence, and wealth that the institution needed in order to succeed. Indeed early lists of leaders and supporters can be re-arranged into overlapping circles encompassing the women's kin, church ac-quaintances, business and political connections, and school associates. Inter-secting circles connected Graham and Bethune with Seton, particularly through Sarah Ogden Hoffman, who became second directress of the organization in 1800 after the deaths of her ill husband and daughter-in-law. An intimate co-worker and exact contemporary of Isabella Graham (both were born in 1742), Sarah Hoffman was doubly related to Elizabeth Seton: first, in 1792 when her daughter Mary Hoffman married William Seton's brother James; and again in 1802 when her son Martin married William's sister Mary. Martin Hoffman and William Seton were partners in an auction house; James Seton operated his insurance business out of the same office.[16] Before her marriage, Mary Hoff-man Seton may have been a student at Graham's school, along with Sarah Hoffman's nieces, Isabella and Catherine Ogden.

Episcopalian church networks also tied Elizabeth Seton to Sarah Hoffman, and to other important supporters, including Sarah Clarke Startin, Seton's wealthy widowed godmother; Catherine Mann Dupleix, Seton's close friend; and Elizabeth Schuyler Hamilton, who became an officer in 1805 after Alexan-der Hamilton's death. Graham and Bethune's ties to the Scotch Presbyterian Church provided recruits with religious and ethnic affinities, including Mary Weygand Chrystie, the widow of a Scots china merchant who was Isabella Graham's neighbor on Maiden Lane and an "intimate" of the Graham-Bethune circle. These women often shared family business and political con-nections as well, including ties to the Hamilton family and that of Jefferson's treasury secretary, Albert Gallatin, and of the federal judges Nathaniel Pendle-ton and William Few. Gallatin and Few married sisters, Hannah and Catherine Nicholson; another Nicholson sister, Maria, was a pupil and disciple of Isabella Graham before her marriage to the Maryland politician John Montgomery; yet another, Adden, married Mary Chrystie's son James, a Presbyterian ("Cove-nanter") minister. In turn, one of the Few daughters, Frances, married another

Chrystie, Albert. Despite their different theological leanings, the Hamilton, Nicholson, Gallatin, and Few families were political insiders, traveling to Philadelphia and then Washington, D.C., then circling back to Manhattan when the opportunity arose. In their households, religious, business, and political matters were part of the air that they breathed, and conversation about one often included another. Their church, family, and political ties provided crucial sources of support to the new organization.[17]

Isabella Graham's students and their families added yet another connecting circle, as many of them labored for the society. In 1804, for example, twenty-nine "young ladies, in rank the first in the city, in the very bloom of life, and full of its prospects, engaged in those pleasures and amusements which generally engross the mind, and shut out every idea unconnected with self," volunteered to teach clients' children "offering (not to contribute towards a school,) but *their own personal attendance to instruct the ignorant.*" Among the twenty-nine were the Nicholson, Murray, and Ogden daughters and Sarah Farquhar, who had studied and taught at Graham's side but who, rather than succeed her "patroness and friend" as her school's principal, became her silent coworker in the Society for the Relief of Poor Widows. When Farquhar married a British missionary and journeyed with him to an assignment in Madras, India, in 1805, Graham felt the loss as though "Sally" had been her own daughter. Yet, as any teacher, she was immensely gratified to see her pupil carrying out her convictions.[18]

Their ability to marshal such extensive religious, economic, political, and social networks in the service of the organization reveals how well positioned Graham, Bethune, and Seton were among New York's comfortable middle and upper classes at turn of the nineteenth century. Whatever challenge the new organization faced, they could command the means to meet it. As the society prospered, their lives changed. The experience of running the endeavor redirected each woman's charitable impulses into organizational channels and recast her religious ambitions (which were necessarily inseparable from secular ones) onto a grander scale. If before 1797, each of them had merely hoped to dispense traditional charity and alms more extensively, by 1806 all had taken definitive steps toward organizing female benevolence into modern shape.

DURING THOSE YEARS, Elizabeth Seton's life underwent the most dramatic changes. In the tumultuous period when William Seton's business failed and then her father died, Elizabeth, with John Henry Hobart's guidance, experienced a religious awakening. As did Joanna Bethune and countless Protestant women before and after her, Elizabeth Seton "renewed my covenant" and began "a new life" by taking communion for the first time in September 1802. She resolved thereafter to celebrate only one birthday, "the birthday of the soul." The arrival of her infant daughter Rebecca in July brought additional happiness, as did her deep spiritual comradeship with the baby's namesake, Rebecca Seton, her coworker in "widow's visits" for the society. Despite her disappointment in William Seton's unawakened state, her life seemed blessed by a strong and harmonious scaffolding.

Its lovely pattern began to disintegrate soon after, just as she agreed to take on extra responsibilities for the Society for the Relief of Poor Widows with Small Children by becoming its treasurer. William Seton, whose delicate health had been a source of concern ever since their marriage, required an ocean voyage, a common prescription for the illnesses of the well-to-do. This time, Elizabeth feared, "there can be no hope of his recovery" from tuberculosis. Upon their arrival in Italy, Elizabeth and William (along with their eight-year-old daughter Anna Maria) were confined to quarantine; Italian authorities feared their ship carried yellow fever. Within a few months, he was dead. Only attendance at Catholic Mass, with its comfortingly repetitive rituals in appealingly ornate settings, seemed to ease her devastation. The tender solicitude and the prayers of her Italian Catholic friends, Amabilia and Antonio Filicchi, were crucial. "How happy we would be," she wrote to Rebecca Seton, "if we believed what these dear [Catholic] Souls believe, that they *possess God* in the Sacrament, and that he remains in their churches and is carried to them when they are sick. . . . [M]y God how happy would I be even so far away from all so dear, if I could find you in the church, as they do." Letters from her pastor offered no succor; indeed, she left most of them unanswered.[19]

Accompanied by Antonio Filicchi, Seton returned to New York in turmoil, only to find Rebecca, her "Soul's Sister," on her deathbed. Within a month of Elizabeth's return, Rebecca too was gone. As the underpinnings of her life crumbled, she felt lost and alone: "The Home of plenty and comfort—the Society of Sisters united by prayers and divine affections—the Evening hymns, the daily lectures, the sunset contemplations, the Service of holy days, the Kiss of Peace, the widows visits—all—all—gone—forever—and is Poverty and Sorrow the only exchange[.] My husband—my Sisters—my Home—my comforts—Poverty and sorrow[.]" Conversion to Roman Catholicism provided both a refuge and an answer to her questions about these terrible events. Catholic rituals, such as making the sign of the cross, seemed "full of meaning." The Church's teaching that suffering could be offered up for one's sins and those of others had great appeal, as did its doctrine of transubstantiation, which promised God's actual presence in the consecrated communion bread. Being able to attend Mass every day provided routine and stability. Letters kept her close to her Italian companion, Amabilia Filicchi, a model of Catholic womanhood; at the same time, observing her own "babes" and "cr[ying] myself to sleep" with thoughts of her long-dead mother, she experienced a deep psychic identification with the sainted mother of God whose image had surrounded her in every church, chapel, and museum during her extended Italian sojourn. In March 1805, at the age of thirty-one, Seton began taking communion as a Catholic.[20]

To the modern eye, the lines between Episcopalian and Catholic belief and practice may seem indistinct, and perhaps in the company of wealthy Florentine merchants Seton found the historic affinities between the sects particularly evident, but in 1805 New York they were worlds apart. The contrast between attending Hobart's Trinity Church and St. Peter's Roman Catholic church was hardly lost on her. In the minds of people of Seton's class, Catholics constituted "a disreputable minority" holding unfathomable beliefs. "Let me be anything in the world but a Roman Catholic" was the horrified comment of her sister, Mary Bayley Post; Catholics were "dirty, filthy, ragged, the church a horrid place of spits and pushing." To her dismay, Elizabeth's initial experience confirmed the impression: "alas—I found it all that indeed," she recalled. As she wrote to Antonio Filicchi in April 1805, one month after her first communion as a Catholic, "it requires indeed a mind superior to all externals to find its real enjoyment" at St. Peter's; "I am forced to keep my eyes always on my Book, even when not using it." She seems not to have considered remaining with the Society for the Relief of Poor Widows, and her departure in 1804 (or rather failure to return after being "necessarily absent" in 1803) went unmentioned in its records. A "very painful conversation (certainly for the last time)" ended her intimacy with John Henry Hobart, but her godmother, Sarah Startin, provided economic support until Elizabeth's example led her sisters-in-law, Cecilia and Harriet Seton, to convert. By 1807, Startin was "very distant and reserved" and "visits me no more." By contrast, Eliza Saidler and Catherine Dupleix exhibited sympathy and understanding, with Saidler suggesting wryly that Elizabeth "had penance enough without seeking it among Catholics" and Dupleix expressing happiness "that anything in this world can comfort and console me." Their friendship sustained her; later Dupleix followed her example and converted to Catholicism. As Seton confirmed her commitment to Catholicism, she moved farther and farther from the economic and social world she had known during the first thirty-five years of her life. Trinity represented that universe; St. Peter's was a new one.[21]

Established in 1785 by twenty-three Catholics under the leadership of Hector St. Jean de Crevecoeur, St. Peter's remained the only Catholic church in the city until 1815. Not yet transformed by the massive influx of impoverished Irish immigrants who came in the 1830s and especially during the famines of the 1840s, New York Catholicism, like its Boston counterpart, often spoke in French-accented tones. Its ranks swelled in the 1790s by exiles from the French and Haitian revolutions seeking refuge in the city, St. Peter's congregation in 1808 consisted of "Irish, some hundreds of French, and as many Germans." Some of the French were slaves, some slave owners. At daily Mass, Seton would have found herself in the company of Pierre Toussaint, hairdresser to New York's elite women, a slave who had been stranded in New York with his owners by the revolution in Haiti. (Trinity's African American communicants were generally free persons; they seceded from Trinity in 1809, forming the Free African Church of St. Philip, which became a diocesan church in 1818.) On Sundays, she would meet parishioners such as Toussaint's owner, Marie Berard Nicolas, whose experience of genteel poverty (for a while, her slave helped support the family) might have resonated with Seton, and wealthy Irish merchants such as Cornelius Heeney, onetime partner of John Jacob Astor, and Dominick Lynch. By 1805, the presence of wealthy French and Irish émigrés had become somewhat muted, as the ranks of parish laymen swelled with unskilled workers, and French parishioners sequestered themselves from involvement in parish affairs.[22] Seton herself drew strength from the spiritual counsel of both Irish and French priests, and from new friends and supporters who rallied to her because of her conversion. After all, the voluntary choice of Catholicism by a woman of her birth and high social standing, as well as by her sisters-in-law, helped counteract widely held stereotypes (repeated by her relatives) about "'Bigotry, Superstition, Wicked Priests' etc. etc." Archbishop John Carroll of Baltimore, presiding bishop of the American church, began to correspond with her in 1804, and performed her confirmation ceremony in 1806.[23]

As Isabella Graham had done thirty years earlier, Seton attempted to turn her education to remunerative use by opening a school, at first without success in New York, and then in Baltimore, where the presence of a group of wealthy Catholic families guaranteed a source of clients and the opportunity to promote "the progress of religion in this country." Increasingly, though, she was attracted to convent life, and in the spring of 1809, she took her first vows as a Roman Catholic nun. With the financial assistance of another convert, Samuel Sutherland Cooper of Philadelphia, Mother Seton, as she was now known, along with Cecilia and Harriet Seton, her five children, and a few other recruits, established a religious community at Emmitsburg, Maryland, site of Mount St. Mary's Seminary. There she began a girls' academy and sought church recognition for her community. The Sisters of Charity of St. Joseph, modeling their rule on that of a French order, received Archbishop Carroll's sanction in 1812.[24]

Eight eventful years had taken Elizabeth Seton from New York and the Society for the Relief of Poor Widows with Small Children to Maryland and the Sisters of Charity. In embracing Catholicism, and especially in taking the veil, she had walked across a personal Bering Strait, and as the waters rushed in to cover her path, she had alighted in territory quite separate from that of former associates such as Isabella Graham and Joanna Bethune. Thereafter, although all three women continued to devote themselves to religious education and relief for the poor, sectarian differences ensured that Seton would do so separately from Graham and Bethune. Yet their experience in the society shaped their lives and labors. Organizations founded and run by women continued to be significant mechanisms by which all sought to achieve their religious and social goals.

AT THE TIME OF Elizabeth Seton's conversion in 1805, Isabella Graham was well into her sixties. Retired from her career as a "school madam" and living with the Bethunes, she devoted her time to the Society for the Relief of Poor Widows with Small Children, personal religious devotions, evangelical teaching, and doing her rounds among poor women, usually in the company of Sarah Hoffman. She dispensed patronage as well as food and fuel, offering teaching jobs to "some of the widows best qualified for the task" (instructing the children of the clients of the Society for the Relief of Poor Widows), and recommending one widow for a job as manager of the Humane Society's Soup House. Spiritual ministrations always accompanied corporal ones; sometimes they sufficed, as Graham dispensed religious advice to clients, friends, and relatives. Besides her own religious journal, she kept up an extensive correspondence on religious subjects with friends on both sides of the Atlantic, using her letters to console, advise, instruct, preach, and theologize. "Young disciples," some of them former pupils, sought her out "as mother, friend, counsellor," and she answered, often providing detailed theological lectures or hortatory sermons. By one account, some poor New Yorkers turned her into a sacred figure: "when she walked in our streets, it was customary with us to come to the door and receive her blessing as she passed." If anything, Graham became even more strictly evangelical in her views and practices during the last decade of her life and narrowed the acceptable range of "worldly" preoccupations.[25]

In these evangelical endeavors, Graham labored in the company of several sets of associates: officials of the Society for the Relief of Poor Widows, New York's Scots Presbyterians and their old country counterparts, her minister and members of his congregation, her former pupils, and most important, Joanna and Divie Bethune. The Graham-Bethune partnership formed the bedrock upon which they could, individually and collegially, construct benevolent edifices. With Divie Bethune's importing business providing a comfortable income, and their religious principles demanding a simple style of living, Graham and the Bethunes had the time and means that access to household help and carefully husbanded finances allowed. Their home in Greenwich Village served as a center and a refuge, a place from which they could sally forth to do battle with the world's evils, then return to its shelter amid "woods and water, flower-garden and fruit-trees." Joanna Bethune's later comment that "I cannot well attend to my duties . . . & to my societies unless I am [living] in a quiet place" reflected the expectation that private family life would be available and the conviction that it was the essential basis for social activism. Their public and private lives interleaved, creating the interdependent layers that constituted the shale of their common endeavor. Despite six pregnancies during the first ten years of her marriage, which brought the disappointment of three stillbirths as well as the joy of three living children, Joanna continued her chosen work when she could. Jessie Bethune was born in 1798, Isabella Graham Bethune in 1800, and George Washington Bethune in 1805. George's entrance into the family circle brought Divie the "man child" for whom he had pined; his name symbolized his immigrant parents' embrace of American identities. Whether by accident or design, Joanna Bethune bore no more children, and as did increasing numbers of northeastern white women, completed her childbearing years while still in her thirties (she was thirty-five in 1805). No longer drained by repeated pregnancies, Joanna gradually undertook additional public burdens while she reared her children. Indeed, their presence gave her new reasons to do so.[26]

The "happy trio" shouldered such burdens as time and circumstance permitted, both as individuals and through voluntary organizations. Divie's involvements were legion, from the St. Andrew's Society to the New York and London Missionary Societies (he served the latter as one of its two foreign directors), to the New York Bible, Tract, and Sunday School Societies. The two women, having changed New York's charitable landscape by institutionalizing traditional forms of female benevolence in their first endeavor, increasingly gave hearts and hours to organizations founded and run by women. When Sarah Hoffman found the five children of a client mourning their dead mother and facing removal to the dreaded almshouse, the decision to form an Orphan Asylum Society seemed reasonable. Children of clients who died needed care. But that decision reflected an assumption possible only since 1797: that Hoffman, Graham, and Bethune could marshal the necessary organizational experience, access to resources, and personnel. They betrayed little hesitation or timidity in pursuing this new undertaking. Whereas Isabella Graham's comments on the early days of the Society for the Relief of Poor Widows described it as "feeble in its origin, the jest of most, the ridicule of many," particularly "the men [who] could not allow our sex the steadiness and perseverance necessary to establish such an undertaking," plans for the Orphan Asylum from the outset were "bold" and public. The earlier society had been organized at Graham's home; the organizational meeting for the Orphan Asylum was held at the City Hotel.[27]

With nine years' experience behind them, they well knew how to structure the new society's leadership in order to harvest the materials necessary to its success. Familiar names dotted the list of officers and trustees: Sarah Ogden Hoffman, Isabella Graham's close friend and coworker, as first directress; Elizabeth Schuyler Hamilton as second directress; and Sarah Clarke Startin as treasurer. Joanna Bethune was a trustee, as was her friend and cocommunicant, the Scots-born Sarah Lindsay, and Eliza Craig Saidler. In other circumstances, the list would also have included Saidler's dear friend Elizabeth Bayley Seton. Sarah Hoffman's "excellent judgment . . . and commanding social position" and Sarah Startin's "high place in society," as well as her willingness to become "personally responsible for large amounts of money," were to be harnessed for the good of the cause. But in the everyday life of the group, Hoffman, Graham, and Bethune took the lead. The orphanage itself was lodged in Greenwich Village, first in a rented house on Raisin Street, then in a three-story building built on some Bank Street lots furnished by Sarah Startin, with loans guaranteed by Divie Bethune. Tapping the wealth and connections at their disposal, they secured $10,000 in building funds from the state legislature and then an annual $500 appropriation, and a portion of the city's Public School Fund, as well as smaller donations and annual subscriptions. On a regular basis, Bethune and Graham could walk or take their carriage to the orphanage in order to teach a lesson, manage a Sunday school class, or handle some matter of business. Eventually, Graham resigned as head of the Society for the Relief of Poor Widows with Small Children, taking on the less onerous position of manager between 1805 and 1810. Her work with the orphans seemed "more suited to her advanced period of life."[28]

Other organizational activities followed. In 1812, when she was seventy, Isabella Graham agreed to head up a women's auxiliary for a Magdalen Society; two years later, when she was seventy-two, she signed a petition and chaired the founding meeting for a House of Industry Society, and became one of its managers. Initiated by Joanna Bethune, the House of Industry planned a work program patterned after that of the Society for the Relief of Poor Widows, and aimed at meliorating the suffering that accompanied the war with Britain. Once again, the Graham-Bethune team channeled benevolent impulses into organizational forms, collecting patrons and supporters as they went. The City Council, lauding the organizers' "respectible [sic] characters & benevolent lives," provided a building and an annual donation; the organizers bought and distributed materials, hiring poor women to turn them into articles of clothing that were then sold. Supporting the House of Industry proved to be Isabella Graham's final organizational project; she did not live to see its first season.[29]

After Graham's death on July 27, 1814, Joanna Bethune continued down the path they had trod together, following signposts pointing to a career in benevolence. But Isabella's death had a profound effect on her self-awareness. The public acclaim that accompanied her mother's passing—a number of memorial tributes and at least two requiem sermons made their way into print— awoke in Joanna a keen awareness of her own place in history. As she mourned "the most exemplary of mothers" and, with Divie Bethune, began sorting through Graham's journals and correspondence to prepare a religious biography for publication, Joanna revisited her own life, and for the first time wrote down an account of her religious struggles and conversion experience. Although in Graham's day conversion accounts had been oral and entered primarily in church records, and religious biographies more often took men as their subjects, by 1814 published versions were commonplace and women were increasingly their protagonists. Propelled into print by the new evangelical magazines of the early nineteenth century, religious biographies and conversion narratives filled a significant niche in evangelical libraries. Joanna had surely read her share of them. At least one deceased friend, Eliza Van Wyck (daughter of her friend and coworker Hannah Ker Van Wyck Caldwell and stepdaughter of Divie's close friend John E. Caldwell) had recently been the subject of a published religious biography. Dated August 18, 1814, twenty-two days after Isabella's passing and four days after John Mitchell Mason's warm and loving memorial sermon, Joanna's religious autobiography partook of many of the genre's conventions. But in a preface that she later inked out heavily, Bethune revealed what was on her mind. Addressed "to My Husband and Children," the preface contained a (now virtually unreadable) justification for the autobiography's composition, and ventured the possibility that "any of my writings should find their way into magazines or other publications." She expected to die before Divie and the children, and she expected her autobiography to be published.[30]

This awareness of her position as the daughter and potential successor of a Protestant saint, coming at a time when New York women's organizations were turning sharply toward evangelical concerns, was surely intensified by the process of compiling and publishing her mother's memoir. Although Divie Bethune wrote the biographical sketch, Joanna helped comb Isabella's detailed journals and extensive correspondence for the excerpts that comprised the bulk of the text. The profound impact of reading those materials reverberated later in her own journals, where her mother's memory served as a source of inspiration and strength. Once published, *The Power of Faith* quickly achieved wide circulation, increasing Isabella Graham's fame and Joanna's devotion to her memory. "She still lives, in her book & does good," an eighty-two-year-old Joanna commented; "O how many it has assisted." As the inked-out preface to Bethune's religious memoir reveals, the expectation that she would achieve some measure of fame herself could never again be far from her consciousness. Crossing it out was her way of dealing with the religious problem of pride that such an expectation presented.[31]

Joanna's energies continued to flow into her family and her societies, but gradually she channeled her organizational labors exclusively into work with children. In this fashion, she defined the shape of her own life, even while acknowledging that her mother's shadow had already drawn the outlines. Leaving the Society for the Relief of Poor Widows to others after one additional stint on the Board of Managers, she devoted her time to the Orphan Asylum and the House of Industry. When the latter was unable to keep pace with demands for its services and folded in 1820, Bethune remained active with the orphanage and with a new society she instigated in 1816, the Female Union Society for the Promotion of Sabbath Schools. Originated in February, one month before Divie helped found a masculine counterpart, the Female Union institutionalized a long-standing concern of both Isabella and Joanna with girls' education and their long-standing practice of teaching Sunday religious classes. It also signaled her interest in providing evangelical associations through which young women could announce their religious commitments. Although the society turned its schools over to the male-run New York Sunday School Union Society and dissolved in 1828, Joanna continued to teach Sunday school classes off and on for the rest of her life. She turned down a request to head up a new Female Tract Society in 1822, but in 1826 began prodding the Public School Society to undertake an experiment with infant schools for children "of the la-

boring poor" aged eighteen months to six years. Receiving little encouragement, she and her longtime friend and coworker Hannah Murray started their
own infant school, then formed the New York Infant School Society in 1827.
God, she believed, had "made plain paths for my feet in bringing me out of the
Sabbath Schl Union [and] assigning to me the delightful work of feeding his
lambs." Thereafter, Bethune concentrated her labors on the Orphan Asylum,
infant schools, and Sunday schools, writing and publishing lesson materials for
infant scholars. The only additional endeavor to which she lent her name was
a colonizationist group raising money for girls' schools in Liberia. In all of these
activities, formally organized societies created the venue for benevolence.[32]

Divie Bethune's unexpected death in 1824 when Joanna was fifty-four dissolved the Graham-Bethune partnership once and for all. Joanna was "desolate." She missed Divie's "great assistance & judicious counsel" dreadfully,
mourned her mother anew, and grieved over a long estrangement from her
only living sibling Isabella Smith. She turned once more to God, "now my Husband, & only Counsellor." The Bethunes' close secular as well as spiritual partnership was fully evidenced in his choice of Joanna as his sole heir and execu-
tor; "my beloved Husb[an]d left me the control of his property," she noted
gratefully, "that I might . . . keep my own house." She would not spend her
widowhood without a key to turn in her own front door, dependent upon the
good graces of a son- or daughter-in-law. Her gratitude reflected her understanding that a wealthy man like Divie Bethune who named his wife sole ex-
ecutor of his estate was an anomaly; as Suzanne Lebsock has demonstrated,
"when there was enough property to make its management a source of considerable power in the family and perhaps beyond it as well," in general husbands left their wives "on the sidelines." Although it cost her sleepless nights,
Joanna was fully in the game, settling accounts, disposing of property, dissolv-
ing Divie Bethune & Co. With her two daughters married and her son preparing for the ministry at Princeton, she found that her new "little *Home*" nicely
accommodated her "faithful friend," Miss V., and her servants, but was too far
from the Cedar Street Church. Sadly, she spent her last Sunday there, mourning another death, that of her "beloved pastor," John B. Romeyn, who had
preached Divie's funeral sermon.[33]

These changes signaled no fundamental shift in her life's direction; in widowhood as in marriage, she sought useful work, an orthodox and caring pastor,
and public recognition. Useful work came in the form of the Orphan Asylum
and Infant School; spiritual sustenance she found, first with her son-in-law,
Robert McCartee, then, most satisfyingly, with James Waddel Alexander, pastor of the Duane Street Presbyterian Church, who preached "admirable" ser-

mons "in the good old way no New School Doctrine nor hopkinsianism but the pure milk of the Gospel."[34]

Public recognition was a more difficult matter. To seek it for oneself was to risk indulging a sinful pride. All glory and credit for one's accomplishments, after all, belonged to God. Just as she had tried to obliterate any evidence of her ambitions by crossing out the preface to her religious autobiography, Bethune annihilated her pride and reshaped it, stone upon stone, into monuments to the family legacy. To honor Isabella's and Divie's memories was to give evidence of her devotion. The public ones included, of course, the organizations they had served, but more conspicuous were successive editions of *The Power of Faith*, especially a completely revised version that she prepared for publication in 1843, and a family grave at the Pearl Street Associate Reformed Church. Over the site, which held Divie's and Isabella's remains and those of two stillborn Bethune daughters, she had a tablet installed, listing Divie's name first, then Isabella's, with the notation that it had been erected by "his bereaved widow and her orphan daughter." (See Figure 3.1.) Joanna planned to be buried there too. Although she wrote and published other books, she seems not to have considered writing Divie's biography, even while she lamented that "no one offered." Her own story, compiled by George W. Bethune after her death in 1860, and published in 1863, added another ornament to the family edifice.[35]

Private monuments were constructed through her religious journals, George's career, and her grandchildren's naming and religious training. Begun three days after Divie's death and continued for most of the rest of her life, Bethune's diary faithfully recorded her observance of the sad anniversary ("As usual, I have spent the day in my room") and returned often to the lost partnership. Of 269 surviving entries, seventy-nine (30 percent) mention Divie or Isabella; thirty-eight of the seventy-nine (48 percent) mention both ("My own blessed mother, & my beloved ever to be regretted Husband"). The traces of her mother's journals were there, too, in language and phrasing modeled on the originals. It was a source of personal and family pride that both her daughters had married Presbyterian ministers—Jessie became Mrs. Robert McCartee and Isabella Mrs. George Duffield in 1817—but she valorized George's ministerial career beyond any achievement of her daughters or sons-in-law. While praying regularly for all her children, Joanna lavished attention on "our dear dear Son," noting his birthday (but not those of her daughters), commenting more than once on how happy his birth and choice of profession had made Divie, and recording the occasions when she heard him preach. "My dear first born Jessy" McCartee and Isabella Duffield appeared most often in the diary

SACRED

TO THE MEMORY OF

DIVIE BETHUNE,

MERCHANT OF THIS CITY,

WHO DIED SEPTEMBER 18, 1824;

AGED 53 YEARS.

and of

ISABELLA GRAHAM,

HIS MOTHER-IN-LAW,

WHO DIED JULY 27, 1814,

AGED 72 YEARS.

THEY WERE BOTH NATIVES OF SCOTLAND.

THIS MONUMENT

Is reared by his bereaved Widow, and her orphan Daughter,
As a testimonial of two servants of JESUS CHRIST;
The one a ruling Elder in his Church, the other a Mother in Israel,
Who, like Enoch, walked with God,
Like Abraham, obtained the righteousness of Faith,
And, like Paul, finished their course with joy.
They were lovely and pleasant in their lives, and they rest here together
in their graves.

" The blessing of him that was ready to perish came upon them; and they caused the widow's heart to sing for joy."--*Job* xxix. 13.

"Oh! how great is thy goodness, which thou hast laid up for them that fear thee; which thou hast wrought for them that trust in thee before the sons of men."--*Psalm* xxxi. 19.

FIGURE 3.1. This memorial inscription, which Joanna Graham Bethune composed for Divie Bethune and Isabella Marshall Graham, reveals Joanna Bethune's devotion to their memories and her sense that they formed a spiritual and temporal partnership. From *The Unpublished Letters and Correspondence of Mrs. Isabella Graham* (New York: John S. Taylor, 1838). (Courtesy of the University of Delaware Library)

when pregnant or giving birth, as Joanna prayed "to rejoice again over a living Mother, and a living Child." Despite being a published poet, Jessie fulfilled her adult role in the family (as did her sister) through motherhood. Jessie eventually had ten children; Isabella bore one child and buried five more before becoming "again the mother of a dear Isabella Graham [Duffield]." Her son

George followed his father and uncles into the ministry, while Jessie's son, Divie Bethune McCartee, became a Presbyterian medical missionary in China. (Isabella also named a son after Divie Bethune). The other Duffield and McCartee children, raised in Carlisle, Pennsylvania, and New York, came in for special prayers (and intense pressure) when they reached the age at which "their mothers . . . came out from the world and took the easy yoke of Christ upon them." To Joanna, every Bethune had a role in reinforcing and polishing the family temple: her daughters by training their children, her son and sons-in-law by service to the church, and her grandchildren through their names and their properly timed conversions. The family's religious history she interpreted as evidence of God's covenant with "my seed and the seed of my mother." As George put it, the "strain of sanctified blood" that ran in the family offered "striking proofs of God's faithfulness in His covenant." In this fashion, both Bethunes interpreted the Presbyterian doctrine of the covenant in highly personal and tribal ways, stressing the significance of "seed" "blood" and mother's milk in transmitting religious belief and practice across the generations. The comment that she had fed George "with milk—spiritual and temporal—the latter from my own breast," revealed her interpretation of the doctrine.[36]

In the histories of Isabella Graham and Joanna Bethune, one sees in concrete fashion how evangelicals captured economic, social, and ideological power in the nineteenth century. The stone jambs of the family economy—commerce and the professions—held the door to middle-class status in early nineteenth-century America. Divie's position as an importing merchant tied the family's fortunes to the international and local economies; purchases of the goods he procured in Europe and the West Indies enabled New Yorkers to define and display their standing in the new urban economy. In 1819, those goods included tobacco, flour, cotton bagging and sheeting, madeira, brandy, glassware, and coffee. Profits invested in Manhattan real estate permitted him not only to buy privacy for his family in the "pleasant home of fruits and flowers . . . by the Hudson's verdant side" that George recalled sentimentally, but also to bequeath upon his widow a reliable source of income. In 1857, Joanna's holdings amounted to $35,150 in real estate and $4,000 in personal wealth. The relatively modest size of her personal account reflected the couple's lifelong habit of simple living and giving "to the poor & every institution."[37]

Commerce had limited appeal as a way of life, however. Like Arthur and Lewis Tappan, Divie found his chosen work useful; his income financed worthy endeavors, and his example in business might inspire others. Yet it was "trying to Christian sensibilities . . . to be constantly among men of the world." (Had he lived longer, he would undoubtedly have been even more troubled;

by the late 1820s, the frost of evangelical disapproval had begun to descend upon brandy- and tobacco-selling.) In their ambitions for their children, Divie and Joanna preferred the church to the counting house, earnestly praying that young George might "'be made a faithful, honored, and zealous minister of the everlasting Gospel'" and celebrating the girls' marriages to ministers. Taking up "the most responsible of all professions" at a crucial moment in its history, men like George W. Bethune, Robert McCartee, and George Duffield helped chisel new lines in the stone. All three trained at college or theological seminary, all took posts at large urban temples built by commercial, manufacturing, and investment wealth, and all used the evangelical press to reach audiences beyond the sound of their voices. Both Bethune and Duffield spoke out on the religious and political issues of their day. Jessie and Isabella Bethune wielded their own tools to match line with grain, creating the position of "minister's wife" by teaching Sunday school, writing for religious magazines, and crafting model evangelical homes.[38]

Teaching and writing, the two quintessentially feminine careers of the nineteenth century, engaged the professional energies of all the Graham-Bethune women. Isabella Graham and Joanna Bethune taught for most of their adult lives, Isabella mostly with pay, Joanna mostly without it. Along with her mother's story, Joanna published organizational reports, infant school lessons and manuals, and religious poetry. Jessie McCartee was also a published poet. By producing cultural artifacts with lessons about values, morality, and behavior, as well as through teaching, child-rearing, and ministering to others, they helped define the world of the middle-class evangelical as surely as their men did. Indeed, the labor of both husbands and wives was essential, first to produce the career that supported the family, and then to reproduce and disseminate the ideals that sustained it.[39]

ALTHOUGH ELIZABETH SETON'S life and the lives of her Protestant coworkers diverged after 1805, her story illuminates the shape of Catholic benevolence, and reveals the different, if overlapping, contours of Catholic and evangelical Protestant practice in this arena. Elizabeth was both a recipient and a dispenser of charity, first in New York as a widow, then in Maryland as a nun. Her sister and brother-in-law furnished living quarters after Seton's school venture fell apart; a former beneficiary of William Seton's patronage then sponsored a brief boardinghouse undertaking. Friends like Antonio Filicchi provided tuition money for her two boys to attend Georgetown Academy, pledges guaranteeing her an income of $1,000 a year, and even money for Anna Maria's dancing lessons. When Cecilia Seton's conversion led to a major family rift and halted payments on income pledges, Filicchi put "unlimited sums" at her disposal, telling Elizabeth, "through you my mercantile interests are blessed by God with uninterrupted success."[40] Despite serious financial reversals, Elizabeth never faced destitution. By combining charity with remunerative work, she avoided any precipitous alteration of her children's standard of living and worldly expectations. The changes, when they came, were more gradual.

In Baltimore, the Filicchi brothers' financial support and that of her friends Julia Scott and John Wilkes enabled Seton to rent a house for her school and employ a servant to do the washing, cleaning, and cooking. The Emmitsburg convent was funded in part by Samuel Sutherland Cooper, a wealthy Philadelphia convert preparing to enter the priesthood. Although at one point Elizabeth envisioned starting "a Manufactory on a small scale which may be beneficial to the poor," her primary benevolent enterprises at Emmitsburg were a school for both paying and charity students and convent training that prepared nuns to run similar institutions. Like Isabella Graham's, Seton's curriculum included both academic and ornamental subjects, but neither elocution nor oratory. Catholic girls attending her school would be trained for domestic, not public roles.[41]

Seton's experience illustrates a key difference between Catholic and Protestant benevolence, and thus between Catholic and Protestant definitions of gender roles and social class. Although New York's Catholic laywomen served on parish charitable committees, and at the behest of their husbands formed a Ladies' Benevolent Society for the support of the Roman Catholic Orphan Asylum, nuns living in religious orders performed the bulk of charitable labor within the church. They, not laywomen, gained the kind of experience acquired from creating a permanent institution, raising endowment funds, attaining corporate status, and behaving as legal entities.[42] Catholic laywomen might develop organizing and fund-raising skills, as members of the Ladies' Benevolent Society did, and they might provide invaluable assistance to their sisters in religious orders, but their relationship to the nuns was always a secondary, auxiliary one. In this, they had Protestant counterparts, such as missionary fund-raising societies. But Catholic laywomen created no comparable institution to the well-endowed, tax-assisted, indenture-granting Orphan Asylum Society. Only nuns did so.[43]

Catholicism placed a high premium on both celibacy and motherhood, but the dominant nineteenth-century American gender conventions envisioned feminine fulfillment exclusively in terms of marriage and childbearing. Regardless of the growing numbers of single women in the United States, the real (if limited) opportunities some enjoyed for economic self-support, and the emerging cultural ideal of "single blessedness," other things being equal, unmarried women's social status remained inferior to married women's. As if to underscore the invaluable social authority that devolved upon those who married, members of Protestant benevolent societies, as we saw in Chapter 2, invariably chose married or widowed women to lead them. Catholic practices both reinforced and challenged these conventions by creating a class of single, celibate women—nuns—who were at one and the same time subordinate and authoritative. Nuns' vow of obedience guaranteed their subjection to male authority within the church's gender hierarchy; their dedication to others through lives of poverty, chastity, and service constituted them as a special class of women permitted to run their own affairs and admired for their selflessness. As teachers, nurses, and orphans' caretakers, they became surrogate mothers while also training young women for actual motherhood and domesticity. Their "maternity of the spirit" underpinned and reinforced the relegation of laywomen to domestic lives.[44]

As a widow with five young children, Elizabeth Seton encountered the status of the nun differently from most of her coworkers; nevertheless, the two themes of subordination and authority were important parts of her experience. Ownership of the Sisters of Charity's land in Emmitsburg, for example, initially belonged to Samuel Cooper and two priests: William Dubourg and John Dubois. (Dubourg served as the sisters' first religious "superior," or supervisor; Dubois was the local priest and their third superior.) Unlike the women of the Society for the Relief of Poor Widows with Small Children, the Sisters of Charity acquired legal title to their institution's property only after almost ten years of male control.[45] Their religious superior, as well as the presiding diocesan bishop, could demand obedience from the sisters, recruit applicants for the order, assign members to new posts, and request services for other Catholic institutions. At the same time, as the community's founder and leader, Seton exercised inviolable authority in many areas of daily life, and found ways to exert her will when priestly demands interfered with her plans. She cheerfully complied with some requests, telling her friend Julia Scott with wry humor, "[I] walk about with my knitting in my hand (we supply or are to supply by knitting and spinning the college and two seminaries of Mr. Du Bourg with socks and cloth,) give my opinion, see that every one is in his place, write letters, read, and give good advice." She gratefully received the petitioners for admittance recommended by Father Anthony Kohlmann (pastor of her old New York parish) and Bishop Jean Cheverus of Boston, believing that the two clerics had community's interests at heart through efforts to increase its numbers. But she came into sharp conflict with Dubourg over his edicts to the community, and resisted another superior's efforts to merge her order with a French one. On both counts, she won her point, first by appealing Dubourg's orders to her friend Bishop John Carroll, then by invoking the higher law of motherhood against the merger plans. "The dear ones have their first claim," she argued, referring to her children; "I could never take an obligation which interfered with my duties to them." Amalgamation with the St. Vincent de Paul sisters could deny her "the uncontrolled privileges of a Mother to my five darlings" by displacing her as community head. "*I am a Mother,*" she told a Baltimore friend. "Whatever providence awaits me consistent with that plea I say Amen to it." Her devotion to her children was indeed intense, yet temporal motherhood offered a source of authority not available to mere spiritual mothers, and permitted Seton to deflect demands for the silent, unquestioning docility that she found so difficult.[46] Some years after her death, the Emmitsburg community did merge with a French order.

Like priests, nuns occupied ill-defined positions within the class structure. Voluntarily poor, they nevertheless retained some trappings of the class status (whether high or low) that they brought with them into their religious orders. With her privileged birth and upbringing, and her continuing ties to Protestant family and friends, Elizabeth Seton moved easily between the worlds of her wealthy benefactors and her pupils. Although a visitor's eye might discern few variations among the Sisters of Charity, all clad in the same simple black-and-white mourning costume, among themselves and among Catholics at large, status differences remained visible. Even after almost a decade of convent life, Seton carried herself in the fashion of an upper-class matron. "I know how difficult it is," she advised her seventeen-year-old daughter Catherine in 1818, "to behave to some persons (who in certain circumstances of life or by coarseness of manners would take our proper reserve for pride and insult)." Only "sweet dignity of charity" and "free[dom] from the least familiarity" would suffice. Seton's warmth and humor enabled her to lead the Emmitsburg community with easy grace and a democratic style, but her ability to command patronage through the possession of high social status contributed significantly to her success. So, too, did her ability to reassemble her family at Emmitsburg, in the persons of her children and sisters-in-law, all of whom provided crucial emotional sustenance. Just as Isabella Graham had done for the Society for the Relief of Poor Widows with Small Children, Seton tapped an extensive set of connections on behalf of the Sisters of Charity.[47]

By the time of her death from tuberculosis in 1821 (she was forty-six), Seton had laid the groundwork for a set of benevolent enterprises as ambitious as that constructed by Graham and the Bethunes. By 1813, for example, nineteen Sisters of Charity, at least one of whom was also a widow with children, resided in the Emmitsburg community, along with ten novices, thirty-two boarding students, a few "pensioners," and two servants. During the summer months, twenty pupils from the town came to school daily. Among the boarding students, Seton could count the daughters of some of the wealthiest and most influential Catholic families on the East coast, including those of Baltimore's Harper and Carroll clans and New Yorkers Robert and Elizabeth Fox. Indeed, despite her initial hope of running "a nursery only for our Saviour's poor country children," by 1817 she found that her academy was "forming *city* girls to Faith and piety as wives and mothers."[48] Two groups of her recruits had left Emmitsburg to staff new Catholic orphanages in Philadelphia (1814) and in New York (1817), where Seton's former co-communicants, Cornelius Heeney and Pierre Toussaint, and laywomen like Elizabeth Fox and Charlotte Crone Lasala offered unstintingly generous support. In later years, the New York Sisters of Charity became a separate order with responsibility for a number of city schools, academies, hospitals, and asylums. Their story was repeated in other cities, such as St. Louis, where Seton's spiritual daughters settled.[49]

Along with the community at Emmitsburg, these enterprises formed Seton's lasting monuments. Like the organizations that Isabella Graham and Joanna Bethune founded, Seton's religious order carried on her work and her name. Like Joanna and the Bethune children, too, Seton's family took up the task of honoring her memory by publishing her letters and religious journals. (Seton had saved a great deal, including drafts of outgoing letters.) Only two of Seton's five children, William and Catherine, lived long enough to have a role in monument building. Tuberculosis claimed her beloved Anna Maria and Rebecca before their seventeenth birthdays, just as it killed Harriet and Cecilia Seton. Richard, whom she had placed with the Filicchi firm in Italy, died within three years of his mother, at the age of twenty-four. But Catherine entered the order of the Sisters of Mercy and William had a career, first with the Filicchis, then in the Navy. It fell to a grandson she never knew, the Catholic priest Robert Seton, to compile Seton's writings for publication and to compose a family history.[50]

In most ways, it was not her biological family so much as the Sisters of Charity who served as the primary keepers of Seton's memory. By preserving her writings, creating an archive for them and for the community's records, tending her grave, and testifying to their founder's holiness of character, her spiritual family helped shape Seton into the saint she later became (the church canonized her in 1975). (See Figure 3.2.) Even in the nineteenth century,

FIGURE 3.2. Original Elizabeth Bayley Seton gravestone, with a later addition, Emmitsburg, Maryland. Seton's remains now rest in an elaborate memorial chapel in Emmitsburg at the home of the religious order she founded. (Courtesy of the Archives of the Daughters of Charity, Emmitsburg, Maryland)

Seton's elevation to the ranks of female worthies outpaced that of her former coworker Isabella Graham, whose own life story entered Seton's library almost as soon as it was published. In the twenty-first century, although one New York social service agency bears Graham's name, Seton's public recognition is much broader, and institutions bearing her name more far-flung. The reasons for this contrast are rooted in Seton's special position as a convert, widow, mother, and native-born founder of a religious community. But they also speak to the organizational form of nineteenth-century Catholicism and the broad consciousness that it seems to have fostered. In part because of its heavily immigrant constituency, and in part because of its Roman center, Catholicism encouraged an awareness that encompassed nation and world, as well as locality. Catholic laywomen might concern themselves both with the affairs of a homeland, such as Ireland or France, by sending money or information home, and with their parish-based and locally focused charities. Nuns often belonged to religious orders with European origins, regularly corresponded with religious superiors in Europe, accepted into their ranks women of varying ethnic and class backgrounds, and, when called upon to establish a new school, hospital, or orphanage, obediently traveled wherever their religious superiors required. Elizabeth Seton's advice to her son William that he avoid "giv[ing] way to national prejudices" during his residence in Italy, but "allow for many customs and manners," may have reflected her own upper-class background, but it was also a habit of mind that her new religion encouraged. Catholicism's centralized organization permitted widespread dissemination of Seton's story; its international constituency learned to revere coreligionists from many backgrounds. Seton's ability to embody all possible varieties of Catholic womanhood—wife, mother, widow, celibate nun—and her status as a convert made her an especially apt candidate for reverence and veneration. After 1821, her story acquired a powerful cultural symbolism for American Catholics; she became, and remains, better known than either of her Protestant coworkers.[51]

Mary Morgan Mason and Henrietta Green Regulus Ray

The lives of two other New York women vary the themes evident in Graham's, Bethune's, and Seton's stories, while also elaborating some significant contrasts to them, especially in the experiential realms of social class and race. Mary Morgan Mason, born in Cork, Ireland, in 1791, and raised in Philadelphia, was a convert to Methodism, the wife of a Methodist minister, and the mother of nine children. Her spiritual struggles, detailed in a journal and letters preserved and published by her daughter, sound similar notes to those that resonated in Joanna Bethune's and Elizabeth Seton's accounts. Some twenty years younger than those women and equally active in women's benevolence, Mason developed a different life pattern, combining lifelong paid labor with Methodist evangelizing and feminine benevolence. Although Henrietta Green

Regulus Ray, born in New York in 1808, left none of the personal documents that enable historians to reconstruct the other women's motives and concerns, she was nevertheless a significant actor in one segment of New York's charitable enterprises. A member of New York's Abyssinian Baptist Church, Henrietta Ray was freeborn at a time when slavery was still a reality in New York State, though its extent was waning in the aftermath of the gradual emancipation law of 1799. In the years following slavery's formal abolition in 1827, she helped shape some pioneering African American women's organizations.[52]

Both Mary Mason and Henrietta Ray participated in their families' econo-mies much more directly than Graham, Bethune, or Seton. Whereas during marriage the latter confined their economic activities to assisting their hus-bands or facilitating the men's careers and took on remunerative work only upon widowhood, both Mason and Ray labored for pay during most of their adult lives. Recruited in 1810 from the Young Ladies' Academy of Philadelphia to teach in a girls' school operated by the Quaker Female Association, Mary Morgan continued in the job after her marriage to the Methodist minister Thomas Mason in 1817. She resigned the following year, when six months' pregnant with her first child, then promptly opened her own school, assisted by her cousin Susan Morgan. Only when expecting her second child in 1820 did she close that school. Other similar endeavors followed, as she interspersed paid labor with bearing and rearing nine children, seven of whom survived to adulthood. The last child, born when she was forty-six, arrived a few months before the eldest married. Aided by a lifelong companion, Sarah Sickles, Mary Mason managed a phenomenally productive career as minister's wife, mother, teacher, Sunday school superintendent, and founder and leader of numerous benevolent societies. That she viewed remunerative labor as inseparable from family labor is suggested by her daughter Elizabeth's comment that a new fam-ily house, built in 1836 from Mary and Thomas Mason's "united savings," needed to be "commodious" in order to accommodate Mary Mason's school as well as "the education of her own children."[53]

Henrietta Ray's economic activities are more difficult to document; the available sources tell us only that she pursued a "useful trade," and that she taught it to others. Given the narrow range of work permitted to free African American women in New York City and the nature of her charitable undertak-ings, it seems likely that she was a seamstress. Married to Laurent (Lawrence) Regulus, whose white French father had brought the "colored child" and his brother Alexandre from St. Thomas, West Indies around 1812, Henrietta was a widow before her twenty-first birthday. Tuberculosis claimed Lawrence in No-vember 1828, when he was just 26. Henrietta and Alexandre then assumed joint ownership of 153 Orange Street, a house and shop from which Lawrence had operated a shoemaking business. Although Orange Street bore little resemblance to the leafy green riverside spot that Isabella Graham and Joanna Bethune had called home—numbers 141, 143, 147, and 149 were all brothels in 1826—Henrietta's control of property set her apart among free African Americans as a person with some resources. Possession of a skill and of full literacy (that is, she could both read and write) added to the advantages she could claim amid a population with a high proportion of former slaves in its midst.[54]

When Henrietta married again in 1834, the house on Orange Street became home also to Charles B. Ray, a New Englander who had come to New York City in 1832. Their combined assets, including the house, Henrietta's trade, and Charles's boot and shoe store on Pearl Street, afforded the Rays some measure of economic security. Unlike many of their impoverished neighbors, they headed their own household (in 1820, almost 38 percent of New York's free black population lived in white households) and had prospects of joining the city's small black elite. Henrietta also enjoyed a close personal relationship with the family of Samuel Cornish, coeditor and co-owner of the city's first black newspaper, *Freedom's Journal*, having lived with the Cornishes for three years. Their relatively high status could not, however, protect the Rays from the disease that ravaged so many families in the nineteenth century (including the Setons), but "proved fatal to twice as many blacks as whites" in New York City: tuberculosis. Henrietta fell seriously ill with it in 1835 and passed it to their daughter, Matilda, who was born early in 1836. Matilda died on July 1 at six months of age, followed by Henrietta on October 27; she was twenty-eight.

After his wife's death, Charles Ray rekindled his ministerial ambitions, which had been crushed by the racial prejudice he experienced at a New England seminary, and sought ordination in the Methodist Church. Soon switching to Congregationalism, he became a well-known New York City minister and missionary, political activist, and editor and owner (1839–42) of a new newspaper, the *Colored American*. After remarrying in 1840, he and his second wife had seven children, one of whom they named Henrietta. An 1857 tax list found him in possession of $3,000 worth of real estate, including the house on Orange Street. We will never know how crucial the first Henrietta Ray's assets proved to Charles Ray's eventual success, but there is no question that the couple's economic edifice rested on delicately balanced pylons: two decent incomes, some property, literacy, marketable skills, resourceful friends, and community ties. (See Figure 3.3.) Only a few other free African Americans were able to replicate such a fortuitous combination; fewer still were able to anchor the family economy in anything resembling secure ground.[55]

The People of the State of New-York,

To Charles B. Ray of the City of New York
late the husband of Henrietta D. Ray late of
said City deceased. Send Greeting

WHEREAS the said Henrietta D. Ray
lately departed this life intestate, being at or immediately previous to her death an
inhabitant of the County of New-York, by means whereof the ordering and granting
Administration of all and singular the goods, chattels, and credits, whereof the said
intestate died possessed, in the State of New-York, and also the auditing, allowing,
and final discharging the account thereof, doth appertain unto us, and we being
desirous that the goods, chattels, and credits of the said intestate, may be well and
faithfully administered, applied, and disposed of, do grant unto you the said

Charles B. Ray

full power by these presents, to administer and faithfully dispose of all and singular,
the said goods, chattels, and credits ; to ask, demand, recover, and receive the debts
which unto the said intestate, whilst living, and at the time of his death did
belong ; and to pay the debts which the said intestate did owe, as far as such goods,
chattels, and credits will thereunto extend and the law require : hereby requiring you
to make or cause to be made, a true and perfect Inventory of all and singular the
goods, chattels, and credits of the said intestate, within a reasonable time, and
return a duplicate thereof, to our Surrogate of the County of New-York, within
three months from the date of these presents : and if further personal property or
assets of any kind not mentioned in any Inventory that shall have been so made,
shall come to your possession or knowledge, to make, or cause to be made, in like
manner, a true and perfect Inventory thereof, and return the same within two months
after discovery thereof : and also to render a just and true account of administration
when thereunto required ; and we do by these presents depute, constitute and appoint
you the said

Charles B. Ray

administrat or   of all and singular the goods, chattels, and credits of the
said   Henrietta D. Ray   deceased.

IN TESTIMONY WHEREOF, we have caused the Seal of Office of the Surrogate of said
County to be hereunto affixed. WITNESS, JAMES CAMPBELL, Surrogate of said
County, at the City of New-York, the twenty fifth day of October
in the year of our Lord one thousand eight hundred and thirty-six and of our
Independence the sixty first

James Campbell

SURROGATE.

FIGURE 3.3. Letter of administration for Henrietta Regulus Ray, 1836. Because she
died intestate, this letter transfers Henrietta Ray's assets to her widower, Charles B.
Ray. Although the letter requires an inventory, none is extant. (Courtesy of the Surrogate's Court, New York County, New York)

In their organizational activities, Mary Mason and Henrietta Ray reflected patterns typical of women who shared their racial and class status, and their engagement with religion. Mary Morgan Mason's conversion from her parents' freethinking to her uncle's Methodism combined elements of Joanna Bethune's and Elizabeth Seton's stories. Like Seton, she faced "bitter persecution" from family members, particularly her mother, for her choice of religion; like Bethune, she endured a conversion experience that included illness, "severe mental struggle," rejection of "vain amusements," and spiritual journal-keeping. As had Seton and Bethune, she attached herself to a spiritual mentor, in this case, her uncle, and discovered new vistas and opportunities in her "new life." Relocated to New York after her rebirth, she found a spiritual family at the John Street Methodist Church and a temporal one with her uncle and cousins. Immersed in her teaching and in Methodist circles, she quickly developed her speaking and leadership talents. Coming of age at a time and in a place where Isabella Graham, Joanna Bethune, and their associates had created an organizational base and a religious rationale for women's collective action, the newly converted Mary W. Morgan found it natural to commit herself both to Methodist undertakings and to pan-Protestant benevolence. She helped found not only the Methodist Female Assistance Society (1813) and Asbury Female Mite Society (1816), but also a women's Missionary Society (1819) and an early Sunday school (1815) at the John Street Methodist Church. After her marriage, she participated in Joanna Bethune's Female Union Society for the Promotion of Sabbath Schools and the Asylum for Lying-In Women.

Mason's Methodism and her early experience teaching for a Quaker association proved both enabling and demanding. In the name of Methodism, and in the cause of Friends' schools, she traveled and spoke in public. Although she rejected Quaker theology and remained wedded to a masculine clerical ideal, Mason found the house of Methodism a spacious enough site for honing her own leadership skills. With its inclusive Arminian theology, democratic worship, continual quest for the Holy Spirit's "second blessing," and lay-led class meetings, Methodism permitted, indeed it demanded, a kind of public female presence more visible than what Graham and Bethune experienced as Presbyterians. Mason claimed to find those demands onerous, depicting herself as a reluctant laborer whose preference for "hid[ing] myself in the most obscure corner" when it appeared that she might be "called upon to exercise by prayer, or speaking publicly" almost made her take the "easy" path of becoming a Quaker. Methodism proffered an alternative to "easy" or "self-indulgent" doctrines; it was attractive precisely because it demanded self-denial. Her public labors, unwanted but required, thus represented mandates from God requiring triumph over the self, even to the extent of leading brothers and sisters in prayer.[56]

Henrietta Regulus Ray was similarly intense about her religious and organizational commitments, though she left no introspective musings. When Samuel Cornish eulogized her, he stressed her long-term dedication "to God and the church," recording that it began when she was seven. As evidence for her "strong mind and sound judgment," he noted her decision to be rebaptized, by immersion, when she joined the Abyssinian Baptist church at the age of nineteen. She took the step only after studying the relative merits of different baptismal theologies. In the Baptist congregation, she would have found a heavily female membership and an exclusively male leadership. In 1833, for example, women constituted at least 75 percent of the 235 members, but all seven deacons, elders, and clerks were men. In thus observing nineteenth-century gender conventions, New York's African Baptists were hardly unusual. Nor did their theological positions on such questions as election, particular redemption, or baptism differ materially from those of white Baptists. Yet in choosing Abyssinian as her religious home, Henrietta Regulus Ray stated her preference for a church run by African Americans themselves, where she could worship freely, rather than being confined to a separate gallery or pew. The emphasis on respectability in the church's standards for membership may have appealed to her as well. Its rules forbade fellowship to drunkards, fornicators, or adulterers; prohibited members from "partiality" in their dealings with each other, "utter[ing] insinuations" against each other's characters, or "tattling"; and labeled "indolent members" as "a blot and a disgrace to the church." Abyssinian Baptist also discouraged formality and fostered intimacy among congregants; even though all members had surnames, the membership list grouped them alphabetically by their *first* names.[57]

These emphases in church practice—self-determination for African Americans as a group, secondary status for women within the group, a concern about respectability, and an emphasis on building communal bonds, protecting the group, self-help and self-discipline—surfaced also in the organizations that Henrietta Regulus Ray helped found and lead. At age nineteen, she became the assistant secretary of the new African Dorcas Association, a mutual aid and sewing society devoted to providing clothing for children attending the African Free Schools. Called into existence and named by the men of New York's Manumission Society, the Dorcas Association was not the product of women's initiative. Nor was it autonomous; the white teacher at the African Free School, William Andrews, wrote its constitution, and an advisory committee of black ministers, which included Henrietta's friend Samuel Cornish, supervised its activities.[58] Nevertheless, the women met weekly on their own, held biweekly sewing classes for each other, paid semiannual dues, and collected clothing and shoes for the schoolchildren. Their organization combined self-help and mutual relief with benevolence, and wrapped it all in notions about free African American women's proper "place" as quiet, steady, and unobtrusive laborers. Whether or not Henrietta fully subscribed to those ideas, her interest in "acquiring literary and scientific knowledge" led her to preside over the New York Female Literary Society from its foundation in 1834 until her death in 1836. A self-improvement group, the Literary Society also raised funds to help runaway slaves and (after Henrietta's death) to promote the cause of abolition. In a short few years, Henrietta Ray's organizational involvements expanded from mutual aid designed to benefit schoolchildren to adult women's self-help and political awareness.[59]

Marriage and life-course stage, both significant factors in shaping the organizational lives of many nineteenth-century women, were of varying importance in Ray's and Mason's histories. As we have seen, both experienced marriage as a direct economic partnership, and both engaged in remunerative work throughout their lives. This relative lack of differentiation in assigning the role of "breadwinner," while common in poor and working-class white and black families, would have been very unusual in families like the Grahams or the Bethunes. Although the Graham and Bethune women were significant economic actors during marriage, their work involved facilitating their husbands' earning power and establishing the family's status; it was curtained and invisible. Only widowhood permitted or forced them to undertake a directly remunerative role. Mary Morgan Mason viewed her marriage in more egalitarian terms, as her references to Thomas Mason indicate ("my dear partner" or "my dear companion"); his death in 1842 brought no immediate changes in either her paid or unpaid work. She continued to teach for ten years, retiring at the age of sixty-one. In the years after Thomas's death, as before, she labored in both Methodist and pan-Protestant benevolence, exhibiting special concern for children's education and women's health. In 1850, she became superintendent of the Methodist mission Sunday school at Five Points and helped run a women's society supporting the Methodist old age home; in 1855, Dr. J. Marion Sims sought her assistance in establishing New York Women's Hospital; and in 1858, she joined the board of the Colored Orphan Asylum. Unlike Joanna Bethune, she did not experience widowhood as a period of narrowing interests, but of continuity in concerns.[60]

Of the women discussed here, only Henrietta Regulus Ray remarried after widowhood. None of the others seems to have considered it, even though two of them, Graham and Seton, were very youthful widows. In deciding to remain unattached, they took a step that many other women in their social and organizational circles followed. In general, when her finances permitted it, a woman usually chose widowhood over remarriage. In this way, she could continue to draw upon the social authority that marriage had provided without facing the limitations and uncertainties a new marriage could impose. Widowhood freed many women for additional work; indeed the widowed stage of life (especially if it came after children were out of leading-strings) often led to new and age-specific organizational involvements. Joanna Bethune's concentration on her infant school, Sunday school, and orphan asylum work illustrates this pattern well. For women like Henrietta Ray, the meanings of marriage and remarriage were doubly and triply complex. Unable to claim the protection and authority that white women, even poor ones, expected from the institution, African American women nevertheless valued marriage as a means of pooling resources, establishing stability, and indicating status. In a community where so many depended upon white employers for work, wages, and shelter, being married and being able to live with one's spouse was a mark of social standing. Remarriage, especially when one was as young a widow as Henrietta Regulus, was probably an economic necessity, in a way that it was not for Isabella Graham or Elizabeth Seton.[61]

By the time of Henrietta Ray's death in 1836, the size, shape, contours, and design of women's benevolent enterprises were considerably different from what they had been in 1797. Building upon the forms pioneered in the early years of the century, women from very different backgrounds had created organizations to achieve a number of social goals while also fulfilling personal imperatives. Her own journey from the meliorist benevolence of the African Dorcas Association to the more politically conscious labor of the Female Literary Society, although taken by few of her contemporaries, reflected one of the directions that female organizing was taking in the 1830s. The formation of the New York Female Moral Reform Society in 1834 and Ladies' New York City Anti-Slavery Society in 1835 not only represented a more reformist turn in women's organizing, but also opened small chinks in the walls separating women's organizational activism along lines of race, class, and religion. If a few white women could commit themselves to a goal dear to the hearts of black women — immediate abolition — and if some middle-class women could make common cause with working women of their own race, then moral reform and abolition might offer what Lori Ginzberg has termed "the radical possibilities of sisterhood."[62]

Neither movement realized those possibilities. Nor did they attract the alle-

MARY W.

RELICT OF REV. THOMAS MASON,

DIED JANUARY 23, 1868,

AGED 76 YEARS, 6 MONTHS.

SHE FOUNDED

THE FIRST METHODIST SUNDAY-SCHOOL IN NEW YORK,

WHERE

SHE LABORED MORE THAN FIFTY YEARS,
FOR THE AGED, THE YOUNG,
AND THE POOR.

WELL REPORTED OF FOR GOOD WORKS;
SHE BROUGHT UP CHILDREN;
SHE LODGED STRANGERS;
SHE RELIEVED THE AFFLICTED;
SHE DILIGENTLY FOLLOWED EVERY GOOD WORK.

FIGURE 3.4. This inscription on Mary Morgan Mason's gravestone honors her memory and establishes her claim on posterity. From Elizabeth Mason North, *Consecrated Talents, or, The Life of Mrs. Mary W. Mason* (New York: Carlton and Lanahan, 1870). (Courtesy of the University of Delaware Library)

giance of more than a tiny minority of organized women, most of whom continued to labor in religiously, ethnically, racially and class-defined groups. Although in 1858 Mary Mason joined the board of the Colored Orphan Asylum, rather than Joanna Bethune's Orphan Asylum Society, she found nothing odd in belonging to an all-white organization running an asylum for black children, and relegating African American women to behind-the-scenes fund-raising. "Favorable financial report," she noted in her journal in 1860; "$1,100 paid by colored ladies who carried on a fair." Among them was Charlotte Burroughs Ray, Charles's second wife, for whom the house on Orange (now Baxter) Street served as a center of community and antislavery activism. Absent from such board meetings but present as fund-raisers, organizers, and activists within their own churches and organizations, "colored ladies" such as Henrietta and Charlotte Ray usually left many fewer permanent monuments to their work. As Joanna Bethune had done for her mother, and expected someone else to do for her, Mary Mason's daughter published her memoir and erected an historically minded headstone over her grave. Inscribed with the (unverifiable) claim that "she founded the first Methodist Sunday-School in New York" and the (unassailable) fact that "she labored more than fifty years, for the aged, the young, and the poor," the "plain, solid, and symmetrical . . . marble monument" bore witness to the life of a formidable woman. (See Figure 3.4.) Without the two-paragraph obituary that Samuel Cornish composed, Henrietta Ray's equally formidable record would have vanished. The differences between the two women's experiences reveal how nineteenth-century social hierarchies manifested themselves in death as well as in life.[63]

Conclusion

Five stories, while not precisely typical of those of the hundreds who managed and ran women's associations in New York and Boston, embody significant themes in women's organizational history. Aside from demonstrating the rapid growth and entrenchment of associational activity in individual lives and individual cities, these capsule biographies enable us to see the flexible nature of organizational involvements and their adaptability to particular circumstances, personal concerns, and stages of life. They also clarify the process whereby the women of the urban middle classes incorporated organizational work into their self-definitions and, when possible, reproduced and perpetuated their interests and concerns. The ability of some and the inability of others to do so speaks clearly to the divisions within nineteenth-century society that gave only certain women the power to shape a city's present and its future.

On any given day during her short adult life, Henrietta Regulus Ray might have passed Joanna Graham Bethune on a New York City street—perhaps even Bethune Street—as each of them hurried to complete some work for her societies. Lacking the assets that Bethune possessed by virtue of her race, education, marriage, connections, inheritance, and progeny, Ray could hardly muster the economic resources or social influence to establish her associations on the same footing as Bethune's. The two women would have little basis for recognizing each other as middle-class New Yorkers practicing appropriately feminine benevolence, although each in her own way fit that description. They would remain strangers in an unequal world.

CHAPTER FOUR

Politics

The rise of permanent women's organizations altered the form and locus of female political activity. Before 1790, with the exception of some Revolutionary-Era activists, women seeking political influence found it as individuals, not in ladies' associations or female mobs, and more often in the parlor or the bedroom than in the press or public square. But during the years that spanned the shift from the republican era of limited suffrage to the democratic era of mass politics, woman-run organizations—whether charitable, religious, mutual aid, or reformist in orientation—moved from the unusual to the commonplace. As they proliferated, formal organizations came to represent a source of collective influence and (at least potentially) an "engine for moving [women's] concerns into the public sphere." Organizations could make those concerns visible and audible in public forums and policy debates. Moreover, women in groups could do many things legally prohibited to individuals, especially wives, including owning property, investing funds, indenturing children, and contracting for services. There was strength in numbers.[1]

Harnessing that strength in the interests of particular issues or specific policies was another matter. Between 1800 and 1830, the female organizational leaders who were most successful at making their voices heard or gaining favors for their associations were white, Protestant, and middle class. For them, political access was rooted in their possession of bourgeois feminine respectability—those intertwined class and gender characteristics that ideologically "conflated femininity and morality" and turned individual women (and some groups of women) into symbols of a social class. Using their symbolic status and employing a deferential political style based on personal connections to powerful men, some women could claim to speak for all women, sweep figuratively past low-status men whose lack of "independence" barred them from the magic circle of enfranchised citizens, and wield their collective influence for the benefit of group projects. Like statesmen's wives, mothers, and daughters, representatives of organizations could speak their groups' requests into listening ears.[2] As they did, they clung steadfastly to the notion that their organizations served no political functions, avoided "exciting public attention," and operated securely within "woman's province." Just as early women leaders adhered to the position that their work never competed with the demands of home, they affirmed their organizations' retirement from all things political.[3]

Yet by their very existence, women's groups altered the political scene. Onto the postrevolutionary ideal of republican motherhood, which envisioned individual mothers raising good citizens for the nation, women organizers grafted an ideal of collective feminine responsibility for the common weal. To the republican concept of a gendered citizenship rooted in masculine independence and control of dependents, they added the notion that women in groups could perform civic duties even while, as individuals, fulfilling their primary duties to their families. Paralleling the new consciousness that men developed as citizens possessing rights and giving their consent to be governed, women in groups became aware of themselves as "the wives mothers and daughters of . . . citizens" operating within a separate and subordinate "province" or "sphere." As the men of their families moved into a new republican world of equal rights, women organizers adopted the deferential politics of influence that men were throwing off, a politics suitable to political subjects.[4] At a time when individual women's political assertiveness was being silenced, and their "engagement in civic culture" closely scrutinized and critiqued, organizational leaders' insistence on duties and deference permitted groups of women to enter the public sphere without directly challenging the republican gendering of politics. The creation of permanent women's organizations made possible the postrevolutionary reverberation of feminine voices speaking on policy matters and the clatter of female feet traversing city sidewalks as "the almoners of public charity."[5]

During the 1820s and 1830s, as the voters' circle opened to embrace most white men (and a few free black men), electoral politics became both more democratic and more exclusively masculine. During the same decades, the growth of working-class white, Roman Catholic, and African American women's charitable and mutual aid societies, and the appearance of reform-oriented Protestant women's organizations, cast deference-based political action into a new light. Sharing their men's outsider status and relative powerlessness, African American women, for example, could voice their organizations' collective concerns only through the mediation of fathers, brothers, or husbands. Because they were denied claims to respectability or ladyhood, they could not approach political figures on behalf of their organizations. Whether black or white, women reformers, especially those seeking to end slavery or challenge the sexual double standard, vocally rejected deference-based political action. In its place, they sought to create a new style of female politics based on mass mobilization rather than class- and race-exclusive influence. As they did, they found themselves vilified for activities in which other women had quietly and collectively engaged for years: assembling in public places, speaking to monthly gatherings, petitioning their rulers, lobbying for legal changes, and controlling property although married. Although denunciations of any woman who "assumes the place and tone of man as a public reformer" targeted abolitionists, not orphanage managers, the latter nevertheless shrank from the spotlight's unwonted glare and rethought their accustomed practices.[6]

By 1840, the line separating "political" from "domestic," or "public" from "private" actions was being redrawn, and earlier practices faced heightened scrutiny. As female reformers articulated their views on women's relative duties to their families and to themselves, and asked questions about the relationship between duties and rights, they wrote another chapter in a continuous historical process of boundary definition. By the 1840s, the bounds of both womanhood and the public arena had been reconstituted. Nevertheless, over the course of four decades, the form, locus, and style of women's politics had changed markedly. Women's political influence was wielded collectively as well as individually, and feminine political utterances had become audible in the masculine public sphere where policy was discussed and formulated.

Women's Organizations and "the Public Sphere": Publicity

Women's organizations first entered the public sphere—that arena of policy discussion and opinion formation so characteristic of modern literate societies—when they named themselves and announced their existences. In doing so, they utilized the existing world of print culture and courted "publicity" for the particular cause they espoused. Because the republican public sphere was a largely masculine space in which individual women's voices were few and muted, the appearance of visible and audible groups of women represented a significant change. Henceforth, women could develop and express opinions on matters related to public policy or the common good both in the singular, as members of families, and in the plural, as collections of public-minded female citizens.[7]

As a means of moving organization members' concerns into arenas of public discussion, publicity was a powerful but unstable resource. From the start, some organizations sought and won publicity, while others hid from it, and still others lacked the power either to court or to renounce it. Women leaders who commanded abundant economic, political, and social resources experienced the largest measure of control over their organizations' public visibility and visage. As the wife of a prominent Baptist minister, for example, Bostonian Hannah Morgan Stillman could expect a newspaper editor to print her words in 1799 when she wrote a letter proposing an asylum for orphaned (white) girls. Stillman's coreligionist, Mary Webb, although from a family of bookbinders, schoolteachers, and shipwrights, enjoyed a similar presumption of favor for her numerous causes, which included several fund-raising missionary organizations, a prostitutes' refuge, and a home for neglected white children, all of which were founded between 1800 and 1833. New Yorker Hannah Ker Van Wyck Caldwell brought to her volunteer work, undertaken through five societies between 1803 and 1840, the financial reserves of two husbands, and the social capital accumulated by her birth family (her father was a minister) and marital connections.[8]

Almost at will, women like Stillman, Webb, and Caldwell could draw (or deflect) attention to their work. As founder and secretary of the Boston Female Missionary Society (1800), Webb initially publicized the group's work by sending written reports to her pastor, Thomas Baldwin, editor of the *Baptist Missionary Magazine*. He published them. Soon, she arranged to have the group's constitution and rules printed in separate pamphlets. Taking an evangelical turn in the 1810s, her organization sought to spread knowledge and communication among female missionary societies up and down the east coast. After inviting correspondence from similar groups, Webb found herself penning letters to seventeen secretaries of missionary societies in 1812, and to a finger-numbing 109 in 1818. That same year, an investigative report compiled by two male urban missionaries brought Webb's missionary society widespread notoriety when the society sponsored and published it. Yet when Webb, after pressing evangelical men of her acquaintance to create a Penitent Females' Refuge for some of the young prostitutes mentioned in the report, became the refuge's matron and secretary of its Ladies Auxiliary, she guided that organization toward almost complete reticence. Learning that some men had attended refuge-sponsored sermons for titillating "purposes the very reverse of those for which they were designed," the refuge ladies concluded that it was impossible to discuss "this vice" openly "without great danger of communicating defilement and pollution as well as information to the public mind." Webb had learned the scandalous potential of some evangelical publicity. The group published no reports between 1825 and 1839, instead circulating copies only among friends.[9]

As did Webb with her penitent magdalens, some other women leaders cultivated and won reclusiveness for their organizations. Their groups were inconspicuous by choice, and could alter the choice without fear of censure. Boston's Widows' Society, founded in 1816 with a strong list of well-off subscribers and "a wish to avoid publicity," went its own way at first, so that "the operations, and even the existence of the Society, have been scarcely known beyond the sphere of its immediate influence." Five years later, finding themselves in financial need, the managers reversed policy, advertised their rented receiving-space in the papers, and solicited donations, revised their constitution, and made a public appeal for funds. Soon, they had also recruited a minister to preach a charity sermon for them, petitioned for incorporation, and begun publishing their annual reports. The city's Corban Society, a group of Congregationalist women providing clothing to ministerial students, incorporated themselves, but otherwise did little to court attention outside the orbit of their subscribers. Primarily a sewing circle, the women focused narrowly on the needs of Andover Seminary students. Indeed, for thirty-seven years, until they closed their sewing baskets once and for all in 1848, the members made a virtue of obscurity, humbly claiming "no splendid achievements, nothing to attract the admiring gaze of the curious," acknowledging merely some "feeble efforts" to promote orthodox ministerial education. In New York, the Female Bethel Union, a group seeking the "moral and spiritual improvement" of sailors, operated quietly at first before deciding to go before "the public" in 1836 by publishing an annual report.[10]

As these examples demonstrate, controlling an organization's public visibility required access to the printed word, through self-publishing, paid advertising, or acquaintance with sympathetic editors. With enough money, women leaders could afford to publish their own annual reports, meeting announcements, charity sermons, and lists of donors. Tract, Sunday school, and infant school societies printed leaflets, pamphlets and books for members' use. Some groups regularly purchased newspaper space to announce meetings or advertise their services. Soon after its founding in 1800, the Boston Female Asylum used an advertisement to notify the public of its readiness to accept female orphans; the Fragment Society did the same for its mission in 1812; and in 1824 New York's Asylum for Lying-In Women placed a notice "that it may be more generally known that a society exists" to assist poor expectant wives. New York's Society for the Relief of Poor Widows with Small Children advertised for clothes-washing work for its clients in 1803; a Boston counterpart publicized its donations receiving room in 1822. Printing costs were a regular item in organizational budgets, a necessary part of courting attention and donations.[11]

Organization leaders' personal connections to male printers, publishers, editors, and writers kept those costs within reason by providing them with free publicity as well. As the early nineteenth-century "print revolution" created a huge demand for words to etch onto pages, women's organizational reports became newsworthy. Evangelical magazines and newspapers were particularly eager consumers of women's collective utterances, as Mary Webb discovered when her pastor regularly printed the Boston Female Missionary Society's annual reports. Moreover, as evangelicals extended their cultural power in the 1810s and 1820s and the number of religious weeklies surged, readers' encounters with the feminine organizational face and voice became routine. Regular reports of fairs, concerts, lectures, sermons and especially annual meetings broadcast well-connected women's concerns. While the gathering of friends, acquaintances, and strangers into churches and meeting halls provided opportunities to pass the collection basket and mention achievements, published stories about such gatherings multiplied their impact. Similarly, putting young children on exhibit in various ways, at anniversaries or public examinations, by means of parades through city streets on specific occasions, or "visiting times" at orphanages and rescue homes commanded attention, but admiring newspaper articles gave the events a lengthy afterlife.[12]

Although religious journals were the primary echoers of such reports, large-circulation papers occasionally printed material made available by women's associations. The manuscript records of New York's House of Industry (1814–20) have long since disappeared into the historical dustbin, but the pages of the *Evening Post* preserve regular reports of the group's activities. The *Post* was unlikely, of course, to devote space to missionary fund-raising; the House of Industry's project was news because city funds underwrote much of it. Nevertheless, the organization women who benefited from free publicity of this and other sorts were those with ties to the publishing world, ties that grew more numerous over the decades as the number of writers (some of them the women themselves), printers, editors, and publishers expanded. (See Table A.10.) One New York group casually noted in its 1837 minutes that Hetty King would arrange to have its by-laws printed "in a neat pamphlet form" and that her husband Charles not only would pay the cost of printing its annual report but would arrange for a free advertisement; Charles King, son of the Federalist politician Rufus King, was editor of the *New York American*.[13]

Notices in city newspapers might be but one speck on a vast strand, but articles or reprints of annual reports in the evangelical press could carry a group's name and cause to shores near and far. When printed circulars or annual reports made their way into religious weeklies, their effects multiplied. The experience of Boston's Society for Promoting Christianity among the Jews was not unusual: a woman in rural New York State forwarded her $3.50 mite after reading about the group in *The Panoplist*. New York's Orphan Asylum Society garnered $770 in donations after an 1810 appeal appeared in city newspapers. Less common was the Boston Female Asylum's experience with a "Juvenile Female Orphan Society," which caught the asylum leadership by surprise in 1821, announcing its commitment to raising money for the asylum. The leaders had not heard of their young benefactors, who clearly were well aware of the asylum. Women's groups with access to the evangelical and secular print worlds amplified their utterances and heard them reverberate in public arenas.[14]

Only some women leaders, of course, had the power to shape the amount and type of publicity their organizations garnered. Shaping required access to the printed page, and all printed pages were not equal. In antebellum cities like New York and Boston, numerous "publics" and "counterpublics," interest groups that constituted themselves through written and published media, competed for attention. Women organizers who sought both to reach a broad audience and to control it needed to scale the steep class, religious, gender, and racial hierarchies that structured the world of print. Hetty Low King and her coworker, Sarah Beach Hall, both married to men who ran well-circulated weekly papers, started the climb much nearer the top than did Henrietta Regulus Ray, officer in two African American women's groups, who could provide publicity for her causes only through her friend Samuel Cornish, editor of two short-lived newspapers.[15]

Women like Ray entered the world of publicity primarily through small-circulation weeklies geared toward particular ethnic, religious, racial, or ideological audiences, but which paid scant attention to specifically female concerns. The presumed reader of most such newspapers was a man. Yet the papers provided some coverage of woman-run organizations, issuing pleas for support, announcing fairs and concerts, and lauding the "estimable ladies" who were arranging the events. Publicity of this sort resembled acts of ventriloquism; the men of the group spoke for the women. Their words also served the larger purpose of promoting group identity and appropriating the prevailing rhetoric of feminine respectability for group use. When Catholic or African American editors covered women's organizational activities, they sought, by highlighting the women's accomplishments, to capture the symbolic associations of womanhood and bolster the entire group's claims to respectability. "We are all," wrote an editorialist in Samuel Cornish's *Weekly Advocate*, "branded with the epithets of vicious, degraded, and worthless." Favorable publicity about black women could "disabuse the public mind of the misrepresentations made of our character."[16]

Ventriloquism was preferable to voicelessness, however, for without coverage of this sort, or the money to print their own materials, women's groups like Ray's lacked a sympathetic source of publicity. Readers of most urban dailies or weeklies, which covered some white Protestant women's organizational activities, would have no inkling about Roman Catholic or African American women's labors, encountering instead only stereotypes. Descriptions of black women in those sources, for example, usually reeked with "literary blackface"; they employed language and characterizations ridiculing black behavior, speech, and appearance. With the arrival of newspapers like *Freedom's Journal* (New York, 1827), the *Emancipator* (New York, 1836), the *Weekly Advocate/ Colored American* (New York, 1837), and the *Liberator* (Boston, 1831), leaders of New York's African Dorcas Association or Boston's Colored Female Charitable Society gained access to the world of printed advertisements and meeting notices.[17]

But even sympathetic sources of publicity could be unreliable; without the ability to control their organizations' public representations, women leaders could find themselves held to gender standards that differed from their own. Consider the scorn and praise that Samuel E. Cornish and John Russwurm, editors of *Freedom's Journal*, handed out to two women's groups. However "decorous," the Daughters of Israel's 1828 anniversary involved "a female procession, dressed in the full costume of their order." The men considered it their "duty to the community . . . to denounce such an uncommon sight." Annual processions, they later explained in an editorial commending the quiet and unobtrusive manner in which the African Dorcas Association carried on its labors, were "pharisee-like" and designed "to proclaim to the world the nature of" the women's work. Held to strict and conflicting gender standards, African American women leaders might wonder how they were to "exert all their power to disabuse the public mind of the misrepresentations made of our character," yet do so without the wrong sort of publicity. Their own printed utterances emphasized "acquiring literary and scientific knowledge," "suppressi[ng] vice and immorality," and cultivating "such virtues as will render us happy and useful to society"—the sorts of self-help and mutual education labors that might escape misrepresentation. Outside of the African American and white abolitionist press, though, even those labors were continually misrepresented and caricatured.[18]

A resource at once powerful and unstable, publicity eventually began to seem problematic even to privileged white women. By the 1830s, their organizations were no longer novel; their numbers were legion. Outside of the evangelical press, interest in publishing their reports and announcements was declining; within it, space considerations precluded giving equal attention to all. More important, the emergence of new reform-oriented associations led to swirling controversies that caught even old, established organizations in their eddies, making them aware of publicity's negative potential and concerned about image management. Although female moral reform and antislavery society leaders sought visibility for their causes—as did their counterparts in tract distribution and infant school organizations—they attained much less control over the public attention that resulted. Clever entrepreneurs transformed moral reformers' brothel exposés into street guides for male sex-seekers; outraged moralists and antiabolitionist mobs turned abolitionist women's meetings into occasions for verbal or physical abuse. To both activist women and their more retiring sisters, the uncontrollable consequences of sought-after public attention were both frightening and frustrating.

Maria Weston Chapman bitterly underscored the dual potential of publicity when she pointed to the differential treatment accorded the Boston Female Anti-Slavery Society and the Fatherless and Widows Society. Female abolitionists, she noted, faced vilification and accusations of "act[ing] with undue publicity" for drawing attention to their cause. Yet the Fatherless and Widows group, despite its use of "advertisements in the daily papers," was amply rewarded by "an approving public," and "designated as 'woman, stepping gracefully to the relief of infancy and suffering age.'" Chapman stretched the argument when she portrayed the Female Anti-Slavery Society as merely "a benevolent association of ladies" holding an annual meeting, hearing a speaker, and publicizing its work. She conceded that the women met hostile mobs, not approving admirers, because of what they represented. "Popular notions of feminine propriety" and appropriately feminine action wound tight limits around efforts to publicize women's causes. Those with the requisite combination of privileged social status and unassailable chosen work, such as leaders of the Fatherless and Widows Society, could manage their group's level of visibility. But when they embraced unpopular causes, even elite white women like Chapman found themselves the targets of unwanted, unfavorable, and distorting publicity.[19]

One way to avoid unflattering publicity was to lower a group's public profile, much as had the women of Boston's Penitent Females' Refuge Ladies Auxiliary Society during the 1820s. By the mid-1830s, they and the women of New York's Female Benevolent Society could take their contemporaries' prize for reticence in print. After the wrenching schism that launched the New York Female Moral Reform Society in 1834, members of the Benevolent Society rejected the sensational exposés favored by moral reformers and concentrated on reforming prostitutes through a refuge. Singed by fiery newspaper-fueled polemics, the women of the Benevolent Society sought to distance themselves from the moral reformers. Although they experienced serious financial difficulty and had trouble informing potential clients about their refuge, they nevertheless refused an 1841 offer of a fund-raising lecture, reasoning that "it might bring the Society too much before the public."[20]

For their part, moral reformers had another solution: woman-run newspapers. The arrival of New York's *Advocate of Moral Reform* (1835) and Boston's *Friend of Virtue* (1838) marked a new departure in women leaders' self-publishing. Rather than hoping that a sympathetic editor would reprint their words, or praying that an unsympathetic editor would not distort them, moral reformers would control their own publicity. Defining the "radical difference" between themselves and the Female Benevolent Society in 1835, members of the New York Female Moral Reform Society underlined their own organizational philosophy: "They believe . . . that what is done on the subject of Moral Reform, *should be done and not said*. We believe in *doing* and *saying too*, and that while *some* good may result from *doing*, the *great* good must result from *saying*." Twenty thousand copies of the *Advocate*, "edited entirely by a lady, whose whole time is devoted to the work," and "EXCLUSIVELY under the direction" of the society, circulating to subscribers in several states, permitted the women to say a great deal more than a thousand or even fifteen hundred printed copies of their annual report.[21]

In their approach to saying as well as doing, moral reformers markedly altered the relationship between women's groups and publicity. Like organizations with less controversial messages, moral reform societies used a collective voice in printed annual reports; like them, they did not usually attach organizational utterances to specific women. The bold byline that adorned reports of the Boston Seamen's Aid Society from 1836 to 1841, "Written by Mrs. Sarah J.

Hale," no doubt sought to harness Hale's literary reputation for the Society's benefit, but it was uncharacteristic. Other well-known public figures, such as the novelist Susanna Haswell Rowson or the historian Hannah Adams, separated their literary and organizational careers, making no effort to identify themselves in published reports. Similarly, articles in the *Advocate of Moral Reform* or *Friend of Virtue* only rarely carried attributions or bylines. (When the *Advocate* carried two signed articles by Sarah M. Grimké in 1837 and 1838, they were reprinted from the New England *Spectator*.) Nevertheless, moral reform organizations spoke in a different collective voice from non-reformist groups. Not only did they control their own bimonthly periodical, but they used it and their annual reports to address printed appeals to women as a group, "to the Ladies of every Religious Denomination"—not merely locally but nationally— "to the Wives, Mothers, and Daughters of our Land" ("Beloved Sisters").[22]

Antislavery activists (many of them also moral reformers) and some temperance reformers followed suit, especially by seeking wide national audiences for their ideas. Printed petitions were one such venue, public appeals to specific constituencies were another, and visual representations of issues were a third. Aside from agreeing to publish their minutes and circulate printed petitions, those attending the three-day Anti-Slavery Convention of American Women, held in New York in 1837, agreed that "anti-slavery prints" were so "powerful" as "'pictorial representations'" of "the speechless agony of the fettered slave," that they should be "multiplied a hundred fold." Indeed, so important did the women consider the task of producing publicity that on the last day, they pledged $357.50 for printing costs alone. Eventually, the convention issued printed proceedings and six publications, including an "Appeal to the Women of the Nominally Free States," a "Letter to Juvenile Societies," an "Address to Free Colored Americans," and a "Letter to the Women of Great Britain." By means of these and other uses of public print, women reformers sought unmediated access to their audiences and control over their own printed representations.[23]

Women's Organizations and "the Public Sphere": Public Policy

Once possessed of access to publicity, women's groups could venture onto the sidelines of politics, advocate for particular public policies, gain access to public funds, and assume the privilege of discharging state functions. Steadfastly disclaiming partisanship, women leaders adopted deferential political strategies that, for a time, proved effective in promoting their groups' interests. The language employed by Hannah Stillman in proposing and founding the Boston Female Asylum conveyed the combination of deferential self-effacement, policy advocacy, and presumed public partnership that characterized the political style of many early women's groups. Boston's women, she suggested, should make it their "glorious prerogative . . . to finish the good work of our political fathers," by providing "patronage," in the form of schooling, for poor orphaned white girls, thereby supplementing "the care taken of them by the Town." Simultaneously, Stillman and her coworkers advocated for a particular public policy (girls' education), pointed to a gap in existing provision (despite "municipal liberality" in funding schools, poor girls could not attend if they could not read), and proposed a remedy (a woman-run charity).[24]

The same combination of advocacy and remedy-seeking marked the activities of many white Protestant women's groups. As advocates, they spoke for groups (children, orphans, poor women) and causes (education, religious training) that fell within the circle of traditional womanly beneficence. And although few organizations went as far as did Boston's Seamen's Aid Society in the 1830s, campaigning for the teaching of "plain needlework" to girls in city schools, they were not reticent when it came to offering opinions about the sort of education children needed. The deficiencies in such training were a regular source of printed commentary. Sunday school organizations promoted children's religious education; women's Bible and missionary societies made enrolling children in a Sunday school a precondition for temporal assistance to their parents. Infant school societies sought to provide "personal and moral culture," along with religious training, to the children of "indigent or uneducated parents." Citing women's duty "to seek out and instruct the rising generation" and "point sinners to th[e] Lamb of God," women's missionary societies stood as advocates for more churches and more schools in poor urban neighborhoods. In promoting their cause, moral reformers and abolitionists issued stinging comments on the racial and sexual inequities in existing systems of schooling. Boys' education was "miserably defective," commented one moral reformer, because of the "rudeness and vulgarity" in which they were permitted to indulge—unlike girls, of whom "the most scrupulous delicacy" was expected. Orphaned African American children "claim our especial care and protection," argued the women of New York's Association for the Benefit of Colored Orphans. Unlike the comparably "destitute portion of our white population," they had no access to institutions to which they could turn.[25]

In a similar way, many white charitable organizations brought into public view the needs of particular groups of impoverished women. As they did, they underscored what they perceived to be gaps in public relief programs, and especially the limitations of the almshouse. Most commonly, they held up for special sympathy "respectable" women who had "been reduced to penury" from "a state of ease or affluence," had known the "elegancies" of life, and were "unused to grappling with adversity." The argument that such women "present to the heart a far more touching appeal than any other class of sufferers" because they "feel more keenly the barbed points of poverty and want" was in essence an endorsement of the standard nineteenth-century distinction between "vicious" and "respectable" poverty. It allied women organizers with city leaders who sought to encourage "the dread of being supported at the public expense" and reduce applications for relief. But it also identified a group whose needs were not being met, promoted women's organizations as superior alternatives to the almshouse, and justified its continued use for individuals who did not fit their clients' profiles.

The almshouse proved a useful symbol, signifying the respectable widow's or the helpless orphan's worst nightmare, a mark of crushing defeat for the deserving poor. Virtually absent from unpublished minutes, except as a location, the almshouse turned up often in material designed for publicity. Explaining why she and her coworkers founded the Asylum for Lying-In Women in 1823, Mary Morgan Mason described New York's almshouse as a place where "the virtuous and the vicious were indiscriminately treated," and where a "virtuous woman wife [sic]" should not have to "seek a home & companionship among degraded, unmarried mothers." The lying-in asylum provided an alternative space, a home-like environment in which poor, "virtuous," married women could give birth. The almshouse was no place for fatherless children, objected women founding orphanages, who often claimed to have "removed . . . a vast number" to their own asylums. "Respectable, aged, indigent" women, "who have known better days," held the almshouse in sheer "dread," argued the directors of a New York old-age charity. So did their counterparts in Boston. "The apprehension seems to arise," commented an official of the Widows' Society in 1819, "from the fear of being thrown into large rooms, with numbers and deprived of liberty."[26]

For such deserving folk, benevolent women suggested, private charitable provision was superior to public provision, and personal methods of relief preferable to institutional methods. Women's benevolence protected deserving clients' tattered dignity and permitted them to retain both privacy and a semblance of respectability. The almshouse was horrifying precisely because of its promiscuous mixing of humans, and its dismissal of customary distinctions of daily life, such as marital status or community standing. Yet such criticisms of public policy seldom entered the record as condemnations of existing arrangements; more often, they were simply pleas for protecting virtuous women from unvirtuous ones, or malleable children from hardened adults. Similarly, when women leaders referred to their clients as "helpless," "neglected," or "forgotten," or accused local churches of abdicating their responsibility to destitute urbanites, their words rebuked male leaders. But in effect, such critical comments fostered an association of the almshouse with vice and degradation, and endorsed the view that some destitute women and some needy children deserved to escape its walls but others did not. Through their service to the deserving, charitable women could imagine their organizations as engaging in partnerships (however unequal) with the public authorities.[27]

This conception enabled women's organizations, like their male counterparts, to seek and win, from "the guardians and rulers of our city," monetary or in-kind grants, lottery sponsorships, tax rebates or exemptions, shares of tax funds, and contracts with governmental agencies. Through such official assistance, women leaders entered the anterooms of politics and attached their groups' concerns to those of male politicians. In 1803, the New York State legislature authorized a lottery to raise $15,000 for the Society for the Relief of Poor Widows with Small Children; the New York City Council supervised the actual lottery, appointing lottery managers, supplying them with an office, and permitting them to advance cash to the ladies. The Orphan Asylum Society received similar help in the form of a $5,000 lottery grant in 1808, and annual $500 contributions beginning in 1811. During its five-year existence, from 1814 to 1819, New York's House of Industry received grants totaling $2,650 from city tax revenues. Besides money, some societies received land on which to build benevolent institutions or rebates on property taxes. In 1817, New York's Female Missionary Society asked the city council to place a lamp opposite their new chapel in Bancker Street; in 1842, the Female Benevolent Society asked for a guard to be posted outside their prostitutes' refuge. New York's city council was considerably more active in this process than Boston's town government, in part because the two cities distributed charitable monies differently. On occasion, the council bought supplies for private charities; often, it saved them storage costs by permitting them to stack winter fuel at the almshouse. One gift offered a particularly pungent symbol of public largesse: in 1808 the aldermen paid a carter $191.50 to collect and deliver manure to the Orphan Asylum Society's kitchen garden.[28]

Contracts or other comparable arrangements with state agencies represented another way in which women sought to mesh their organizational concerns with the political interests of local leaders. In 1812, New York's Society for the Relief of Poor Widows with Small Children negotiated a contract whereby the state prison would shoe the small children's feet at five shillings a pair. A few years later, some of the same women, now involved in running the House of Industry, sought their own contract with the United States Navy: to furnish regulation clothing (via the House of Industry workroom) to sailors stationed in New York. The proposal lost out to a lower bidder. Boston's Seamen's Aid Society met with more success, however temporarily, in 1843. After three years of trying, the society secured an experimental contract with the Navy Bureau of Provisions and Clothing, whereby its workers (sailors' wives, widows, and daughters) would sew naval uniforms. Once fulfilled, however, the contract was never renewed.[29]

Less formal contract-like arrangements, in which city functionaries enlisted women's organizations to deliver city services, were considerably more common. Mary Ryan's term, "a private project in the public interest," is an apt description of the New York Orphan Asylum Society, which accepted fatherless white children from the city almshouse, and of Boston's Penitent Females' Refuge, one-fourth of whose magdalens arrived on the doorstep with an official escort, having been sent directly from the courtroom, the house of correction, or the workhouse. For another half, the refuge became a detour from the grim path to jail, a bypass fashioned by city missionaries who haunted the courthouse seeking to head off girls "whose departure from virtue has been the least aggravated, either in character or duration," in other words, who had just entered the prostitute's life. Because the managers of New York's Female Benevolent Society took "inmates of the Female Penitentiary" into their magdalens' refuge, they felt entitled to the small grants the city bestowed. But if the refugees proved troublesome, the women felt equally entitled to send them back, or insist upon more city money. In 1840 the Benevolent Society complained that the city sent too many "persons of the lowest grade and character." "We cannot possibly receive [them] into this establishment in future," the women protested, "unless one Dollar or half a dollar [a] week shall be paid for their board and lodging." On occasion, the transfer of clients was reversed. The white women who had opened New York's Colored Orphan Asylum by shepherding five youngsters out of the almshouse, two years later sought to protect the institution's healthy residents by banishing two seriously ill children to the almshouse.[30]

Although unequal, and available only to some women's associations, these partnerships with politicians rested upon the assumption, clearly evident in the language of both women and politicians, that women's institutions could serve public interests in much the same way as men's: by delivering specific services at substantial savings to the public treasury. Recommending that the newly formed House of Industry receive $500 to create work for poor women, a New

York City Council committee simply lifted words from the women's 1814 petition: quite apart from the "intrinsic merit" of its program, the House of Industry would "be a real saving to the City[;] it will greatly relieve the pressure on the public charity." Four years later, a similar committee repeated the women's claim that their "Institution has already kept from the Alms House a number of persons who . . . would . . . have become a public charge." A $750 grant to the Society for the Relief of Poor Widows with Small Children was approved on the grounds that it had "rendered to the Community great and essential services" saving hundreds of widows and children from "the necessity of taking refuge in the Alms House." And an 1824 city council committee, although reluctant "to establish any more precedents for annual donations to charitable Institutions," nevertheless agreed that the Orphan Asylum Society deserved $500 because, without its work, the city "would have been compelled to support many of the Orphans who are thus taken care of by this society." Such language placed women's charitable organizations on the same political footing as men's, and established the principle that because they were "efficient auxiliaries" to local officials, they had "a reasonable right to expect support and encouragement from the public authorities."[31]

"Reasonable rights," however, accrued only to women's associations whose leaders enjoyed some access to city leaders. And even well-connected women leaders, unlike their men, could never expect to *be* the public authorities. Whereas the volunteer male managers of New York's House of Refuge counted among their ranks sundry "commissioners of the poor" (who oversaw the almshouse), elected officials, and political operatives, and Boston's Overseers of the Poor took pride in their combined philanthropies, the most that women in either city could hope for was patronage achieved through personal access or petitions to men in power. Moreover, philanthropic women could not turn their enterprises into wholly or primarily public ones. Within a decade of founding the House of Refuge in 1824, for instance, the men who created the Society for the Reformation of Juvenile Delinquents controlled a $8,000 annual state and a $4,000 city subvention, and soon public money was so available that "private contributions constituted a small fraction of" the group's income. The group's managers counted among themselves the same men who voted the payments. Like the House of Refuge, other men's volunteer efforts benefited from their leaders' ability to walk directly into spittoon-furnished rooms and disburse public funds. But as long as only men (and only some of them) could participate in the electoral system, women's politics operated along the sidelines of electoral politics and in the anterooms of public policy-making. They developed a political culture that dictated the use of deferential and personal tactics.[32]

In such a context, women leaders could readily describe work that took them out of their homes, into church vestries and city hotels, onto oratorical stages, and out among impoverished strangers in far-flung neighborhoods as, on the one hand, "a public charity" and on the other, "within woman's province." In their minds, politics involved partisanship and conflict. Individual women could be, and were, political partisans, and could even seek to influence male relatives on this or that issue. But collectively, as members of groups or organizations, women had to disavow partisanship. As long as they did, the boundaries of the feminine domain would stretch to encompass organizational work of many varieties. When a group became "a party in any public contest," though, as the officers of the Boston Female Asylum put it in 1806, its members pushed up against the limits of collective female activism. Although willing to petition legislators and quasi-public groups (such as the trustees of a will) on behalf of their charges, the Female Asylum leaders thought twice about joining a local landowners' formal plea to the legislature. They were hardly spineless; not only had they vehemently defended their organization's autonomy when their male advisers proposed entrusting its finances to a male board of trustees, but the landowners requesting their signatures were the very same men, and had donated the land their institution occupied. Moreover, in their families resided a number of elected or appointed officials; the women were not strangers to partisan politics. But because "distinguishing themselves as a party in any public contest" opened the possibility of open partisanship and visible confrontation for the group they represented, it lay outside the expansive limits of their domain.[33]

Within that domain, a deferential female political culture shaped organizational leaders' strategies. Choosing well-connected women as officers and using powerful men as intermediaries were two sides of the tactical coin. At a time when women's organizations were a novelty, the Boston Female Asylum's leadership found it politic to have Sarah Bowdoin, wife of a prominent state politician (whose own father had been governor), serving as a manager and "giving it her name and influence, . . . thereby encouraging its friends and adding to its respectability." Through women like Sarah, the Female Asylum had access to men who could oil the political gears when it needed something done. Her husband, James Bowdoin, Jr., drafted the articles of incorporation, making the group the first Massachusetts women's society to incorporate; a member of the state senate then sponsored the legislation and ushered it through. When the Widows' Society sought incorporation in 1828, its vice president ("second directress," to use her official title), Maria Theresa Gold Appleton, offered the assistance of her husband, Nathan Appleton, the wealthy textile manufacturer who had served three terms in the Massachusetts legislature and would soon be elected to Congress. And New York's Orphan Asylum and Infant School Societies basked in the warm patronage of DeWitt Clinton, mayor and then governor, who willingly attached his name to legislative petitions and fund-raising appeals. Clinton's first wife, Maria Franklin, had for three years been an officer of the Society for the Relief of Poor Widows with Small Children, and he retained a cordial interest in Joanna Graham Bethune's projects, just as he did other "private projects in the public interest," such as the New-York Historical Society, the New York Free School Society, and the New York House of Refuge.[34]

For groups with the necessary connections and access, deferential politics made sense, and paid tangible rewards. But cultivating favors took work and a degree of political savvy. When the managers of New York's Asylum for Lying-In Women needed space to build a new facility, they shrewdly dispatched a committee of ladies to consult informally with the mayor and aldermen before writing their petition for a land grant. After being advised that they were unlikely to receive a city-owned lot, the asylum managers instead requested a $3,000 donation. They received $1,500. Some groups issued special invitations to political leaders to show off their programs, as when the trustees of New York's House of Industry requested that city council members attend meetings, "examine the proceedings" of the house, and judge for themselves its "beneficial effects." Such visits invariably evoked a panegyric on the group's contributions to the city—and another donation.[35]

Defined as appropriately feminine because its goal was influence for particular women's organizations, not collective political power for all women, deferential politics was effective in many circumstances. Not only did it bring perceptible benefits to organizations, but it deflected the occasional criticisms that came the way of organized women in the early years of the century. In addition, deferential politics enabled some women's groups to use their collective voice to comment on public policy, without fear of arousing controversy. Reflecting the view that women sought "influence," not power, deferential politics wrapped its practitioners—and by extension, their organizations—in the mantle of domesticity, their voluntarism encircled within the bounds of "woman's sphere."[36]

Deferential politics had its limits, however, particularly when city revenues fell short during hard times or shifting political winds swept some men out of office and others in. At those times, supplicating women could only watch to see whether the new breeze still scattered funds their way. The experience of New York's Female Assistance Society is instructive: between 1815 and 1836, the Methodist group petitioned the city council at least seven times, receiving four grants. Two of those arrived during Roger Strong's tenure on the council; his wife was a manager of the Assistance Society. Women officials could be keenly sensitive to the prevailing winds and tailor their applications to existing realities. When rejection of a petition signaled that the current solons were tightening the city's purse strings, some simply stopped requesting funds, and bided their time. The leaders of New York's Orphan Asylum Society, for example, made no requests to the city council between 1809, when a plea was rejected, and 1817, when the council began to show itself willing to support comparable charities again. During those tight economic times, as a national trade embargo and then war with England froze the meager portion of the poor, some of the same women actively sought and won yearly grants for the House of Industry they initiated in 1814. As a supportive newspaper editor put it, the women sought, not "a donation to a charitable society," but "an appropriation of part of the city fund which is allotted to the support of the poor." Clearly, they understood what the aldermen would and would not underwrite.[37]

Deferential politics also rested upon an assumed personal acquaintanceship between women and politicians, and especially the women's possession of appropriate "reputations." The language of approbation that city leaders used for the women's charities they supported reflected these realities. The "very respectable and exemplary character" of New York's House of Industry's leadership inspired the "full confidence" of city councillors, not least because the ladies' "respectible [sic] characters and benevolent lives" rendered their work "highly beneficial to the community & worthy of public patronage." Twenty years later, in an era of rapid political change that undercut most support for charitable donations, a city council committee justified a $500 grant to the Association for the Relief of Respectable, Aged, Indigent Females because it was "conducted by ladies of elevated character, most of them known to our Committee." Politicians' reflexive emphasis on women's reputation, respectability, and character, and their unabashed claims to personal acquaintanceship with deserving "ladies" conveyed significant messages about the racial and class hierarchies that underlay women's claims to any public money.[38]

However flattering, politicians' encomiums on their "respectable" or "exemplary" characters did not alter benevolent women's vulnerability to political storms and sea-changes, as voting tides ebbed and flowed. The Respectable, Aged, Indigent Females relief group learned through experience how to ride out the crosscurrents of political change. Although earlier city council committees had made monetary awards, and others would do so later, in 1822 the group's petition was denied on the grounds that "all public charity should be dispensed through the Alms House, [and] if those charitable societies do exist they should be wholly supported by individual subscriptions or donations." The Female Assistance Society had a similar experience in 1829; accustomed to affirmative responses to their requests, the ladies must have been surprised when a new committee concluded that however "invaluable" the "services and the great good" accomplished by the society, the men "cannot think it is of that *Public Character* that it ought to be supported by the Common Council." Although later committees restored grants to both groups, their experiences demonstrated how unequal and unstable was any alliance between elected officials and charitable organizations that relied on personal ties and deferential petitions.[39]

Some women's groups, of course, had little power to cultivate public favors. Gender-defined racial, religious, and class barriers kept their structures out of sight, and confined their endeavors largely to unseen locales. Free African American women, for example, enjoyed no entrée (not even the highly circumscribed access some men possessed) into the corridors of city hall, the state house, or the courthouse. Whereas African American men incorporated several mutual relief and literary societies in New York between 1810 and 1830, at least one with the sponsorship of Mayor DeWitt Clinton, women's societies achieved no such legal status. No members with prominent names or influential husbands represented their cause. No doors opened to deliver public contracts, nor did recorders inscribe testimonials to their "respectable and exemplary" characters onto official parchment. And despite the prevalence of desperate, life-destroying poverty in urban free black communities, they collected no monetary or other crumbs from the municipal table. Instead, African American women's groups fashioned their daily bread from hard-pressed members' meager resources, from friends, and occasionally from sympathetic whites.[40]

Even for Roman Catholic laywomen, it was not enough that they be respectable white women engaged in charitable work. Insofar as Roman Catholics managed to pry tax money loose from city coffers, it was men's organizations, not women's, that wielded the tool. When New York's city council, for example, turned down an 1829 request for assistance from the Union Emigrant Society, a group helping Irish immigrant men find jobs in the city, the weekly *Truth Teller* printed the names of all who voted against the measure. Surely the councillors got the message, one that no Catholic lay women's society could send. And if anyone knew that truth, it was Catherine Dupleix, president of the Roman Catholic Asylum for the Children of Widows and Widowers. In an earlier life, as an Episcopalian, she had witnessed the patronage conferred on her organizations, both the Society for the Relief of Poor Widows with Small Children and the House of Industry. Indeed, until 1814 she was one of the ladies whose "respectible [*sic*] characters and benevolent lives" warranted "public patronage" for the House of Industry. But now, as Catherine Dupleix, Catholic, her benevolent labors lay outside the pale of publicly patronized feminine respectability.[41]

Deferential Women in a Democratic Age

During the 1820s and 1830s, the limits of a political culture based on reputation, deference, and influence began to become evident even to white Protestant women leaders. As the rapid expansion of voting privileges reworked the political script in those decades, in both New York and Boston, established political dynasties and men used to wielding power found themselves rudely challenged for positions on the public stage by new voters demanding radical changes in the long-running show. By the 1830s, the patrician incumbent with whom the members of the Boston Female Asylum had genteelly negotiated their incorporation petition was becoming a rare performer; in his place stood the plebeian upstart whose power depended upon a very different voting audience. Hannah Nicholson Gallatin's sarcastic suggestion that "in this *happy free country*" her mother's "illiterate" servant "will be a candidate for the common council, and at last will be one of the great men of New York," reflected one perspective on how things were changing. And if Hannah's sister, Catherine Few, or her coworkers in the Society for the Relief of Poor Widows with Small Children needed any reminder that the old-style political show was closing, a series of contests over access to tax money called their attention to the changing marquee.[42]

Most prominent among these were arguments over Roman Catholics' right to two pools of public money: school and orphanage funds. In New York, where the battles began earlier and lasted longer, the issue centered particularly on the Common School Fund. Created in 1805, the fund gradually became the focus of bitter wrangling over which voluntary societies' schools were entitled to shares. At issue was a larger debate over labeling various free and charity schools "public" and giving control of them to a politically powerful men's association, the Free School Society, founded the same year as the fund. By 1825, when they changed their name to the Public School Society, the group had shifted control of the Common School Fund from the state legislature to the city council, assumed control of it and convinced the council to deny shares to "sectarian" schools, that is, charity schools run by individual churches. Although Bethel Baptist Church, with its three schools and hundreds of pupils, was the largest single loser, Catholic institutions such as the free school at St. Peter's parish also forfeited income. Between 1806 and 1823, for example, St. Peter's school had received 43 percent of its operating budget from the Common School Fund. Indeed, in some years, particularly between 1814 and 1821, public money had paid at least 90 percent of the parish schooling costs. (On occasion, School Fund monies amounted to more than 100 percent of costs.) When the contributions stopped, the Roman Catholic Orphan Asylum lost out because its children attended the free school at St. Patrick's Cathedral, along with the parish youngsters. Yet the school held at Joanna Bethune's Orphan Asylum Society, deemed non-"sectarian" by the Public School Society managers' partisan logic, continued to receive its portion of the Common School Fund; indeed in 1828, the asylum school, with 175 pupils—2.8 percent of the total receiving city support—collected over 3.5 percent of the fund.[43]

Access to state money for orphanages was similarly disputed. In addition to a one-time benefit of $5,000 from a state lottery, beginning in 1811 Bethune's Orphan Asylum Society received $500 annually from Albany, from a fund designated for "the foreign poor." Yet the Roman Catholic Orphan Asylum received nothing, despite its being, in the words of a Protestant layman (and benefactor of the orphanage), "overwhelmed with orphans, so many poor Irish die after a short residence in this city." Only as pupils attending the parish free school every day could Catholic orphans benefit from the flood of money washing over charity schools. Once that monetary flow dried up, leaving Catholic parish schools stranded, the male trustees of the Roman Catholic Orphan Asylum sought other means of access to both the city's wallet (the Common School Fund) and the state's purse (the orphanage money). By turning to partisan, electoral politics to achieve their goals, they gave organized Protestant women an object lesson in the limits of a deferential, influence-based political culture.[44]

As did their female Protestant counterparts, the male trustees of the Roman Catholic Orphan Asylum made a practice of inviting city councillors to see for themselves the benevolent workings of their institution. In addition, the affiliated Ladies' Association held regular fund-raising concerts, sermons and fairs at St. Patrick's Cathedral and other churches, and conducted public examinations of the children at their annual meetings. Moreover, just as wealthy Catholic laymen such as Dominick Lynch contributed their "favor and interest" to the Protestant Orphan Asylum Society at fund-raising events, Protestant benefactors regularly assisted the Catholic orphanage and its sister institution, the

Asylum for the Children of Widows and Widowers.[45] But the events of the 1820s brought the Catholic and Protestant orphanages' interests into conflict, and tension replaced tolerance (or indifference) in their relationship. Reopening the issue of city funding for Catholic school pupils, in 1831 the Roman Catholic Orphan Asylum's trustees convinced the city council that "every principle of equity" entitled their orphans to a "share of the school fund" comparable to that furnished "the Greenwich Asylum" (Bethune's Orphan Asylum Society) and its school. Rejecting the argument that their orphanage was "sectarian," the trustees noted its lay management, claimed that it "receive[s] orphans without distinction as to creed country, or sex," and accused the Orphan Asylum Society of "partak[ing] as much of sectarianism as any institution can." Joanna Bethune's beloved orphanage should enjoy no special status; the two institutions should be treated similarly. Not only did the city council agree, and provide funding to Roman Catholic Orphan Asylum students in 1832, but it soon included the Catholic institution in a special appropriation for orphanages pushed beyond capacity by the cholera epidemic. In 1833, too, the state legislature began providing the same $500 annual check that the Orphan Asylum Society had been cashing since 1811.[46]

Perhaps more than anything else, the eighteen-month struggle over access to the school fund demonstrated how to get things done by mobilizing voters. New York's *Truth Teller*, a weekly newspaper founded in 1825 as the voice of Irish New York but soon transformed into the voice of Irish Catholic New York, kept the tally. After the first petition in 1831, the editor published the names of aldermanic supporters and opponents, then underscored the contributions of Roman Catholic orphans' champions who deserved special credit for their efforts. Any voter who missed the message could take the paper's endorsement list with him to the next ward elections. Soon, he could also read the full text of a speech by Democrat John Rhinelander, the paper's candidate in the Sixth Ward, attacking the Public School Society's claims to non-sectarianism, questioning why it included the African School in its largesse while the excluding the Catholic orphanage (which now had its own school), and directly criticizing Bethune's group. "Must we have our sensitivity exerted in favor of a race whose moral and intellectual characters are inferior to our own?" Rhinelander asked, using the ace of racial privilege to trump the Protestant suit. Revealing his whole hand, Rhinelander embraced Catholics as "our own brethren, who are born to the same principles, . . . exercise the same functions in the State, and participate in the same equal rights." His inference was clear. Concluding with a slap at the Orphan Asylum Society, he pointed out that it "teaches Protestantism," then asked, "have we ever heard the cry of sectarianism against them?" His answer: "Never! but now that a Catholic Institution asks the same privileges, the whole city is in a ferment."[47]

Beyond the unpleasant notoriety that it brought to the Orphan Asylum society, and beyond its role as a skirmish in the larger struggle over educational funding that, eight years later, escalated into a major political battle at the state level, the 1831–32 controversy reflected the changing politics of the era. To be sure, the Orphan Asylum Society continued receiving city funds until 1894, when its officials refused further cash, feeling that the strings attached under the Freedom of Worship Act would compromise its Protestant character. Catholic New Yorkers would wait many decades before they could claim a right to equal treatment for their charitable institutions. But after 1832, grant-giving practices could no longer avoid the glare of party politics, in part because politics itself was changing, in part because donations of city funds were increasingly the subject of partisan scrutiny and disputation. One result was another redefinition of the line between "public" and "private" charities, as reflected in the inward-turning behavior of groups like the Boston Female Asylum. When its officers suggested in 1840 that they would "sit quietly in our usefulness" rather than "place ourselves before the public," they repudiated an earlier assertion of public visibility for their organization. For other societies, the new location of the line came as a surprise. When the city council turned down a routine grant request in 1839, the Society for the Relief of Poor Widows' leaders were forced to acknowledge that although they had always seen themselves and the city as "co-workers" in assisting the urban needy, the current crop of aldermen took a different view. Accustomed to using feminine influence to pluck favors from the political tree, women in groups like these had to inure themselves to being mere spectators, watching while groups of voters scrambled to capture a share of the windfall. City agencies continued to work with women's groups in managing the needs of urban residents, but formalized procedures and contracts increasingly took the place of petitions and ad hoc grants in the ongoing process.[48]

Democratic Women in a Democratic Age

If some women leaders preferred to "sit quietly in our usefulness," others responded differently to the altered situation. Renouncing the political sidelines, women involved in moral reform and abolitionist organizations forged a new style of female politics, based on mobilizing groups to pursue broad political and social change. They directly addressed a wide range of public policy matters previously viewed as outside respectable women's purview. Moral reformers condemned "licentiousness in high places," pledged to influence the votes of their fathers, brothers and husbands, and used collective petitioning and lobbying to promote legislative goals. Abolitionists, advocating the destruction of slavery, made forthright pronouncements on matters of national concern. In addition, they willingly voiced criticisms of other women's organizations. Reformist women were unabashed in acknowledging their intrusion into political matters, their desire to change public policy, and their interest in mobilizing women as a group. In this fashion, they rejected deferential, exclusionary tactics and inaugurated a new kind of women's politics, one frankly oriented toward influencing votes and mobilizing for broad-based political change.[49] Eventually, they used the power of the printed collective utterance, a tactic pioneered by benevolent women, to speak for women as a group rather than simply for the interests of a class- or race-privileged organization. By 1840, they had fundamentally reshaped ongoing conversations about women's political rights.

In their hands, petitions, special pleas for assistance or favors with a time-honored place in the histories of women's organizations, became instruments of political pressure, public education, and mobilization. Whereas benevolent women deferentially addressed specific requests to political leaders who knew them (or knew their families), female activists collected untold numbers of individual signatures, then delivered the ink-laden scrolls to the legislative hall. Dubbing petitioning "the only right which we ourselves enjoy—the right which our physical weakness renders peculiarly appropriate," the women of the Boston Female Anti-Slavery Society endorsed petitioning as a means of "urg[ing] men to cease to do evil, and learn to do well." Disseminating petition forms headed, "the undersigned, women of" Anytown, U.S.A., they remade the female petition from a instrument of special pleading into a tool of mass canvassing and mass mobilization. Moral reformers combined both styles, seeking individual "influence" or occasional favors but backing up legislative demands with mountains of petitions. Any woman, regardless of age, marital status, race, ethnicity, religion, or social class, could sign. Actual practice meant that printed petition forms traveled the routes taken by reform newspapers, employing the dispersing mechanisms of the press and the mail to drop petitioning power at particular women's doorsteps. Circulating and signing the forms enabled these women to act politically, as individuals separate from husbands fathers or brothers, within a democratic context. For them, petitioning became a means to demand, not simply request, and to do so as a collection of political subjects, equals to each other and, in this one arena, male voters.[50] (See Figure 4.1.)

Reform-minded women mustered petition campaigns for varied causes, at

FIGURE 4.1. Like antislavery societies, female moral reform societies circulated printed petitions designed to mobilize masses of women for a particular cause. This petition form, at the bottom of the back page of the June 15, 1843, *Advocate of Moral Reform,* could be torn off and circulated. It demanded laws punishing seduction, adultery, and brothel-based prostitution. (Courtesy of the Library Company of Philadelphia)

both the national and state levels. The 1836 Boston Female Anti-Slavery Society petition targeted the slave trade in Washington, D.C. Later antislavery demands included ending slavery in the capital, outlawing the internal slave trade, preventing Texas's annexation, and ending churches' tolerance of slaveholding. Moral reformers printed petition forms in their magazines, enabling members to pressure state legislatures into rendering seduction and adultery as crimes punishable by imprisonment. "We must," argued the New York Female Moral Reform Society, "*petition* those in authority until our voice is heard and our prayer granted." Only "the still small voice of petition" spoken into the "ears of our legislators," as Female Moral Reform Society official Julia Reed put it in 1839, could enable voteless women to achieve legislative goals; they "may not come forward into the arena of public debate, or appear in the halls of legislation." But in the 1840s, Reed's coworkers did precisely that, lobbying legislators and testifying in legislative committees for antiseduction laws, the education of "destitute and neglected" children, and truancy statutes. Concurrently, temperance advocates pressured for state laws restricting liquor sales.[51] These women utilized both publicity and politics to pursue their goal of collective and public feminine influence.

Yet another avenue—the convention—led women activists to the broader road of politics. Conventions took attendees a step beyond the anniversary meetings on which they were modeled, breaking down parochialism and bringing activists together to formulate expansive, coordinated agendas. At the first Anti-Slavery Convention of American Women in 1837, for example, officers, delegates, and attendees from nine states spent three days in New York City thrashing out a number of resolutions and plans of action, including a national petition campaign, and approving a printed "appeal" to all the women of the North. Rejecting the position that slavery was "a *political* subject with which women have nothing to do," and urging abolitionist women to use their "natural and inalienable . . . right of petition" to pursue specific ends, the delegates explicitly embraced politics as a means. The following year, a thousand women reconvened on the same dates, in the same location (the Third Free Church), to press the cause of moral reform and connect it to abolition. Some of the delegates then traveled to Philadelphia for the second Anti-Slavery Convention of American Women, where an antiabolitionist mob burned down the meeting hall. Once again, women's "unalienable" right to petition received ringing endorsement. And in 1839, after New York moral reformers, in convention with delegates from across the northeast, had agreed to transform their organization into the American Female Moral Reform Society, a delegation once again trekked to Philadelphia for the third Antislavery Convention. Such experiences were crucial, not only for organizing, training, and rallying devotees to the cause, but also for creating alliances across causes, and destroying existing "class-based patterns of political deference."[52]

Women who set out onto the main political thoroughfare met a very different reaction from those who kept to the existing byways. Far from questioning women's right to form organizations—that issue had been settled decades earlier—critics focused on particular organizations' methods and tactics. The occasional voice arguing for women's literal confinement to hearth and home was small indeed. Instead, the loudest condemnations, such as that issued by a group of Massachusetts Congregationalist clergymen, focused on women's potential independence from masculine authority. After all, the statement's primary author, Nehemiah Adams, was married to a Director of the Boston Female Auxiliary Bible Society and Second Vice-President of the Fatherless and Widows Society. Women reformers made men's "care and protection . . . seem unnecessary," the clergymen argued; their "character[s]" were "unnatural" because, rather than accept that "the power of woman is her dependence," they sought to "assume the independence and overshadowing nature" assigned to men. Similar assumptions underlay Catharine Beecher's criticism of female abolitionist lecturers. Whereas men could appropriately seek "power" and "conquests," women who felt "the promptings of ambition, or the thirst for power" lost the essence of womanhood, which was to be "dependent and defenceless." Women were to seek influence "in the domestic and social circle," not power in the political arena, though clearly their domain encompassed many types of voluntary association. For these reasons, Beecher argued, women who sent "petitions to congress, in reference to the official duties of legislators" were "out of their place"; "men are the proper persons to make appeals to the rulers whom they appoint." Sarah Josepha Hale used her own access to the printed page to make a similar argument.[53]

A primary effect of these criticisms, as Lori Ginzberg has cogently argued, was to redraw ambiguous past practices into strict boundaries between acceptable and unacceptable public activities for women, define deferential political practices as acceptable because "unobtrusive," "unostentatious," and "private," and depict reformist women as the first of their sex to participate in politics. Even as the organization she headed sought a contract with the federal government in 1840, for example, Sarah Josepha Hale decried "meddling with public matters or politics" as "always unsuitable to the female character," and abjured "the public interference or petitioning of women." Instead she urged using "our personal and moral influence" to sway "the hearts and consciences of all with whom in private life we stand connected." So long as her group, the Seamen's Aid Society, secured its sewing contract in silent, deferential, and nonpartisan fashion, Hale did not construe its action as political.[54]

A coterminous and equally important effect was to force reformist women to sharpen and clarify their own understandings of their political rights. Indeed, these boundary-drawing exercises produced significant public discussions among both moral reformers and abolitionists as they advanced ideas in print, mulled them over, and then moved on or retreated from the positions they had staked out. On only one question did they agree consistently: women's political activism should be nonpartisan. "The voice of principle," argued Sarah Towne Smith in the *Advocate of Moral Reform*, "cannot be heard at the ballot box," but it can "come up to the ears of the men who ride into office on the shoulders of party," through women's petitions. After all, women were the only "portion of their constituents who have never bowed down before the Dragon of partisan idolatry." Above partisanship and lacking "a voice in electing our law makers," Smith suggested, women nevertheless had political rights and obligations. Beginning with the right of petition, she and other abolitionists and moral reformers moved on to defend their "human rights" to free speech and free association, to weigh in on public controversies, and to become involved in "the affairs of *State*."[55] They also joined growing public conversations about women's wages and the property rights of married women. "A Friend to Equal Rights" commented feelingly in 1838 on "a grievance which is felt by hundreds of wives": husbands' control over family money. "Shall the husband be the keeper of his wife's conscience," asked this moral reformer, "simply by means of holding the purse-strings?" Indeed, moral reformers proposed a right to remain single. "A woman may be happy, and eminently useful in a state of celibacy," commented one; "our sex [will] rise to a full sense of their duties or capabilities" only when each woman understands that "it is not *absolutely essential* to her happiness or usefulness to be married."[56]

By 1837, the year of the first national women's antislavery convention and of the Pastoral Letter, both abolitionists and moral reformers were in the midst of wide-ranging discussions on questions of women's rights. The development of simultaneous conversations is unsurprising. The two groups overlapped substantially in leadership, and both antislavery and moral reform conventions attracted the same attendees. Subtle differences of emphasis, however, differentiated those who spoke a language of rights, duties, and equality from those whose words stressed duties and spheres alone.

Among abolitionists, the Boston group staked out an assertive defense of women's right to advance "the sacred cause of freedom" and rejected the argument that women should "eschew . . . every enlarged and comprehensive purpose, as masculine, and unsuited to our sex." Directly confronting the ancient argument that men earned rights by bearing arms, Maria Weston Chapman invoked "the strength and firmness" of New Englanders' Revolutionary "maternal ancestors," and proposed that "strength of purpose" take an equal place with "strength of arm" as a standard of citizenship. New York's Daughters of Abyssinia, meeting in September 1837 on the heels of the Pastoral Letter's publication and only four months after the members' participation in the antislavery convention, announced pointedly that at this, their fifth annual gathering, they would "be addressed by several distinguished speakers, both male and female." The women clearly did not intend to be constrained by white ministerial decrees. By contrast, the all-white leadership of the Ladies' New York City Anti-Slavery Society fell back upon the language of women's "appropriate sphere" to define the group's range of action. Renouncing "any thing that would interfere with the sacredness of the feminine character," they proposed pursuing only antislavery labor that could be done "without calling [women] from their own firesides or identifying them with the scenes of political strife."[57]

Among moral reformers, the Boston group sounded a similar theme. Their work, they asserted, "will elevate woman to her proper standing in society, without moving her from her 'appropriate sphere.'" Responding to the Pastoral Letter, they agreed that "in maintaining the *rights* of women, we will not neglect her appropriate *duties*." The New York Female Moral Reform Society, however, embraced Sarah Grimké's approach to "the Province of Woman" and directly criticized the Pastoral Letter. "We are styled 'public reformers,'" wrote Sarah Towne Smith in response, "but 'names are not arguments,' and a sneer . . . [is not] calculated to convince." On moral issues, she concluded, women "*must* claim the privilege of thinking and acting for ourselves." Shortly thereafter, she published Grimké's views on rights and duties: "Duties belong to *situation*, not to sex; . . . the rights and responsibilities of men and women as moral beings are identical."[58]

A confusion of tongues was evident in such simultaneous conversations about rights and duties, however, and tangled up the pages of the *Advocate of Moral Reform*. Between 1837 and 1839, for example, amid printed petitions addressed to state legislatures, strongly worded articles by Sarah Grimké, and tart editorials rebuking the Massachusetts Congregational clergy and sarcastically naming one of them as a critic of "unsexed *lecturesses*" like herself, editor Sarah Towne Smith drew the line at female irreligion, speeches to "promiscuous assemblies," and neglect of "our domestic duties." Standing firmly on the side of women's "privilege of thinking and acting for ourselves," she nevertheless denounced Fanny Wright as a "high priestess of infidelity" and urged her readers to consult both their rights and their duties. In order to think and act for themselves, she believed, women must always possess "*sanctified* intellect, directed by the word of God."[59]

In the cacophonous context of the late 1830s, inherent contradictions like these soon turned conversation to argumentation, and talk of rights joined with duties became harder to hear amid calls to duty alone. In Boston, as Debra Gold Hansen has demonstrated, the Female Anti-Slavery Society went through a wrenching schism, dividing Garrisonians from anti-Garrisonians, and driving a wedge between those who had been simultaneously active in the Boston (later New England) Female Moral Reform Society and those who had not. In New York, the leadership of the Ladies' Anti-Slavery Society, more timid souls than the Boston group, in part because of closer ties to the evangelical churches and in part because of their experience with the bloody racist riots of 1834, resisted pressure to challenge clerical authority. "There is still moral power sufficient in the church, if rightly applied, to purify it" they pleaded in 1838 as their coworkers set about repudiating churches that permitted slaveholders to take communion. In both cities, it gradually became more difficult—and dangerous—for individual women to speak about women's rights without being assailed as irreligious, sexually promiscuous, and unrespectable. Only the very privileged or the very committed could stand up to the onslaught. Among the most committed were African American women; among the most privileged were wealthy white Unitarians. Both were disproportionately represented among radical Garrisonians in the Boston Female Anti-Slavery Society's schism.[60]

Yet another set of boundaries had been drawn, with religious symbols as the most prominent markers. Women who underscored the issue of rights without highlighting the corresponding matter of duties were likely to have their religious credentials questioned. Regardless of how personally religious they were, women who put too much emphasis on equal rights could be exiled to the land of irreligion, a country where sexual laxity and racial "amalgamation" supposedly thrived. Evangelical faith and submission to a masculine clergy offered some sanctuary to those whose abolitionist principles and opposition to the sexual double standard put them in danger of symbolic expatriation. Moral reformers' retreat from attacking slavery because slave women "are our sisters" toward a critique of its effects on white women provides just one bit of evidence about how effective the cry of "amalgamation" could be. So, too, does the deep division at the 1837 Anti-Slavery Convention of American Women over whether "corrupt custom and a perverted application of Scripture" had concealed the "rights and duties [that] are common to" both women and men.[61]

Almost at those very moments, of course, the issue of women's rights was taking on a new urgency, as male reformers debated their own relation to the political realm, and especially to the efficacy of voting. Women's exclusion from that central privilege of citizenship, once a mark of dependency as well as gender, and shared with low-status men, now served primarily as a gender signifier. As reformist men turned increasingly to electoral politics to achieve their goals, women's lack of suffrage and other rights became more noteworthy. "As the significance of voting grew," notes Lori Ginzberg, "so did the significance of votelessness." Similarly, wives' enforced seclusion within the walls of coverture seemed increasingly out of touch with women's experiences and with the rapidly changing economy. In the years following 1840, both wives' right to control property and women's right to participate in the governmental process took on new political import. Although actual conventions bearing the label "women's rights" did not take off until the late 1840s and 1850s, by 1840 some terms of the argument over rights as opposed to duties had been established, and some women had acquired a language that they could continue to employ in opposition to "corrupt customs and a perverted application of the Scriptures."[62]

Conclusion

In 1839, "old lady Hamilton," Elizabeth Schuyler by birth, Mrs. Alexander Hamilton by marriage, and New York Orphan Asylum Society leader by career, "walked down from St. Mark's Place" to the law offices of George Templeton Strong in order to conduct some business, "and was going to walk back," a feat Strong considered remarkable "for an old lady of her degree of antiquity." Now eighty-two, Hamilton had served on the Orphan Asylum Society board for thirty-three years, and would continue to preside over it for another ten. During that time, she had helped draft more than one petition to a city council whose members included close family friends, as well as partners and legal executors of her late husband. (Some had been most helpful when she petitioned personally to the U.S. Congress for her revolutionary widow's pension. See Figure 4.2.) But in 1839, neither the city, its council, nor its political culture much resembled those of her earlier years. If she read the moral reform papers, with their direct attacks on "licentiousness in high places," she might experience an especially personal reminder of how much had changed. In the 1790s, when her husband had admitted to an adulterous affair, such printed attacks were the purview of scurrilous newspapermen, not groups of organized, politically active women.[63]

As the daughter of a prominent political family, and the widow of a founding father (and keeper of his flame), Elizabeth Schuyler Hamilton had called by name many leading statesmen of her day. As a republican mother raising eight children along with an adopted daughter in postrevolutionary New York and Philadelphia, she had prepared her sons for citizenship in the new repub-

REPORT

OF THE

Committee of Claims,

ON

THE PETITION

OF

ELIZABETH HAMILTON.

JANUARY 11, 1810.

Read and committed to a committee of the whole house on
Wednesday next.

CITY OF WASHINGTON :

A. & G. WAY, PRINTERS.

....

1810.

FIGURE 4.2. Title page of the 1810 *Report of the Committee of Claims on the Petition of Elizabeth Hamilton*, concerning Elizabeth Schuyler Hamilton's petition for Alexander Hamilton's Revolutionary War pension. The petition from an individual woman requesting a favor was a long-standing feature of political life. (Courtesy of the Library Company of Philadelphia)

lic and her daughters to follow in her footsteps. As second directress (1806–21) and then first directress (1821–49) of the Orphan Asylum Society, she led a group of devout women, mostly Episcopalians like herself, who assumed responsibility for the needs of white orphaned children and secured city and state aid for the job. In all these roles, she possessed and wielded political influence, though in different ways. As a daughter, wife, mother, and widow, she could express her views and attempt to influence individual men. But as a leader of the Orphan Asylum Society, Hamilton enjoyed vastly expanded opportunities to influence public discussions and public policies, particularly those related to the care of dependent children. As she and her asylum coworkers translated individual into social mothering, they brought a collective feminine voice and influence into city politics, and used it to shape welfare policy. In acquiring funds for their orphanage, they created a partnership with urban leaders and established their woman-run institution as one segment in the city's patchwork system of social provision.[64]

By 1839, the year she strolled down to visit George Templeton Strong, Hamilton and women like her could see the results of their labors manifested on the city's topography, through identifiable buildings, such as an orphanage or an old age home, newspaper offices and employment bureaus, and rented storefronts or workrooms. Rising on the urban scene and usually labeled with the group's name, such edifices embodied one version of collective feminine responsibility for the public good. In that same year, as she presided over the opening of a new asylum building on the banks of the Hudson River, several miles north of its original location and away from "the noisey [sic] scenes of the city," Hamilton knew that, whatever brief future she might enjoy on this earth, her organization and the institution it managed would live on. Deference-based politics had paid many dividends, the unpleasant publicity surrounding the orphanage's access to public money had been weathered, and the orphanage was well established. If she chose, Elizabeth Hamilton could simply ignore the new sort of publicity and new style of politics evident among other New York women. Like their counterparts in the Boston Female Asylum, she and her associates could "sit quietly in our usefulness," secure in the "knowledge that all is well with us."[65]

Other women's collective labors were not so well rewarded, nor could other women easily shield their work from potentially negative publicity. The endeavors of Boston's Samaritan Asylum for Colored Children or New York's Abyssinian Benevolent Daughters of Esther Association were blankly invisible on city streets. Even the white women establishing a Colored Orphan Asylum in New York in 1836 found that "the force of prejudice" made it impossible for them to rent living quarters for the children; they begged and borrowed the money to purchase— very quietly—a small house. When the meeting hall of a racially integrated group of abolitionist women was torched in Philadelphia in 1838, the mob "seemed to direct their malice particularly toward" black women. In 1839, as Elizabeth Hamilton made her way around Manhattan, the status-based tradition of female influence that she represented appeared to have little in common with the mass-based politics that abolitionist women pursued. Indeed, women in organizations such as hers actually gained from the negative associations that surrounded white women abolitionists. Hamilton and her coworkers were not the rebellious wives and spinsters, "'female brethren,'" "amazons," and "oratoresses" who appeared in press reports.[66]

Yet there were overlaps among the various female political traditions, especially in the use of petitions, and in women's access to public print. More important, both the rise of women's organizations and changes in politics itself had altered the form and location of women's political action. To be sure, individuals continued to approach male politicians with ideas, opinions, requests, and demands, and visible and audible groups of women appeared at partisan political gatherings and in the galleries of state and national legislatures. Now, however, the lone woman petitioner and the "woman politico" had company in the townhouse drawing room, the office anteroom, and the legislative hall; individuals speaking as representatives of organizations presented requests and petitions, and lobbied for legislative changes, hoping to convey the wishes of hundreds, or thousands, or even of "Woman." Later, during the eras of Reconstruction and Progressive reform, when local and national women's groups pressed to place their causes onto political agendas, they would use all these means of access. Yet they would continue to worry whether, even though individual women, or women attending party rallies, could vocally express their partisanship, women's organizations should be nonpartisan. The argument that women's organizations lost their effectiveness when they became partisan was one that leaders of Elizabeth Hamilton's generation would have recognized. Expressing in 1806 their "peculiar solicitude to avoid distinguishing themselves as a party in any public contest," the leaders of the Boston Female Asylum argued precisely that position. And as Nancy Cott has cogently demonstrated, women's groups faced the conundrum well into the twentieth century: should they try to wield political influence "indirectly or directly— through the voluntarist, lobbying and pressure group mode or through . . . partisan politics"?[67]

CHAPTER FIVE

Economies

E very year for the eighteen years she spent as treasurer of the
Boston Female Asylum, Eleanor Peirce Davis compiled neat
columns of figures into brisk one-page financial statements. Her
counterpart at the Widows' Society, Frances Erving, did the same
for nine years, and Deborah Torry Lerow performed the service
for the Children's Friend Society for fifteen. In New York Sarah Clarke Startin
served as treasurer of the Orphan Asylum Society from 1807 until just before
her death in 1822, while her goddaughter Elizabeth Bayley Seton completed
the task for the Society for the Relief of Poor Widows with Small Children for
one year; Sarah Bane managed the African Dorcas Association's finances for at
least two years; and Julia Gouge Lockwood did the same for the Female Anti-
slavery Society, also for at least two years. When published, these treasurers' reports, occasionally accompanied by an auditor's approving stamp, succinctly
totted up an organization's financial status. (See Figure 5.1.) In most instances,
the accounting appeared at the end of the report, almost as an afterthought,
calling little attention to itself; the bulk of the report was its written text, where
an organization's managers elaborated on their plans, goals, accomplishments,
and social ideals. The connection between a report's text and its one-page
financial balance sheet often went unremarked.[1]

Dr.	Seaman's Aid Society in account with Mrs. William Grigg, Treasurer.	Cr.

1837.	$ cts.		$ cts.
Jan. 9, Balance of Cash from last year's account	100 92	Cash paid for articles for Store	5681 16
Cash received from subscription of members	358	do. do. to Workwomen	1423 03
Donations	1975	do. do. Rent of Store	140 00
Sales at Store	5560 48	do. do. Sundry drafts of the President for charitable purposes	426 25
	$7994 40	Cash paid for books for Library	50 00
		do. do. Repairs of School room	15 46
		do. do. Miss Millet, Instructress of Sewing School	104 00
		Cash paid for Printing Reports & Notices	74 51
		do. do. Stationery for School, &c	10 25
		do. do. Distributing Reports, Notices, Advertising	15 50
		Cash paid for use of Amory Hall,	10 00
		do. do. Insurance of stock in Store, for 1836 & 7	20 00
		Total, 7970 16
Examined and approved by the Board of Managers.		Balance in Treasury	24 24
			7994 40

FIGURE 5.1. This one-page financial summary, prepared in 1837 by Boston Seamen's Aid Society treasurer Eunice Faxon Grigg and approved by the organization's managers, represents a typical statement included in organizations' annual reports. (Courtesy of the Boston Public Library)

Raising and spending money was an essential part of any organization's work—work that took place within an increasingly complex and competitive market economy. Analyzing how an organization's leaders made getting and spending decisions and aligned those decisions with their collective goals helps connect the one-page financial statements at the back to the rest of the thirty-page annual reports—and to the larger urban economies of New York and Boston. And because organizations' treasurers, women such as Eleanor Davis and Sarah Bane, also participated in their families' economies, sometimes as business managers or wage-earners, but more often as wives, mothers, or daughters, examining the links between familial and organizational economies can help clarify individuals' economic ideas and the distinctions they made (in the arena they termed "retired" or "private") between their personal lives as members of families and their collective lives as officers of women's organizations. For in the day-to-day work of directing their organizations, especially when operating asylums or other institutions, women leaders imagined the labor required to sustain the enterprise as *both* a market commodity *and* something apart from the world of market relations. Although engaging regularly in the process of getting, spending, earning, saving, investing, hiring, and firing for their organizations, they did not locate their own activities within the same arena as the one where their husbands, fathers, brothers, and sons accumulated wealth, formed capital, bought and sold labor-power, and arranged to transfer material well-being to the next generation. Only their clients' labor appeared to belong to that realm.

The underlying scaffolding, the one that undergirded their own and their clients' family economies, bracing some but letting others collapse, was largely invisible to them. Most of them saw their world in a clear light, full of busy, self-denying activity that protected unfortunate women and children from winter's worst gales and smoothed the icy edges of an inexorable economic climate with caring compassion. Religious concern was a central element in that compassion; for them, temporal and spiritual care were intertwined. Although not an inaccurate image, theirs was nevertheless partial. In insisting that family and benevolent society labor occupied a place apart from the cold world of cash valuation, even while clients' labor was located within it, they helped formulate a set of ideas that have remained powerful down to the present day. The comforting notion that bourgeois family life, and by extension voluntary civic labor, represented alternatives to or bulwarks against the torrent of free-market self-interest, was one to which they gave form, and one they helped anchor in place. The contours of this view, and the contradictions within it, become visible when we examine how organizations raised, spent, and invested their money, what women organizers believed were their clients' most pressing needs, how they conceptualized the problems that clients faced in fast-changing urban economies, and how clients used the charitable or benevolent assistance they received.[2]

Fund-Raising

Although the scope of fund-raising and investing varied considerably from organization to organization, all women's groups made decisions about how to get money for their endeavors, how to allocate it once they had it, and how to plan financially for both the short and the long term. As they made those decisions, women leaders shaped their organizations into economic actors that would have some impact the economies of the cities in which they were located. And in accumulating budgets, organization leaders shifted money from their own household accounts, persuaded members to do the same, sought contributions from friends and strangers alike, and learned investment strategies. Once women's organizations became regular sights on the urban scene, those whom they targeted as sources of funds (whether friends, husbands or city councillors) either reallocated their charitable budgets or increased them in order to meet organizational needs.

All of this decision-making took place within a chaotic and rapidly changing economic context. Between the 1790s and the 1830s, the end of colonial mercantilism and the emergence of market capitalism brought new opportunities for wealth creation, accumulation, and loss, a new cash nexus of valuation, as well as a new wage system and the social relations that accompanied it. The boom-and-bust cycle that characterized the new economy could be giddyingly enriching or terrifyingly impoverishing, or both. Because economic security was difficult to come by and could disappear in a international crisis, a business failure or a general panic (major ones occurred in 1819 and 1837), well-off individuals sought to invest their economic gains in ways that might enable them to ride out economic squalls and transfer accumulated wealth to succeeding generations. To the time-honored practice of buying real estate, they added newly minted forms of investment, especially in the stock of banks and savings institutions, insurance companies, and transportation or manufacturing concerns. At the other end of the economic scale, those who dug the canals, tended the new factory machines, cooked the meals and cleaned the chandeliers at merchants' townhouses, sewed shirts by candlelight for $1.50 a week, sold sexual services to sailors, or hired out as wet nurses, faced a continual struggle to earn enough to subsist. The seasonal nature of a good deal of wage work and the rock-bottom prices that most women's work fetched turned daily existence into a struggle for survival.[3] As organization leaders sought to mitigate the most brutal aspects of that contest, their actions shaped and were shaped by the new urban economy at all levels.

Like a group of entrepreneurs starting a business, the founders of women's organizations had to raise funds for their work. The volume of funds raised depended in part upon the organization's ambitions and in part upon its access to resources. An orphanage or old age home needed more and different sorts of funding than a tract or clothing distribution society. Similarly, a mutual aid society run by working-class women drew upon different funding resources from those mined by middle-class groups supplying paid work to sailors' wives or widows. But collectively, women's organization very quickly emerged as significant economic entities in both cities. By 1820, they were raising and spending substantial budgets in both New York and Boston; by 1840, the combined value of their annual budgets exceeded $50,000; with endowment funds and buildings added in, it easily reached $200,000 in New York, $100,000 in Boston. (See Table A.11.)

To create such assets, organizational leaders tapped a variety of sources. They sold annual and life memberships; solicited donations of goods and money; collected savings account interest and stock dividends; sponsored church collections; sold client-made goods or services; rented out organizational space; held fund-raising fairs, sermons, or concerts; accepted legacies and bequests; sought tax monies (by means of city and state donations, subsidies, lotteries, and abatements); and took out loans. The particular blend varied from group to group. In 1837 and 1838, for example, while Boston's Seamen's Aid Society and New York's Orphan Asylum Society raised their $7,000 budgets from donations (including those from city and state coffers), subscriptions, rents, investments, and sales, the Ladies' New York City Anti-Slavery Society's $375 budget and the (African American) Female Assistant Benefit Society's $360 budget derived almost entirely from member donations. (See Table A.12.)

At base, however, the best-funded groups were those that promoted ambitious institutional projects (a refuge or asylum), served clients who could be deemed deserving, had access to wealthy supporters, and enjoyed significant political connections. Even the most liberal donors were unlikely to give as much to a prostitutes' refuge as to an orphanage, and orphanage supporters preferred to send money to children resembling their own. Although New York Protestants gave to the Roman Catholic Orphan Asylum, and Boston's Unitarian elite contributed one-fifth of the amount needed to build Holy Cross Catholic Church, and although Boston's Catholic shepherds proved "beneficent donors" to several Protestant charities, the bank notes passed across the denominational fence generally came in small denominations. New Yorker George Templeton Strong commented that the $456 annual collection taken up in St. Patrick's Cathedral for the Roman Catholic Orphan Asylum seemed to his friend Charles Shea "very large," but to Strong himself "rather small"; their different conclusions reflected the different expectations (and realities) that denominational preferences created. Similarly, New York's Colored Orphan Asylum and Boston's Samaritan Asylum for Colored Children — the one sponsored by Quakers, Methodists, and Presbyterians, the other by Unitarians and Congregationalists — struggled for donations in cities that supported white orphaned children more generously.[4]

Tapping Protestant donors alone, and requiring less operating capital than asylums or refuges, missionary, Bible, tract, and Sunday school societies nevertheless raised significant budgets for their labor. Devoted primarily to raising funds, these organizations had virtually no overhead. Raising a small amount meant doing less, raising a lot meant doing more, but short of raising nothing, a missionary or tract society could plug along year after year. Both New York's Female Tract Society and Boston's Female Auxiliary Bible Society spent varying amounts annually; in some years, the Boston group's spending reached over $800, but in others, $200 was a stretch. Despite "comparatively small" budgets, the women believed themselves to be fulfilling their mission, especially in supporting the American Bible Society. Between 1814 and 1836, they forwarded $1,465 in donations and $2,277 in purchase orders to the Bible Society's New York headquarters. In addition, they amassed an interest-bearing permanent fund of $2,510, which in 1836 they transferred to the national society. Although relying heavily on volunteer labor and donated schoolrooms, the New York Female Union Society for the Promotion of Sabbath Schools needed some spending money; in 1818–19, six percent of its $1,520 budget went for cleaning, heating and renting school spaces. Most of it, however (89 percent), paid for printing, binding and buying books, a cost that disappeared in the early 1820s as the group gave up on publishing its own materials. By 1823, the women were spending much less, about $350 a year, mostly to warm and clean schoolrooms.[5] (See Table A.12.)

During its start-up years, Boston's Society for the Promotion of Christianity among the Jews took the plugging-along principle to an extreme. Between 1816 and 1828, the group put together a permanent fund of almost $3,800 by sequestering high proportions of its annual collections (one year, 52 percent) in U.S. stock and in interest-bearing loans to the American Board of Commissioners for Foreign Missions (ABCFM). As the Fund grew, the women cast their remaining bread upon the waters, sending donations to a London men's missionary society, a school educating Jewish children in Bombay, a group circulating Christian books among Palestine's Jews, and a Maine organization seeking "to obtain Jewish children" (orphaned boys) to educate as Christians. But by its eleventh year, as the group's income continued to outrun its endeavors, "some of our Auxiliaries began to look with a suspicious eye on the movements of the Parent Society, and to inquire to what good purpose their charities were appropriated." The answer that the women were simply investing group funds while seeking worthy uses for the rest was no longer "satisfactory." Finally, in 1827, they secured an ABCFM Middle Eastern missionary whose labors they could sponsor, and gave up fishing for causes.[6] Comparable organizations matched expenditures to income by expanding or contracting their activities as needed. Yet for some, simply plugging along on small budgets was unacceptable. The urgency of the cause demanded continual increases in spending. To New York's Ladies' Anti-Slavery Society, the $358 they raised in 1836–37, $185 of which (51 percent) went to the American Anti-Slavery Society, seemed paltry indeed. And what would not the women of the Female Assistant Benefit Society have given to enjoy the luxury of a $3,800 permanent fund and leisurely consideration of how to spend it?[7]

From year to year, too, and over the decades, as organizations matured, sources flowed or dried up, and urban economies boomed or crashed, the blend of their assets changed. Most notably, the individual "subscription," a yearly pledge generally amounting to between fifty cents and three dollars, declined in significance as a source of organizational income for benevolent groups. (The exceptions were mutual aid society subscriptions, which took the form of dues, not donations, and Female Moral Reform Society subscriptions, which purchased a periodical.) Although long lists of subscribers and donors often filled the back pages of annual reports, the crisp, one-page treasurers' reports were more telling. They revealed a secular shift from away from the annual pledge as the primary financial well from which benevolent groups drew. (See Table A.13.) Indeed, almost every organization's subscription history traced an arc, with the number of subscribers reaching a peak within ten or twenty years of the founding date, then dropping to a plateau. Within nine years of its origin, and four of its incorporation, Boston's Corban Society recorded "a lamentable diminution in Subscribers." New York's Society for the Relief of Poor Widows with Small Children, begun in 1797, recorded its first noticeable decline in subscriptions in 1807. Divining sources of new contributors was one solution, but most long-lived groups filled their financial wells from alternate springs.[8]

The declining significance of subscription income is worth chronicling, especially because organizations' abilities to elicit and redeem those pledges can serve as one measure of membership base and support. Benevolent society leaders considered subscriptions a crucial initial mechanism for generating budgets, and every new announcement of a worthy cause was accompanied by a subscription list. A few assigned a standing crew of apprentices—young women in training to join organizational boards—to spend their time as collectors. On occasion, men were hired to do the same. In 1805 and again in 1809 the Boston Female Asylum paid male subscription collectors to visit delinquent members; in 1817, the Fragment Society did the same. Yet over time, every benevolent organization in both cities experienced a secular decline in the number of its subscribers. This despite population growth, increases in organizational visibility, and organizations' relative sense of need. Thus, the Boston Female Asylum, which collected $1,245 from 415 subscribers in 1803, in a city with about 30,000 inhabitants, could count only 73 subscribers in 1841, amid a population of 94,000. In its peak year, 1813, the group collected $1,362 from 454 subscribers. Similarly, New York's Orphan Asylum Society had 615 subscribers in 1810, but 421 in 1827.[9]

Yet many of these organizations not only remained financially solvent, some grew positively sleek on other income sources. By 1840, for example, the Boston Female Asylum's approximate net worth was a hefty $100,000. For such groups, legacies, bequests, interest, and dividends produced the largest quantities of alternate income. In 1828, for example, about 44 percent of the New York Orphan Asylum Society's $11,500 budget derived from large bequests and stock certificates; 12 percent came from subscriptions; 19 percent from small donations. Between 1800 and 1834, the Boston Female Asylum accumulated a permanent fund totaling $65,000; $27,000 of that came from bequests alone. The two orphanages fattened their budgets with extra rations from the tables of new wealth, by means of accumulated capital disbursed as charity during benefactors' lives or as bequests after their deaths, and direct investment in government bonds and corporate stocks. Indeed, the creation of permanent funds (or in some instances, more targeted building funds) to produce reliable yearly cash flows could be described as the one financial move that marked the most comfortable and long-lived organizations. Many created and enlarged their permanent funds by setting aside all life memberships purchased by or for supporters. Nor was it simply asylum and refuge-builders whose balance sheets benefited from these strategies, though institution building cost more than Bible distributing. A Boston sewing circle turned $200 (about 30 percent) of its first year's income into a permanent fund in 1812; with additions from another defunct circle, the fund reached $950 in 1831. Although the sewing ceased in 1848—"we languish as a society and must soon *die*," wrote the secretary dramatically, and accurately—the money still accumulated interest. Similarly, long after closing the school for which it had begun soliciting permanent fund contributions in 1811, New York's Female Association continued to parcel out the fund's proceeds, mostly to other local Protestant women's charities. (See Table A.14.)[10]

Women leaders were proud of their endowments and of their ability carefully to manage the money entrusted to them. Organizational money management strategies replicated those their families employed in husbanding family fortunes. In the new economy, capital accumulation and wealth generation were better done by means of long-term strategies than by living from paycheck to paycheck or annual meeting to annual meeting. Eventually, the wealthiest women's organization in Boston, the Female Asylum, by freeing itself almost totally from reliance on subscription income, was able to abandon annual public meetings entirely (and annual pleas for new subscribers) as unnecessary and perhaps impolitic. Suppose someone questioned "our need of that which many are so forward to claim?" asked Abigail Frothingham Wales in 1840, alluding to the multiplication of benevolent societies and their concomitant demands upon the public. Indeed, her sister Priscilla, the group's "collecting secretary" of nineteen years' standing, successfully recommended abolishing her own position because the asylum's altered "pecuniary arrangements" made it superfluous. Dispensing with public anniversaries and with Priscilla's services were cause, not for concern, but for congratulations; the organization was in rosy financial shape.[11]

The ability of organizations like the Female Asylum to become less dependent on squeezing or cajoling a yearly mite from supporters and to develop more stable funding sources was certainly a major step in securing economic autonomy and control over resources. Having to conduct the annual equivalent of a pledge drive or bake sale rendered women's groups highly vulnerable to economic downturns, as well as to geographically mobile or aging membership bases, and to competition from other worthy causes. Moreover, because most subscribers to women's organizations were married women (men were more likely to be donors than subscribers, even when the organization did not limit subscriptions to women), their treasuries were as dependent on husbands' generosity as were individual wives' domestic allowances. Joanna Bethune's grateful comment that her husband gave her all the money she needed "both for the families of myself & children & to give to the poor & every institution" had an unspoken dimension best articulated by an embarrassed Bostonian who told a young subscription-collector: "I have not a quarter in the house. I will ask my husband when he comes home; can't you call tomorrow?" As cash became the measure of value, and wives became managers of family economies, they got used to asking husbands for quarters. But as organization leaders, administering institutional economies, they preferred to minimize their dependence on income cadged from household budgets.[12]

Creating permanent funds that generated substantial portions of organizational income was a strategy beyond many groups' resources, however. It could also be at odds with group goals, especially because it was likely to widen the gulf separating members from managers. Mutual aid societies, for example, operated entirely on dues payments, with the occasional smidgen of savings bank interest. Dependent on members' own wages, operating with minuscule budgets, and paying out fifty cents here or a dollar there to cover sickness or funeral expenses, few had the luxury of setting aside investment monies. Small wonder that few African American women's church aid groups could compile and preserve the leather-bound record books that might enable historians to chronicle their labors.[13] Similarly, Roman Catholic women's parish societies seldom had the means to seek long-term funding; they sought to relieve immediate need and contribute to existing institutions. The handwritten subscription list for Boston's citywide Roman Catholic Female Charitable Society vividly captures the fifty-cent and one dollar scraps from which the women stitched their charity; of 311 donations made in 1832 and 1833, 187 (60 percent) came in amounts of one dollar or less; 291 of the 311 (93.5 percent) did not go beyond two dollars.[14] (See Figure 5.2.) New York's Methodist Female Assistance Society might have found the means to create a permanent fund, but did not; as a result, the cup of compassion it offered clients needed to be remade every year. Nevertheless, assembling the shards of subscriptions and donations into a usable vessel created close bonds between members and officers, who saw their collective labor as service to their God. That sense of common devotion received reinforcement when officers gave their annual accounting in a public or quasi-public setting.[15] When the Boston Female Asylum abandoned anniversaries and retreated into the orphanage building for annual meetings, the group's invested wealth subsidized the move away from a broad membership base (while ensuring institutional stability). By contrast, the New York Female Moral Reform Society transformed itself into the American Female Moral Reform Society by multiplying its newspaper subscription base five- and ten-fold.

Indeed, because creating permanent funds involved sequestering a portion of current budgets, organizations might defer client needs or deny client requests in order to amass reserves. (Building funds were a different story; organizations usually conducted targeted capital campaigns for the specific purpose of erecting an asylum or orphanage. The money thus raised was separate from yearly fund-raising.) Boston's Fragment Society provides a telling example of the process. Begun in 1812 by a group of young women in their twenties, most of them from families involved in mercantile and printing businesses, and including at least two income-earners, the Fragment Society leadership, managing annual budgets of around $1,000, decided in 1815 to set aside $200 — or 20 percent of the year's income — for a permanent fund. With additions every year, by 1838 the fund stood at over $2,400. As decade followed decade, and Boston's poor became more desperate, more Irish, and more Catholic, the Fragment Society board became more exclusive, elite, and extravagant. By the 1870s, they had remade the annual meeting into something that "assumed the style and proportions of an elegant party," with members attending by invitation only, dressed in evening clothes and wearing jewelry. Soon, they restricted access to membership, making lineage the sole criterion for joining; new recruits hoping to take one of the 200 available slots had to demonstrate kinship or descent from current or past members.[16]

However extreme and atypical, the example of the Fragment Society high-

The Names of the first Subscribers, at the suggestion of the Bishop, on the 18th of March, 1832 — the same being the second Sunday of Lent in that year.

		Paid Doll²	Paid Cents
1	Rosanna Burns	$ 1	
2	Mary Ann Casey		
3	Marg.t Eliz.th Garrity	1	
4	Ann Garrity		50
5	Ann Smith	1	
6	Esther Sarsfield, an. sub.	1	50
7	Mary Cahill, an. sub.	2	
8	Eliz.th Dalton		
9	Mrs Charrier, an. sub.	2	
10	Hanna Duff an. sub	2	
11	Pat.k Keenan		50
12	Marg.t P. Marten, an. sub.		50
13	Tho.s Murtha	3	
14	Mary Ann E.J. Page	1	50
15	M.rs Beverely, an. sub.	2	
16	Cath. Peterson, an. sub.	2	
17	Sarah A. C. Russel, an. sub.	2	
18	Mary Ward, an. sub.	2	
19	Mary Ann Ward, an. sub.	11	
20	Unice Ward, an. sub.	11	
21	Bridget Mc Elroy, an. sub.	2	
22	Hannah Lee, an. sub.		50
23	Abby Donohoe ann. sub.		50
24	Susanna Mc Laughlin, an. sub	1	50
25	M.rs Morgan, an. sub.		
26	Ann Gaffeny, an. sub.		
27	Miss Flynn, an. sub.	1	
28	M.rs Lally	1	
29	Eliz.th Debella, ann. sub.		
30	M.rs Mc Namara, an. sub.	1	50	50
31	Judith Rooney, an. sub.	1	
32	Eliz.th Dormandy, an. sub.		50	50
33	Mary Desmond	2	
34	Bridget Jordan	1	
35	Mary A Jackman	1	
36	Mary A. Wakefield, an. sub.	2 2	
37	Mary A. Butler, an. sub.	2	
38	Ann M. Teresa Gyps, an. sub.		
39	Mary Killebran, an. sub.	1	
40	Mrs James Sullivan, an. sub.		50	50
41	Mary A. Nowlan, an. sub.		50

FIGURE 5.2. First page of a subscribers' list, Roman Catholic Female Charitable Society, Boston, 1832. Note the small sums pledged at the society's first meeting. (Courtesy of the Archives of the Archdiocese of Boston)

lights the reasons why other fund-raising methods—particularly fund-raising fairs, sermons, and concerts—gained in popularity over the decades. They served additional purposes, especially education and mobilization, incidental to some organizations, but inseparable from the work of others. Sermons and concerts had roles early and late. The 1836 event that George Templeton Strong observed had its counterparts in the annual sermons preached for the Boston Female Asylum between 1801 and 1812 and the practice of designating specific Sunday collections for orphans or Sunday schools. Concerts of sacred music were particularly useful means of corralling Protestants' dollars for Catholic causes, or whites' money for African American needs. New Yorker John Pintard regularly attended such events at St. Patrick's Cathedral, as did Strong. And the popularity of African American choirs, both adults' and children's, provided extra income sources for black schools and antislavery labors.[17]

Fund-raising fairs, essentially unknown in both cities until the 1830s, grew more numerous and elaborate as time went by. Boston, the smaller and less heterogeneous of the two cities, offered the loamier environment for such events. The two Infant School Societies, the Fragment Society, the Seamen's Aid Society all advertised fairs (in 1830, 1831, and 1836 and 1840, respectively). In New York, fund-raising fairs were largely congregational and parish affairs, as women's associations sold goods to benefit church benevolent societies and schools. "It is a new thing for Catholics to hold a Fair for any such purpose," noted a local newspaper in 1834, announcing that the "charitable ladies" supporting the Roman Catholic Asylum for the Children of Widows and Widowers planned a three-day event at Niblo's Saloon just before Christmas. Such occasions did not long remain novel. Between 1837 and 1839, Catholic women's parish charitable associations at St. Mary's, St. Peter's, St. James's, and Transfiguration Church all sponsored fund-raising fairs, with the St. James event taking place at the Apollo Association's exhibition space on Broadway and lasting five days. Designed "for the extension of education among the poor and indigent," the event benefited the girls' school attached to the church. Similarly, the Tappan Female Benevolent Society held the first of several fairs in 1840, not at the sponsoring First Colored Presbyterian Church, but at the much larger Broadway Tabernacle, in order to tap white abolitionist support. The group rescheduled its 1841 fair from December to May, in order to coincide with "Anniversary Week," when large numbers of sympathetic visitors would be in town.[18]

But it was antislavery fairs, the first of which the Boston Female Anti-Slavery Society sponsored in 1834, that eventually became the lodestars for others. As historians of abolition have pointed out, the antislavery fair was a key source, not only of income, but more importantly of mobilization and movement momentum. Supporters mingled with organizers, fingering, discussing, and purchasing homemade or store-bought donations, many of which bore reminders of the cause in which they all labored. Carrying home a pincushion inked with an abolitionist motto or a work bag embroidered with a pathetic scene linked the purchaser with the creator and reinforced the movement's message long after the fair doors closed. (See Figure 5.3.) Moreover, like concerts at African American churches, fairs helped expose the curious, the uninformed, and the uncommitted to abolitionist principles. Attracted by the displays of goods, at which pincushions and work bags shared space with elegant, unusual, and imported items, shoppers became targets of moral suasion and perhaps even picked up lessons in antislavery beliefs within a world of consumer goods. The Boston Fair run by Maria Weston Chapman in particular served such purposes, escalating in size and scope until by 1849 it was a several-day affair held at Faneuil Hall. By common estimate, twenty-four fairs held by the Boston Female Anti-Slavery Society between 1834 and the 1860s raised $65,000. On a smaller scale, the 1839 St. Peter's Catholic Church fair at the Apollo gallery permitted curious or hostile New Yorkers to see Catholic women in a setting other than the townhouse scullery or the convent. The sponsors' emphasis on the fair's "expense," and the "style" and "rich variety" of the "exquisite specimens of taste" proffered for sale, sought to undercut the increasingly common image of Catholic women as uniformly oppressed and impoverished. Yet the expectation that someone would purchase the central item, "an entire suit of Clerical vestments . . . finished with expensive elegance and taste," underscored the fair's mobilizing function.[19]

If fairs provided contemporaries with object lessons in how to combine fund-raising with cause-building, they also revealed organizers using the rapidly expanding consumer marketplace for both purposes, and fashioning their own varying moral economies of consumption. Before fairs became commonplace, if a benevolent or charitable organization sold anything, it was clients' services or client-produced goods. (Boston's Female Auxiliary Bible Society did on occasion request a contribution from clients, but most received their Bibles gratis.) Magdalens resident at Boston's Penitent Females' Refuge earned $325 in 1825 for "washing, ironing, spinning, knitting, and picking wool." In the early 1820s, the Society for Employing the Female Poor hired women to wash, iron, and sew for donors' families; the society's store sold items made by clients with donated cloth. New York's House of Industry had operated along similar lines until closing up shop in 1820. Even the Boston Female Asylum collected $191 in 1831 for work done by its orphans. Most often, however, organizations

FIGURE 5.3. Pincushion, ca. 1835. Items inscribed with abolitionist messages and sold at antislavery fairs raised money for the cause. (Courtesy of the Friends Historical Library, Swarthmore College)

donated raw materials; clients then used or sold their own rough and ready products. But because poor women seemed capable only of "*coarse* work, *plain* washing and ironing, and *coarse* sewing," demand for the products of their labor was limited and inelastic. Organizations' turn to fairs that sold more stylish or genteel products represented a new appreciation that middle-class desires for decorative goods exhibiting their owners' refinement could be harnessed for social mobilization. Stylish fairs also raised questions about the morality of conspicuous spending and consuming, and whether morality and consumption could be reconciled.[20]

Except for Quakers, women organizers from across the political spectrum recognized no contradiction between their embrace of fairs as cash-producing bonanzas and their collective goals. When fairs gained popularity in the 1830s, only some organizations sponsored them, but nonsponsoring groups expressed no principled opposition to them. Because fairs were significant arenas for sustaining a movement culture or educating an opposition, however, sponsoring societies occasionally worried about what they should be selling. Boston abolitionists, for example, quarreled among themselves about whether home-embroidered or home-baked goods represented more virtuous selling and consuming than did fancy imported items. While the upper-class radical Maria Weston Chapman sought out rare, unusual, and elegant porcelains, silks, and laces, advertising them as the "most recherché articles of taste and fancy from the old world," the middle-class teachers Martha and Lucy Ball preferred that abolitionist money come from the sale of useful items such as socks and toys. "Fancy" goods "should have upon them appropriate devices or mottoes." Still, Chapman's approach was the more common one. The similarity between her language and that of New York's Catholic "Ladies of St. Peter's Congregation" who promised an 1839 fair that "will be of a style surpassing any thing of the kind that has yet been seen in this city," is emblematic both of the aspirations of middle- and upper-class Catholics and women leaders' general acceptance, across various social barriers, of refined and "elegant" consumption as socially acceptable for those who could afford it.[21]

In its own way, as each sponsoring group came to a decision about what to sell, it delineated a range of personal consuming options for participating women (organizations' consumption was a separate matter). At one end lay the kind of morally engaged, consciously utilitarian approach that characterized the middle-class Boston abolitionists, and that middle-class evangelicals such as Joanna Bethune favored. At the other, a morally engaged but expansive consumption dedicated both to social change and to personal refinement. Each approach had a role to play in shaping women organizers' attitude toward and involvement in the expanding marketplace of the antebellum years. Some proposed that benevolent women's personal spending convey lessons in frugality, usefulness, middle-class restraint, self-discipline, and proper husbanding of resources. Others saw consumer spending as a source of personal delight and pleasant recreation, and a means of expressing taste or displaying refinement. (And indeed both of these approaches to the consumer marketplace left traces that remained visible in later women's organizing.) All saw it as a means of generating greater wealth for their groups, mobilizing supporters, reaching out to the uncommitted, and teaching lessons about a particular cause.[22]

These disagreements and decisions aside, fair-sponsoring groups were almost uniformly silent about the enormous donations of unpaid labor that filled tables with saleable goods. Indeed, in reformist and benevolent circles alike, a set of larger issues usually went unmentioned, including what value voluntary labor added to goods and services, what a woman's time and labor were worth, and what effect the unpaid labor of charitable ladies had on the wages paid their female clients. On occasion, equations between time and money appeared in published reports, as when a Boston group pledged "by the more faithful use of our time, influence and capacity" to compensate for inadequate funds, or when New York's Anna Shotwell commended her "colored friends" for the time and labor they devoted to an 1860 fund-raising fair. And, as we shall see below, the issue of wages received some attention during the 1830s. But in general, organizational fund-raising shared the fate of other types of unpaid female labor; it was "pastoralized" into a leisure activity accomplished at the kitchen table or the parlor sewing basket, or by unmarried girls with time to spare. Fairs represent a particularly clear example of the process, as organizers eclipsed their feverish labor with soothing displays of neatly organized or elegantly turned out sale items. But other fund-raising labors—including taking up collections, seeking bequests and legacies, and soliciting donations—similarly obscured women's economic activity, as ministers pleaded from the pulpit on organizations' behalf and organizational leaders combined visits to family grocer with requests for donated barrels of flour.[23]

To note this point is not to suggest a contemporary awareness of the pastoralizing process. Female fund-raisers simply did not measure their time or their labor in cash terms, or calculate the market value of their activities, any more than they considered home, child, and family care to be parts of the economic realm. On occasion, especially when justifying an appeal for public funds, an organization might put a dollar value on its labors. Thus, in 1836, as they prepared to lay the cornerstone for a new building and sought $15,000 from the New York State legislature, the women of the Orphan Asylum Society calculated the average amount spent caring for each orphan: $41.17 per year, or eleven and one-half cents per day. Such calculations were rare, though; even in appealing for public funds, women leaders preferred simply to assert that their work "will be a real saving to the City" rather than attempt to measure the value of that saving. In avoiding such one-dimensional tallies, they produced and embodied the views that Sarah Josepha Hale and Catharine Beecher articulated in print: that domestic values were superior to those of the commercial marketplace; and that value should not be measured exclusively or even primarily in cash terms.[24] The practice of paying men to collect yearly pledges, but assuming that women would do so gratis, reflected these beliefs in all their contradictions. Some things, both women and men did, but women did them for love, men for pay.[25]

Investing

Like pledge-collections, fairs, and fund-raisers, investing was unpaid labor that produced income. But it was also an economic activity hard to befog behind clouds of domestic imagery. Whatever their stake in a domestic ideology that pastoralized their labor, women organizers established on the pages of every annual report their competence to manage the money entrusted to them. They took the principal on their permanent or building funds, invested it, and collected the interest; they conducted their own audits of treasurers' books. And although some groups' treasurers were considerably more precise about their financial practices than others, all expected members to comprehend information about those practices: that operating funds were separate from permanent funds; that principal was sequestered, then increased through reinvested interest; and that interest income was a source of operating expenses. Clearly, too, they assumed that members understood what investing in "six per cent stock of the United States," or "18 shares in Mechanics Bank" meant.[26]

Women leaders' money-managing competence derived from both personal experience of paid labor and family ties. Businesswomen formed a particularly important core leadership group within white early republic-era organizations. Elizabeth Peck Perkins, for example, keeper of a well-known glass, tea, and wine shop in Boston's King Street, real estate investor, and mother of two highly successful merchants, James and Thomas Handasyd Perkins, served the Boston Female Asylum as treasurer during some crucial early years. Similarly, Mary Chrystie was still attending to her china shop on Manhattan's Maiden Lane when she joined her friend Isabella Graham in the work of the Society for the Relief of Poor Widows with Small Children in 1807; Sarah Bane and her husband Peter ran an oyster house and also offered board to "respectable persons of colour" at their home on Leonard Street during the time that Sarah served as treasurer of the African Dorcas Association; and Boston's Mary Bowers combined family labor at a shop on Cornhill with extensive evangelical organizational commitments. School founders such Isabella Graham and Susanna Rowson, and authors such as Rowson and Hannah Adams had valuable aptitude at starting and managing economic enterprises. Adams's writing career, crafted in an era when successful authors often vied fiercely for shares of textbook and other markets, made her something of a managerial and public relations expert. And women with considerable skill in managing family investments, such as New York's Sarah Clarke Startin and Boston's Eleanor Peirce Davis, contributed insiders' knowledge of the commercial and financial worlds of the new economy. According to her friend and personal beneficiary

Elizabeth Bayley Seton, Startin was a stickler for financial precision: she "always requires of me a Receipt for whatever money I recieve [sic] from her, in order to keep her books correct."[27]

Over time, the boards of white Protestant benevolent societies could count fewer such redoubtable matrons in their midst, as paid labor, business experience and entrepreneurship became less common sources of personal income for middle- and upper-class women, replaced by investment managing and annuity collecting. With the exception of groups founded by Boston's indefatigable Mary Webb, benevolent organizations became less and less likely to have wage-earners on their boards at all. Indeed, by 1830, reform, mutual aid, and parish charitable societies could often be distinguished from strictly benevolent organizations simply by the presence of employed women at meetings. And now, employed women's personal knowledge of investing or financial planning was more likely to come from wage- and salary-earning than from independently managing a shop or school. Moreover, as the commercial economy roared into high gear, those employments themselves changed subtly. Among women educators, teaching replaced owning an independent girls' seminary as a source of employment. By the 1820s, most teachers serving on organizational boards were salaried employees, not entrepreneurs; moreover, the entrepreneurs among them, such as Bostonians Mary Perry, Martha Ball and Lucy Ball, served a very different clientele from the elite girls who had attended Susanna Rowson's academy in the preceding era. Sixty-year-old Mary Perry, while serving on the boards of the evangelical Female Auxiliary Bible Society and Corban Society, needed to rent out her Newbury Street schoolroom for $4 in 1819 to the elite, Unitarian-led Widows' Society. In later years, too, authors were more likely to work on contract for religious publishing houses than as free agents, and some employed women leaders in the 1830s earned their living as employees of the organizations they served, or labored in other women's homes. Elizabeth Jackson Riley, president of both the Boston Afric-American Female Intelligence Society and the Colored Female Union Society in the 1830s, nursed the sick and dying; Mary Irena Treadwell Hubbard both served and was employed by the New York Female Moral Reform Society and its successor organizations for over forty years. The money-managing experience of teachers, nurses, missionaries, or writers during the 1820s and 1830s might be of a different sort from that of the business or investment managers of the 1800s and 1810s, and the funds to which they had access were certainly of a different order; still, through paid labor they acquired economic knowledge that, in turn, served their organizations' needs.[28]

Both early and late, in the 1790s and the 1830s, family ties permitted women leaders to draw upon the knowledge, expertise, and cultural authority of their husbands, brothers, or sons for the benefit of their volunteer involvements. Aside from an occasional official auditor or financial adviser, continuing formal male involvement in women's groups was rare, at least until the 1840s. Instead, women leaders drew upon expertise acquired as amanuenses to fathers and husbands, or asked for and received advice from male family members and friends. The conditions of dependence or deference under which they did so are unclear, however. To be sure, self-supporting widows such as Sarah Josepha Hale complained in the 1830s on behalf of the newly dependent wife who "must go to her husband to beg money for her charities!" Yet the available evidence suggests that we should be careful about accepting retrospective assumptions of routine deference. When one of Eleanor Davis's successors at the Boston Female Asylum looked back upon Davis's years of buying bank stocks and public securities, she imagined Davis fretting over this "complicated and anxious duty for a lady," and lauded Davis's associate Benjamin West for his assistance. But Davis's account book tells a very different story. There, Davis appears clearly in charge, directing West and others in decisions about her land and her sugar business. Similarly, although one of the many losses the widowed Joanna Bethune lamented in her diary was Divie Bethune's "great assistance and judicious counsel," the diary makes clear her firm hold upon matters relating to liquidating his "mercantile concern," "manag[ing] his estate" and property, "provid[ing] for his family" and "free[ing herself] from a Chancery suit." Sharing one's bed or dining table with a man who ran a partnership or store, served on a bank board or founded a savings institution, or published a magazine or newspaper, could prove very valuable to one's organizational involvements, and unpublished minutes include routine references to relatives' informal assistance.[29]

Whether drawing upon family members' advice or their own money-managing experience, women leaders were generally cautious investors. Seeing themselves as guardians of assets entrusted to them, they sought to avoid risky ventures in favor of steady, solid returns. In rejecting an 1815 bequest, for example, the women of the Boston Female Asylum explained that they "could not with propriety receive the legacy in the offered stocks the value of which is so fluctuating and uncertain." They preferred that Samuel Smith's bequest come to the asylum in stocks they considered reliable. That preference for dependable over variable income expressed itself in a fairly narrow investment range, including government securities, insurance companies, and banks. After its founding in 1819, the Massachusetts Hospital Life Insurance Company became the primary beneficiary of Boston women's organizational investing. During the late 1830s, it had the use of close to $75,000 in women's organizational funds, especially those of well-endowed groups such as the Boston Female Asylum. New York women preferred United States securities and New York City stock as safe, interest-generating places to tuck their assets. By means of such investment strategies, women leaders secured their groups' futures, while also establishing reputations for prudent money management, hence augmenting the confidence of future donors and legators.[30]

But particular strategies had broad consequences, certainly broader than the women themselves would have recognized. In seeking security, women's organizations bolstered the power of the institutions to which they entrusted their money, hardening new enterprises such as banks and insurance companies into diamonds. Moreover, they made the money available for reinvestment in some of the commercial, mercantile, and industrial ventures of the era. No doubt the Boston Fragment Society's and Female Asylum's permanent funds indirectly financed railroads, cotton mills, and shipping companies across New England. After all, by 1850, the Massachusetts Hospital Life Insurance Company was "the largest commercial lender in New England and a key player in underwriting the region's textile and railroad industries." Indirectly, too, the funds helped crown King Cotton, enrich his mercantile servants, and tighten his slaves' chains. As Sarah and Angelina Grimké pointed out in 1837, "ten thousand cords of interest . . . link [the North] with the southern slaveholder," whether in New England mills processing slave-grown cotton or New York businesses insuring slaveholders' property—human and otherwise. In a similar manner, the building fund or permanent fund deposits made in local banks by New York's Association for the Relief of Respectable, Aged, Indigent Females or Association for the Benefit of Colored Orphans helped sponsor the city's real estate boom. By 1860, mortgages constituted about half of city banks' investments. Women leaders watched their organizations' bottom line improve as mortgage prices increased and landlords raised rents. Eventually, too, those deposits facilitated the emergence of a manufacturing sector based in the city's tenements and cellars. By a relentless turn of the economic wheel, the success of some organizations' investments produced the misery that required another organization's fund-raising, benevolent donation, or mutual assistance.[31]

Although women's groups in both cities pursued similar economic strategies to those of the men of their families, the local legal and economic structure gave those strategies a particular cast in each city. Bostonians, especially those whose wealth derived from mercantile and merchant-manufacturer pursuits, faced state laws that were "inimical to the transmission of large fortunes between generations." Money secured in trust for widows and children bypassed such legal restrictions, made capital available for investment in the broader city and state economy, and turned trustees into members of a powerful financial class. With its small and homogeneous elite, Boston quickly became a city where family trustees were the same men managing educational and charitable corporations' endowments, and amassing substantial political and economic power from the pooled resources they managed. The result was a new elite class: the Brahmins. New York law, by contrast, permitted families to accumulate enormous fortunes (such as that of the Astors), but limited bequests to charities, subjected charitable institutions to state regulation, and restricted the amount of wealth they could hold. Wealth accumulation and transmission thus looked different in each city, especially where charitable corporations were concerned. Whereas in Boston the management of philanthropic endeavors such as Massachusetts General Hospital often intertwined with that of for-profit corporations such as the Massachusetts Hospital Life Insurance Company, in New York the new rich required some other motive, such as religion, to turn their pursuit of profit into philanthropy. Nevertheless, in both cities, assets invested by women's benevolent corporations bolstered the power of already powerful economic institutions.[32]

Women leaders were hardly bystanders in the new economy; they understood and were often personally acquainted with these financial maneuverings. After all, the trustees of Ann Amory McLean's widow's portion, her two brothers, had to face court charges in 1829 that their efforts to maximize her gain jeopardized the $50,000 principal, which upon her death was to go to two of her late husband's philanthropies, Harvard University and Massachusetts General Hospital. Ann and her sisters, Catherine Codman and Rebecca Lowell, could list numerous organizational leadership posts on their resumes. Singly and together, the Amory sisters had roles in planning the present and future of the Boston Female Asylum, Female Auxiliary Bible Society, Widows' Society, Fatherless and Widows Society, Penitent Females' Refuge, and Children's Friend Society. Surely parlor conversations with brothers and husbands, as well as estate-planning meetings with lawyers, enabled them to speak as easily of solid investment income as Jane Austen's characters spoke of having "three thousand pounds." In New York, comparably wealthy women such as Hannah Murray displayed a clear understanding of how to be one of the "faithful stewards of the riches" she inherited, an understanding she shared through her extensive benevolent involvements.[33]

Among the other lessons these women learned at parlor fireside and solicitor's desk were the relative importance of women's and men's philanthropies. John McLean's will, while endowing the psychiatric hospital that later bore his name and providing generously for Massachusetts General and Harvard, dropped a mere $500 into the Boston Female Asylum's permanent fund. But McLean was not alone in slighting his wife's philanthropies; upon her death in 1834, Ann McLean Lee showered $53,500 in cash bequests upon various worthy causes, but only $500 of it went to the Fragment Society, none to the Female Asylum. To be sure, during her lifetime, Ann had been accustomed to multiply her annual dues one hundred times or more, donating $100 here and $200 there, but her testatory decisions clearly favored institutions managed by male trustees, such as her brothers, not those to which she and her sisters had devoted time, talent, skill, and financial know-how. Other wealthy decedents behaved similarly. New Yorker Hannah Murray left $1,000 to the Society for the Relief of Poor Widows, $500 to the Infant School Society. Only the most obtuse observer would not have noticed the relative pittances women bestowed from beyond the grave, or the imbalance between wealthy men's and women's gifts. Between 1800 and 1844, for example, seventeen men bequeathed $19,600 to the Boston Female Asylum and twenty-seven women bequeathed $10,600. The largest woman's donation amounted to $3,000; the largest man's to $5,000. Between 1820 and 1849, the New York Orphan Asylum Society received eight bequests, $34,800 from six male decedents, $7,500 from two female, the first of which arrived in 1839. When Sarah Clarke Startin died in 1822, her will included cash gifts to Episcopal Bishop John Henry Hobart, Orphan Asylum superintendent John McFarlane and his family, and family members, but nothing to the orphanage itself. These behaviors reflected both broad societal assumptions about the appropriate size of women's and men's charities, and wealthy women's preference for donating to their favorite causes while in this life rather than after departing it. During her years as Orphan Asylum Society treasurer, for example, Startin had "bec[o]me personally responsible for large amounts of money" through no-interest loans, loan guarantees, and outright grants.[34]

Despite the apparent skill and ease with which women leaders managed their organizations' capital, by the 1850s many groups had established formal male advisory boards with which to consult on building projects or investment funds. The appointment of male treasurers remained in the future; only Boston's Widows' Society, which asked men to audit its books from its founding in 1816, officially designated a man as treasurer, in 1862. Formal "Committees of Gentlemen" advised some groups from the start, but with considerable variation in the conditions under which women accepted the advice. New York's African Dorcas Association had its work overseen by "an advising committee" of ministers from "each African Church in this city"; the Roman Catholic Asylum for the Children of Widows and Widowers' three "Gentlemen" advisers included the city's presiding bishop; and the Protestant Half-Orphan Asylum's 1839 Act of Incorporation vested corporate power in nine male trustees; Jewish women's charities always did the same. An expectation of feminine deference was clearly built into those arrangements. In Boston, the male "Committee of Advice" selected by the Society for Employing the Female Poor did all public speaking for the women managers in the 1820s. But the Children's Friend Society, with a male "Board of Advisors" identified in its constitution and Act of Incorporation, specified explicitly that the "Board of Ladies" ran the institution. In later decades, men's advisory committees served more uniformly to limit women's collective independence, although at least one organization, the Penitent Females' Refuge, passed from men's direction to women's in the 1850s. New York's state legislators permitted the American Female Guardian Society (formerly the New York Female Moral Reform Society) to incorporate in 1849 only under the oversight of male "counselors" needed to approve all real estate transactions. By doing so at the same time they were adopting laws protecting married women's rights as individuals to control property, the lawmakers sent the message that improved individual rights would not undermine women's dependent status.[35]

These departures from informal consultation, the prevalent advisory mode early in the century, evidenced a discomfort, not with women's financial practices, but with the growing disjunction between femininity and financial management. Just as the professionalization of medicine and law masculinized the associations surrounding them and excluded occasional or casual practitioners (many of whom were women), once banking and investing became full-time occupations, they came to be seen as the exclusive and appropriate occupations of men. Whereas before the 1850s, most bank directors had been volunteer trustees, by the 1860s their duties were being performed by salaried professional staffers with titles such as "comptroller" and "treasurer." And once salaried treasurers were always men, treasurers' work was always masculine. The real lives of women investors such as Elizabeth Peirce Davis and Sarah Clarke Startin disappeared from public view, and the lasting stereotype of women as not "man enough" to handle money was born. Women leaders themselves, by formalizing the position of male advisers within their organizations, separated their "home" and "work" roles more fully than had their predecessors. At the same time, however, they reinforced contemporary appraisals of women's money-management talents as amateurish and unprofessional.[36]

Spending and the Purposes of Charity

Women leaders' economic activities went beyond the investments they made in banks, buildings, government securities, and insurance companies, beyond the fund-raising fairs and concerts they sponsored. Organizational budgets purchased paper and ink, thread and tea, wood and shoes, books and tracts; paid wages and rents; and contracted for services. Some organizations owned institutions housing scores of orphans; others operated workrooms providing wage work to hundreds of poor wives and widows; still others provided tiny supplements to or substitutes for women's wages. The beneficiaries of all this spending were not only the clients targeted for assistance, but those hired to supply it. Orphanages, old age homes, prostitutes' refuges, and children's homes routinely hired full-time superintendents, matrons, teachers, cooks, nurses, and servants, and paid as needed for the services of physicians, chaplains, carpenters, masons, painters, tinmen, carters, and haulers. Noninstitutional groups paid individuals to manage shops and storehouses, superintend workrooms, and teach children. And evangelical, mutual aid, and reform organizations hired missionaries, agents, canvassers, and lecturers. Local merchants, including organization leaders themselves, provisioned organizations of all types. Money thus spent entered urban economies by many different paths.[37]

Spending a group's money involved making innumerable decisions—both large and small—about how best to meet its collective goals, within the limits set by organizational resources. In order to keep the treasurer writing in black ink rather than red, organization leaders strictly accounted for every penny spent and, when necessary, set limits on group benevolence. Although every organization at some point found itself stretching scarce resources, those providing direct assistance to poor urban women and children confronted the limits of benevolence most directly and most frequently. Their initial response, that they would separate the deserving from the unworthy, and assist only the "respectable" poor, underwent a few changes as they encountered the hard realities of a constantly changing urban poverty. The new politics of the 1820s and 1830s precipitated new forms of cost accounting, renewed discussions of the causes of poverty and dependence, and altered some decisions about the proper uses of their charity. Organizational practices embodied those decisions.

In deciding how clients' needs were best served, benevolent women assumed the superiority of private over public charitable provision, and of personal over institutional methods of relief. With a few exceptions, they rejected bare-bones cash transactions, instead offering a combination of money, goods, services, and personal attention. Whether aid recipients received, to use the terminology of the day, "outdoor relief" in their cellars and garrets or "indoor relief" in orphanages or lying-in homes, the currency was similar. The "pensioners" supported by New York's Association for the Relief of Respectable, Aged, Indigent Females received a dollar or two per winter month, firewood, a monthly visitor who might "wipe away the tear which passes down the furrowed cheek of decrepit age," and an occasional gift of tea or sugar. Boston's Fragment Society members handed out advice, instruction and Bibles along with the "trifling benefaction" of clothing, shoes, or bedding. Poor children boarding at the Boston Children's Friend Society's asylum absorbed food, clothing, and shelter, along with schooling, religious instruction, work, the company of others in the institutional "family," and the "care and guidance of wise & affectionate" substitute parents. And mutual aid societies, although providing primarily illness or death insurance, included home visits as part of the package for dues-paying members.[38]

Rather than "trusting them with a few dollars themselves," or combining money with necessaries, charitable women preferred to assist outdoor relief clients with goods. Between November 1808 and November 1809, New York's Society for the Relief of Poor Widows with Small Children purchased for 216 widows (each with about three children) 7,695 pounds of meal; 729 loads of wood; 441 pairs of shoes; 1,138 yards of flannel and wool and 482 yards of linen and cotton (all to be turned into clothing); thirty-one pounds of candles; twenty-two pairs of stockings; fifteen pounds of yarn; and small quantities of other foodstuffs such as sugar, tea, meat, wine, and butter. The women's preference for wool and candles over cash went beyond their belief, especially entrenched by the 1820s, that personal attention and religious instruction were equal in importance to more tangible contributions. As stewards of organizational accounts, they sought to spend wisely. Buying wood during warmer months, storing it at the almshouse and distributing it in the winter saved an organization from paying high peak-demand and small-quantity prices. Buying in bulk or securing raw materials to be turned into finished clothing were economizing strategies no doubt derived from their management of family economies. Other outdoor relief societies followed similar practices, seeking to husband donations and to embody the principle that "administering comfort to the afflicted, and supply to the needy" were equally significant obligations.[39]

There were other messages in the preference for goods over money, however. Distributing items of daily need enabled givers to decide what recipients lacked, enforced upon poor women certain domestic norms, and conferred powers of intervention and surveillance. Clients of most outdoor relief societies had to apply personally to a manager, then agree to regular visits involving "close . . . questioning" designed to "ascertain the[ir] real character and true situation." By entering "the lonely dwelling," cheering, "the desponding heart," and offering "consoling assurance," commented the president of one such society, the managers made themselves "acquainted with the objects [they] relieve" and evaluated clients' "wants, . . . habits and dispositions." The actual goods provided varied according to conditions. Clients of the Society for the Relief of Poor Widows with Small Children, for example, could have a little sugar, tea, meat, wine, or butter when they were ill; ordinarily, they were entitled only to items of basic human comfort: wood and clothing for warmth, candles for light, and cornmeal ("Indian meal") or bread for sustenance. Indoor relief organizations carefully laid out diet and clothing specifications. At the Boston Female Asylum's midday dinner, girls ate plain, nourishing fare such as soup, or beans with pork; but on Sundays, the smell of "roast meat and pudding" wafted across the table. Dressed alike in "plain and simple" dresses, they absorbed messages about the clear distinction between necessities and luxuries, and how they should conduct their lives.

Organizations' rules for client behavior, specifying circumstances under which individuals could be cut off, voiced other lessons clearly. Visiting committees scrutinized spending habits in order to separate good clients from bad. The latter could be found drinking or selling liquor; "dressing & going to dances"; "spend[ing] their earnings in Articles of Dress improper for their station"; or exhibiting "habits inimical to their own comfort." One African American women's mutual aid society refused "aid or sympathy" to members "who shall rashly sacrifice their own health"; another excluded "any person addicted to inebriety or having a plurality of husbands." Worthy clients were frugal and hard-working, "clean and tidy," and managed on pittances, as evidenced by the "patched bed quilt" and "much-mended" dress described in annual reports. As they swept into "abodes of poverty" bearing both friendly consolation and firewood vouchers, benevolent and observant visitors carried the message that clients needed to adopt the same frugal style of consumption that their benefactors' organizations practiced, and the same habit of long-term planning. By collectively exhibiting "benevolence and frugality," the women of Boston's Fragment Society believed, they not only walked in Jesus's footsteps "gathering up the fragments," but also showed others the way.[40]

Like these Bostonians, members of other women's groups held up their organizational, not individual, spending habits as models when they lectured clients on household management. Whether they referred to "the society" or "this charity," they imagined the group as an entity outside of and partially separate from their personal lives, one that conferred upon its representatives an authority different from what they possessed as individuals. Thus the friendly visitor, who "descend[ed] into the dwellings of misery, as they abound in this city," bearing the gift of household items and the lesson on careful spending, could teach that lesson because she represented the larger collectivity. This distinction between personal and collective lives helps explain the deaf ear that most organization members turned to calls for personal "retrenchment" in the 1820s. Women managers on occasion passed the hat to replenish an empty treasury, but suggestions that members rework their personal finances in order to do more for the cause were rare indeed. The New York Female Missionary Society's 1818 argument that "the retrenchment of a few superfluities, and needless ornaments, used by professing Christian females *in this City*, would support a number of Missionaries," was unusual. "Shall we value our ornaments while souls are perishing?" pleaded the group's spokesperson. (A comparable cry did echo from women's antislavery conventions in the late 1830s, though.)[41] As individuals, group leaders might respond by seeking to increase their missionary mites; but as leaders, many rejected the question's premise and, as we have seen, used the very attraction of "needless ornaments" to raise money and momentum at fairs. Similarly, they evaluated liquor sales and the wearing of finery differently in different contexts. After all, their boards contained women whose families trafficked in brandy and spirits, or whose wealth depended upon the sale of fashionable frippery. And at least one organization entered "paid workmen for drink: $25" as a line in its list of building expenses.[42]

In the economy of charitable spending, the time that organizational leaders devoted to their work was a source of still additional lessons. The value of personal contact between charitable donor and recipient, strongly endorsed by benevolent women from the start, acquired even greater salience as many benevolent leaders intensified their groups' identification with evangelicalism during the 1810s and 1820s. An expressly evangelical faith that personal contact could transform clients' lives was one element in the evangelical turn that many groups took during those decades. Although they continued to distinguish between the undeserving and the deserving poor, women leaders also embraced the view that poverty could be a moral (or cultural) problem, and that temporal assistance provided by a caring spiritual adviser could help eradicate it. To their calculus of poverty's antidotes, including industry, frugality, modesty, self-help, and respectability, they added spiritual counsel and eventual conversion. And for the few blameless individuals, who were too young, too old, or too ill to need those remedies, religious visitors could relieve immediate want while also applying the soothing balm of consolation and nurturing the virtues of patience and submission. It was possible to imagine a world transformed by the power of feminine religious benevolence.[43]

Yet almost from its first glimmer, that dream threatened to dissipate in the face of changing urban realities, especially the limits of organizations' money and members' time. However much these women might imagine a personal benevolence bestowed through regular personal contact, by the 1820s population growth and geographical expansion seemed to be turning their vision into an evanescent mist. Their familiar cities were becoming unmanageable or unrecognizable. The opening of New York's Erie Canal in 1825 changed the city almost overnight. In 1822, Boston's newly created city government began to scrutinize rising poor relief costs and tax rates. In both cities, discussions about poverty moved to the center of urban political debate. In New York, the newly founded Society for the Prevention of Pauperism, led by influential male philanthropists such as Thomas Eddy, pointed a stern finger at private charities (many of which they themselves had created), suggesting that, along with public relief programs, charities actually helped promote and perpetuate the poverty they aimed to alleviate. In Boston, similar arguments reverberated as an energetic new mayor, Josiah Quincy, empowered by a new city charter, pursued a major overhaul of the public welfare system. Reform — of welfare and all forms of public relief and private charity — became the watchword of the decade.[44]

For their part, benevolent women generally echoed the newly unsentimental sentiment. With group resources seldom stretching to meet insistent demands and association donors more frequently asking for a careful accounting of their collective mite, benevolent women's public pronouncements reflected their common dilemma: how to provide temporal and spiritual assistance individually while coping with urban growth and a political climate hostile to charitable endeavors. In her annual remarks to New York's Society for the Relief of Poor Widows with Small Children, Hannah Caldwell blended observations on the increased numbers "who as widows and strangers have a claim on our benevolence" with concerns that expanding demands "precluded the Managers from paying that attention to each individual family" that would permit them "to convey instruction . . . to the immortal spirit." By 1819, the society had bought city maps for managers' use on visits to clients; in 1821 and again in 1840, the society hired a widow whose job it was to direct supplicating clients to managers. In 1823, the group suggested that making a "careful selection" among many deserving supplicants would be more likely to lead to "moral result[s]" than would continuing past practice. In 1824, the women set geographical limits on their benevolence, and in 1827 provided a carriage to enable two managers to visit all city neighborhoods served by the society.[45]

Although Boston remained geographically manageable, some of the city's benevolent women, confronting a shifting and increasingly (to them) alien population, turned to an old practice — residency tests — as a means of meeting their goals. In 1819 and again in 1825, the Fragment Society explicitly identified as preferred clients "our own poor," in contrast to the "multitudes of . . . Indigents," many of them "the poor of foreign nations," arriving daily in the city. In 1827, the women firmed up the preference by imposing a three-year residency rule. The Society for Employing the Female Poor had a two-year rule from its start in 1820. "Our own" meant something different to the Boston Children's Friend Society, whose officers decided in 1835 to exclude Roman Catholic children from further assistance. Bitterly denouncing the "insolence" of a local priest, who insisted that the children did not belong in a Protestant asylum, the women considered it "advisable to leave that people to provide for their poor from their abundant resources"; the society would "look more immediately to the necessities of our own." Their casual assertion that Catholics enjoyed "abundant resources," along with their expressed preference for assisting "our own" poor, revealed the women's acceptance of the new politics of poverty.[46]

The growth of white Roman Catholic and African American Protestant women's benevolent and mutual aid efforts in the 1820s, while following dynamics internal to those groups, constituted as well a direct challenge to such negative attitudes. As they gave their time to "the visiting of widows and orphans in their affliction" or "the improvement of the mind," African American and Catholic women sought to alter the public discourse that shaped representations of themselves. "I am a true-born American — your blood flows in my veins, and your spirit in my breast," declared Maria W. Stewart in 1832. Catholic leaders employed a similar strategy, rejecting portrayals of needy immigrants as "foreign poor," and instead presenting them as citizens, "persons of industry and of enterprise," who had "cleared [the country's] woods, built its houses, dug its canals, paved its streets, and superintended its literary seminaries" (and, they might have added, cooked its meals, nursed its children, laundered its clothes, and staffed its orphanages). Merely suffering "the vicissitudes of fortune" or needing "refuge in old age" should not render a citizen ineligible for charitable assistance. In addition, by identifying incidents of white Protestant intolerance or labeling Protestant women's groups hypocritical, they challenged those women's claims to universal, selfless benevolence and bourgeois respectability. Because an attempt by "those respectable ladies" of

New York's Asylum for Lying-In Women strictly to limit the number of Catholic clients was "actuated by the blindest, and most deplorable bigotry," argued the editor of the city's Irish newspaper, then their asylum was "a sectarian institution" not worthy of rank among "institutions designed for universal charity."[47]

But of course, challenging representations was not the same as changing them. The power to shape public discourses on poverty, foreignness, respectability, and sectarianism remained primarily in other hands, as did the ability to dispense most charitable assistance. In the changed urban climate of the 1820s and 1830s, as overt restriction and exclusion became the watchwords of groups that had long made claims, however spurious, to universality, white Protestant women's organizations began to spell out explicitly who would receive their donations. Whereas in the past, they might in practice have restricted client lists to whites, to Protestants, to long-term residents, or to children, now they made the restrictions explicit. And they underlined their efforts personally to visit clients on a regular basis, assuring donors that their redoubled vigilance produced only clients who were "respectable, and deserving of the bounty of the society." Moving a client population the within the walls of an asylum, refuge, or "home" was another narrowing strategy. In 1834, for example, New York's Association for the Relief of Respectable, Aged, Indigent Females first limited the number of regular aid recipients to 150 and then began planning an asylum—an old age home—for them. When completed in 1839, the building, set "apart from the noisy scenes of the city," had a capacity of only one hundred, on whom association members focused most of their time (while continuing to give small sums to another fifty or so still living at home). All clients, in addition, had to meet a three-year residency requirement. By the late 1830s, both existing and new organizations found the institution or the asylum an increasingly appealing and manageable form for their benevolent labors. Both New York's Protestant Half-Orphan Asylum, founded in 1835, and the Society for the Relief of Worthy, Aged, Indigent Colored Persons (1839) wrote planned homes into their constitutions, as did Boston's Children's Friend Society (1834); the New England Female Moral Reform Society (founded in 1835) opened its Temporary Home for Fallen Women in 1838.[48]

Other, noninstitutional approaches also reassured donors that organizational resources were properly husbanded. Asserting that they could quickly "discriminate between real and pretended want" by means of home visits, and simultaneously emphasizing their faith in the personal touch, organization leaders lengthened the lists of conditions that disqualified potential clients, including being "totally destitute and of the lowest grade" of poverty, marrying, refusing to work, begging, and lying. Even so, simply living in an "inaccessible" area, on a street of "disreputable character" or "bad reputation" or in urban "retreats of vice and infamy . . . improper for Ladies to visit," or spending too much time "in Streets where the Managers cannot visit with Propriety," rendered supplicants ineligible for assistance. As Christine Stansell has pointed out, decisions like these favored clients who closely resembled their bourgeois benefactors in their preference for the "retirement of the domestic circle" over the street, the "consolation" of religion over that of the bottle.[49]

Even so, the women's published reports offered repeated confessions that the "prying eye" of personal scrutiny was often inadequate to the task of separating worthy from unworthy applicants, and that restrictive policies could not stretch organizational resources to cover all worthy clients. Amid the growing cacophony of the antebellum city, charitable women publicly despaired of adequately distinguishing among the various appeals that fell on their ears. They offered recurring tales of applicants who lied, dissembled, or sold donated goods to buy liquor, and repeated legends about "foreign imposters" or "great numbers of aged poor . . . constantly emigrating from Europe" to impose upon generous, gullible native-born Americans. Increasingly, they adopted a political discourse that sought poverty's causes in personal inadequacies and found its solutions in a personal spiritual transformation. Likewise, the tight grip replaced the open hand in dispersing organizational largesse. When Bostonians create a central clearinghouse in 1834, the Committee of Delegates from Benevolent Societies, some twenty-two white Protestant women's and men's charities agreed to compare client lists in order to "detect imposition." By "getting rid of" unworthy recipients in this fashion, leaders of Boston's Fragment Society, Fatherless and Widows Society, Mite Society, and Widows' Society argued, they could "do more for those who come strictly within the letter of the constitution." Although New Yorkers attempted nothing comparable, by the 1850s, at least one women's charity thought it prudent to require an annual comparison of its rolls to that of the almshouse.[50] In these and other instances, organizational leaders budget-stretching preferences revealed a limited vision of what those who benefited most from the new economy owed to those who benefited least.

Wages, Prices, and Rents:
The Necessity of Charity

Yet this general endorsement of punitive or exclusionary policies was never complete, nor was it consistently uttered from year to year. Instead, women leaders experienced occasional faltering moments when they called into question their own easy assumption that the urban poor could be classified as either deserving or unworthy. Such moments occurred most frequently in times of economic crisis, and were especially commonplace during the 1830s. In those moments, their awareness of three volatile matters shaping the political economy of the antebellum city—rents, prices, and women's wages—led them to wonder, in the words of Sarah Josepha Hale, if what poor women needed was not charity, but "a charity of wages."[51]

Faith in paid labor as the ticket to female self-dependence was a recurring theme in benevolent society reports. "If employment could be found" for able-bodied poor women, suggested members of New York's Society for the Relief of Poor Widows with Small Children in 1803, "their distress would be alleviated, & their situation rendered more comfortable and independent." A decade later, the women's new House of Industry added "habits of virtuous activity" to the list of benefits; paid labor would also "do away with the necessity of begging, and foster self-respect in the honest poor." Without it, they later suggested, women who were merely poor would "sink to indigence," a state they deemed almost irredeemable. Work and especially wages, argued Sarah Josepha Hale in 1835, operated "like a charm to incite them to hope and energy." These women imagined few of their beneficiaries joining the ranks of independent artisans; their goal was to provide a "prop to poverty," a cushion against complete destitution, and an incentive to work rather than to beg at back doors or join the wretched throng at the almshouse. Poverty, in their minds, especially the respectable poverty they sought to support, was "in itself . . . not an evil, but essential to civilized life." If "the female poor" could "supply their own wants by their own exertions," suggested the Boston Society for Employing the Female Poor, then "the dependencies that so usefully and kindly subsist between the rich and the poor" could continue, with wage labor replacing handouts in the equation.

The belief that wage labor had the power to lift women out of indigence and into respectable poverty explains why proposals for workhouses, houses of industry, jobs programs, and employment bureaus—what would later be termed "workfare"—recurred regularly throughout the era. Despite the contrary experiences of women in their own and other cities, each new work-based proposal arrived with faith and hope that it could be the substitute for charity. Charitable institutions could be accused of simply "widening the breach they mean to close," suggested the women of New York's House of Industry in 1819, employing a wisdom that had already become conventional. "No such objections" tainted their work project. Likewise denouncing "the pernicious effects of those systems of charity, which hold out to the poor the hope of support without self-exertion," Sarah J. Hale announced that her new Seamen's Aid Society would be different. Through "the furnishing of work" to sailors' wives, widows, and daughters, the society offered "the best and most effectual charity," that of wages, she wrote, offering no acknowledgement that the Society for Employing the Female Poor was still struggling, even as she dipped her nib into the inkwell, to "excite and reward industry" by providing "a frugal subsistence" through paid labor.[52]

When the supply of laborers outran the demand for their labor, however, benevolent women's confidence in the magical power of waged work flagged, and they occasionally questioned their own assumptions. During the "peculiar situation" wrought by the War of 1812, for example, as the numbers of poor widows seeking work began to overwhelm them, the New York society relieving poor respectable widows became "thoroughly convinced . . . that it is an impossibility for a widow, with the labour of her own hands, to support her infant family." A group of them soon proposed the House of Industry to tackle the problem. Five years later, "richer in experience and poorer in funds," they had to close it. Despite a three-fold increase in the numbers of "workwomen" applying for work, a precipitous drop in retail prices cut the value of the goods the workers had spun, woven, sewed, and knit, rendering the House of Industry insolvent. Providing poor wives and mothers with regular, paying work as an alternative to charity required, it seemed, plenty of pump-priming funds (the House of Industry collected almost $8,500 in donations alone between 1814 and 1819) and countless hours of unpaid labor contributed by charitable benefactors. Once again, in 1837, the Society for the Relief of Poor Widows with Small Children cited "the want of employment" the preceding winter as the reason "many respectable" self-supporting widows "were unwillingly obliged to seek assistance from" them. Being willing to work and being able to find work were two different things.[53]

Even relatively prosperous times, when jobs were available, could spark nagging questions, if benevolent leaders noticed wage differentials between women and men. The 1826 report of New York's Society for the Relief of Poor Widows, for example, rebutted the argument that anyone could make a decent living by noting that while men were "well paid" for their labor, women often earned only twenty-five cents per day. There followed the story of a widow struggling to support six children, four of them crippled. The 1829 report was more explicit: when a male breadwinner died, "in a moment the individual is reduced from a comfortable living to absolute poverty"; moreover, the "low rate of wages" ensured that in seeking to support "her helpless children, . . . even with every exertion, she cannot make more than is barely sufficient." The ideal solution, of course, was to marry another breadwinner. And surely some ladies listening to the report in the Brick Presbyterian Church Session Room that November evening, or reading it in their comfortable parlors on a December day, experienced a chill as they considered their own economic dependence, their own vulnerability. Perhaps a collective shudder ran through those attending a January meeting when they voted a ten-dollar gift to former donors, "reared in the bosom . . . of affluence" but now reduced by the death of a breadwinner "to the labor of their own hands for subsistence."[54]

In raising as an issue "the low rate of wages" paid to women, the New Yorkers partially challenged the terms of the well-developed discourse on poverty, its causes and its cures. Like Matthew Carey, the Philadelphia reformer whose writings on the wage system introduced the issue into public consciousness, the women situated poor women's dilemma, not merely in their difficulty of finding wage work, but also in the price female labor-power commanded. This was a new awareness. Until the late 1820s, these women and others like them evinced little concern over wage rates; their focus had been on creating or providing work at the going rate, or even less. In 1817, for example, the women of New York's House of Industry had expressed no objection when a City Council committee, in approving a $400 donation, advised them to "regulate . . . the price of labour" and strictly limit the number of "Articles manufactured" in order to balance their books. Boston's Society for Employing the Female Poor was explicit about its practice of paying "considerably lower than the ordinary rate of wages" to its clients. At the same time, by charging market rates to its customers, the society sought to avoid undercutting washerwomen and seamstresses who contracted for their services on the open labor market, or further depressing women's wages. In theory, the society's customers would shift unpaid family labor into the paid labor market, thereby "add[ing] to the stock of labour," not forcing poor women to compete for scarce jobs. In actuality, of course, benevolently inclined housewives often did precisely the latter by switching the family washing from an independent contractor to the society's workers. The low price paid to female labor received little attention from these women. During the 1810s and 1820s, concern about the issue came almost exclusively from labor reformers such as Carey and women workers themselves; Louise Mitchell, leader of New York's United Tailoresses' Society, underscored "the inequality of our wages with that of men," in a speech that pronounced women needleworkers "literally *slaves*" lacking both "liberty" and "Independence."[55]

After 1830, however, benevolent society reports included more frequent remarks on women's wages. They ranged from the empathetic, such as those in the 1829 report of the Society for the Relief of Poor Widows, to the openly angry denunciations that marked Sarah Josepha Hale's annual accounts of the Seamen's Aid Society. Beginning in 1834 with pointed remarks derived from her reading of Carey ("the best and most effectual charity would be the furnishing of work at a *just* price"), Hale quickly moved on to more fiery language, complete with italics, capital letters, exclamation marks, and lengthy footnotes. "Combinations of selfish men are formed to beat down the price of female labor," she charged in 1836, "and then forsooth, they call the diminished rate the market price." She pledged her organization's utmost exertions until "it should be accounted a shame for any one, who writes himself *man*, to make a fortune out of the handy-work of poor females!" Challenging "the creed of political economists . . . that the market price of labor is the just price," in 1840 she singled out federal government military uniform contracts as important influences on wage rates, and proposed a minimum payment of about twenty-five cents per day to each female shirt-sewer, hardly enough to ensure her comfort, but enough to "keep her from starving." One of the most lucrative of those contracts, ironically enough, belonged to the Irish immigrant entrepreneur Andrew Carney, who became wealthy during the depression of the late 1830s precisely by "beating down the price of female labor" (to use Hale's language); Carney became a real estate investor and a generous donor to Boston's Catholic charities. Despite the remarkably confused nature of Hale's analysis—she advocated simultaneously for wage work as an incentive to industry and for barely-above-starvation wages—her influence was evident. Organizations as different as the New York and New England Female Moral Reform Societies, the Boston Fatherless and Widows Society, and the Boston Fragment Society echoed her arguments in varying tonalities.[56]

Along with wages, prices and rents came in for their share of critical commentary in 1830s discussions of poverty. Previously merely a subject for passing notation—they rose, fell, or remained stable—in the 1830s both became topics for collective handwringing, especially during the hard times of the depression. Rent "among the poor is often extravagantly high," one organization leader informed members in 1835, proposing an asylum to concentrate the group's elderly beneficiaries and save labor and travel for its officials. "The very poorest people" living in "mean, wretched tenements" paid "rents nearly double in proportion to those paid by the occupants of elegant dwellings," announced Sarah Hale. Information on the hardships that high city rents imposed usually came as news to members, who learned that escalating costs drove elderly women to urban fringes where they no longer qualified for assistance, or forced working widows to use the bulk of their earnings on hovel-like dwellings. Injunctions to beneficiaries about emulating middle-class organizations' frugality were likely to ring hollow when urban commodity prices rose, as Sarah Hale noted pointedly. Not only did impoverished people pay 20 to 100 percent more than their affluent neighbors (because they could not buy groceries in bulk or winter fuel in summer), but some were "obliged to buy tea by the ounce, wood by the foot, and coal by the peck." Some, indeed, purchased "wood by the *stick*."[57]

Printed conversations about rents and prices, like those dealing with wages, devoted some lines to possible solutions. Few of the proposals, however, challenged in any fundamental way the economic arrangements that rendered women's wages, urban rents, and commodity prices so problematic. By focusing on their particular group of clients, benevolent society leaders generally avoided considering the broader questions that arose when they bemoaned high rents and low wages. Meliorative solutions, or assumptions that little could be done, held sway. Proposals for low-cost tenement apartments or asylums serving limited numbers of clients, however heartfelt in their concerns or thoughtful in their planning, did little to address the fundamental causes of poor women's desperate plight. And despite Sarah Hale's fiery rhetoric and tough-minded compassion, the Seamen's Aid Society had relatively little new to offer women and girls attempting to support themselves in a sex-segregated wage economy, where a stick of wood or a few square feet of living space could, at the drop of a sewing needle, be priced beyond their pockets. By 1840, Hale and her energetic coworkers were not only running a sewing business offering higher payments than the local "slop-shops," and operating a school at which sailors' daughters studied "the common branches of an English education . . . needlework, . . . [and] the social, moral and religious duties of females," they were working on a bulk-buying scheme to lower the cost of winter fuel for clients, and on contracting with the Navy Bureau of Provisions and Clothing to sew uniforms for solid wages. Worthy projects, all. (See Figure 5.4.) But even at the height of their exertions, the women served at most sixty seamstresses and thirty schoolgirls; moreover, the school closed in 1844 for want of funds, and the Navy contract, once secured, expired without renewal.[58]

These examples suggest just how intractable were the economic conditions that groups such as the Seamen's Aid Society attempted to meliorate; they also underline the extent to which Hale and other concerned organization leaders were enmeshed in contemporary assumptions about the role and the value of women's labor-power within family and urban economies alike. A breadwinner herself, fighting tooth and nail for her own right (and that of other women)

SEAMEN'S AID SOCIETY

CLOTHING STORE,

UNDER THE SEAMEN'S BETHEL,

NORTH SQUARE, BOSTON.

THE Society still keep constantly for sale a good assortment of ready-made Garments for Seamen and other gentlemen, comprising, among other articles, *Fine Shirts, Cotton do., Flannel do., Gingham do., Bosoms and Dickeys, Fancy Silk Handkerchiefs, Stocks, Cravats, Gloves and Hosiery, Hats, Drawers, Boots and Shoes, Frock Coats, Vests, Round Jackets, Pea do., Monkey do., Pantaloons, Trousers, Storm Oil Dresses, Life Preservers, Cork Mattresses, Blankets, &c. &c.*

Seamen going to sea can be supplied, at short notice, with Chests, and every suitable article to fill them.

The Store is established by a Society of Ladies, for the following purposes:

1st. To assist in *relieving the sick and disabled Seamen,* and their suffering families.

2d. To afford aid and encouragement to the poor and industrious females belonging to the families of Seamen.

3d. To promote the education of Seamen's children and improve the condition of Seamen and their families.

The establishment is therefore entirely devoted to the benefit of Seamen and their families. The garments are all made by the wives, widows, and daughters of Seamen, who are employed by the Society, and *paid a just price* for their labor. The articles are warranted to be well made, and of the best quality. Those who purchase, need fear no imposition; and the profits are to be wholly employed in doing good to the unfortunate, promoting the comfort, and encouraging the improvement of Seamen and their families.

Seamen, and the friends of Seamen, will you not call at the Store of the Seamen's Aid Society?

FIGURE 5.4. Back cover of the Boston Seamen's Aid Society's 1843 *Annual Report* advertising its clothing store, designed to provide work for sailors' wives, widows, and daughters. Note the assurance, in the next to last paragraph, that seamstresses would be "*paid a just price* for their labor." (Courtesy of the Library Company of Philadelphia)

to earn a living from genteel feminine pursuits such as writing, Hale never-theless could not escape the unquestioned assumption that women's labor within family economies would usually be secondary, nor the belief that the work force should be sex-segregated, and that feminine work should command lower wages than masculine. Despite her deep concern for the sailors' wives and widows whom her organization sought to assist, Hale had little power to keep the Andrew Carneys of Boston from buying poor seamstresses' labor-power at the lowest possible rate. And despite her own experience as a wid-owed mother supporting five children, Hale's notion of a just wage for seam-stresses was three dollars a week.[59]

Conclusion

Working women themselves had their own notions of charity and just wages or prices. Some, such as Louise Mitchell and her compatriots in the United Tai-loresses' Society, attempted to form unions for the benefit of women workers as a group. Although short-lived, their associations articulated an alternative anal-ysis of the new economy, one that directly questioned "the inequality of our wages with that of men" and thereby challenged middle-class women's casual assumption that wage labor in and of itself secured economic independence. Asserting "their just claims to a share of the boasted Independence" through a living wage (as opposed to a woman's wage), these women formulated a vision of themselves very different from the depictions found in even the most sym-pathetic middle-class organizational reports. Not the starving seamstresses rep-resented so pitiably in Sarah Hale's writings, and in the pages of innumerable novels, these were self-reliant wage earners associating together to pursue their rights as women workers. Some years later, a Boston working woman went one step further, holding up for contempt the twenty-five cent daily wage offered by "the charitable institutions of the city," and asking what price charity ex-tracted from women workers, in the "loss of self-respect, of independence."[60]

However brave these women's words and deeds, the rugged topography of working-class life required sturdy survival strategies. For most, these included wage work for all eligible family members, self-protection through mutual aid societies, charity for the neediest within their communities, and when possible, the use of wealthier women's benevolence to help them manage their family economies. For as Peter Mandler has shrewdly observed, "poverty and charity went hand in hand as integral parts of urban life" in the nineteenth century, but "the aims of charity are not the same as its uses." In the ongoing dance of urban survival, poor women continually sought to choreograph middle-class women's charitable impulses to meet their own purposes. The ladies of the Boston Female Asylum confronted this reality in 1841 when they found their orphanage numbers declining, "notwithstanding a rapidly increasing population among which there is a full proportion of the poor." After forty years of sheltering girls between the ages of three and twelve (386 had walked through the asylum door since its opening), then indenturing them until age eighteen, the women found only three families in the entire city willing to commit their daughters to their care. Poor families that might once have sent their daughters for training and education now preferred to send them out to service themselves. After all, when "a capable girl, long before she is Eighteen can obtain wages . . . [and] the feeling of independence" attendant upon wage earning, why should her family surrender her to an asylum offering only "to clothe and instruct [her] . . . in return for her services?" Facing the music, the women amended their rules to include cash payments at the completion of a girl's indenture and an expanded definition of who qualified to enter the asylum. In this and other instances, poor women's family designs and needs, including the search for living wages, forced alterations in charitable rules and practices.[61]

The one-page financial statements that organizations' treasurers prepared each year could never quite capture the changing world that this decision revealed. While accumulating their "donation fund" of $73,573 (about $12.5 million today), the women of the Boston Female Asylum never connected the economy that facilitated their wealth accumulation with the economy within which their clients sought work, lodging, and sustenance. Although they themselves hired and paid adult servants in their homes, they were genuinely troubled that many families to whom they indentured twelve-year-olds sought only "to obtain a selfish convenience—the most service at the least price," and thereby "in the idea of the servant lose sight of the child." And although they knew that a girl might derive a fleeting "feeling of independence" from earning cash wages, they believed that their own unselfish civic labor in caring for children offered an alternative to a world in which money was the primary measure of value. Perhaps it did. But as they learned, their clients' evaluated such alternatives differently. However warmly they offered and delivered their benevolence, to their clients it often provided cold comfort indeed.[62]

T he stories recounted here—both of organizations and of women—
had their counterparts in other American cities. From Worcester
to Philadelphia, Petersburg to Charleston, women in the new
nation formed associations to achieve personal and group goals,
and in the process shaped new experiences, representations, and
expectations of womanhood. The enduring power of such experiences and expectations could also be found in later settlements—whether Rochester or
Chicago, Denver or San Francisco—as women formed associations almost at
the moment the barge, prairie schooner, clipper ship, or railway carriage
reached its destination. Some indeed were sister and daughter organizations to
those in New York and Boston, as family circumstances lifted individuals from
familiar streets and set them down in raw lanes, cleared fields, and newly built
houses across the country. Transplanted by marriage to Jacksonville, Illinois,
New Yorker Elizabeth Caldwell Smith Duncan, for instance, replicated the
career patterns she had learned from her mother and her aunts, all key leaders of New York benevolent associations. In addition to bearing and rearing
nine children, she labored for a Maternal Association, sewing society, colonization society, Ladies Education Society (promoting girls' schooling), and
temperance society. Similarly, Serena DeGrasse Downing carried her
mother's example into antislavery and civil rights activism in Newport and
Providence, Rhode Island.[1]

As in New York and Boston, the women's associations that arose independently throughout the antebellum North could almost have been cut from the same cloth. Once a first generation had outlined the pattern, organizations founded and run by women became legitimate, recognizable, and permanent elements of urban life. Assuming responsibility for solving some of the social problems facing the new republic, their leaders married collective feminine responsibility for the common weal to a distinctly evangelical vision of womanhood, offered welfare services to poor women and children, provided mutual assistance in poor neighborhoods, and (in the 1830s) undertook radical reform efforts. Once early associational leaders had learned to piece their domestic and organizational responsibilities together into a seamless whole, their successors could—and did—repeat the pattern, fill in the details, or vary the model. Women moving to new towns or coming of age in middle-class families could assume the existence of organizational networks and incorporate organizational leadership into their own domestic lives. Working-class women could hope to join a mutual aid society and perhaps depend on middle-class benevolence if their wages shriveled so much as to preclude dues payments. By the 1840s, individuals and local associations had begun to create a small but significant number of national women's networks laboring for causes as varied as fund-raising for home and foreign missions, protecting or rescuing urban female migrants, abolishing slavery, and expanding free women's legal rights.

Wherever they arose in the urban North, women's associations embodied and disseminated new ideas about gender, ideas befitting an era of democratic republicanism and market capitalism. Through their organizations, women leaders expressed their understanding of their combined class, racial, and gender identities. Through their organizations, too, women helped make political and economic change comprehensible, especially through a new ideology emphasizing women's difference from men but permitting women's groups to assume quasi-masculine roles in politics and the economy. The gender ideology of the antebellum years, which posited the existence of male and female "spheres," functioned to mitigate some of the contradictions within the new political and economic order, especially women's subordinate status, the interlocked nature of the family and market economies, and the power that some women exercised over other women. Women's associations offered their members opportunities to act politically to help shape the nation's present and future, and to participate directly in the new economy of investment and wealth accumulation, but as elements in the collectivity, not as independent citizens.[2]

Individuals' enthusiastic response to these opportunities was evident in the broad spectrum of associations they formed. Like New York and Boston, cities as varied as Chicago, Providence, Rochester, Utica, Philadelphia, and Worcester were home to prominent benevolent groups led by middle-class white Protestants, small but significant numbers of reform associations, Catholic laywomen's parish societies, and working-class mutual aid societies. Uniformly, Protestant benevolence occupied "the most acceptable, applauded, and affluent" space on the spectrum. Uniformly, too, separate networks of women leaders labored for particular causes, often in ignorance of each other's activities. And despite the example of Rebecca Gratz in Philadelphia, Jewish and Catholic women found it nearly impossible to scale the walls of religious exclusivity that surrounded the largest coterie of organizations in most cities: Protestant benevolent associations. Thus, although one can pinpoint local variations in patterns of organizing in the North, the variations were in the detail, not in the overall form. In some cities, for instance, maternal associations were more prominent than in others. Similarly, whereas both women and men formed missionary and tract societies, and women constituted the majority of Sunday school teachers, women's Sunday school organizations were short-lived, while women's missionary associations flourished.[3]

By 1820, southern as well as northern women had embraced the organizational form. But although women leaders in Charleston as well as Boston helped broaden the field of social action available to themselves and their coworkers, southern free women's organizational compass was never as expansive as that of their northern counterparts. Significant differences marked the shape of women's associations in the North and South, as well as the behavior and experiences of women leaders and the possibilities contained within the organizational form. Most notably, the range of associations found in Charleston or Richmond was considerably narrower than in New York and Boston. The slave labor–based economies of southern towns and cities simply had no place for certain types of organizations. Charleston might have its Female Domestic Missionary Society and Ladies Benevolent Society, Petersburg its Female Orphan Asylum, and Richmond its ladies' auxiliary to the American Colonization Society, but in no part of the South was it possible to form permanent associations devoted to undermining slavery. Free women abolitionists became expatriates. Even women's colonization societies, which used collective petitions to voice some faint disquiet over the slavery system, did so largely by appealing for the protection of elite white women and the creation of a lily-white region. Moreover, by the late 1830s, along with sympathetic coworkers in the North, they had turned their energies away from petitioning and toward fundraising for Liberian girls' education. To be sure, southern white women's associations received showers of praise and encouragement from the men of the region, but only so long as they confined themselves to a narrow range of (mostly) charitable labors and did nothing to question the larger economic and legal institutions that structured the privileged position of whites. In the South, even more than in the North, women's associations served to reinforce unequal class relations and inequalities among women, although women leaders in both regions often spoke the same language of femininity.[4]

The urban reform organizations that emerged in the 1830s were an especially northern phenomenon. Completely absent from the South, antislavery, moral reform, and radical temperance societies nevertheless took different shapes in different northern cities. The contrast between New York's and Boston's female antislavery societies, for example—the one cautiously unwilling to stray too far onto the path toward racial and gender egalitarianism, the other blazing the trail—represents one of the starkest differences between two cities that in many respects followed similar organizational models. Philadelphia's female abolitionists had yet another experience, managing to avoid the bitterly divisive battles that sundered the Boston group and the fear of alienating evangelicals that rendered the New York group ineffective. Both united and effective, the Philadelphia women labored harmoniously for decades, not only within their own organization but also as members of gender-integrated antislavery societies. With a significant and visible black membership, and a strong representation of both black and white Hicksite Quakers, the Philadelphia women shaped their own version of a social reform organization. Indeed, the presence or absence of Quaker women—especially Hicksite and Congregational Friends—might be seen as a central factor shaping the character of social reform circles. As David Brion Davis and others have demonstrated, Quakers were among the first groups to challenge millennia-old assumptions about the naturalness of human inequality and to imagine the possibility of radical equality, including women's equality with men.[5]

The emergence of these antislavery and moral reform associations sparked fierce debates both within and without the meeting rooms, lecture halls, and convention centers where women met. The resulting renegotiations of gender ideology and gender relations, of boundaries between "public" and "private" life and between "political" and "partisan" activities, refashioned existing patterns of women's organizing in the urban North and drew new models. Like the 1790s, the 1830s were a crucial decade in the history of women's organizing. If by creating permanent associations in the 1790s some women opened up new fields of social action that they and their successors could traverse familiarly for decades, others in the 1830s sought to claim and mark off new expanses and by doing so to challenge restrictive codes about race and gender.

After 1840, women's associations and associational networks were both the same and different from what they had been earlier. Citywide Roman Catholic laywomen's societies lost much of their rationale once institutions run by nuns gained access to public funds. Increasingly, nuns claimed both the city and the parish as their territory, while laywomen served primarily the parish and neighborhood. In 1870s New York, for example, St. Joseph's Industrial Home, at which the Sisters of Mercy cared for 900 children, received 96 percent of its funding ($77,000 in 1880) from the city. Laywomen's associations now took the form of devotional societies (sodalities and confraternities) and parish charitable organizations; gone were the Ladies Association of the Roman Catholic Benevolent Society and the Roman Catholic Association for the Children of Widows and Widowers, which in the 1820s and 1830s had brought laywomen together from across the city to support two orphanages staffed by nuns. Not until the turn of the twentieth century would Catholic laywomen begin to form urban Catholic women's leagues and national associations to represent their interests as laywomen.[6]

Among Protestants, networks of missionary, Bible, and charitable organizations devoted to spiritual and temporal service continued to represent respectable feminine benevolence. And while some women reformers pursued careers that took them into gender-integrated (though never fully equal) associations, others found new forms of woman-only labor more in keeping with their ideals, beliefs, and personalities. Martha and Lucy Ball, the white sister-schoolteachers who had taught a school for African American girls in the 1830s and had been significant leaders of the Boston Female Anti-Slavery Society, took a different road from their coworker Maria Weston Chapman when the Female Anti-Slavery Society split in 1840. Whereas Chapman enthusiastically embraced gender-integrated antislavery associations, the Ball sisters turned their energies to supporting men's antislavery labors and women's missions, but especially toward the rescue of young white women through moral reform. When she died in 1894, Martha Ball left the proceeds of a lifetime of paid work to groups that were the labors of her love: the Woman's Baptist Foreign Missionary Society, the Woman's American Baptist Home Mission Society, the New England Moral Reform Society, the Ladies' Baptist Bethel Society, the Woman's Union Missionary Society of America for Heathen Lands, the Clarendon Street Baptist Church Sabbath School Fund, and the Boston Woman's Christian Temperance Union.[7]

Martha Ball's membership in the Woman's Christian Temperance Union (WCTU), founded in 1874, and in the Woman's American Baptist Home Mission Society (WABHMS), founded in 1878, bore significant connections to her antebellum voluntary career. With its interest in protecting women from behavior identified with masculine culture (prostitution, the sexual and physical abuse of women) and in establishing a single (feminine) standard of sexual morality, the WCTU represented some of the same strains in social reform that the Boston Female Anti-Slavery Society and Boston Female Moral Reform Society had championed. But with its unambiguous endorsement of women's suffrage, it stepped into politics in ways that Martha would not earlier have envisioned or sanctioned. Moreover, it was a national association, centrally organized with state and local affiliates in both North and South—something quite unknown in her younger days. Through its sponsorship of African American women missionaries in the South and its encouragement of their speaking tours in New England and the Midwest, the WABHMS directly tapped two significant elements in Martha's abolitionism: her deep religiosity and her interest in the "elevation" of the "colored population." Perhaps most notably, Martha's simultaneous involvement in local Boston groups, regional New England associations, and a nationally organized "women's crusade" for temperance and suffrage represented one of the new possibilities for women's voluntary action in the postbellum era.[8]

In her later years, Martha labored in the company only of other white women. If the African American women who had been her associates in the Boston Female Anti-Slavery Society disappeared from the meetings that Martha and her sister Lucy attended, they continued to serve as members of African American women's associations, community leaders, church workers, and political actors. Lavinia Ames Hilton and her sister Eunice Ames Davis, along with their daughters and granddaughters, remained devoted to the antislavery cause, fought to desegregate Boston's public schools, and in the postbellum years, joined the new women's clubs and associations that engaged the energies of black women and embodied their own ideas about racial "uplift." Eunice, who died in 1900 at age one hundred, also claimed her right to join the new Daughters of the American Revolution (founded in 1892); the Ames sisters' father, Prince Alexander Ames, had served his country in the War for Independence.[9]

By 1894, when Martha Ball died, many possibilities for voluntary action were available in Boston and other northern cities. Indeed, the visibility of new women's voluntary groups often overshadowed the continuing role of older-style benevolent societies in providing charitable assistance to urban residents, rescuing prostitutes and unmarried pregnant girls, or selling women's handiwork at urban exchanges. The new undertakings went by modern-sounding names such as "settlement houses" and "scientific charity" or, by the early twentieth century, "social work." Many of the new associations were considerably more visible on urban landscapes, as they constructed apartment houses and boardinghouses, club buildings, exchange rooms, and work spaces, and plunked them down on busy downtown thoroughfares. As Sarah Deutsch has suggested, women now filled and "enjoyed urban spaces they had created themselves," rather than spaces "created for them." Increasingly, women volunteers supported the work of paid professionals, who themselves were often educated white single women pursuing careers as scientifically trained experts who knew how to do "case work." (Black women social workers were usually married and involved simultaneously in professional careers and voluntary community labor.) Increasingly, too, women volunteers could sense the subtle inexorable shift that turned the tables on them; labor that had once been valuable because it was voluntary and unpaid now seemed sentimental, old-fashioned, unscientific.[10]

In the new era, if few antebellum organizations survived in their original form, many of them nevertheless found ways to adjust to new conditions. Their adaptations are perhaps best seen in their changing names. Antebellum founders thought it natural, when seeking to describe their organizations, to combine words like "female" and "ladies" with words like "benevolent," "asylum," "refuge," "mite," and "relief." And when they described their clients as "respectable, aged, indigent females," "lying-in women," "half-orphans," "penitent females," "poor widows with small children," or "the sick poor," they imagined that they were simply being precise. By the 1890s, most such organizational names had disappeared, along with the memorable biblical terms that women founders had once so reflexively employed. Groups such as the Abyssinian Benevolent Daughters of Esther Association, whose name at once evoked an ancient African nation and a woman who saved an entire people from annihilation, were succeeded by more prosaically named societies, such as the Woman's Convention. The Society for the Relief of Poor Widows with Small Children became simply the Society for the Relief of Women and Children; Boston's Female Asylum in 1910 changed its name to the Society for the Care of Girls, and then merged in 1923 with the city's Children's Aid Society. Similarly, Boston's Children's Friend Society, after becoming an adoption agency, merged with the Children's Services Association in 1960. None of the moral reform or prostitute-rescue societies maintained its original mission. Instead, like the Penitent Females' Refuge (renamed the Bethesda Society in 1854) and new "homes" established by Roman Catholic nuns, they shifted their attention to "wayward" or "homeless" girls and single mothers. The Female Benevolent Society endures today as Inwood House; the New York Female Moral Reform Society became the American Female Guardian Society and then Woodycrest Youth Services; Martha Ball's New England Female Moral Reform Society eventually became the Talitha Cumi Maternity Home and Hospital before closing in the 1960s. At the start of the twenty-first century, New York's Graham-Windham Services continues the work of the Orphan Asylum Society, while Boston's Fragment and Widows' Societies still survive under their original names.

Two hundred years after the founding of the earliest permanent women's organizations, and one hundred years after the emergence of professional social work, Americans still debate the value of unpaid volunteer labor and the role of voluntary civic associations in the larger life of the nation. My findings should cause readers to think hard about the interests that specific voluntary associations serve, the exclusions they practice, and the mechanisms whereby they claim to speak for the common weal.[11] There can be little doubt that when small groups of women in the 1790s created permanent organizations, they took an extraordinary historical step, one that forever altered the social field in which women could undertake collective religious, political, ideological, and economic activities. That move had unintended consequences, as subsequent groups with very different goals reworked the organizational form into new shapes, including working-class women's self-help and labor associations and societies devoted to radical social reform. Still, the best-funded and most densely connected associations in antebellum New York and Boston, the groups that spoke into politicians' ears and pressed city fathers to allocate tax monies for their benefit, were those led by the wealthiest and most privileged women. The ability of such women leaders to wield political and economic power, even if never as unalloyed as that of their husbands and fathers, nevertheless set them off from their less well situated sisters and reinforced differences in the conditions of their lives, deepening the chasms of religion, race, class, and legal status that separated them from each other.

Women's Organizations

New York

Year	Organization	Programs
1797	Society for the Relief of Poor Widows with Small Children	Provided winter relief to widows with at least two children under age ten; ran a school; opened a workroom to provide wage work to widows
1798	Female Association	A Quaker charitable organization; later opened a day school and a sewing school for girls
1806	Orphan Asylum Society	Began as an orphanage for Widows' Society clients; eventually admitted other white children; one-third to one-half of clients had one living parent
1813	Female Assistance Society	A Methodist charitable organization "for the relief & instruction of the sick poor"

	Association for the Relief of Respectable, Aged, Indigent Females	Provided small annuities to elderly single and widowed white women (some of them superannuated servants); in the 1830s opened an old age home for clients
1814	Female Society for the Aid of Foreign Missions	Raised money to send to the American Board of Commissioners for Foreign Missions; appears to have been short-lived
	House of Industry	Ran a workroom providing jobs to impoverished women; closed in 1820
1816	Female Union Society for the Promotion of Sabbath Schools	Opened Sunday schools taught by volunteer teachers; published materials for their use; taught literacy to white and black adult women; dissolved in 1828 and transferred its schools to the New-York Sunday-School Union Society
	Female Auxiliary Bible Society	Raised money to buy Bibles (through the American Bible Society) and distribute them in poor neighborhoods; later offered charitable relief and visits to poor
	Female Missionary Society	Raised money for city missions; became involved in building urban mission chapels
1817	Ladies Association Auxiliary to Roman Catholic Benevolent Society	A laywomen's organization raising money for the Roman Catholic Orphan Asylum and especially for the religious order running the asylum
1818	Maternal Association	Brought mothers together for monthly child-rearing discussions and prayer
1820	Female Hebrew Benevolent Society	A charitable society affiliated with Temple Shearith Israel
1822	Female Tract Society	A women's auxiliary to the Religious Tract Society; raised money for tracts and charity
1823	Asylum for Lying-In Women	Opened a birth center for "respectable married women" as an alternative to the almshouse

1820s	Daughters of Israel	An African American women's mutual benefit society
1827	Infant School Society	Provided day care for children (aged eighteen months to six years) of poor working mothers; taught religion, reading, and numbers
	African Dorcas Association	Raised money and sewed clothing for children attending the African School
1829	Roman Catholic Asylum for the Children of Widows and Widowers	An orphanage for "half-orphans" founded by laywomen; supported the religious order that staffed the orphanage
1831	Female Asylum Society	Short-lived group; visited a Magdalen Asylum run by men; see Female Benevolent Society, 1832
	United Tailoresses' Society	A short-lived union of skilled female garment workers
1832	Female Bethel Union	Provided assistance and religious instruction to sailors and their families
	Female Branch of Zion	A charitable society affiliated with the AME Zion Church
	Daughters of Abyssinia	A.k.a. Rising Daughters of Abyssinia; a mutual aid society at the Abyssinian Baptist Church
	Female Benevolent Society	Opened a refuge for repentant prostitutes; split in 1834 when the Moral Reform Society was founded
1833	Female Mite Society	A charitable society at the AME Zion Church
	Ladies' Depository	Sold genteel clients' needlework at a "depository" or retail store

1834	Female Moral Reform Society	Founded by dissident members of the Female Benevolent Society, it attacked prostitution by challenging the double standard, criticizing male sexual behavior, and publishing a newspaper; eventually became the national American Female Guardian Society
	Colored Ladies Literary Society	A.k.a. Female Literary Association; a book-discussion and essay-writing group; also raised money for abolitionist causes
	Female Baptist Association	A charitable association at the Abyssinian Baptist Church
1835	Protestant Half-Orphan Asylum	Ran an orphanage for white children with one deceased parent
	Ladies' New York City Anti-Slavery Society	Affiliated with the American Anti-Slavery Society; raised money for the cause and sponsored abolitionist speakers; the leadership was all white
1836	Colored Orphan Asylum	Founded by white women; provided a home for African American orphans
	United Daughters of Conference	Supported the work of the AME Zion Church
1837	Juvenile Daughters of Rush	Named for Christopher Rush, pastor of the AME Zion Church; a mutual aid society
	Society for the Support of Schools in Africa	Founded by white women, it raised money to "colonize" freed slaves in Liberia and support schools for girls in Liberia
1838	Female Assistant Benefit Society	An African American mutual benefit society
	Female Education Society of the First Presbyterian Church of Color	Raised money to support the church, promote girls' education, and assist candidates for the ministry

	Ladies Association for the General Instruction of Children of the Jewish Persuasion	Raised money to educate children of Shearith Israel congregation (Protestant groups were attempting to convert them by offering free schooling)
1839	Abyssinian Benevolent Daughters of Esther Association	A mutual aid society located at the Abyssinian Baptist Church
	Society for the Relief of Worthy, Aged, Indigent Colored Persons	Founded by white women; ran an old age home that took elderly impoverished African Americans from the almshouse
1840	Tappan Female Benevolent Society	A charitable society located at the First Colored Presbyterian Church; named for Arthur Tappan, a white abolitionist
	Manhattan Abolition Society	A.k.a. Manhattan Anti-Slavery Society; a biracial, gender-integrated abolition society
1841	Colored Female Vigilance Committee	An auxiliary to a men's organization; aided runaway slaves
	Female Trading Association	An African American women's group; ran a shop in which all goods sold were products of "free labor" (i.e., not produced by slaves)
	Martha Washington and Lady Howard Temperance Benevolent Societies	Women's auxiliaries to men's societies, formed by working-class white women; promoted total abstinence and provided mutual aid to members' families

Boston

Year	Organization	Programs
1800	Female Asylum	Ran an orphanage for white girls over age three, most of whom were indentured at age twelve
	Female Society for Missionary Purposes	Initially collected money for Baptist and Congregationalist missions; in 1817, began sponsoring missions to the city's poor

1811	Corban Society	Raised money to send ministerial students to Congregationalist seminaries; sewed clothing for seminarians
1812	Fragment Society	Aided indigent sick women and children by giving or lending clothing and bedding
1814	Female Auxiliary Bible Society	Initially collected money to buy Bibles; in the 1820s, began visiting and aiding the poor
1815	Female Society for Promoting Christianity among the Jews	Collected money for a London missionary society; later supported a missionary in the Middle East
1816	Widows' Society	Aided "destitute and infirm widows and aged single women of good character" who were reduced from affluence to poverty
	Female Tract Society	Collected money to print and distribute religious tracts and pamphlets
	Female Auxiliary Society for the Moral and Religious Instruction of the Poor	A Sunday School organization auxiliary to a men's organization
1817	Fatherless and Widows Society	Gave winter relief (food, fuel, clothing) to widows and their children
	Graham Society	Sewed clothing for men studying to be Congregationalist ministers
	Female Samaritan Society	A Universalist Church group aiding poor women with food, fuel, and clothing
1820	Society for Employing the Female Poor	Provided work (washing, ironing, sewing) for poor white women; folded in 1837
1822	Female Philanthropic Society	Gave small donations to poor white women
1825	Penitent Females' Refuge, Ladies Auxiliary	Visited repentant prostitutes at the refuge, prayed with them, provided clothing, and supervised the refuge

1828	Infant School Society	Provided day care for children (aged 18 months and up) of poor working mothers; hired teachers who taught religion, reading, and numbers
1829	Roman Catholic Clothing Society	A "young women's" group that sewed clothing for Catholic schoolchildren; a.k.a. Roman Catholic Charitable Clothing Society, Female Clothing Society
1830	Colored Female Union Society	A mutual aid society; members paid small dues and received aid if ill or dying
1832	Colored Female Charitable Society	Visited widows and orphans "in their afflictions"; gave aid and comfort; buried the dead
	Afric-American Female Intelligence Society	A literary society that also worked against "vice and immorality," promoted temperance, and sponsored lectures (Maria W. Stewart delivered one in 1832)
	Roman Catholic Ladies Charitable Society	Raised money to support the Sisters of Charity and the school they operated
1833	Seamen's Aid Society	Provided work for wives and widows of sailors; ran a school for their daughters; sold their handiwork in a store
	Colored Ladies' Temperance Society	Promoted temperance among the city's African American population
	Garrison Society	A black women's literary society; met weekly to discuss history, read useful books, write essays, and "converse upon the sufferings of our enslaved sisters"
	Female Anti-Slavery Society	An integrated organization that worked for the immediate abolition of slavery; raised money, planned conventions, hired lecturers
	Mutual Lyceum	A mixed-sex organization run by African Americans; sponsored lectures and discussions

1834	Children's Friend Society	Provided a home and a school for poor children who were neglected by their parents or whose mothers had to work
1835	Female Moral Reform Society	Worked to eradicate prostitution and the sexual double standard; ran a newspaper, hired a female missionary; opened a refuge for prostitutes
	American Female Home Education Society	Promoted girls' education, the training of female teachers, and temperance
1838	Samaritan Asylum	Ran an orphanage for black children; also aided neglected black children
	Ladies' Society for Promoting Education in Africa	A white women's organization promoting colonization of African Americans and supporting schools in Liberia
	St. Vincent de Paul Society	A Roman Catholic group raising money for the Sisters of Charity's free school and later their orphanage; all officers were men, but there was a female Board of Trustees; in 1840, 71.3 percent of the members were female

APPENDIX 2

Tables

Note: Tables A.1–A.10 are based on my reconstruction of the life histories and leadership careers of 722 New York organizational leaders and 420 Boston leaders. The reconstructions involved standard techniques of record matching using organizational records, city directories, marriage and death records, historical biographical dictionaries, genealogies, and church records. In rare instances, I was able to combine quantitative information with qualitative materials, such as letters or diaries. I compiled the data into two databases, one for each city, and created the tables from these databases. I will gladly make the databases (or material from them) available to interested scholars. Tables A.11–A.14 are based on my analysis of available treasurers' reports and financial data.

TABLE A.1 Religious Affiliations of Officers in Selected Organizations

New York

	Presbyterian	Reformed Dutch	Protestant Episcopal	Methodist Episcopal	Baptist	Friend	Unitarian/ Congrega- tionalist	Roman Catholic
Society for the Relief of Poor Widows with Small Children (N=44)	43.2%	9.1%	45.5%[a]	6.8%	0%	4.5%	0%	0%
Female Association (N=39)	0	0	0	0	0	100.0	0	0
Orphan Asylum Society (N=19)	31.6	0	63.2	5.3	0	0	0	0
Female Assistance Society (N=30)	10.0	6.7	3.3	80.0	0	0	0	0
Association for the Relief of Respectable, Aged, Indigent Females (N=32)	53.1	12.5	28.1	0	6.3	0	0	0
House of Industry (N=18)	50.0	5.6	33.3	0	0	0	0	11.1[a]
Female Union Society for the Promotion of Sabbath Schools (N=30)	33.3	6.7	23.3	23.3	6.7	0	6.7	0
Female Auxiliary Bible Society (N=44)	50.0	18.2	18.2	4.5	2.3	4.5	2.3	0
Female Missionary Society (N=18)	83.3	5.6	5.6	5.6	0	0	0	0
Ladies Association of the Roman Catholic Benevolent Society (N=15)	0	0	0	0	0	0	0	100.0
Maternal Association (N=9)	88.9	11.1	0	0	0	0	0	0
Female Tract Society (N=63)	58.7	20.6	7.9	3.2	4.8	0	4.8	0
Asylum for Lying-In Women (N=80)	41.3	15.0	21.3	7.5	2.5	7.5	5.0	0

New York

	Presbyterian	Reformed Dutch	Protestant Episcopal	Methodist Episcopal	Baptist	Friend	Unitarian/ Congrega- tionalist	Roman Catholic
African Dorcas Association (N=5)	40.0	0	0	40.0	20.0	0	0	0
Female Benevolent Society (N=32)	65.6	12.5	12.5	3.1	3.1	0	3.1	0
Female Bethel Union (N=4)	25.0	0	25.0	0	25.0	0	25.0	0
Female Moral Reform Society (N=29)	58.6	0	3.4	20.7	6.9	3.4	6.9	0
Protestant Half-Orphan Asylum (N=7)	71.4	14.2	14.2	0	0	0	0	0
Ladies' New York City Anti-Slavery Society (N=20)	75.0	0	5.0	0	5.0	5.0	10.0[b]	0
Association for the Benefit of Colored Orphans (N=28)	10.7	0	10.7	10.7	0	67.9	0	0

TABLE A.1 (continued)

Boston

	Congrega-tionalist	Unitarian	Congrega-tionalist/ Unitarian	Baptist	Protestant Episcopal	Methodist Episcopal	Friend	Other
Female Asylum (N=44)	20.5%	54.5%	4.5%	6.8%	11.4%	0%	0%	2.2%[c]
Female Society for Missionary Purposes (N=9)	33.3	0	0	66.6	0	0	0	0
Corban Society (N=30)	93.3	3.3	0	0	3.3	0	0	0
Fragment Society (N=35)	34.3	28.6	2.9	28.6	5.7	0	0	0
Female Auxiliary Bible Society (N=47)	46.8	10.6	4.2	8.5	27.7	0	0	2.1[c]
Society for Promoting Christianity among the Jews (N=31)	42.0	9.7	9.7	12.9	25.8	0	0	0
Widows' Society (N=31)	25.8	35.5	6.5	9.7	22.6	0	0	0
Fatherless and Widows Society (N=37)	35.1	0	0	56.8	8.1	0	0	0
Penitent Females' Refuge Ladies Auxiliary (N=15)	60.0	0	0	40.0	0	0	0	0
Infant School Society (N=22)	45.5	13.6	0	27.3	9.1	0	0	0
Seamen's Aid Society (N=7)	0	71.4	0	0	14.3	14.3	0	0
Female Anti-Slavery Society (N=28)	21.4	32.1	0	32.1	0	0	7.1	14.2[d]
Children's Friend Society (N=23)	43.5	13.0	0	43.5	0	0	0	0
Female Moral Reform Society (N=13)	69.2	0	0	23.1	0	0	7.7	0

TABLE A.1 (*continued*)

Note: The number in parentheses indicates the number of women for whom I could confirm religious affiliation. New York's Presbyterians, Reformed Dutch, and Associate Reformed were very close in theology and church polity until the 1830s. Some women shifted back and forth between the denominations; I counted each woman's affiliation at the time of her involvement in a society. In Boston, some individuals shifted their affiliation from Congregationalist to Unitarian while serving in a society. Those individuals are listed separately in the third column. Still, this snapshot portrait cannot fully capture the dynamic quality of some women's religious leanings.

[a]Includes Catherine Dupleix, who converted to Catholicism in 1812.

[b]Includes one Unitarian.

[c]Catherine Hickling Prescott was a Unitarian, but all her children were baptized at Trinity Episcopal Church, where her husband was a vestryman. She may have switched allegiances at some point.

[d]Henrietta Sargent was a Universalist; Mary Handy Himes was a member of the First Christian Society on Summer Street, where her husband Joshua was minister; both Himeses later became Adventists.

TABLE A.2 Membership in Organizational Networks

New York

High Leadership Overlap	Mid-level Leadership Overlap
Network 1 Society for the Relief of Poor Widows with Small Children (1797) Orphan Asylum Society (1806) House of Industry (1814) Female Auxiliary Bible Society (1816)	*Network 9* Society for the Relief of Poor Widows with Small Children (1797) Association for the Relief of Respectable, Aged, Indigent Females (1813) Female Union Society for the Promotion of Sabbath Schools (1816) Female Tract Society (1822)
Network 2 Association for the Relief of Respectable, Aged, Indigent Females (1813) Female Auxiliary Bible Society (1816) Female Tract Society (1822)	*Network 10* Female Association (1798) Association for the Benefit of Colored Orphans (1836)
Network 3 Female Auxiliary Bible Society (1816) Female Tract Society (1822) Asylum for Lying-In Women (1823)	*Network 11* Association for the Relief of Respectable, Aged, Indigent Females (1813) Female Union Society for the Promotion of Sabbath Schools (1816)
Network 4 Female Union Society for the Promotion of Sabbath Schools (1816) Female Tract Society (1822) Asylum for Lying-In Women (1823)	*Network 12* Female Union Society for the Promotion of Sabbath Schools (1816) Female Auxiliary Bible Society (1816)
Network 5 Female Missionary Society (1816) Maternal Association (1818) Asylum for Lying-In Women (1823) Female Benevolent Society (1832)	*Network 13* Female Auxiliary Bible Society (1816) Female Missionary Society (1816) Maternal Association (1818)
Network 6 Female Tract Society (1822) Asylum for Lying-In Women (1823) Female Benevolent Society (1832)	*Network 14* Female Tract Society Protestant Half-Orphan Association
	Network 15 African Dorcas Association (1828) Colored Ladies Literary Society (1836)

New York

High Leadership Overlap

Network 7
Female Baptist Association (1834)
Assistant Benefit Society (1838)
Female Trading Association (1841)

Network 8
New York Female Moral Reform
  Society (1834)
Ladies New-York City Anti-Slavery
  Society (1835)

Mid-level Leadership Overlap

Network 16
African Dorcas Association (1828)
Female Education Society of First Colored
  Presbyterian Church (1840)

Boston

Network 1
Female Missionary Society (1800)
Female Auxiliary Bible Society (1814)
Society for Promoting Christianity
  among the Jews (1816)
Widows' Society (1816)

Network 2
Fragment Society (1812)
Female Auxiliary Bible Society (1814)

Network 3
Female Auxiliary Bible Society (1814)
Corban Society (1811)
Society for Promoting Christianity
  among the Jews (1815)
Widows' Society (1816)

Network 4
Corban Society (1811)
Female Auxiliary Bible Society (1814)
Society for Promoting Christianity
  among the Jews (1815)

Network 7
Female Society for Missionary Purposes
  (1800)
Corban Society (1811)
Fragment Society (1812)
Fatherless and Widows Society (1817)
Penitent Females Refuge (1825)
Children's Friend Society (1834)

Network 8
Colored Female Union Society (1830)
Afric-American Female Intelligence
  Society (1832)

Boston

High Leadership Overlap	Mid-level Leadership Overlap
Fatherless and Widows Society (1817) Penitent Females Refuge (1825)	
Network 5 Colored Ladies Temperance Society (1833) Garrison Juvenile Society (1833)	
Network 6 Female Anti-Slavery Society (1833) Female Moral Reform Society (1835)	

Note: By comparing leadership lists, I determined which organizations had high levels of overlap in leadership (between 15 and 45 percent of one group's leaders also led another at some point) and which had mid-levels of overlap (between 10 and 14.9 percent of one group's leaders also led another at some point). For the purposes of this table, I did not separate leadership overlaps that were simultaneous from those that were sequential. The organization's year of founding, when known, is in parentheses. In analyzing how moral reform society leaderships overlapped with antislavery society leaderships, I took into account officers' attendance as delegates at one or more of the three Anti-Slavery Conventions of American Women, as well as service on the board of a women's Anti-Slavery Society. Sixteen of the fifty-three officers (30 percent) of the New York Female Moral Reform Society, for example, fit those criteria.

TABLE A.3 Patterns of Leadership

	New York		Boston	
Number of women leaders	722		420	
Number (and percentage) of women who led one organization	545	(75.4)	324	(77.1)
Number (and percentage) of women who led two organizations	117	(16.2)	56	(13.3)
Number (and percentage) of women who led three organizations	38	(5.3)	21	(5.0)
Number (and percentage) of women who led four organizations	11	(1.5)	9	(2.1)
Number (and percentage) of women who led five organizations	6	(0.8)	9	(2.1)
Number (and percentage) of women who led six organizations	5	(0.6)	1	(0.2)
Number (and percentage) of women who led more than one organization	177	(24.5)	96	(22.9)
Simultaneously	110	(62.1)	77	(80.2)
Serially	67	(37.8)	19	(19.8)

TABLE A.4 Occupations of Household Heads among Leaders of Selected Organizations

New York

Organization	Merchant/ Manufacturer	Physician	Lawyer/ Judge	Minister	Other Professional	Shopkeeper	Artisan	Widow[a]	Self- Supporting[b]	Not Found
Society for the Relief of Poor Widows with Small Children (N=123)	22.0%	5.7%	11.4%	1.6%	14.6%	0%	0%	3.3%	2.4%	39.8%
Female Association (N=39)	15.4	0	0	2.6	2.6	0	0	0	0	79.5
Orphan Asylum Society (N=43)	32.5	9.3	9.3	2.3	18.6	0	0	7.0	2.3	18.6
Female Assistance Society (N=55)	14.5	5.5	9.1	1.8	12.7	1.8	18.2	5.5	3.6	27.3
Association for the Relief of Respectable, Aged, Indigent Females (N=55)	47.3	0	10.9	1.8	9.1	3.6	5.5	7.3	3.6	10.9
House of Industry (N=37)	27.0	8.1	2.7	0	8.1	0	0	0	2.7	51.4

TABLE A.4 (*continued*)

New York

Organization	Merchant/ Manufacturer	Physician	Lawyer/ Judge	Minister	Other Professional	Shopkeeper	Artisan	Widow[a]	Self-Supporting[b]	Not Found
Female Union Society for the Promotion of Sabbath Schools (N=58)	29.3	1.7	6.9	6.9	6.9	5.2	8.6	1.7	5.2	27.6
Female Auxiliary Bible Society (N=68)	36.8	4.4	14.7	19.1	5.8	2.9	1.4	4.4	1.4	8.8
Female Missionary Society (N=29)	27.6	0	3.4	6.9	6.9	13.8	6.9	0	6.9	27.6
Ladies Association of the Roman Catholic Benevolent Society (N=15)	33.3	0	0	0	0	13.3	6.7	0	0	46.7
Maternal Association (N=12)	33.3	0	8.3	8.3	33.3	8.3	0	0	0	8.3
Female Tract Society (N=99)	42.4	5.0	10.1	10.1	11.1	3.0	3.0	1.0	1.0	13.1
Asylum for Lying-In Women (N=94)	48.9	6.4	10.6	7.4	10.6	2.1	4.3	3.2	1.1	5.3

TABLE A.4 (*continued*)

New York

Organization	Merchant/ Manufacturer	Physician	Lawyer/ Judge	Minister	Other Professional	Shopkeeper	Artisan	Widow[a]	Self-Supporting[b]	Not Found
African Dorcas Association (N=20)	0	0	0	5.0	0	10.0	15.0	0	10.0	60.0
Roman Catholic Asylum for the Children of Widows and Widowers (N=11)	9.1	0	0	0	45.5	0	0	9.1	0	36.4
Female Benevolent Society (N=43)	37.2	7.0	2.3	18.6	16.3	0	2.3	2.3	0	14.0
Female Moral Reform Society (N=54)	9.2	11.1	0	16.7	11.1	1.8	1.8	0	14.8	33.3
Ladies New York City Anti-Slavery Society (N=36)	25.0	8.3	2.8	5.5	13.9	5.5	0	0	2.8	36.1
Association for the Benefit of Colored Orphans (N=43)	34.9	2.3	4.7	11.6	11.6	4.7	9.3	0	4.7	16.2

TABLE A.4 (*continued*)

Boston

Organization	Merchant/ Manufacturer	Physician	Lawyer/ Judge	Minister	Other Professional	Shopkeeper	Artisan	Widow[a]	Self-Supporting[b]	Not Found
Female Asylum (N=68)	44.1%	2.9%	8.8%	4.4%	5.9%	4.4%	0%	1.5%	4.4%	23.5%
Female Society for Missionary Purposes (N=15)	6.7	0	13.3	0	6.7	6.7	0	0	20.0	46.7
Corban Society (N=43)	20.9	0	0	11.6	7.0	4.7	4.7	0	7.0	44.2
Fragment Society (N=52)	28.9	1.9	3.8	3.8	15.4	1.9	7.7	0	3.8	32.7
Female Auxiliary Bible Society (N=61)	36.1	3.3	8.2	18.0	8.2	1.6	1.6	1.6	4.9	16.4
Female Society for Promoting Christianity among the Jews (N=44)	27.3	4.5	6.8	15.9	9.1	4.5	4.5	0	6.8	20.5
Widows' Society (N=47)	42.6	2.1	12.8	6.4	6.4	0	0	0	0	29.8
Fatherless and Widows Society (N=67)	13.4	0	3.0	11.9	9.0	4.5	13.4	3.0	6.0	35.8

TABLE A.4 (*continued*)

Boston

Organization	Merchant/ Manufacturer	Physician	Lawyer/ Judge	Minister	Other Professional	Shopkeeper	Artisan	Widow[a]	Self- Supporting[b]	Not Found
Penitent Females' Refuge (N=24)	25.0	0	12.5	4.2	12.5	8.3	16.7	4.2	0	16.7
Infant School Society (N=37)	35.1	0	5.4	13.5	10.8	2.7	5.4	0	0	27.0
Seamen's Aid Society (N=14)	0	7.1	0	7.1	14.3	28.6	7.1	14.3	7.1	14.3
Colored Ladies Temperance Society (N=3)	0	0	0	0	0	33.3	33.3	0	33.3	0
Female Anti-Slavery Society (N=42)	14.3	0	4.8	9.5	4.8	11.9	4.8	0	19.0	31.0
Children's Friend Society (N=32)	18.7	3.1	3.1	6.3	15.6	12.5	12.5	3.1	6.3	15.6
Female Moral Reform Society (N=19)	10.5	0	0	5.3	15.8	10.5	21.1	10.5	10.5	15.8

Note: Because most women derived their class status from the occupation and income of a father, husband, or brother, this table classifies women leaders according to the occupation of the head of household. Some women, of course, worked in family businesses alongside their husbands.

[a]The category "widow" includes only those widows about whom I had no household information.
[b]The category "self-supporting" includes only those women who worked for all or most of their own incomes.

TABLE A.5 Percentages of Married and Single Officers in Selected Organizations

New York

Organization	Years Covered	% Married	% Single	% Single/Married	% Unknown
Maternal Association (N=12)	1818, 1834	100	0		
Asylum for Lying-In Women (N=94)	1823–40	100	0		
Ladies Association of the Roman Catholic Benevolent Society (N=15)	1817, 1827, 1831, 1838	93.3	6.6		
Female Benevolent Society (N=43)	1834–40	93.1	6.9		
Female Bethel Union (N=38)	1836–38	92.1	7.9		
Protestant Half-Orphan Asylum (N=11)	1835, 1839	90.9	9.1		
Female Moral Reform Society (N=54)	1834–40	88.9	11.1		
Female Auxiliary Bible Society (N=69)	1816–38	82.6	17.4		
Female Assistance Society (N=55)	1818–36	81.8	18.2		
Society for the Relief of Poor Widows with Small Children (N=123)	1797–1840	79.7	19.5	0.8	
House of Industry (N=37)	1814–19	75.7	24.3		
Assistant Benefit Society (N=4)	1837–38	75.0	25.0		
Ladies New-York City Anti-Slavery Society (N=36)	1836–39	75.0	22.2		2.7
Female Missionary Society (N=29)	1818–21	79.3	20.7		

TABLE A.5 (*continued*)

New York

Organization	Years Covered	% Married	% Single	% Single/Married	% Unknown
Female Tract Society (N=99)	1822–40	78.8	21.2		
Association for the Relief of Respectable, Aged, Indigent Females (N=55)	1814–40	78.2	21.8		
Orphan Asylum Society (N=43)	1806–40	76.7	18.6		4.6
Roman Catholic Asylum for the Children of Widows and Widowers (N=11)	1829, 1833	63.4	36.4		
Female Union Society for the Promotion of Sabbath Schools (N=58)	1817–28	58.6	41.4		
Association for the Benefit of Colored Orphans (N=43)	1836–40	55.8	32.6		11.6
African Dorcas Association (N=20)	1828–29	40.0			60.0
Female Association (N=39)	1799–1837	23.0	51.3	5.1	20.5

TABLE A.5 (continued)

Boston

Organization	Years Covered	% Married	% Single	% Single/Married	% Unknown
Penitent Females' Refuge (N=24)	1825, 1839	100	0		
Female Moral Reform Society (N=19)	1834–40	94.7	5.3		
Children's Friend Society (N=32)	1833–40	90.6	9.4		
Seamen's Aid Society (N=14)	1834–38	85.7	14.3		
Female Asylum (N=68)	1800–1840	77.9	17.6	4.4	
Female Auxiliary Bible Society (N=61)	1814–36	75.4	24.6		
Colored Female Temperance Society (N=4)	1833	75.0	25.0		
Fatherless and Widows' Society (N=67)	1817–40	71.6	26.9		1.5
Infant School Society (N=37)	1829, 1831	70.3	29.7		
Corban Society (N=43)	1811–40	69.8	23.3	6.9	
Society for Promoting Christianity among the Jews (N=44)	1816–27	61.4	38.6		
Fragment Society (N=52)	1812–40	57.7	38.5	3.8	
Female Society for Missionary Purposes (N=15)	1800–1816	53.3	46.7		
Female Anti-Slavery Society (N=42)	1834–40	47.6	45.2		7.1
Widows' Society (N=47)	1816–40	46.8	51.1	2.1	

TABLE A.6 Distribution of Ages at Which Women Joined Selected Organizations, 1797–1840

New York

Organization	Number (and Percentage) for Whom Age Is Known	Age at Joining					
		<20	20–29	30–39	40–49	50–59	60+
Society for the Relief of Poor Widows with Small Children	54 (43.9)	1.8%	31.4%	33.3%	22.2%	7.4%	3.7%
Female Association	25 (64.1)	16.0	52.0	20.0	12.0	0	0
Orphan Asylum	28 (65.1)	0	17.8	28.6	35.7	3.5	14.3
Female Assistance Society	16 (29.1)	0	18.7	37.5	18.7	25.0	0
Association for the Relief of Respectable, Aged, Indigent Females	22 (40.0)	0	27.3	27.3	40.9	4.5	0
House of Industry	18 (48.6)	0	22.2	33.3	22.2	11.1	11.1
Female Union Society for the Promotion of Sabbath Schools	24 (41.3)	4.2	33.3	37.5	25.0	0	0
Female Auxiliary Bible Society	49 (71.0)	0	14.3	34.6	26.5	18.4	6.1
Female Missionary Society	11 (37.8)	0	9.1	72.7	18.2	0	0
Maternal Association	9 (75.0)	0	11.1	66.7	22.2	0	0
Female Tract Society	60 (60.6)	0	25.0	43.3	18.3	11.7	1.7
Asylum for Lying-In Women	63 (67.0)	0	20.6	34.9	39.6	3.1	1.5
Female Benevolent Society	24 (55.8)	0	12.5	41.6	12.8	25.0	8.3
Female Moral Reform Society	23 (42.6)	8.7	26.1	47.8	4.3	13.0	0
Ladies New-York City Anti-Slavery Society	19 (52.8)	5.2	36.8	31.6	15.8	10.5	0
Protestant Half-Orphan Asylum	6 (54.5)	0	0	16.6	50.0	16.6	16.6
Association for the Benefit of Colored Orphans	30 (69.8)	3.3	13.3	30.0	23.3	26.6	3.3

TABLE A.6 (*continued*)

Boston

Organization	Number (and Percentage) for Whom Age Is Known	Age at Joining					
		<20	20–29	30–39	40–49	50–59	60+
Female Asylum	57 (83.8)	0%	17.5%	31.5%	29.8%	10.5%	10.5%
Female Missionary Society	8 (53.3)	0	12.5	62.5	12.5	12.5	0
Corban Society	24 (55.8)	0	33.3	45.8	12.5	8.3	0
Fragment Society	39 (75.0)	10.2	43.6	23.1	10.2	10.2	2.6
Female Auxiliary Bible Society	51 (83.6)	0	11.8	33.3	27.4	19.6	7.8
Society for Promoting Christianity among the Jews	34 (77.3)	2.9	23.5	35.3	14.7	20.6	2.9
Widows' Society	33 (70.2)	6.1	27.3	42.4	18.2	6.1	0
Fatherless and Widows Society	34 (50.7)	0	23.5	47.1	17.6	11.8	0
Penitent Females' Refuge	17 (70.8)	0	5.9	35.3	35.3	11.8	11.8
Infant School Society	23 (62.2)	0	30.4	47.8	17.4	4.3	0
Seamen's Aid Society	9 (64.3)	0	11.1	44.4	22.2	11.1	11.1
Female Anti-Slavery Society	28 (66.7)	7.1	42.9	35.7	10.7	3.6	0
Children's Friend Society	19 (59.4)	0	5.3	21.1	52.6	15.8	5.3
Female Moral Reform Society	9 (47.4)	0	22.2	55.5	11.1	11.1	0

TABLE A.7 Percentage of Officers in Selected Organizations under Age 40 at Time of Joining and Median Ages of Officers and Founders

New York

Organization	% of Officers under Age 40 at Time of Joining	Median Age at Which Officers Joined	Median Age of Founders
Female Association	88.0	25	
Female Moral Reform Society	82.6	32	33
Female Missionary Society	81.8	34	34
Maternal Association	77.8	34	
Female Union for the Promotion of Sabbath Schools	75.0	32	29
Ladies New-York City Anti-Slavery Society	73.6	30	34
Female Tract Society	68.3	37	41
Society for the Relief of Poor Widows with Small Children	66.5	35	
Female Assistance Society	56.2	36	
Asylum for Lying-In Women	55.5	38	35
House of Industry	55.5	38	37
Association for the Relief of Respectable, Aged, Indigent Females	54.6	37	43
Female Benevolent Society	54.1	39	35
Female Auxiliary Bible Society	48.9	39	40
Association for the Benefit of Colored Orphans	46.6	40	40
Orphan Asylum Society	46.4	41	
Protestant Half-Orphan Asylum	16.6	43	47

Boston

Organization	% of Officers under Age 40 at Time of Joining	Median Age at Which Officers Joined	Median Age of Founders
Female Anti-Slavery Society	85.7	29	25
Corban Society	79.1	32	37
Fragment Society	78.9	29	26
Infant School Society	78.2	33	32

Boston

Organization	% of Officers under Age 40 at Time of Joining	Median Age at Which Officers Joined	Median Age of Founders
Female Moral Reform Society	77.7	35	
Widows' Society	75.8	32	34
Female Society for Missionary Purposes	75.0	37	
Fatherless and Widows Society	70.6	33	
Society for Promoting Christianity among the Jews	61.7	35	32
Seamen's Aid Society	55.5	39	42
Female Asylum	49.0	39	42
Female Auxiliary Bible Society	45.1	41	43
Penitent Females Refuge	41.2	45	44
Children's Friend Society	26.4	44	45

TABLE A.8 Number of Organizational Affiliations per
Married Woman by Number of Children Borne

Number of Children Borne	Average Number of Affiliations per Woman	
	New York	Boston
0[a]	2.1 (N=22)	2.0 (N=18)
1	1.9 (N=9)	1.8 (N=12)
1+[b]	1.7 (N=14)	1.6 (N=12)
2	1.5 (N=11)	1.8 (N=14)
2+	1.7 (N=8)	1.3 (N=11)
3	1.8 (N=13)	1.2 (N=9)
3+	1.3 (N=7)	
4	2.0 (N=12)	1.6 (N=15)
4+	1.5 (N=2)	
5	1.7 (N=18)	1.5 (N=11)
5+	1.0 (N=2)	
6	1.8 (N=19)	2.2 (N=9)
7	1.5 (N=17)	1.8 (N=9)
8	2.0 (N=14)	1.0 (N=6)
9	1.8 (N=6)	1.0 (N=2)
10	1.4 (N=7)	1.6 (N=3)
11	1.0 (N=2)	1.3 (N=4)
12	1.0 (N=3)	1.0 (N=2)
13	1.0 (N=2)	1.0 (N=1)
14	2.0 (N=3)	1.5 (N=2)
15	3.0 (N=1)	

Note: Childbearing histories could be reconstructed for 192 New York women and
140 Boston women.

[a]Excludes childless women who married for the first time at age forty-five or older
(two in New York; three in Boston).
[b]In cases where childbearing histories are incomplete, the plus symbol indicates that
the woman bore *at least* the designated number of children but probably more.

TABLE A.9 Creation of Male Advisory Boards

New York

Organization	Founded	Board Created or Amended
Society for the Relief of Poor Widows with Small Children	1797	1857
Orphan Asylum Society	1806	1851
Female Missionary Society	1817	1817
Asylum for Lying-In Women	1823	1823, 1827, 1899[a]
African Dorcas Association	1828	1828
Roman Catholic Asylum for the Children of Widows and Widowers	1829	1829[b]
Female Benevolent Society	1832	1850s
Female Moral Reform Society	1834	1845, 1849[c]
Protestant Half-Orphan Asylum	1835	1839[b]
Association for the Benefit of Colored Orphans	1836	1837

Boston

Organization	Founded	Board Created or Amended
Widows' Society	1816	1862[d]
Fatherless and Widows Society	1817	1918[d]
Society for Employing the Female Poor	1820	1820
Penitent Females' Refuge Ladies Auxiliary	1825	1854[e]
Infant School Society	1828	1828
Seamen's Aid Society	1833	1868[f]
Children's Friend Society	1834	1834
Female Moral Reform Society	1835	1852
St. Vincent de Paul Society	1838	1838[g]

[a]In 1823, six physicians controlled the appointment of medical officers to the asylum; in 1827, a Building Committee of Gentlemen was created to advise on a new building; in 1899, the asylum merged with the Infant Asylum, and men were admitted to the board.

[b]The Roman Catholic Asylum for the Children of Widows and Widowers (in 1835) and the Protestant Half-Orphan Asylum (in 1839) each incorporated, with corporate power vested in male trustees, not the women organizers.

[c]In 1845, a Board of Counselors was created to advise on a building project; in 1849, the Act of Incorporation required that a majority of men approve mortgages and real estate sales.

[d]The Widows' Society (1862) and the Fatherless and Widows Society (1918) chose male treasurers or auditors.

[e]The Penitent Females Refuge began as an auxiliary to the men's organization, but in 1854 the women's auxiliary took over the organization and renamed it the Bethesda Society.

[f]In 1868, the Seamen's Aid Society merged with the Boston Port Society, all of whose officers were male; the new board's officers were men, but the assistant secretary and assistant treasurer were women; twelve of the managers were men and eight were women.

[g]The St. Vincent de Paul Society had two branches, male and female, which met in alternate months. Governance was vested in the male branch, but membership on the Board of Trustees was divided evenly between women and men.

TABLE A.10 Women Leaders' Connections to the World of Print

Published Authors

New York	Boston

New York	Boston
Sarah Ingraham [Bennett]	Hannah Adams
Joanna Graham Bethune	Mary Hooker Cornelius
[Anna] Jane Dunbar Chaplin	Sarah Josepha Hale
Almira Francisco Loveland	Louisa Davis Minot
	Susanna Haswell Rowson

Editors

New York	Boston
Sarah R. Ingraham [Bennett]	Maria Weston Chapman
Cornelia Green Ely	Sarah Josepha Hale
Sarah Towne Smith [Martyn]	

Through Close Relatives

New York

Name	Organization(s) Led	Relative
Martha Abbott Bannister	Female Moral Reform Society Ladies Anti-Slavery Society	Wife of Ridley Bannister, printer
Anna Maria Bayard Boyd	Society for the Relief of Poor Widows with Small Children Female Bible Society Female Tract Society Orphan Asylum Society House of Industry Asylum for Lying-In Women	Sister of Margaret Bayard Smith, author
Elizabeth Collins	Association for the Benefit of Colored Orphans	Sister of Robert B. Collins, bookseller in firm of Collins, Keese, & Co.
Mary Kerr Day	Association for the Benefit of Colored Orphans	Wife of Mahlon Day, printer and bookseller
Sarah Street Durrall	Female Assistance Society	Wife of William Durrall, printer and bookseller
Eleanor Boyd Dwight	Association for the Relief of Respectable, Aged, Indigent Females	Wife of Theodore Dwight Jr., editor of Protestant magazines, author of advice and anti-Catholic books
Mary Reed Eastman	Maternal Association Female Tract Society	Wife of Ornan Eastman, secretary of American Tract Society and author of religious works

TABLE A.10 (continued)

New York

Name	Organization(s) Led	Relative
Sarah Beach Hall	Female Union Society for the Promotion of Sabbath Schools Female Assistance Society Asylum for Lying-In Women Female Tract Society Female Benevolent Society Association for the Benefit of Colored Orphans	Wife of Francis Hall, co-owner of *New York Commercial Advertiser*
Fanny Lathrop Hallock	Female Tract Society	Wife of Rev. William Hallock, secretary of American Tract Society and editor of *American Messenger*
Maria Arcularius Harper	Female Assistance Society	Wife of James Harper, printer and partner in Harper Bros. Publishers (later mayor of New York City)
Hetty Low King	Association for the Benefit of Colored Orphans	Second wife of Charles King, editor of *New York American*
Sarah Williams Leavitt	Female Benevolent Society Female Moral Reform Society	Wife of Joshua Leavitt, editor of *New York Evangelist*
Eliza Lewis	Association for the Relief of Respectable, Aged, Indigent Females	Wife of Zechariah Lewis, co-owner of *New York Commercial Advertiser*

New York

Name	Organization(s) Led	Relative
Julia Gouge Lockwood	Ladies Anti-Slavery Society	Wife of Roe Lockwood, bookseller
Jessie Bethune McCartee	Orphan Asylum Society	Daughter of Joanna Graham Bethune, author
Eliza Piercy	Ladies Anti-Slavery Society	Wife of Henry R. Piercy, printer
Henrietta Regulus Ray	African Dorcas Association	Before marriage, lived with family of Samuel L. Cornish, owner and editor of
	Colored Ladies Literary Society	*Freedom's Journal*
Elizabeth Downer Sayre	Female Missionary Society	Wife of John Sayre, bookseller
Elizabeth Southard	Female Moral Reform Society	Wife of Rev. Nathaniel Southard, editor of *Youth's Cabinet*; later edited
		Adventist papers
Susannah Wayland Stone	Asylum for Lying-In Women	Sister of Francis Wayland, Baptist minister, author, and president of Brown
		University; wife of William Leete Stone, editor of *New York Commercial*
		Advertiser and author of controversial books, including an exposé of Maria
		Monk
Electa Barrell Wilder	Female Tract Society	Wife of Sampson V. S. Wilder, president of American Tract Society
Mrs. Ransom Williams	Ladies Anti-Slavery Society	Wife of Ransom G. Williams, publisher

Boston

Name	Organization(s) Led	Relative
Martha Hooper Adams	Female Bible Society Fatherless and Widows Society	Wife of Rev. Nehemiah Adams, author and editor
Abigail Walker Armstrong	Female Bible Society Society for Promoting Christianity among the Jews Widows' Society Corban Society	Wife of Samuel T. Armstrong, bookseller and publisher of *The Panoplist* and *The Missionary Herald*
Margaret Duncan Baldwin	Female Asylum Society for Promoting Christianity among the Jews Children's Friend Society	Wife of Thomas Baldwin, minister and editor of *Baptist Missionary Magazine*
Anne Greene Chapman	Female Anti-Slavery Society	Sister of Maria Weston Chapman
Mary Gray Chapman	Female Anti-Slavery Society	Sister of Maria Weston Chapman
Hannah Lane Clapp	Fragment Society	Wife of William Warland Clapp, publisher of *Boston Repertory, Daily Advertiser*, and other papers
Louisa Willis Dwight	Infant School Society Graham Society	Daughter of Nathaniel Willis, owner of *Boston Recorder*; sister of Nathaniel Parker Willis, author
Mehetabel Barnes Evarts	Female Bible Society Society for Promoting Christianity among the Jews	Wife of Jeremiah Evarts, editor of *The Panoplist*, and *The Missionary Herald*

TABLE A.10 (*continued*)

Boston

Name	Organization(s) Led	Relative
Mary Moore Francis	Fragment Society	Wife of David Francis, bookseller
Prudence Clark Morris Loring	Fatherless and Widows Society	Second husband was James Loring, editor of the Baptist *Christian Watchman*
	Penitent Females Refuge	
Elizabeth Breese Morse	Female Bible Society	Wife of Rev. Jedidiah Morse, textbook author
Louisa G. Purdy	Female Moral Reform Society	Wife of Edward G. Purdy, printer
Ann Cauldwell Sharp	Society for Promoting Christianity among the Jews	Wife of Rev. Daniel Sharp, editor of *American Baptist Magazine*
	Fatherless and Widows Society	
Elizabeth Skinner Stow	Fragment Society	Wife of Rev. Baron Stow, writer for Baptist and evangelical magazines
	American Female Home Education Society	

TABLE A.11 Yearly Budgets of Selected Women's Organizations

	Around 1820			Around 1840	
Year	Organization	Budget	Year	Organization	Budget
1816	New York Female Association	$1,620	1836	Ladies New York City Anti-Slavery Society	$358
1817	Boston Society for Promoting Christianity among the Jews	1,153	1836	New York Female Assistance Society	5,314
1818	New York Female Assistance Society	926	1836	New York Orphan Asylum Society	7,000
1819	Boston Female Bible Society	577	1837	Boston Widows' Society	2,550
1819	Boston Fragment Society	863	1837	New York Association for the Relief of Respectable, Aged, Indigent Females	3,114
1819	New York Female Sabbath School Union	1,520	1838	New York Female Assistant Benefit Society	360
1819	New York Society for the Relief of Poor Widows with Small Children	5,253	1839	Boston Children's Friend Society	3,347
1820	Boston Widows' Society	216	1839	Boston St. Vincent de Paul Society	809
1820	New York Association for the Relief of Respectable, Aged, Indigent Females	1,819	1839	New York Association for the Benefit of Colored Orphans	4,262
1823	New York Asylum for Lying-In Women	4,000	1840	Boston Female Bible Society	244
1823	New York Female Tract Society	606	1840	Boston Fragment Society	1,009
1827	New York Orphan Asylum Society	11,473	1840	Boston Seamen's Aid Society	14,437
			1840	New York Female Benevolent Society	2,120
			1840	New York Female Tract Society	2,500
			1840	New York Society for the Relief of Poor Widows with Small Children	4,238
			1841	Boston Fatherless and Widows Society	1,800
Total		30,026	Total		53,462

Note: Budget figures indicate the amount an organization actually spent in a given year (as far as I could determine from financial statements); they do not include money sequestered in permanent funds or building funds.

TABLE A.12 Sample Annual Budgets of Organizations

New York Orphan Asylum Society, 1817–1818

Total budget: $6,288

Income			Expenditures		
Subscriptions	$1,977	31.4%	Repairs and maintenance	$1,145	18.2%
Donations and collections	2,326	37.0	Stock purchases	850	13.5
Interest income	208	3.3	Superintendent's salary	450	7.1
Grant from legislature	500	7.9	Clothes, shoes, bedding	694	11.0
Common school fund	370	5.8	Fuel	263	4.2
Legacies (2 female decedents)	350	5.6	Stationery and printing	80	1.3
Legacy (male decedent)	500	7.9	Medicine	63	1.0
Sale of cow and calf	35	0.5	Food, groceries	2,677	42.6
Balance from last year	22	0.3	Subscription collector's fee	62	1.0
			Balance	4	

New York Orphan Asylum Society, 1827–1828

Total budget: $11,473

Income			Expenditures		
Subscriptions	$1,343	11.7%	Land purchases	$1166	10.2%
Donations	2,169	18.9	Repairs	454	3.9
Interest income	100	0.8	Taxes	442	3.8

TABLE A.12 (continued)

	Income		Expenditures	
Stock income	548	4.7	Stock purchase	515	4.5
Grant from legislature	500	4.3	Insurance	34	0.3
Common school fund	728	6.3	Superintendent's salary	500	4.4
Legacy (male decedent)	4,000	34.8	Clothing, shoes, bedding	724	6.3
Legacy (female decedent)	500	4.3	Fuel	575	5.0
Loan	1,000	8.7	Money loaned out	1,000	8.7
Balance from last year	584	5.0	Stationery and printing	22	0.2
			Medicine	77	0.7
			Food, groceries	4,685	40.8
			Balance	1,279	11.1

New York Female Union Society for the Promotion of Sabbath Schools, 1818–1819

Total budget: $1,520

	Income		Expenditures	
Subscriptions and donations	$683	44.9%	For books	$172	11.3%
Proceeds from a benefit concert	246	16.2	For printing	861	56.6
Collections made in six churches	252	16.6	For binding	320	21.0
Society publications sold	339	22.3	Rent, heating, and cleaning of schoolrooms	89	5.8
			Counterfeit money	4	0.2
			Balance owed treasurer	74	4.9

TABLE A.12 (*continued*)

Boston Female Auxiliary Bible Society, 1816

Total budget: $635

Income			Expenditures		
Balance from last year	$224	35.3%	To permanent fund	$200	31.5%
Subscriptions	240	37.8	Purchase of Bibles	440	69.3
Life subscription	30	4.7	Miscellaneous expenses	3	0.5
Donations	141	22.2	Remaining in treasury	1	
Interest on cash loaned	9	1.4			

Seamen's Aid Society, Boston, 1836–1837

Total budget: $7,994

Income			Expenditures		
Balance from last year	$101	1.3%	For articles for store	$5,681	71.0%
Subscriptions	358	4.5	Cash to workwomen	1,423	17.8
Donations	1,975	25.3	Rent for store	140	1.8
Sales at store	5,560	71.3	Charity dispensed by president	426	5.3
			Books for library	50	0.6
			Schoolroom repairs	15	0.2
			Sewing school teacher's salary	104	1.3
			Printing	75	0.9
			Stationery for school	10	0.1
			Advertising	15	0.2
			Insurance	20	0.3
			Rental of hall	10	0.1
			Remaining in treasury	25	0.3

TABLE A.12 (continued)

Ladies New York City Anti-Slavery Society, 1836–1837

Total budget: $358

Income			Expenditures		
Balance from last year	$8	2.2%	To American Anti-Slavery Society	$185	51.7%
Subscriptions and donations	149	41.6	For printing	122	34.1
From Anti-Slavery Sewing Society	175	48.9	Purchase of antislavery publications	9	2.5
Donation from Third Free Church			Remaining in treasury	42	11.8
Ladies Anti-Slavery Society	26	7.3			

TABLE A.13 Number of Annual Subscribers and Subscription Income in Selected Organizations

Number of Subscribers

	1800	1803	1805	1810	1813	1815	1817	1820	1825	1827	1828	1830	1833	1834	1835	1836	1838	1839
Boston Female Asylum	415	413	290	454				244				126			89			73
New York Orphan Asylum Society			615							421								
Boston Fragment Society				544	600	459	554											
New York Association for the Relief of Respectable, Aged, Indigent Females						332	364		280			222			218			
Boston Widows' Society									238			189			172			168
New York Asylum for Lying-In Women											169	219						

Subscription Income

	1800	1803	1805	1810	1813	1815	1817	1820	1825	1827	1828	1830	1833	1834	1835	1836	1838	1839
Boston Female Asylum	$291	$1,245	$1,239	$1,362														
New York Female Association						621		475										
New York Orphan Asylum Society							1,977			1,343								
Boston Fragment Society					965		964		555	559	558			254	269	247	229	242
Boston Seamen's Aid Society													118	227	215	258	514	

TABLE A.14 Creation of Organizations' Permanent Funds
and Growth of Boston Female Asylum Permanent Fund

Organization (Year of Founding)	Year Permanent Fund Created
New York Society for the Relief of Poor Widows with Small Children (1797)	1812
Boston Female Asylum (1800)	1800
New York Orphan Asylum Society (1806)	1806
Boston Corban Society (1811)	1812
Boston Fragment Society (1812)	1815
Boston Female Auxiliary Bible Society (1814)	1815
New York Society for the Relief of Respectable, Aged, Indigent Females (1813)	1835 (building fund)
Boston Society for Promoting Christianity among the Jews (1815)	1826
Boston Widows' Society (1816)	1817
Boston Society for Employing the Female Poor (1820)	1820
New York Asylum for Lying-In Women (1823)	1824
Boston Children's Friend Society (1834)	1837 (building fund)
New York Association for the Benefit of Colored Orphans (1836)	1838 (building fund)

Boston Female Asylum Permanent Fund

Year	Amount in Fund
1801	$912
1806	7,300 plus a building fund of $10,000
1829	54,218
1834	64,000
1837	68,000
1838	69,000
1841	73,500

Introduction

1. Mary R. Beard, *Woman's Work in Municipalities* (1915; reprint, New York: Arno Press, 1972); Mary Bosworth Treudley, "'The Benevolent Fair': A Study of Charitable Organization among American Women in the First Third of the Nineteenth Century," *Social Service Review* 14 (September 1940): 509–22; Eleanor Flexner, *Century of Struggle: The Woman's Rights Movement in the United States* (1959; rev. ed., Cambridge: Harvard University Press, 1995). The best recent survey is Anne Firor Scott, *Natural Allies: Women's Associations in American History* (Urbana: University of Illinois Press, 1992). See also Keith Melder, *Beginnings of Sisterhood: The American Woman's Rights Movement, 1800–1850* (New York: Schocken, 1977); and Barbara Berg, *The Remembered Gate: Origins of American Feminism—The Woman and the City, 1800–1860* (New York: Oxford University Press, 1978).

2. The historiography on postbellum and Progressive Era organizations is enormous, but key works include Ruth Bordin, *Woman and Temperance: The Quest for Power and Liberty, 1873–1900* (Philadelphia: University of Pennsylvania Press, 1980); Jack S. Blocker, *"Give to the Winds Thy Fears": The Woman's Temperance Crusade, 1873–1874* (Westport, Conn.: Greenwood Press, 1985); Barbara Leslie Epstein, *The Politics of Domesticity: Women, Evangelism, and Temperance in Nineteenth-Century America* (Middletown, Conn.: Wesleyan University Press, 1980); Karen Blair, *The Clubwoman as Feminist* (New York: Holmes & Meier, 1979); Anne Firor Scott, *The Southern Lady: From Pedestal to Politics* (Chicago: University of Chicago Press, 1968); Linda Gordon, ed., *Women, the State, and Welfare* (Madison: University of Wisconsin Press, 1990); Robyn Muncy, *Creating a Female Dominion in American Reform* (New York: Oxford

University Press, 1991); Theda Skocpol, *Protecting Soldiers and Mothers: The Political Origins of Social Policy in the United States* (Cambridge: Harvard University Press, 1992); Peggy Pascoe, *Relations of Rescue: The Search for Female Moral Authority in the American West, 1874–1939* (New York: Oxford University Press, 1990); Kathryn Kish Sklar, *Florence Kelley and the Nation's Work* (New Haven: Yale University Press, 1995); Patricia R. Hill, *The World Their Household: The American Woman's Foreign Mission Movement and Cultural Transformation, 1870–1920* (Ann Arbor: University of Michigan Press, 1985); Jane Hunter, *The Gospel of Gentility* (New Haven: Yale University Press, 1984); Dorothy Salem, *To Better Our World: Black Women in Organized Reform, 1890–1920* (New York: Carlson, 1990); Deborah Gray White, *Too Heavy a Load: Black Women in Defense of Themselves, 1894–1994* (New York: W. W. Norton, 1998); and Sarah Deutsch, *Women and the City: Gender, Space, and Power in Boston, 1870–1940* (New York: Oxford University Press, 2000).

3. See Flexner, *Century of Struggle*, 38–66; Melder, *Beginnings of Sisterhood*, 30–61; and Berg, *Remembered Gate*, 145–75.

4. For critiques of the idea of a linear progression from early organizing to women's rights activism, see Anne M. Boylan, "Women in Groups: An Analysis of Women's Benevolent Organizations in New York and Boston, 1797–1840," *Journal of American History* 74 (December 1984): 497–522; and Nancy Hewitt, *Women's Activism and Social Change: Rochester, New York, 1822–1872* (Ithaca: Cornell University Press, 1984), 69–73.

5. Nancy F. Cott, *The Bonds of Womanhood: "Woman's Sphere" in New England, 1780–1835* (New Haven: Yale University Press, 1977), 155–59; Suzanne Lebsock, *The Free Women of Petersburg: Status and Culture in a Southern Town, 1784–1860* (New York: W. W. Norton, 1984), 195–236; Blanche Glassman Hersh, *The Slavery of Sex: Feminist-Abolitionists in America* (Urbana: University of Illinois Press, 1978), 4; Hewitt, *Women's Activism and Social Change*, 54, 69. See also Carroll Smith Rosenberg, *Religion and the Rise of the American City: The New York City Mission Movement, 1812–1870* (Ithaca: Cornell University Press, 1971); Mary P. Ryan, *Cradle of the Middle Class: The Family in Oneida County, New York, 1790–1865* (New York: Cambridge University Press, 1981); Barbara Miel Hobson, *Uneasy Virtue: The Politics of Prostitution and the American Reform Tradition* (New York: Basic Books, 1987); and Boylan, "Women in Groups," 497–522.

6. It is instructive, for example, to compare the extensive leather-bound collection of impeccably penned records relating to the Boston Female Asylum, 1800–1923, found at the Massachusetts State Library, with the incomplete and creatively spelled "Order Book" from the Daughters of Africa, 1821–29, found at the Historical Society of Pennsylvania. The latter, parts of which are reprinted in Dorothy Sterling, ed., *We Are Your Sisters: Black Women in the Nineteenth Century* (New York: W. W. Norton, 1984), 106–7, constitute one of the only extant manuscript records of an antebellum free black women's association. See also Dorothy B. Porter, "The Organized Educational Activities of Negro Literary Societies, 1828–1846," *Journal of Negro Education* 5 (October 1936): 555–75; Gerda Lerner, *Black Women in White America: A Documentary History* (New York: Vintage, 1972); Linda Perkins, "Black Women and Racial 'Uplift' prior to Emancipation," in *The Black Woman Cross-Culturally*, ed. Filomina Chioma Steady (Cambridge, Mass.: Schenkman, 1981): 317–34; and Anne Firor Scott, "Most Invisible

of All: Black Women's Voluntary Associations," *Journal of Southern History* 56 (February 1990): 3–22.

7. See the essays by Amy Swerdlow, Julie Winch, Carolyn Williams, and Deborah Van Broekhoven in *The Abolitionist Sisterhood: Women's Political Culture in Antebellum America*, ed. Jean Fagan Yellin and John Van Horne (Ithaca: Cornell University Press, 1994); Shirley J. Yee, *Black Women Abolitionists: A Study in Activism, 1828–1860* (Knoxville: University of Tennessee Press, 1992); Debra Gold Hansen, *Strained Sisterhood: Gender and Class in the Boston Female Anti-Slavery Society* (Amherst: University of Massachusetts Press, 1993); Julie Roy Jeffrey, *The Great Silent Army of Abolitionism: Ordinary Women in the Antislavery Movement* (Chapel Hill: University of North Carolina Press, 1998); Catherine E. Kelly, *In the New England Fashion: Reshaping Women's Lives in the Nineteenth Century* (Ithaca: Cornell University Press, 1999); Carolyn J. Lawes, *Women and Reform in a New England Community, 1815–1860* (Lexington: University of Kentucky Press, 2000); Elizabeth Varon, *"We Mean to Be Counted": White Women and Politics in Antebellum Virginia* (Chapel Hill: University of North Carolina Press, 1998); Ruth M. Alexander, "'We Are Engaged as a Band of Sisters': Class and Domesticity in the Washingtonian Temperance Movement, 1840–1850," *Journal of American History* 75 (1988): 763–85; Lori D. Ginzberg, *Women and the Work of Benevolence: Morality, Class, and Politics in the Nineteenth-Century United States* (New Haven: Yale University Press, 1990). See also the essays in *Women of the Commonwealth: Work, Family, and Social Change in Nineteenth-Century Massachusetts*, ed. Susan Lynne Porter (Amherst: University of Massachusetts Press, 1996); Porter, "Benevolent Asylum — Image and Reality: The Care and Training of Female Orphans in Boston, 1800–1840" (Ph.D. diss., Boston University, 1984); Hobson, *Uneasy Virtue*; and Mary Hershberger, "Mobilizing Women, Anticipating Abolition: The Struggle against Indian Removal in the 1830s," *Journal of American History* 86 (June 1999): 15–40.

8. The literature on republican motherhood starts with Linda K. Kerber's *Women of the Republic: Intellect and Ideology in Revolutionary America* (New York: W. W. Norton, 1980); the literature on domesticity starts with Barbara Welter, "The Cult of True Womanhood, 1820–1860," *American Quarterly* 18 (1966): 151–74. But see also Anne L. Kuhn, *The Mother's Role in Childhood Education: New England Concepts, 1830–1860* (New Haven: Yale University Press, 1947).

9. Kerber, *Women of the Republic*, 269, 285; Cott, *Bonds of Womanhood*, 146–48; Susan Juster, *Disorderly Women: Sexual Politics and Evangelicalism in Revolutionary New England* (Ithaca: Cornell University Press, 1994), 109–43; Ruth H. Bloch, "The Gendered Meanings of Virtue in Revolutionary America," *Signs* 13 (1987): 37–60. See also Christine Leigh Heyrman, *Southern Cross: The Beginnings of the Bible Belt* (New York: Knopf, 1997), 161–205; Ruth H. Bloch, "American Feminine Ideals in Transition: The Rise of the Moral Mother, 1785–1815," *Feminist Studies* 4 (June 1978): 100–126; and Joan R. Gunderson, "Independence, Citizenship, and the American Revolution," *Signs* 13 (1987): 61–77. Margaret A. Nash's suggestive essay, "Rethinking Republican Motherhood: Benjamin Rush and the Young Ladies' Academy of Philadelphia," *Journal of the Early Republic* 17 (Summer 1997): 171–91, offers an important approach to reconceptualizing republican motherhood as a historical model.

10. Juster, *Disorderly Women*, 188, 177; Elaine Forman Crane, "Dependence in the

Era of Independence: The Role of Women in a Republican Society," in *The American Revolution: Its Character and Limits*, ed. Jack P. Greene and J. R. Pole (New York: New York University Press, 1987), 253–75. See also Crane, *Ebb Tide in New England: Women, Seaports, and Social Change, 1630–1800* (Boston: Northeastern University Press, 1998), 206–41; and Susan Juster, "To Slay the Beast: Visionary Women in the Early Republic," in *A Mighty Baptism: Race, Gender, and the Creation of American Protestantism*, ed. Susan Juster and Lisa Mac Farlane (Ithaca: Cornell University Press, 1996), 19–37. For incisive analyses of the class- and race-exclusivity that were essential to the ideology of domesticity, see Christine Stansell, *City of Women: Sex and Class in New York, 1789–1860* (New York: Knopf, 1986), 19–37; and Jeanne Boydston, "The Woman Who Wasn't There: Women's Market Labor and the Transition to Capitalism in the United States," *Journal of the Early Republic* 16 (Summer 1996): 184–206.

11. On this point, see especially Daniel Walker Howe, "The Evangelical Movement and Political Culture in the North during the Second Party System," *Journal of American History* 77 (March 1991): 1222–35; Howe, "Protestantism, Voluntarism, and Personal Identity in Antebellum America," in *New Directions in American Religious History*, ed. Harry Stout and D. G. Hart (New York: Oxford University Press, 1997), 206–35; Kathryn Kish Sklar, *Catharine Beecher: A Study in American Domesticity* (New Haven: Yale University Press, 1973); and Ann Braude, "Women's History *Is* American Religious History," in *Retelling U.S. Religious History*, ed. Thomas A. Tweed (Berkeley: University of California Press, 1997), 87–107.

12. Gabriel P. Disosway, *The Earliest Churches of New York and Its Vicinity* (New York: James G. Gregory, 1865); Patricia Bonomi, *Under the Cope of Heaven: Religion, Society, and Politics in Colonial New York* (New York: Oxford University Press, 1986); Dee Andrews, *The Methodists and Revolutionary America: The Shaping of an Evangelical Culture* (Princeton: Princeton University Press, 2000); John H. Wigger, *Taking Heaven by Storm: Methodism and the Rise of Popular Christianity in America* (New York: Oxford University Press, 1998); James C. Odiorne, "A Complete List of the Ministers of Boston of All Denominations, from 1630 to 1842, Arranged in the Order of Their Settlement," *New England Historical and Genealogical Review* 1 (1847): 134–37, 240–43, 318–21; Anne C. Rose, *Transcendentalism as a Social Movement, 1830–1850* (New Haven: Yale University Press, 1981), 229–33.

13. Hyman B. Grinstein, *The Rise of the Jewish Community of New York, 1654–1860* (Philadelphia: Jewish Publication Society of America, 1945); Jonathan D. Sarna and Ellen Smith, eds., *The Jews of Boston* (Boston: Combined Jewish Philanthropies, 1995); Ronald D. Patkus, "A Community in Transition: Boston Catholics, 1815–1845" (Ph.D. diss., Boston College, 1997); Robert H. Lord, John E. Sexton, and Edward T. Harrington, *History of the Archdiocese of Boston in the Various Stages of Its Development, 1604 to 1943*, 3 vols. (New York: Sheed & Ward, 1944); John Gilmary Shea, *The Catholic Churches of New York City* (New York: Lawrence G. Goulding, 1878).

14. Leonore Davidoff, "Regarding Some 'Old Husbands' Tales': Public and Private in Feminist History," in *Feminism, the Public, and the Private*, ed. Joan Landes (New York: Oxford University Press, 1998), 165–85.

15. On this point, see especially Nancy Fraser, "Rethinking the Public Sphere: A Contribution to the Critique of Actually Existing Democracy," in *Habermas and the*

Public Sphere, ed. Craig Calhoun (Cambridge: MIT Press, 1992), 110–34; and Leonore Davidoff and Catherine Hall, *Family Fortunes: Men and Women of the English Middle Class, 1780–1850* (Chicago: University of Chicago Press, 1987), 416–49. Fraser explores the extent to which the very concept of a civil society or public sphere was "a masculinist ideological notion" that legitimated the existing political order.

16. The literature on "civil society," much of it by sociologists and political scientists, took off in the 1990s in response to the fall of the Soviet Union. This literature often reflects an interest in finding alternatives to state provision in social welfare and state parties in politics, although it also considers the conditions of citizenship and the functions of a "public sphere" in modern societies. Much of it is also decidedly triumphalistic in its treatment of the American experience, even when Jeremiah-like authors scold contemporary Americans for their lack of civic virtue; indeed, analyses of American "civil society" are often explicitly prescriptive. See, for example, *Community Works: The Revival of Civil Society in America*, ed. E. J. Dionne (Washington, D.C.: The Brookings Institution, 1998); and *Seedbeds of Virtue: Sources of Competence, Character, and Citizenship in American Society*, ed. Mary Ann Glendon and David Blankenhorn (Lanham, Md.: Madison Books, 1995). The most influential statement claiming a decline in American civic engagement is Robert Putnam, *Bowling Alone: The Collapse and Revival of American Community* (New York: Simon & Schuster, 2000). Frank Trentmann provides an excellent, nuanced introduction to the history of the term "civil society" and scholars' uses and misuses of it; "Introduction: Paradoxes of Civil Society," in *Paradoxes of Civil Society: New Perspectives on Modern British and German History*, ed. Frank Trentmann (New York: Berghahn Books, 2000). For a critique of the masculinist assumptions behind concepts of "civil society" and "the public sphere," see the essays by Nancy Fraser and Mary Ryan in Calhoun, *Habermas and the Public Sphere*.

Chapter One

1. Worcester, quoted in Conrad Edick Wright, *The Transformation of Charity in Postrevolutionary New England* (Boston: Northeastern University Press, 1992), 51.

2. Linda K. Kerber, *Women of the Republic: Intellect and Ideology in Revolutionary America* (Chapel Hill: University of North Carolina Press, 1980), 269–88; Lori D. Ginzberg, *Women and the Work of Benevolence: Morality, Politics, and Class in Nineteenth-Century America* (New Haven: Yale University Press, 1990), 2–8.

3. Christine Stansell, *City of Women: Sex and Class in New York, 1790–1860* (New York: Knopf, 1986), 20–22; Joan R. Gunderson, "Independence, Citizenship, and the American Revolution," *Signs* 13 (Autumn 1987): 59–77; Kathryn Kish Sklar, *Catharine Beecher: A Study in American Domesticity* (New Haven: Yale University Press, 1973), 168–75; Stephanie McCurry, *Masters of Small Worlds: Yeoman Households, Gender Relations, and the Political Culture of the Antebellum South Carolina Low Country* (New York: Oxford University Press, 1996), 121–29.

4. A number of historians have made this point, but see especially Nancy F. Cott, *The Bonds of Womanhood: "Woman's Sphere" in New England, 1780–1835* (New Haven: Yale University Press, 1977), 154–59; Ginzberg, *Women and the Work of Benevolence*,

22–25; Stansell, *City of Women*, 69–75; and Linda K. Kerber, "Separate Spheres, Female Worlds, Women's Place: The Rhetoric of Women's History," *Journal of American History* 75 (June 1988): 9–39.

5. Ginzberg, *Women and the Work of Benevolence*, 24. See also Ginzberg, "'The Hearts of Your Readers Will Shudder': Fanny Wright, Infidelity, and American Freethought," *American Quarterly* 46 (June 1994): 195–225.

6. Ginzberg, *Women and the Work of Benevolence*, 18–25; Stuart Blumin, *The Emergence of the Middle Class: Social Experience in the American City, 1760–1900* (New York: Cambridge University Press, 1989), 192–229; Mary P. Ryan, *Cradle of the Middle Class: The Family in Oneida County, New York, 1790–1865* (Cambridge: Cambridge University Press, 1981), 105–44; Peter Dobkin Hall, *The Organization of American Culture, 1700–1900: Private Institutions, Elites, and the Origins of American Nationality* (New York: New York University Press, 1982); John S. Gilkeson, *Middle-Class Providence, 1820–1940* (Princeton: Princeton University Press, 1986), 8–13. Blumin, Hall, and Gilkeson focus on men's associations. For the British context, see Leonore Davidoff and Catherine Hall, *Family Fortunes: Men and Women of the English Middle Class, 1780–1850* (Chicago: University of Chicago Press, 1987), 419–36.

7. The phrase is Jane Addams's, used to explain the reasons why settlement houses emerged a hundred years later: *Twenty Years at Hull House* (1910; reprint, New York: Signet, 1960), 90.

8. Society for the Relief of Poor Widows with Small Children Minutes, December 20, 1797, New-York Historical Society, New York City; Female Association, "Rules for the Schools . . . and Minutes of the Trustees," 1805, New York Female Association Records, 1798–1988, Friends Historical Library, Swarthmore College, Swarthmore, Pa.; *Constitution of the Boston Female Society for Missionary Purposes, Organized October 9, 1800* (Boston: n.p., 1816), 3; Ginzberg, *Women and the Work of Benevolence*, 15. The literature on benevolent organizations is lengthy, but see Mary Bosworth Treudley, "'The Benevolent Fair': A Study of Charitable Organizations among American Women in the First Third of the Nineteenth Century," *Social Service Review* 14 (1940): 509–22; Keith E. Melder, *Beginnings of Sisterhood: The American Woman's Rights Movement, 1800–1850* (New York: Schocken, 1977), 49–76; Barbara J. Berg, *The Remembered Gate: Origins of American Feminism—The Woman and the City, 1800–1860* (New York: Oxford University Press, 1978), 149–75; and Anne Firor Scott, *Natural Allies: Women's Associations in American History* (Urbana: University of Illinois Press, 1993), 11–36. See also David J. Rothman, *The Discovery of the Asylum: Social Order and Disorder in the New Republic* (Boston: Little, Brown, 1971).

9. Joanna Bethune, ed., *The Power of Faith, Exemplified in the Life and Writings of the Late Mrs. Isabella Graham*, rev. ed. (New York: American Tract Society, 1843), 130; Nancy F. Cott, *The Bonds of Womanhood: "Woman's Sphere" in New England, 1785–1835* (New Haven: Yale University Press, 1978). On Quaker traditions, see Sydney James, *A People among Peoples: Quaker Benevolence in Eighteenth Century America* (Cambridge: Harvard University Press, 1963); Joan Jensen, *Loosening the Bonds: Mid-Atlantic Farm Women, 1750–1850* (New Haven: Yale University Press, 1986); Bruce Allen Dorsey II, "City of Brotherly Love: Religious Benevolence, Gender, and Reform in Philadelphia, 1780–1844" (Ph.D. diss., Brown University, 1993), 5–58; and Margaret

Morris Haviland, "Beyond Women's Sphere: Young Quaker Women and the Veil of Charity in Philadelphia, 1790–1810," *William and Mary Quarterly* 51 (July 1994): 419–46. On religious developments, see Catherine A. Brekus, *Strangers and Pilgrims: Female Preaching in America, 1740–1845* (Chapel Hill: University of North Carolina Press, 1998), 23–113; and Jon Butler, *Awash in a Sea of Faith: Christianizing the American People* (Cambridge: Harvard University Press, 1990). On changes in ideology and education, see Mary Sumner Benson, *Women in Eighteenth-Century America: A Study in Opinion and Social Usage* (New York: Columbia University Press, 1935); and Kerber, *Women of the Republic*, 185–264. On economic activities, see Lisa Wilson Waciega, "A 'Man of Business': The Widow of Means in Southeastern Pennsylvania, 1730–1850," *William and Mary Quarterly*, 44 (1987).

10. New York Female Association Records, 1799; Boston Female Asylum Minutes, October 27,1800, Massachusetts State Library, Boston, Mass.; Susan Lynne Porter, "Benevolent Asylum—Image and Reality: The Care and Training of Female Orphans in Boston, 1800–1840" (Ph.D. diss., Boston University, 1984), 66–68, 74, 96–98, 101 (in 1800, the founders' median age was 42; the median value of their families' real estate holdings was $10,000); Carl Seaburg and Stanley Paterson, *Merchant Prince of Boston: Colonel T. H. Perkins, 1764–1854* (Cambridge: Harvard University Press, 1971), 16–19, 22–29; *Notable American Women*, s.v. "Perkins, Elizabeth Peck"; Eleanor Davis Receipt Book, 1812–23, Caleb Davis Papers, Massachusetts Historical Society, Boston, Mass.; Mary Chrystie Receipt Book, 1800–1806, New-York Historical Society, New York City; George Washington Bethune, *Memoirs of Mrs. Joanna Bethune* (New York: Harper & Bros., 1864), 79–84; Bethune, *Power of Faith*, 58–82; Boston Female Asylum Minutes, September 26, 1800; Albert Vail, *Mary Webb and the Mother Society* (Philadelphia: American Baptist Publication Society, 1914), 49–50; Ruth H. Bloch, "The Gendered Meanings of Virtue in Revolutionary America," *Signs* 13 (Autumn 1987): 57. On the changing experiences of young women, see Cott, *The Bonds of Womanhood*, 52–62. On transatlantic evangelicalism, see Carroll Smith Rosenberg, *Religion and the Rise of the American City: The New York City Mission Movement, 1812–1870* (Ithaca: Cornell University Press, 1971), 49–51; and Susan O'Brien, "Eighteenth-Century Publishing Networks in the First Years of Transatlantic Evangelicalism," in *Evangelicalism: Comparative Studies of Popular Protestantism in North America, the British Isles, and Beyond, 1700–1900*, ed. Mark A. Noll, David W. Bebbington, and George A. Rawlyk (New York: Oxford University Press, 1994), 38–57. On the growing significance of reading in the revolutionary era, see Cathy Davidson, *Revolution and the Word: The Rise of the Novel in America* (New York: Oxford University Press, 1986); and Kerber, *Women of the Republic*, 233–64.

11. *Constitution and By-Laws of the Orphan Asylum Society in the City of New York* (New York, 1810), 10 (emphasis added); Boston Female Asylum Minutes, September 26, 1800.

12. "Address to Young Ladies, 1804," in Bethune, *Power of Faith*, 232; "Curtius" articles in the *Worcester Aegis*, 1803, quoted in Porter, "Benevolent Asylum," 80; *An Account of the Boston Female Asylum . . .* (Boston, 1803), 3–4. Beginning in 1801, the Female Asylum held its annual meetings in churches or at the asylum building; from 1803 until 1825, the Society for the Relief of Poor Widows' annual meeting was at the City Hotel; after 1825, the group met annually at various Presbyterian churches.

13. By contrast, men's voluntary associations, especially those involved in partisan and factional politics, seem to have been more vulnerable to continuing attack; see Albrecht Koschnik, "Voluntary Associations, Political Culture, and the Public Sphere in Philadelphia, 1780–1830" (Ph.D. diss., University of Virginia, 2000).

14. Suzanne Lebsock, *The Free Women of Petersburg: Status and Culture in a Southern Town, 1784–1860* (New York: W. W. Norton, 1984), 200–201; Ginzberg, *Women and the Work of Benevolence*, 48–53. The incorporation of private associations remained a controversial legal practice throughout the era, especially in New York (which did not have a general incorporation statute for charitable associations until 1848), but women's groups were seldom singled out for criticism. On the rare occasions when petitions for incorporation were denied (the Female Benevolent Society had that experience in 1840), female incorporators' sex was not the cause. See Hall, *The Organization of American Culture*, 95–114; Ronald E. Seavoy, *The Origins of the American Business Corporation, 1784–1855: Broadening the Concept of Public Service during Industrialization* (Westport, Conn.: Greenwood Press, 1982), 3–21; Oscar Handlin and Mary Flug Handlin, *Commonwealth: A Study of the Role of Government in the American Economy, Massachusetts, 1774–1861*, rev. ed. (Cambridge: Harvard University Press, 1968), 213–17; and Pauline Maier, "The Debate over Incorporations: Massachusetts in the Early Republic," in *Massachusetts and the New Nation*, ed. Conrad Edick Wright (Boston: Massachusetts Historical Society, 1992), 73–117.

15. Kerber, *Women of the Republic*, 99–106; David Montgomery, "The Working Classes of the Pre-Industrial American City," *Labor History* 9 (1968): 3–22; Society for the Relief of Poor Widows with Small Children Minutes, November 1805; Boston Female Asylum Minutes, April 1805; Melder, *Beginnings of Sisterhood*, 70–71.

16. Association for the Relief of Respectable, Aged, Indigent Females Minutes, September 1815, Records of the Association for the Relief of Respectable, Aged, Indigent Females, 8 vols., New-York Historical Society, New York City; Widows' Society, *First Annual Report* (Boston, 1817), 2; *Constitution of the Fatherless and Widows Society, Including the Report for 1832* (Boston, 1832), 3. On the Fragment Society, see Scott, *Natural Allies*, 27–36.

17. Female Auxiliary Bible Society, *Second Annual Report* (New York, 1818), 2; Records of the Graham Society, January 1817, Congregational Library, Boston, Mass.; *Constitution of the Female Tract Society of Boston and Its Vicinity, Instituted September 19, 1816* (Boston, 1820), 3; David F. Allmendinger, Jr., "The Strangeness of the American Education Society," *History of Education Quarterly* 11 (1971): 3–22. Members of the Corban and Graham Societies defined orthodoxy in terms of the theological principles outlined in the Westminster Assembly's Shorter Catechism, that is, through Congregationalism or Presbyterianism. A "corban" is an offering of money or service dedicated to God. On Boston Unitarianism, see Anne C. Rose, *Transcendentalism as a Social Movement, 1830–1850* (New Haven: Yale University Press, 1981), 4–30.

18. Society for the Relief of Poor Widows with Small Children Minutes, November 25, 1816, November 16, 1820, November 3, 1823; Orphan Asylum Society in the City of New York, *Twelfth Annual Report* (New York, 1818), 4; *A Brief Account of the Origin and Progress of the Boston Female Society for Missionary Purposes . . .* (Boston, 1818), 6; *Boston Recorder and Religious Telegraph* 15 (January 6, 1830): 4; Vail, *Mary Webb*,

62–74; Stansell, *City of Women*, 65–75. Barbara Bellows found a similar shift among white Protestant women in Charleston; see *Benevolence among Slaveholders: Assisting the Poor in Charleston, 1670–1860* (Baton Rouge: Louisiana State University Press, 1993), 40–41.

19. Association for the Relief of Respectable, Aged, Indigent Females Minutes, November 8, 1814; Fragment Society Minutes, October 9, 1815, Fragment Society Collection, Schlesinger Library, Cambridge, Mass.; Society for the Relief of Poor Widows with Small Children Minutes, October 3, 1814. On the evangelical impetus within Episcopalianism, see Smith Rosenberg, *Religion and the Rise of the American City*, 125–26; and Diana Hochstedt Butler, *Standing against the Whirlwind: Evangelical Episcopalians in Nineteenth-Century America* (New York: Oxford University Press, 1995).

20. Female Association Records, October 4, 1811 (Quaker involvement in cross-denominational societies became an important issue in 1827 when the group split into Orthodox and Hicksite wings); Boston Female Asylum Minutes, August 1810; Samuel L. Knapp, *The Life of Thomas Eddy* (New York: Connor & Cooke, 1834), 123–26; *Dictionary of American Biography*, s.v. "Griffin, Edward Dorr"; Porter, "Benevolent Asylum," 180–87; Hamilton Andrews Hill, *History of the Old South Church (Third Church), Boston, 1669–1884*, 2 vols. (Boston: Houghton Mifflin, 1890), 2:340–42. As Susan Porter demonstrates, Susanna Bacon's tenure as superintendent was stormy, in part because she was seen as too severe. It seems likely that the managers perceived her as severe because their liberal Unitarianism encompassed different approaches to child-rearing than her orthodox Congregationalism. Porter, "Benevolent Asylum," 180–87. See also Philip Greven, *The Protestant Temperament: Patterns of Child-Rearing, Religious Experience and the Self in Early America* (New York: Knopf, 1977).

21. The classic article on the "true woman" is Barbara Welter, "The Cult of True Womanhood, 1820–1860," *American Quarterly* 18 (1966): 151–74. Carroll Smith Rosenberg makes this point in *Religion and the Rise of the American City*, 3–5, but dates the transition to be somewhat later, and particularly ties it to Charles Grandison Finney's revivals.

22. Boston Female Auxiliary Bible Society, *Ninth Annual Report* (Boston, 1823), 1; *Christian Herald* 1 (May 18, 1819): 120–21. The Female Union Society for the Promotion of Sabbath Schools predated the men's group in New York by a month. On the relationship between the two organizations, see Anne M. Boylan, *Sunday School: The Formation of an American Institution, 1790–1880* (New Haven: Yale University Press, 1988), 121.

23. Raymond W. Mohl, *Poverty in New York, 1780–1825* (New York: Oxford University Press, 1971); Smith Rosenberg, *Religion and the Rise of the American City*; Amy Bridges, *A City in the Republic: New York and the Origins of Machine Politics* (New York: Cambridge University Press, 1984). Bruce Dorsey documents a similar development in Philadelphia in the following decade; see "City of Brotherly Love," 110–48.

24. Rose, *Transcendentalism as a Social Movement*; Mary Kupiec Cayton, "Who Were the Evangelicals?," *Journal of Social History* 31 (1997): 85–107.

25. "Memoir of Mrs. Lydia Morris Malcom," *The American Baptist Magazine* 13 (August 1833): 289–303. See also Ruth Bloch, "Religion and Ideological Change in the American Revolution," in *Religion and American Politics from the Colonial Period to the 1980s*, ed. Mark A. Noll (New York: Oxford University Press, 1990), 44–61.

26. New York Female Tract Society, *Annual Report* (New York, 1827), 3–4; Female Auxiliary Bible Society, *Ninth Annual Report* (Boston, 1823), 1–9; New York Maternal Association Minutes, November 28, 1832, Minutes of the New York Maternal Association, 1832–69, Presbyterian Historical Society, Philadelphia, Pa.; Boston Widows' Society Minutes, June 1829, Schlesinger Library, Cambridge, Mass.; J. F. Richmond, *New York and Its Institutions*, 1607–1872 (New York: E. B. Treat, 1872), 425; Boston Fatherless and Widows Society, *Seventeenth Annual Report* (Boston, 1834); *Twelfth Annual Report of the New York City Tract Society . . . with the Sixteenth Annual Report of the Female Branch* (New York, 1838), 103–5; *Christian Herald* 1 (September 21, 1816): 411–12; *Fifth Annual Report of the New-York Female Juvenile Bible Association* (New York, 1823), 24; Orphan Asylum Society in the City of New York, *Twelfth Annual Report* (New York, 1818), 10. On the Robinson family, see R. Burnham Moffett, *The Barclays of New York: Who They Are, and Who They Are Not* (New York: Robert Grier Cooke, 1904), 106, 117, 130–31. I have information about the ages of three of the nine founders of the Juvenile Female Tract Society; all were thirteen or fourteen years of age. Of the sixteen officers of the Female Juvenile Bible Association in 1823, the three for whom I have age data were between twenty and twenty-three years old. In 1826, feeling that the term "juvenile" "rather dampened than stimulated" members' efforts, the group renamed itself the Young Ladies' Bible Society. See *Eleventh Annual Report of the New York Female Auxiliary Bible Society and First Annual Report of the Young Ladies' Bible Society* (New York, 1827), 19. Sunday school teaching also became a means of formalizing a conversion experience. See Boylan, *Sunday School*, 101–4.

27. Boston Female Asylum Minutes, September 26, 1800; February 26, 1801; Kerber, *Women of the Republic*, 251–57; *Notable American Women*, s.v., "Warren, Mercy Otis." See also Ruth Bloch, "The Gendered Meanings of Virtue in Revolutionary America," *Signs* 13 (Autumn 1987): 39–56; and Cott, *Bonds of Womanhood*, 63–72.

28. Society for the Relief of Poor Widows with Small Children Minutes, November 16, 1815; Boston Female Asylum Minutes, September 1840; [A. F. Wales], *Reminiscences of the Boston Female Asylum* (Boston: n.p., 1844), 30; Vail, *Mary Webb*, 53–54; Female Branch of the New York Religious Tract Society Minutes, March 25, 1824, New York City Mission Society, New York City. Webb's invocation of Miriam, Deborah, Priscilla, and Phebe—the first two Old Testament prophetic figures, the second two New Testament "helpmeets" of Christian men—provides an interesting contrast with the heroines whom Esther DeBerdt Reed praised in her 1780 "Sentiments of an American Woman." Reed's inspirations included Deborah, but also two considerably fiercer Old Testament individuals, Judith and Esther, as well as Roman matrons and Europe's queens. See Kerber, *Women of the Republic*, 274–77.

29. Keith J. Hardman, *Charles Grandison Finney, 1792–1875: Revivalism and Reform* (Syracuse: Syracuse University Press, 1987), 172–91, 212–38; Richard Carwardine, "The Second Great Awakening in the Urban Centers: An Examination of Methodism and the 'New Measures,'" *Journal of American History* 59 (September 1972): 327–40; Barbara M. Cross, ed., *The Autobiography of Lyman Beecher*, 2 vols. (Cambridge: Harvard University Press, 1961), 1:xvii–xxx; 2:33–56, 62–80; Rose, *Transcendentalism as a Social Movement*, 1–37.

30. David Hosack, *Memoir of DeWitt Clinton* (New York: J. Seymour, 1829), 174;

Boston Recorder and Religious Telegraph 13 (May 9, 1828): 76; Maris Vinovskis and Dean May, "'A Ray of Millennial Light': Early Education and Social Reform in the Infant School Movement in Massachusetts, 1826–1840," in *Family and Kin in Urban Communities, 1700–1830*, ed. Tamara K. Hareven (New York: Franklin Watts, 1977), 62–99; *Truth Teller* 5 (October 24, 1829): 342; *Circular, Act of Incorporation, Constitution, Government, and By-Laws of the Boston Children's Friend Society* (Boston, 1834).

31. [Mary W. Mason], "An Account of the New York Society for Lying-In Women," 1823, Records of the Asylum for Lying-In Women, New York Weill-Cornell Medical Center Archives, New York City; *A Short Account of the Penitent Females' Refuge* (Boston, 1834), 14; Female Benevolent Society, *First Annual Report* (New York, 1834), 14; Barbara Miel Hobson, *Uneasy Virtue: The Politics of Prostitution and the American Reform Tradition* (New York: Basic Books, 1987), 118–23; Larry Howard Whiteaker, "Moral Reform and Prostitution in New York City, 1830–1860" (Ph.D. diss., Princeton University, 1977), 157–96. On the condition of working women in New York, see Stansell, *City of Women*, 11–18. Middle-class white women's efforts to assist women prisoners had a similar protective character in the 1830s, as did women's depositories, such as the Ladies' Depository Association of New York (1833), which sold genteel women's needlework. See Estelle B. Freeman, *Their Sisters' Keepers: Women's Prison Reform in America, 1830–1930* (Ann Arbor: University of Michigan Press, 1981), 22–30; and Mari Jo Buhle, "Needlewomen and the Vicissitudes of Modern Life: A Study of Middle-Class Construction in the Antebellum Northeast," in *Visible Women: New Essays on American Activism*, ed. Nancy A. Hewitt and Suzanne Lebsock (Urbana: University of Illinois Press, 1993), 145–65.

32. Anne M. Boylan, "Benevolence and Antislavery Activity among African-American Women in New York and Boston, 1820–1840," in *The Abolitionist Sisterhood: Women's Political Culture in Antebellum America*, ed. Jean Fagan Yellin and John C. Van Horne (Ithaca: Cornell University Press, 1994), 119–38; Ruth M. Alexander, "'We Are Engaged as a Band of Sisters': Class and Domesticity in the Washingtonian Temperance Movement, 1840–1850," *Journal of American History* 75 (December 1988): 770–77; *Colored American*, June 3, 1837, 4. African American women in Philadelphia had created the Female Benevolent Society of St. Thomas in 1793; see Dorothy Sterling, ed., *We Are Your Sisters: Black Women in the Nineteenth Century* (New York: W. W. Norton, 1984), 105. On mutual aid societies in New York, see Mohl, *Poverty in New York*, 154–57. On Roman Catholic women's parish groups, see Robert H. Lord, John E. Sexton, and Edward T. Harrington, *History of the Archdiocese of Boston*, 3 vols. (New York: Sheed & Ward, 1944), 1: 654. On Jewish women's synagogue societies, see Jacob Rader Marcus, *United States Jewry, 1776–1985* (Detroit: Wayne State University Press, 1989), 1:315–44. See also Peter Holloran, *Boston's Wayward Children: Social Services for Homeless Children, 1830–1930* (Cranbury, N.J.: Fairleigh Dickinson University Press, 1989), 63–69.

33. Boylan, "Benevolence and Antislavery Activity," 122–23. On the economic conditions of free blacks, see Rhoda Golden Freeman, *The Free Negro in New York City in the Era before the Civil War* (New York: Garland, 1994), 268–311; and Donald Martin Jacobs, "A History of the Boston Negro from the Revolution to the Civil War" (Ph.D. diss., Boston University, 1968). The same point could be made about the United Tai-

loresses' Society, one of the few laboring women's organizations from this era. In an address to the society in 1831, Louise Mitchell urged unity among women workers and asserted their right to act for themselves. See Dolores Janiewski, "Making Common Cause: The Needlewomen of New York, 1831–1869," *Signs* 1 (1976): 779–81; and Stansell, *City of Women*, 134–36.

34. On the De Grasse family, see William C. Nell, *The Colored Patriots of the American Revolution* (Boston: Robert F. Wallcut, 1855), 316–17; "John Van Surl[e]y De Grasse," in *Dictionary of American Negro Biography*, ed. Rayford W. Logan and Michael R. Winston (New York: W. W. Norton, 1982), 169; *Longworth's American Almanac . . . and New-York City Directory* (New York: Longworth, 1816, 1823, 1831, 1838, 1842); *Liberator* 11 (December 10, 1841); *New York City Methodist Marriages*, comp. William Scott Fisher, 2 vols. (Camden, Maine: Picton Press, 1994); *Minutes of the Common Council of the City of New York, 1784–1831*, 19 vols. (New York: City of New York, 1917) 9:419, 509, 565, 592; 13:59, 617; 15:62; *New York Evening Post*, May 27, 1862; 1850 Census of New York City, 5th Ward, 047–048, microfilm, New York Public Library. For a genealogy of Maria Van Surley De Grasse, see Henry B. Hoff, "Frans Abramse Van Salee and His Descendants: A Colonial Black Family in New York and New Jersey," *New York Genealogical and Biographical Record* 121 (1990): 65–71, 157–61, 205–11. On the 1834 riots, see Paul A. Gilje, *Mobocracy: Popular Disorder in New York City, 1763–1834* (Chapel Hill: University of North Carolina Press, 1987).

35. Gerda Lerner, *Black Women in White America: A Documentary History* (New York: Random House, 1972), 438–39; Dorothy Porter, "The Organized Educational Activities of Negro Literary Societies, 1828–1846," *Journal of Negro Education* 5 (October 1936): 555–76; *Emancipator*, November 24, 1836, 119; Dorothy Sterling, ed., *Turning the World Upside Down: The Anti-Slavery Convention of American Women, Held in New York City, May 9–12, 1837* (New York: Feminist Press, 1987), 22; *Colored American* 2 (May 3, 1838): 3. See also Julie Winch, "'You Have Talents—Only Cultivate Them': Philadelphia's Black Female Literary Societies and the Abolitionist Crusade," in Yellin and Van Horne, *The Abolitionist Sisterhood*, 101–18.

36. Alma Lutz, *Crusade for Freedom: Women of the Antislavery Movement* (Boston: Beacon, 1968); Blanche Glassman Hersh, *The Slavery of Sex: Feminist-Abolitionists in America* (Urbana: University of Illinois Press, 1978), 11–16; Debra Gold Hansen, *Strained Sisterhood: Gender and Class in the Boston Female Anti-Slavery Society* (Amherst: University of Massachusetts Press, 1993), 13–28; Ginzberg, *Women and the Work of Benevolence*, 25–35; Smith Rosenberg, *Religion and the Rise of the American City*, 97–124; Hobson, *Uneasy Virtue*, 53–70; *A Short Account of the Penitent Females' Refuge*, 9. For a similar typology of women's groups in Rochester, see Nancy Hewitt, *Women's Activism and Social Change: Rochester, New York, 1822–1872* (Ithaca: Cornell University Press, 1984), 39–42.

37. "The Province of Woman," *Advocate of Moral Reform* 3 (September 15, 1837): 325; (October 1, 1837): 333; Boston Female Anti-Slavery Society, *Second Annual Report* (Boston, 1836), 6n; Ginzberg, *Women and the Work of Benevolence*, 113–14.

38. Joanna H. Mathews, comp., *A Short History of the Orphan Asylum Society in the City of New York* (New York: Anson D. F. Randolph, 1893), 7–11; *New York Evening*

Post, July 5, 1814; Stansell, *City of Women*, 16; Vail, *Mary Webb*, 73; *A Short Account of the Penitent Females' Refuge*, 3–4.

39. Female Branch of the New York Religious Tract Society, Constitution and Minutes, March 27, 1822; Female Bible Society of Boston and Its Vicinity, circular letter from Philadelphia Female Bible Society, June 5, 1814, Female Bible Society of Boston and Its Vicinity, Corresponding Secretary's Records, 1814–83, Schlesinger Library, Cambridge, Mass.; *Advocate of Moral Reform* 2 (June 1, 1836): 73.

40. On Elizabeth Jackson Riley, see *Liberator* 3 (August 31, 1833): 137; 5 (September 5, 1835): 143; and the documents transcribed in Carol Buchalter Stapp, *Afro-Americans in Antebellum Boston: An Analysis of Probate Records* (New York: Garland, 1993), 522–42. Riley also joined the Boston Female Anti-Slavery Society, though she was never an officer. There is an obituary in *Frederick Douglass's Paper* 8 (February 2, 1855): 2. In rural areas, as Catherine E. Kelly has argued, these connections between class identity and voluntary society involvement seem to have been considerably less salient; see *In the New England Fashion: Reshaping Women's Lives in the Nineteenth Century* (Ithaca: Cornell University Press, 1999), 14–15, 199–203.

41. See Appendix 2 for a discussion of the sources and methodology underlying these conclusions. On the key distinction between participation density (the number of people actually participating in an organization) and organizational density (the number of existing associations), see Jason Kaufman, "Three Views of Associationalism in 19th-Century America: An Empirical Examination," *American Journal of Sociology* 104 (March 1999): 1339. The situation in Philadelphia seems to have been quite different; Bruce Dorsey found none of the leadership overlaps there that I have found in New York and Boston. See "City of Brotherly Love," 140–42.

42. *New York City Methodist Marriages*; *Christian Advocate and Journal*, September 30, 1846; Elizabeth Mason North, *Consecrated Talents; or, The Life of Mrs. Mary W. Mason* (New York: Carlton & Lanahan, 1870), 61; Joanna Bethune Diary, September 13, 1846, Bentley Library, University of Michigan, Ann Arbor, Mich.; Vail, *Mary Webb*.

43. F. W. Chapman, *The Coit Family: or, the Descendants of John Coit* (Hartford: n.p., 1874), 1267. Her sister, Susan Howland Aspinwall, was active in the Orphan Asylum Society for several decades; another sister, Harriet Howland Roosevelt, joined her in working for the Bible Society and Tract Society. On Ann Safford, see Edward S. Safford, "The Saffords in America," typescript, Boston Public Library, Boston, Mass. Ann (1802–74) was Daniel Safford's fourth wife, having married him in 1833; her sister Abby had been his second wife. Safford's firm built the iron fence around Boston Common; Safford himself was a deacon in the Park Street (Congregationalist) Church and a pillar of men's evangelical labor in Boston.

44. Anne M. Boylan, "Henrietta Green Regulus Ray," *Black Women in America: An Historical Encyclopedia*, ed. Darlene Clark Hine (Brooklyn: Carlson, 1993), 866; *The Liberator* 3 (April 20, 1833): 63; Adelaide M. Cromwell, *The Other Brahmins: Boston's Black Upper Class, 1750–1950* (Fayetteville: University of Arkansas Press, 1994), 224–25; Gloria Oden, "The Black Putnams of Charlotte Forten's Diary," *Essex Institute Historical Collections* 126 (October 1990): 237–53; Franklin A. Dorman, *Twenty Families of Color in Massachusetts, 1742–1998* (Boston: New England Historic Genealogical So-

ciety, 1998), 117–42; *The Boston Directory* (Boston: 1834–47); Stapp, *Afro-Americans in Antebellum Boston*, 583–605; C. Peter Ripley, ed., *The Black Abolitionist Papers*, vol. 3, *The United States, 1830–1846* (Chapel Hill: University of North Carolina Press, 1991), 307.

45. See, for example, *The Constitution and Laws of the Orphan Asylum of the City of New-York* (New York, 1818); *The Constitution, and First and Second Annual Reports of the Proceedings of the Association for the Relief of Respectable, Aged, Indigent Females* (New York, 1818), 3–4; Seamen's Aid Society, Boston, *First Annual Report* (Boston, 1834). See also Ginzberg, *Women and the Work of Benevolence*, 11–35.

46. Jay P. Dolan, *The Immigrant Church: New York's Irish and German Catholics, 1815–1865,* (Baltimore: Johns Hopkins University Press, 1975), 135–36; *Truth Teller* 5 (October 10, 1829): 324; Ronald D. Patkus, "A Community in Transition: Boston Catholics, 1815–1845" (Ph.D. diss., Boston College, 1997), 101–2; Hyman Grinstein, *The Rise of the Jewish Community of New York, 1654–1860* (Philadelphia: Jewish Publication Society of America, 1945), 151–52. One New York Protestant woman, Magdalen Sidell Isaccs, whose husband Jacob was Jewish, served for many years as a manager of the Asylum for Lying-In Women, but only after her husband's death. See *New York Evening Post*, July 8, 1858.

47. *Notable American Women*, s.v. "Gratz, Rebecca"; Dianne Ashton, *Rebecca Gratz: Women and Judaism in Antebellum America* (Detroit: Wayne State University Press, 1997), 93–148; Richard C. Murphy and Lawrence J. Mannion, *The History of the Friendly Sons of St. Patrick in the City of New York, 1784–1958* (New York: n.p., 1962), 186–204; Thomas S. Meehan, "A Self-Effaced Philanthropist: Cornelius Heeney, 1754–1848," *Catholic Historical Review* 4 (April 1918): 3–17; Karen Kennelly, "Ideals of American Catholic Womanhood," in *American Catholic Women: A Historical Exploration*, ed. Karen Kennelly (New York: Macmillan, 1989), 1–16. On Catherine Mann Dupleix, see Annabelle Melville, *Elizabeth Bayley Seton, 1774–1821* (New York: Charles Scribner's Sons, 1954), 197; and *Truth Teller* 5 (October 24, 1829): 342. Other philanthropic converts included Cincinnati's Sarah Worthington King Peter; see Debra Campbell, "Reformers and Activists," in Kennelly, ed., *American Catholic Women*, 152–81; and *Notable American Women*, s.v. "Peter, Sarah Worthington King." Catholic laywomen's sodalities and confraternities, while comparable in some respects to Protestant women's missionary societies, remained parish-based during this era. See Ann Taves, *The Household of Faith: Roman Catholic Devotions in Mid-Nineteenth-Century America* (Notre Dame, Ind.: University of Notre Dame Press, 1986), 16–19.

48. On French laywomen's societies, see Rachel Fuchs, "Preserving the Future of France: Aid to the Poor and Pregnant in Nineteenth-Century Paris," in *The Uses of Charity: The Poor on Relief in the Nineteenth-Century Metropolis*, ed. Peter Mandler (Philadelphia: University of Pennsylvania Press, 1990), 92–100. On the differences between American and French orders, see Mary Ewens, *The Role of the Nun in Nineteenth Century America* (1971; reprint, New York: Arno Press, 1978), 32–64, 108–35; and Barbara Misner, *Highly Respectable and Accomplished Ladies: Catholic Women Religious in America, 1790–1850* (New York: Garland, 1988), 53–74. See also Maureen Fitzgerald, "Irish-Catholic Nuns and the Development of New York City's Welfare System, 1840–1900" (Ph.D. diss., University of Wisconsin, 1992), 243–72. Technically, the

term "nun" refers only to members of Catholic sisterhoods who lead cloistered lives; general usage, however, applies the term to cloistered and noncloistered women alike. See Carol K. Coburn and Martha Smith, *Spirited Lives: How Nuns Shaped Catholic Culture and American Life, 1836–1920* (Chapel Hill: University of North Carolina Press, 1999), 228 (n. 3).

49. Anne Firor Scott, "Most Invisible of All: Black Women's Voluntary Associations," *Journal of Southern History* 56 (February 1990): 3–22; Boylan, "Benevolence and Anti-slavery Activity," 119–38; Nell I. Painter, "Difference, Slavery, and Memory: Sojourner Truth in Feminist Abolitionism," in Yellin and Van Horne, *The Abolitionist Sisterhood*, 156–58; Hoff, "Frans Abramse Van Salee," *New York Genealogical and Biographical Record*, 205–11; Charles Lee Lewis, *Admiral de Grasse and American Independence* (Annapolis: U.S. Naval Institute, 1945).

50. Moses S. Beach and Rev. William Ely, *The Ely Ancestry* (New York: The Calumet Press, 1902), 181–82, 302; *New York Evening Post*, January 18, 1823, December 1, 1823; July 6, 1826; Laight Street Presbyterian Church, Catalogue of Members, 1812–42, Presbyterian Historical Society, Philadelphia; *Manual of the New York Free Presbyterian Church* (New York: n.p., 1832), 15; Hardman, *Charles Grandison Finney* 133–91, 239–65; Bertram Wyatt-Brown, *Lewis Tappan and the Evangelical War against Slavery* (Cleveland: Case Western Reserve University Press, 1969), 105–11; John Mc-Kivigan, *The War against Pro-Slavery Religion: Abolitionism and the Northern Churches, 1830–1865* (Ithaca: Cornell University Press, 1984), 210; Gilbert H. Barnes and Dwight L. Dumond, eds., *Letters of Theodore Dwight Weld, Angelina Grimké Weld and Sarah Grimké, 1822–1844*, 2 vols. (New York: n.p., 1934), 1:197; Larry Howard Whiteaker, "Moral Reform and Prostitution in New York City, 1830–1860" (Ph.D. diss., Princeton University, 1977), 157–281; Flora L. Northrup, *The Record of a Century, 1834–1934* (New York: American Female Guardian Society, 1935), 13–22; Sarah M. Grimké, "What Are the Duties of Woman at the Present Time," *Advocate of Moral Reform* 4 (January 1, 1838), 3–4; *New York Herald*, January 12, 1852. By some accounts, Cornelia and William were converted to perfectionism by John Humphrey Noyes, who later began experimental communities in Vermont and in Oneida, New York. During this time, Finney was also experimenting with perfectionist ideas, and Methodist perfectionism was gaining a strong foothold in New York City. On religious perfectionism, see Timothy L. Smith, *Revivalism and Social Reform: American Protestantism on the Eve of the Civil War* (1957; reprint, New York: Harper, 1965), 103–34. For an insightful examination of Frances Wright and "Fanny Wrightism," see Ginzberg, "'The Hearts of Your Readers Will Shudder,'" 195–227.

51. Charles Platt, Jr., *Newbold Genealogy* (New Hope, Pa.: n.p., 1964), 63, 108; Henry Miller Cox, *The Cox Family in America* (New York: n.p., 1912), 28, 91–93; "A List of the Members of the New York Yearly Meeting at the Time of the Separation, 1828," New York Yearly Meeting Records, Swarthmore College, Swarthmore, Pa.; "Catalogue of the Names, Accidents, and Numbers of the Communicants and Baptisms of the Laight Street Presbyterian Church, 1829," Presbyterian Historical Society, Philadelphia; McKivigan, *War against Proslavery Religion*, 207. Abraham Cox served as surgeon-in-chief with the Army of the Cumberland in the Civil War, dying at Lookout Mountain, Tennessee, in 1864.

52. Wyatt-Brown, *Lewis Tappan*, 114; *Old Spring Street Presbyterian Church: The One Hundred and Twentieth Anniversary, May 10, 13, 15, 1931* (New York: n.p., 1931), 13–14; *New York Genealogical and Biographical Record* 5 (July 1874); Larry Ceplair, ed., *The Public Years of Sarah and Angelina Grimké: Selected Writings, 1835–1839* (New York: Columbia University Press, 1989), 88. Henry Ludlow was pastor of the Spring Street Church between 1828 and 1837, later moving to New Haven and Poughkeepsie charges. One of the two Ludlow children, FitzHugh Ludlow, became a "racy writer"; the other, Helen W. Ludlow, became a teacher at the Hampton School for African Americans in Virginia. *Dictionary of American Biography*, s.v. "Ludlow, FitzHugh." On the Willcoxes, see *New York Weekly Museum*, September 26, 1807; *New York Evening Post*, January 21, 1837; and Arlene Norton, *Henrietta* (Sun City, Ariz.: Privately printed, 1986), 7–37.

53. Francis Jackson, *History of the Early Settlement of Newton, County of Middlesex, Massachusetts. From 1639 to 1800* (Boston: n.p., 1854), 348; Charles Henry Pope, *Merriam Genealogy in England and America* (Boston: Charles H. Pope, 1906) 250. Eliza Jackson Meriam was a daughter of Francis Jackson, a wealthy abolitionist and close associate of William Lloyd Garrison. Eliza's son Francis Meriam accompanied John Brown on the Harpers Ferry raid in 1859, but escaped capture. After Charles Meriam's death in 1845, Eliza married James Eddy, whose fecklessness and dishonesty (he kidnapped their two young daughters and took them to Europe) led her to bequeath $50,000 in her will to Susan B. Anthony and Lucy Stone "for the advancement of woman's cause." Elisabeth Griffith, *In Her Own Right: The Life of Elizabeth Cady Stanton* (New York: Oxford University Press, 1984), 92n, 179.

54. Hansen, *Strained Sisterhood*, 114.

55. On abolitionist women's organizational culture, see Julie Roy Jeffrey, *The Great Silent Army of Abolitionism: Ordinary Women in the Antislavery Movement* (Chapel Hill: University of North Carolina Press, 1998), 78–84. For an interesting longitudinal study of one organization, see Toni Cascio, "Continuity and Change: The Organizational Culture of Jewish Family and Children's Services of Philadelphia, 1822–1995" (Ph.D. diss., University of Pennsylvania, 1996).

56. Porter, "Benevolent Asylum," 62–102; Carl Seaburg and Stanley Paterson, *Merchant Prince of Boston: Colonel T. H. Perkins, 1764–1834* (Cambridge: Harvard University Press, 1971), 16–19, 22–29, 39, 136; *Notable American Women*, s.v. "Perkins, Elizabeth Peck," *Dictionary of American Biography*, s.v. "Stillman, Samuel," "Bowdoin, James," "Mason, Jonathan."

57. *Notable American Women*, s.v. "Hamilton, Elizabeth Schuyler"; T. Sharp, *The Heavenly Sisters; or, Biographical Sketches of Thirty Eminently Pious Females* (New Haven, Conn.: N. Whiting, 1822), 116–44; William W. Wheeler, *The Ogden Family in America* (Philadelphia: n.p., 1897), 105–6; Margherita A. Hamm, *Famous Families of New York*, 2 vols. (New York: G. P. Putnam's Sons, 1902), 1:171. See also Jeanne Boydston, *Home and Work: Housework, Wages, and the Ideology of Labor in the Early Republic* (New York: Oxford University Press, 1990), 120–63.

58. Frank Sylvester Parks, *Genealogy of the Parke Families of Massachusetts* (Washington, D.C.: n.p., 1909), 235; Vail, *Mary Webb*, 5–37, 70–72; Frederick Tuckerman, "Thomas Cooper, of Boston, and His Descendants," *New England Historical and Ge-*

nealogical Review 44 (January 1890): 58; Boston Vital Records, City Hall, Boston; *The Boston Directory* (1800–40).

59. The social class backgrounds of these and other women are ably chronicled in Hansen, *Strained Sisterhood*, 64–92. On Maria Weston Chapman, see Jane H. Pease and William H. Pease, *Bound with Them in Chains: A Biographical History of the Antislavery Movement* (Westport, Conn.: Greenwood Press, 1972), 28–59. On Mary Parker, see *The Letters of William Lloyd Garrison*, ed. Walter M. Merrill (Cambridge: Harvard University Press, 1971), 1:547. On Margaret Scarlett, see the documents transcribed in Stapp, *Afro-Americans in Antebellum Boston*, 583–605.

60. Smith Rosenberg, *Religion and the Rise of the American City*, 97–124 and 102n; Annette K. Baxter and Barbara Welter, *Inwood House: One Hundred and Fifty Years of Service to Women* (New York: Inwood House, 1980), 11–16.

61. Hobson, *Uneasy Virtue*, 118–24. The quotation is from *A Short Account of the Penitent Females' Refuge*, 9.

62. Gabriel P. Disosway, *The Earliest Churches of New York and Its Vicinity* (New York: J. G. Gregory, 1865), 13–38, 63–93, 181–204; [Isaac Smith Homans], *History of Boston, from 1630 to 1856. Illustrated with One Hundred and Twenty Engravings* (Boston: F. C. Moore & Co., 1856), 62–119.

63. Smith Rosenberg, *Religion and the Rise of the American City*, 102–4; Marlou Belyea, "The New England Female Moral Reform Society, 1835–1850: 'Put Down the Libertine, Reclaim the Wanderer, Restore the Outcast'" (paper delivered at the Third Berkshire Conference on the History of Women, Bryn Mawr College, 1976), table 1; Lawrence J. Friedman, *Gregarious Saints: Self and Community in American Abolitionism, 1830–1870* (Cambridge: Cambridge University Press, 1982), 45–48; Susan Hayes Ward, *The History of the Broadway Tabernacle Church from Its Organization in 1840 to the Close of 1900* (New York: n.p., 1901), xi–xii; New York Free Presbyterian Church, *Church Manual* (New York: n.p., 1832), 3–16.

64. *Longworth's Almanac . . . and New-York City Directory* (1817–30). On the Lasala family, see *New York Weekly Museum*, December 31, 1814; *New York Evening Post*, November 28, 1829; and Constance Denise Sherman, "Baptismal Records of St. Peter's Church, 1787–1800," *New York Genealogical Society Quarterly* 68 (1980): 133. On the Mooney family, see *New York Herald*, March 1, 1853; and Ray C. Sawyer, ed., "Index of Letters of Administration for New York County, 1801–1856," 20 vols., typescript, New York Public Library, 1837, 1853, New York City. On Francis Cooper, see William H. Bennett, "New York's First Catholic Legislator," *Historical Records and Studies* 12 (June 1918): 29–38.

65. George W. Sheldon, "Old Shipping Merchants of New York," *Harper's* 84 (February 1892): 464–65; Bayard Tuckerman, ed., *The Diary of Philip Hone, 1828–1851*, 2 vols. (New York: Dodd, Mead & Company, 1910), 1:149; "The Late Mortimer Livingston," *U.S. Democratic Review* 42 (August 1858): 146–62; Clare Brandt, *An American Aristocracy: The Livingstons* (Garden City, N.Y.: Doubleday, 1986), 182; Sawyer, "Abstracts of Wills," 9:5; *Truth Teller* 10 (November 29, 1834): 382; 10 (December 6, 1834): 391; 15 (April 13, 1839): 119.

66. Boydston, *Home and Work*, xiv–xv; Kerber, "Separate Spheres, Female Worlds, Woman's Place," 22–28; Hewitt, *Women's Activism and Social Change*, 43–45.

67. Kathryn Kish Sklar, "The Historical Foundations of Women's Power in the Creation of the Welfare State, 1830–1930," in *Mothers of a New World: Maternalist Politics and the Origins of Welfare States*, ed. Seth Koven and Sonya Michel (New York: Routledge, 1993), 51–52. Originally named the New York Female Moral Reform Society, the organization reorganized into the American Female Moral Reform Society in 1839, and adopted the name American Female Guardian Society when it incorporated in 1849. See Smith Rosenberg, *Religion and the Rise of the American City*, 108, 203. On the American Bible Society, see Peter J. Wosh, *Spreading the Word: The Bible Business in Nineteenth-Century America* (Ithaca: Cornell University Press, 1994), esp. 62–88.

Chapter Two

1. Catherine Prescott letter quoted in *The Papers of William Hickling Prescott*, ed. C. Harvey Gardiner (Cambridge: Harvard University Press, 1971), 234; Boston Female Asylum Minutes, 1800–45, Massachusetts State Library, Boston. One of her two surviving sons, William Hickling Prescott, aged seventeen in 1813, became a noted historian; her daughter Catherine E., was fourteen in 1813. Catherine herself was also active in the Female Bible Society (starting in 1814), the Bunker Hill Monument Association (in the 1830s), and the Lying-In Hospital (in the 1840s). The Appleton Fund was a new endowment designed to provide a small sum to each asylum girl when she finished her indenture; see Boston Female Asylum Minutes, June 1845.

2. Nancy F. Cott, *The Bonds of Womanhood: "Woman's Sphere in New England, 1780–1835"* (New Haven: Yale University Press, 1977), 74, 64. Historians and social theorists have engaged in spirited discussions of the "home/work" and "public/private" dichotomies. For good introductions to the key issues, see Linda K. Kerber, "Separate Spheres, Female Worlds, Women's Place: The Rhetoric of Women's History," *Journal of American History* 75 (June 1988): 9–39; *Feminism, the Public and the Private*, ed. Joan B. Landes (New York: Oxford University Press, 1998), especially the essays by Landes, Leonore Davidoff, and Mary P. Ryan.

3. Lori Ginzberg provides a subtle and insightful analysis of the "business of benevolence" in *Women and the Work of Benevolence: Morality, Politics, and Class in the 19th-Century United States* (New Haven: Yale University Press, 1990), 36–66.

4. See Appendix 2 for a description of the methods used to analyze leadership lists and for the organizations included in Table A.5. It is worth stressing here that with the exception of women's antislavery societies, the leaders of these organizations *were* the members and did all the group's work. Antislavery societies often delegated important duties to members as well as officers.

5. On maternal associations, see Mary P. Ryan, *Cradle of the Middle Class: The Family in Oneida County, New York, 1790–1865* (New York: Cambridge University Press, 1981), 89–91; and Richard Meckel, "Educating a Ministry of Mothers: Evangelical Maternal Associations, 1815–1860," *Journal of the Early Republic* 2 (Winter 1982–83): 403–32. On the Asylum for Lying-In Women, see Virginia Metaxas Quiroga, *Poor Mothers and Babies: A Social History of Childbirth and Child Care Institutions in Nineteenth-Century New York City* (New York: Garland, 1989), 47–78. On the Penitent Fe-

males Refuge, see Barbara Miel Hobson, *Uneasy Virtue: The Politics of Prostitution and the American Reform Tradition* (New York: Basic Books, 1987), 118–23. For an insightful study of single women's status, see Lee Chambers-Schiller, *Liberty, A Better Husband: Single Women in America, The Generations of 1790–1840* (New Haven: Yale University Press, 1984).

6. Female Benevolent Society, *First Annual Report* (New York, 1835), 5–8; *Third Annual Report of the Boston Female Moral Reform Society, October 3, 1838* (Boston, 1838), 12. See also Hobson, *Uneasy Virtue*, 118–23; Larry Howard Whiteaker, "Moral Reform and Prostitution in New York City, 1830–1860" (Ph.D. diss., Princeton University, 1977); and Marlou Belyea, "The New England Female Moral Reform Society, 1835–1850: 'Put Down the Libertine, Reclaim the Wanderer, Restore the Outcast'" (paper delivered at the Third Berkshire Conference on the History of Women, Bryn Mawr College, 1976).

7. Margaret Morris Haviland has explored Quaker women's benevolence in Philadelphia during this period. Although her conclusions differ from mine, the patterns she found are similar. See "Beyond Women's Sphere: Young Quaker Women and the Veil of Charity in Philadelphia, 1790–1818," *William and Mary Quarterly* 51 (July 1994): 419–46.

8. Fragment Society, *Constitution* (Boston, 1816), 6; *Boston Pilot* 2 (May 18, 1839): 135; letter of Henrietta Willcox Norton to Augusta Willcox Marvin, January 25, 1848, in Arlene Norton, *Henrietta* (Sun City, Ariz.: Privately printed, 1986), 89; Records of the Graham Society, 1817–31, letter inserted in entry for January 2, 1830, Congregational Library, Boston, Mass. On the role of sewing in women's lives, see Catherine E. Kelly, *In the New England Fashion: Reshaping Women's Lives in the Nineteenth Century* (Ithaca: Cornell University Press, 1999), 47–51; and Carolyn J. Lawes, *Women and Reform in a New England Community, 1815–1865* (Lexington: University of Kentucky Press, 2000), 48–54. The Graham Society was a sewing arm of the Corban Society and merged with it in 1831. On women abolitionists, see Ginzberg, *Women and the Work of Benevolence*, 63–65; Debra Gold Hansen, *Strained Sisterhood: Gender and Class in the Boston Female Anti-Slavery Society* (Amherst: University of Massachusetts Press, 1986), 13–28; and Julie Roy Jeffrey, *The Great Silent Army of Abolitionism: Ordinary Women in the Antislavery Movement* (Chapel Hill: University of North Carolina Press, 1998).

9. Quaker women did not use titles within their own groups, including the New York Female Association. Until the 1830s, whenever female Friends joined cross-denominational groups, they followed standard titling practice. Margaret Morris Haviland suggests that Philadelphia groups comparable to New York's Female Association emerged because young single women could not be active leaders of the Friends Monthly Meeting; see "Beyond Women's Sphere," 442–45.

10. On Margaret Dominick, see Association for the Relief of Respectable, Aged, Indigent Females *Annual Reports* (New York: 1816–24, 1832) and obituary in *New York Evening Post*, December 1, 1831; on Mary Parker, see Milton Meltzer, ed., *Lydia Maria Child: Selected Letters, 1817–1850* (Amherst: University of Massachusetts Press, 1982), 66 n. 6, and Hansen, *Strained Sisterhood*, 108–9.

11. Mrs. Jonathan Odell, comp., *Origin and History of the Orphan Asylum Society in the City of New York, 1806–1896*, 2 vols. (New York: n.p., 1896), 1:104–5; William

Ogden Wheeler, *The Ogden Family in America* (Philadelphia: Privately printed, 1897), 105–6; Boston Fragment Society Minutes, 1812–26, Fragment Society Collection, Schlesinger Library, Cambridge, Mass.; *Sixth Annual Report of the New York Female Auxiliary Bible Society* . . . (New York: 1822); Female Bible Society of Boston and Its Vicinity, Secretary's Records, October 7, 1814, Schlesinger Library, Cambridge, Mass. On common-law statutes, see Norma Basch, *In the Eyes of the Law: Women, Marriage, and Property in Nineteenth-Century New York* (Ithaca: Cornell University Press, 1982), 42–69.

12. Albert L. Vail, *Mary Webb and the Mother Society* (Philadelphia: American Baptist Publication Society, 1914); Association for the Benefit of Colored Orphans, *First Annual Report* (New York, 1837); William Wade Henshaw and Thomas Worth Marshall, *Encyclopedia of American Quaker Genealogy*, 6 vols. (Baltimore: Genealogical Publishing Company, 1969–77), 3:289 (on the Shotwells); *New York Evening Post*, June 13, 1811, May 1, 1865; *The Descendants of John Conrad Codwise and the Ancestry of James Codwise* (New York: Academy of Genealogy, 1966).

13. Chambers-Schiller, *Liberty, A Better Husband*, chapter 6. On attitudes toward marriage and singleness in general, see Amy M. Froide, "Marital Status as a Category of Difference: Singlewomen and Widows in Early Modern England," in *Singlewomen in English Society*, ed. Judith M. Bennett (Philadelphia: University of Pennsylvania Press, 1998), 236–69; Norma Basch, *Framing American Divorce: From the Revolutionary Generation to the Victorians* (Berkeley: University of California Press, 1999); and Kelly, *In the New England Fashion*, 115–22. On marriage as a public institution, in which the state had significant vested interests, see Nancy F. Cott, *Public Vows: A History of Marriage and the Nation* (Cambridge: Harvard University Press, 2000), 6–23.

14. Josiah Quincy, *Figures of the Past*, rev. ed. (Boston: Little, Brown, 1926), 276; *Notable American Women*, s.v. "Adams, Hannah"; "Rowson, Susanna Haswell"; Hannah Adams, *A Memoir of Miss Hannah Adams, Written by Herself. With Additional Notices, by a Friend* (Boston: Gray and Bowen, 1832); Elias Nason, *A Memoir of Mrs. Susanna Rowson* (Albany, N.Y.: Joel Munsell, 1870); Eve Kornfeld, "Women in Post-Revolutionary American Culture: Susanna Haswell Rowson's American Career, 1793–1824," *Journal of American Culture* 6 (Winter 1983–84): 56–62.

15. Adams, *Memoir of Hannah Adams*, 1–2. As Karen Halttunen points out, despite Adams's "unusually public and intellectual life," she was eulogized for "'her sensibility, the warmth of her affections, her sincerity and candor,'" not her literary achievements. See *Confidence Men and Painted Women: A Study of Middle-class Culture in America, 1830–1870* (New Haven: Yale University Press, 1982), 57. For an insightful analysis of the female writer's persona, see Mary Kelley, *Private Woman Public Stage: Literary Domesticity in Nineteenth-Century America* (New York: Oxford University Press, 1984).

16. Gardiner Spring, *A Pastor's Tribute to One of His Flock: The Memoirs of the Late Hannah L. Murray* (New York: Robert Carter & Bros., 1849), 58–59. An aristocratic British traveler invited to dine at the Murray residence in 1827 described Hannah and her sister Mary as "elderly maiden ladies approaching to fifty," still living with their mother and married brother "as is so common in America." Mrs. Basil Hall also professed astonishment that the Murrays employed "but two servants to wait on sixteen per-

sons." Una Pope-Hennessy, ed., *The Aristocratic Journey: Being the Outspoken Letters of Mrs. Basil Hall . . .* (New York: G. P. Putnam's Sons, 1931), 121. Catherine E. Kelly provides a nuanced portrait of the meanings of marriage and spinsterhood to rural New England women in this era; Kelly, *In the New England Fashion*, 107–22.

17. See Chambers-Schiller, *Liberty, A Better Husband*, chapter 1; Maureen Fitzgerald, "Irish-Catholic Nuns and the Development of New York City's Welfare System, 1840–1900" (Ph.D. diss., University of Wisconsin, 1992), 209–89; Colleen McDannell, *The Christian Home in Victorian America, 1840–1900* (Bloomington: Indiana University Press, 1986), 4–5. Catholics defended themselves by emphasizing the womanliness of nuns' self-sacrificing behavior. See, for example, "Sisters of Charity," *Truth Teller* 8 (September 8, 1832): 294; 8 (September 15, 1832): 302.

18. Jenny Franchot, *Roads to Rome: The Antebellum Protestant Encounter with Protestantism* (Berkeley: University of California Press, 1994), 112–62; Maureen A. McCarthy, "The Rescue of True Womanhood: Convents and Anti-Catholicism in 1830s America" (Ph.D. diss., Rutgers University, 1996), 101–46. Franchot's richly rewarding analysis points particularly to the parallels between captivity narratives (including prostitution stories) and convent exposés, and the appalled fascination with which Protestants viewed nuns' seemingly simultaneous liberty and enslavement. Other writers have noted the use of religious terms for brothel-keepers and inmates. For a good example of such an expose, written by a New York abolitionist and minister's wife, see "Hyla" [Jane Dunbar Chaplin], *The Convent and the Manse* (Boston: John P. Jewett and Co., 1853).

19. Joseph G. Mannard, "Maternity . . . of the Spirit: Nuns and Domesticity in Antebellum America," *U.S. Catholic Historian* 5 (1986): 305–24; Franchot, *Roads to Rome*, 132–33; McCarthy, "Rescue of True Womanhood," 153–58.

20. *Truth Teller* 13 (December 9, 1837): 391; 13 (December 16, 1837): 399; *Boston Pilot* 2 (January 4, 1840): 408. My findings here differ from those of Maureen Fitzgerald for the later era; in post-1850 New York, she found a distinct favoritism toward female singleness among lay Catholics. See "Irish-Catholic Nuns and the Development of New York City's Welfare System," 305–12. See also McDannell, *The Christian Home in Victorian America*, 56–66.

21. On nineteenth-century Catholicism, see Jay P. Dolan, *The Immigrant Church: New York's Irish and German Catholics, 1815–1865* (Baltimore: Johns Hopkins University Press, 1975), 121–40; McDannell, *Christian Home in Victorian America*, 52–58; Ronald D. Patkus, "A Community in Transition: Boston Catholics, 1815–1845" (Ph.D. diss., Boston College, 1997), 91–152; and Ann Taves, *The Household of Faith: Roman Catholic Devotions in Mid-Nineteenth-Century America* (Notre Dame, Ind.: University of Notre Dame Press, 1986). On Catherine Mann Dupleix, see Annabelle Melville, *Elizabeth Bayley Seton, 1774–1821* (New York: Charles Scribner's Sons, 1951), 197. On the Roman Catholic Asylum for the Children of Widows and Widowers, see *Truth Teller* 5 (October 24, 1829): 342; and Marie de Lourdes Walsh, *The Sisters of Charity of New York*, 3 vols. (New York: Fordham University Press, 1960), 1: 81–88. On the Boston group, see Patkus, "A Community in Transition," 101–2.

22. Shane White, *Somewhat More Independent: The End of Slavery in New York City, 1770–1810* (Athens: University of Georgia Press, 1991), 166–71; Graham Russell Hodges, *Root and Branch: African Americans in New York and East Jersey, 1613–1863* (Chapel

Hill: University of North Carolina Press, 1999), 200–213, 232–35; James Oliver Horton and Lois Horton, *Black Bostonians: Family Life and Community Struggle in the Antebellum North* (New York: Holmes & Meier, 1979), 15–27; Suzanne Lebsock, *The Free Women of Petersburg: Status and Culture in a Southern Town, 1784–1860* (New York: W. W. Norton, 1984), 90.

23. Rhoda Golden Freeman, *The Free Negro in New York City in the Era before the Civil War* (New York: Garland, 1994), 268–311, 322; for the African Dorcas Association's officers, see *Freedom's Journal*, February 15, 1828, 187; on their husbands' occupations, see *Longworth's American Almanac . . . and New York City Directory* (New York, 1828); on their deaths, see New York City Death Registers, 1790–1865, 1830 (Margaretta Quinn/Quin) and 1836 (Henrietta Regulus Ray), microfilm, New York Public Library; and Ray C. Sawyer, comp., "Abstracts of Wills for New York County 1801–1856," 1840 (Sarah Bane), typescript, New York Public Library, New York City.

24. Benjamin B. Wisner, *Memoirs of the Late Mrs. Susan Huntington of Boston, Massachusetts* (Boston: Crocker & Brewster, 1826), 120; Boston Female Asylum Minutes, March 4, 1845, August 1852, Massachusetts State Library, Boston, Mass.; Susan Lynne Porter, "Benevolent Asylum — Image and Reality: The Care and Training of Female Orphans in Boson, 1800–1840" (Ph.D. diss., Boston University, 1984), 91–92.

25. *Jesuit, or Catholic Sentinel* 1 (November 28, 1829): 100. As Barbara Misner notes, between 1790 and 1840, the median age of convent entrants ranged from 19 to 26, but it generally declined after a community's founding years; *Highly Respectable and Accomplished Ladies: Catholic Women Religious in America, 1790–1850* (New York: Garland, 1988), 127–33. See also Carol K. Coburn and Martha Smith, *Spirited Lives: How Nuns Shaped Catholic Culture and American Life, 1836–1920* (Chapel Hill: University of North Carolina Press, 1999), 72–77. On Silvie Depau, see *Truth Teller* 10 (November 29, 1834): 382; 10 (December 6, 1834): 391; 15 (April 13, 1839): 119; Ray C. Sawyer, "Abstracts of Wills for New York County," 9: 5.

26. Howard P. Chudacoff, *How Old Are You?: Age Consciousness in American Culture* (Princeton: Princeton University Press, 1989), 27; Carroll Smith-Rosenberg, "The Female World of Love and Ritual: Relations between Women in Nineteenth-Century America," *Signs* 1 (Autumn 1975): 1–30; Kelly, *In the New England Fashion*, 77–84, 98. Because young educated single women could expect marriage to produce a major discontinuity in their lives, as Catherine Kelly notes, they may have had little incentive to join organizational boards filled with married leaders, at least until they reached the point when they assumed they would be spinsters. Once married, middle-class women were anchored within their communities.

27. The median age at which women joined the Female Missionary Society was 34, while that for the Female Auxiliary Bible Society was 39. Although I calculated median age data, I find them less revealing of a society's age structure than analysis by decade, mostly because the median age at which women joined most societies was in the thirties. (See Table A.7.) In New York, the median age ranged from a low of 25, in the Female Association, to a high of 43 in the Protestant Half-Orphan Asylum Society. In Boston, the range began at 29 in the Female Anti-Slavery and the Fragment Societies and included three societies with median ages in the 40s: the Female Bible Society (41), Children's Friend Society (44), and the Penitent Females' Refuge Ladies Auxiliary (45).

28. Harriet and Mary Otis were Harrison Gray Otis's stepsisters. See Samuel Eliot Morison, *Harrison Gray Otis, 1765–1848: The Urbane Federalist* (Boston: Houghton Mifflin, 1969), 39n.

29. For good brief introductions to the concept of the "life course" and the field of family history, see Tamara K. Hareven, "Life Course," *Encyclopedia of Gerontology* (New York: Academic Press, 1996), 2: 31–40, and "The History of the Family and the Complexity of Social Change," *American Historical Review* 96 (1991): 95–124.

30. Marion Reynolds, *The History and Some of the Descendants of Robert and Mary Reynolds (1630?–1931) of Boston, Massachusetts* (New York: The Reynolds Family Association, 1931), 137–38; "A Newburyport Wedding One Hundred and Thirty Years Ago," *Essex Institute Historical Collections* 87 (October 1951): 209–32. See also Dean May and Maris A. Vinovskis, "A Ray of Millennial Light: Early Education and Social Reform in the Infant School Movement in Massachusetts, 1826–1840," in *Family and Kin in Urban Communities, 1700–1930*, ed. Tamara K. Hareven (New York: Franklin Watts, 1977), 62–99.

31. The three were Joanna Graham Bethune, Hannah Murray, and Mary Bleecker. Philadelphia's Infant School Society was begun by men.

32. Gertrude Meredith, *The Descendants of Hugh Amory, 1606–1805* (London: n.p., 1901), genealogical chart; Cora Codman Wolcott, *The Codmans of Charlestown and Boston, 1637–1929* (Brookline. Mass.: n.p., 1930), 21, 65; Ferris Greenslet, *The Lowells and Their Seven Worlds* (Boston: Houghton Mifflin, 1946), 88; *Dictionary of American Biography*, s.v. "Ropes, William"; Jane Pease and William Pease, *Ladies, Women, and Wenches: Choice and Constraint in Antebellum Charleston and Boston* (Chapel Hill: University of North Carolina Press, 1990), 125–27.

33. Female Association Records, 1798–1810, Friends Historical Library, Swarthmore College, Swarthmore, Pa.; Hinshaw and Marshall, *Encyclopedia of American Quaker Genealogy*, vol. 3. On Augusta Rogers, see James Swift Rogers, *James Rogers of New London, Ct., and His Descendants* (Boston: n.p., 1902), 242; her homesick letters can be found in the Winthrop-Rogers-Parkin-Moore Collection, Rare Books and Manuscripts, New York Public Library, New York City; she died in childbirth in December 1828. The quotation is from her neighbor, John Pintard; see *Letters from John Pintard to His Daughter, Eliza Noel Pintard Servoss*, ed. Dorothy C. Barck, 4 vols. (New York: New-York Historical Society, 1940), 3:50. In her study of women exhorters, Catherine A. Brekus found that by the 1830s, marriage led them to give up their labors; *Strangers and Pilgrims: Female Preaching in America, 1740–1845* (Chapel Hill: University of North Carolina Press, 1998), 252.

34. *Columbian Centinel*, April 15, 1812; September 18, 1819; Corban Society Minutes, September 29, 1834, Congregational Library, Boston, Mass. The comment was occasioned by news of Harriet's death. Hamilton Andrews Hill, *History of the Old South Church (Third Church) Boston, 1669–1884*, 2 vols. (Boston: Houghton Mifflin, 1890), 2:396–97.

35. On Sophia Cross Badger, see Boston Female Asylum Minutes, May 1834; Boston Marriages, 1830, Vital Records, City Hall; West Church Records, *New England Historical and Genealogical Review* 3 (April 1939): 116; and *Columbian Centinel*, November 11, 1820. On Louisa May Greele, see Porter, "Benevolent Asylum," 99; and Samuel

May, *Genealogy of the Descendants of John May . . .* (Boston: Franklin Press, 1878), 12, 22. Louisa, who died in 1828, was Samuel Greele's second wife. A sister, Abigail May, married Bronson Alcott in 1830; a brother, Samuel J. May, became a well-known abolitionist.

36. On Abby Frothingham Wales, see Porter, "Benevolent Asylum," 91–92; *Columbian Centinel*, June 30, 1832; "Records of the First Church, Boston," *Publications of the Colonial Society of Massachusetts* (Boston: The Society, 1895), 40:454. On Betsey Lane Jackson, see James Hill Fitts, *The Lane Genealogies*, 2 vols. (Exeter, N.H.: n.p., 1897), 2:234–36; Vail, *Mary Webb*, 87; and *Boston City Directory* (1825, 1834).

37. On Judith Anthon, see [Stuyvesant Fish], *Anthon Genealogy* (n.p., n.d.), 6–7; on her lawyer husband, see *Dictionary of American Biography*, s.v. "Anthon, John." On Julia Hyde, see Moses Beach, *The Ely Ancestry* (Boston: New England Historic Genealogical Society, 1902), 301; and Asylum for Lying-In Women, Board of Managers Minutes, December 6, 1831, New York Weill Cornell Medical Center Archives, New York City. Julia served on the board from April 1823 through December 1831; the three of her ten children born during that time arrived in 1824, 1826, and 1828; her year-old son Robert died in 1823, her eight-year-old daughter Sarah in 1825. Her sister was Harriet Cornelia Ely Green, discussed in Chapter 1 above.

38. The "numerous cares" comment was made by Anna Jenkins Havens when she attempted to resign from the Association for the Relief of Respectable, Aged, Indigent Females; see Minutes, October 26, 1815, New-York Historical Society, New York City. On Mary Wyckoff, see Mr. and Mrs. M. B. Streeter, *The Wyckoff Family in America: A Genealogy* (Rutland, Vt.: The Tuttle Co., 1934), 275. Mary and Elizabeth Robertson had very likely been pupils of Isabella Graham. Helen Robertson Rodgers was sixteen years older than Mary, nineteen years older then Elizabeth. On Elizabeth, see Jean Strouse's biography of her granddaughter: *Alice James: A Biography* (New York: Houghton Mifflin, 1980), 3–5. On Helen, see Sawyer, "Abstracts of Wills for New York County," 4: 6.

39. Clara J. Stone, *Genealogy of the Descendants of Jaspar Griffing* (n.p., 1881), 49–50.

40. Letter to friend and journal entries, January 3, 5, 1815, in Wisner, *Memoirs of Mrs. Susan Huntingon*, 120–22. At the time, Susan Huntington was an officer of three organizations, the Female Bible Society, the Corban Society, and the Fragment Society; she later added a fourth, the Society for Promoting Christianity among the Jews. Huntington died of tuberculosis in 1823, at age thirty-two.

41. Hansen, *Strained Sisterhood*, 66–67, 108; *Notable American Women*, s.v. "Grew, Mary"; Sarah H. Southwick, *Reminiscences of Early Anti-Slavery Days* (Cambridge, Mass.: Privately printed, 1893), 5; Francis Jackson, *History of the Early Settlement of Newton, County of Middlesex, Massachusetts. From 1639 to 1800* (Boston: n.p., 1854), 348.

42. *Third Annual Report of the Boston Female Moral Reform Society, October 3, 1838* (Boston, 1838), 12; "What Can Unmarried Females Do in This Cause?," *Advocate of Moral Reform* 2 (September 15, 1836): 133; *First Annual Report of the Ladies' New-York City Anti-Slavery Society* (New York, 1836), 3. For data on use of titles, I checked the two societies' officer lists against those in the *Proceedings of the Anti-Slavery Convention of American Women* (New York, 1837); attendees chose whether to be designated by title. Of the fifteen Philadelphia women in attendance, none chose to use a title, but the Philadelphia Female Anti-Slavery Society, unlike the Boston and New York groups, had a strong Quaker contingent.

43. *Advocate of Moral Reform* 2 (February 15, 1836): 31; 2 (March 1, 1836): 40. These articles, though unusual in mentioning the rape and subsequent death of a "respectable married colored woman," nevertheless failed to connect her individual tragedy to the broader issue of free African American women's sexual vulnerability.

44. William Riley, a clothing dealer and real estate owner, was Elizabeth's second husband. Her older daughters were Ann Jennette Jackson and Sarah Rebecca Jackson; the younger children were William Riley, George Putnam Riley (born in 1833 and named for another Boston activist), and Eliza Dianna Riley Smith. See Carol Buchalter Stapp, *Afro-Americans in Antebellum Boston: An Analysis of Probate Records* (New York: Garland, 1994), 122–24, 350–64, 519–42; and *Frederick Douglass's Paper* 8 (February 2, 1855): 2. See also "Constitution of the Afric-American Female Intelligence Society," in *Black Women in White America: A Documentary History*, ed. Gerda Lerner (New York: Random House, 1972), 438–40.

45. Sara M. Evans notes the importance of African American "mamas" as role models for white female civil rights workers in the 1950s south; *Personal Politics: The Roots of Women's Liberation in the Civil Rights Movement and the New Left* (New York: Knopf, 1979), 51–53.

46. *First Annual Report of the Ladies' New York City Anti-Slavery Society* (New York, 1837); Boston Female Anti-Slavery Society, *Right and Wrong in Boston, in 1836 . . .* (Boston, 1836), 24; Hansen, *Strained Sisterhood*, 140–56; Christopher Dixon, *Perfecting the Family: Antislavery Marriages in Nineteenth-Century America* (Amherst: University of Massachusetts Press, 1997), 46–82.

47. On Abigail Ordway, see Hansen, *Strained Sisterhood*, 78, 80, 144, and *Vital Records of West Newbury, Massachusetts, to the End of the Year 1849* (Salem: Essex Institute Historical Collections, 1903), 44, 115; on Sarah Ingraham [Bennett], see *New York Daily Tribune*, April 26, 1882: 5; on Mary Irena Treadwell [Hubbard], see *New York Daily Tribune*, January 12, 1883, 2; on Margaret Barrett Allen Prior, see Sarah R. Ingraham, *Walks of Usefulness: or, Reminiscences of Mrs. Margaret Prior* (New York: American Female Moral Reform Society, 1843); on Sarah Towne Smith, see *Dictionary of American Biography*, s.v. "Martyn, Sarah Towne Smith." Abigail Ordway (b. ca. 1805) was widowed in 1830; Margaret Prior (b. 1773) was widowed in 1808 and again in 1830. Sarah Ingraham (b. 1806) came to New York City as a widow in the 1830s and remarried in 1849, to James O. Bennett; Irena Treadwell (b. 1812) married Joel M. Hubbard in 1838; Sarah Towne Smith (b. 1805) married Job H. Martyn in 1841.

48. In addition to the sources cited in note 47, see Ginzberg, *Women and the Work of Benevolence*, 113–14.

49. On this point, I am indebted to Brekus, *Strangers and Pilgrims*, 261–62.

50. Hansen, *Strained Sisterhood*, 109, 112.

51. See Asylum for Lying-In Women Minutes, December 28, 1825–December 5, 1828; during this period, while continuing her service as one of the asylum's six "directresses," Julia Hyde gave birth to two children. The quotations are from Boston Female Asylum Minutes, October 1826, and September 26, 1800. Christine Stansell demonstrates brilliantly how to use organizational accounts to understand clients' lives; *City of Women: Sex and Class in New York City, 1789–1860* (New York: Knopf, 1986), 14–16, 70–73.

52. Society for the Relief of Poor Widows with Small Children Minutes, November 19, 1818, November 15, 1838, New-York Historical Society, New York City. At the February 1833 meeting of the New York Maternal Association, for example, Sarah Cleveland Dodge discussed her children's religious conversions; at the February 1835 meeting, twenty-four mothers brought fifty-eight children for whom to pray, and mourned the death of one member's four-year-old; see New York Maternal Association Minutes, 1832–69, Presbyterian Historical Society, Philadelphia. On women's work culture in a later era, see Susan Porter Benson, *Counter Cultures: Saleswomen, Managers, and Customers in American Department Stores, 1890–1940* (Urbana: University of Illinois Press, 1986), 265–66. The quotation about "numerous and multiplied cares" can be found in the Female Bible Society of Boston and Its Vicinity, Secretary's Records, March 23, 1825, Schlesinger Library, Cambridge, Mass. Published memoirs penned by coworkers, such as Sarah Ingraham's biography of Margaret Prior, did, of course, include personal data, but such books were not part of an association's official record.

53. Mary P. Ryan's work is the essential starting point for understanding middle-class family life in the nineteenth century; see *Cradle of the Middle Class*, esp. 145–85. See also Jeanne Boydston, *Home and Work: Housework, Wages, and the Ideology of Labor in the Early Republic* (New York: Oxford University Press, 1990), 75–119; and, on rural patterns, Kelly, *In the New England Fashion*, 175–84.

54. James I:27, Revised Standard Version; Society for the Relief of Poor Widows with Small Children Minutes, November 16, 1820; Boston Female Asylum Minutes, June 1803; New York Orphan Asylum Society, *Fifth Annual Report* (New York, 1811), 3; Carroll Smith Rosenberg, *Religion and the Rise of the American City: The New York City Mission Movement, 1812–1870* (Ithaca: Cornell University Press, 1971), 113; *Advocate of Moral Reform* 3 (June 1, 1837): 265; Association for the Relief of Respectable, Aged, Indigent Females, *Twenty-Fourth Annual Report* (New York, 1837), 4; Association for the Relief of Respectable, Aged, Indigent Females, "Journal of Visits to the Asylum," March 25, 1839, New-York Historical Society, New York City; Boston Children's Friend Society, *Circular, Constitution and By-Laws* (Boston, 1837), 5. Interestingly, although references to fatherlessness are fairly common in modern translations of the Bible, motherlessness is nowhere to be found. See index entries under "fatherless" and "motherless" in *The New Strong's Concordance of the Bible* (Nashville: T. Nelson, 1985), 603. On the use of familial terminology to describe nineteenth-century female preachers, see Brekus, *Strangers and Pilgrims*, 150–54.

55. Asylum for Lying-In Women, Board of Managers Minutes, December 5, 1828; Boston Children's Friend Society, *Sixth Annual Report* (Boston, 1839), 6; *Twenty Second Annual Report of the Widows' Society. Instituted 1816* (Boston, 1839), 4; Porter, "Benevolent Asylum," 224. See also Jay Fliegelman, *Prodigals and Pilgrims: The American Revolution against Patriarchal Authority, 1750–1800* (Cambridge: Cambridge University Press, 1982).

56. Porter, "Benevolent Asylum," 69–70; Boston Female Asylum Minutes, September 26, 1800; Orphan Asylum Society Petition, 1809, quoted in *A Short History of the Orphan Asylum Society in the City of New York*, comp., Joanna H. Mathews (New York: Anson D. F. Randolph, 1893), 27; *Truth Teller* 8 (November 3, 1832); Asylum for Lying-In Women, Visiting Committee Minutes, March 2, 1831, New York Weill Cornell Uni-

versity Medical Center Archives, New York City; Female Benevolent Society, *First Annual Report* (New York, 1834), 25; Mannard, "Maternity . . . of the Spirit," 319.

57. *Colored American* 1 (September 23, 1837): 3; Ruth Alexander, "'We Are Engaged as a Band of Sisters': Class and Domesticity in the Washingtonian Temperance Movement, 1840–1850," *Journal of American History* 75 (December 1988): 770–77; *Liberator* 3 (February 16, 1833): 26; *Advocate of Moral Reform* 4 (June 1, 1838): 83; 2 (February 15, 1836): 31; 2 (March 1, 1836): 40; 4 (November 1, 1838): 165; *Liberator* 4 (March 1834).

58. *Advocate of Moral Reform* 5 (October 15, 1839): 155. American Female Guardian Society, *Annual Report* (New York, 1849). The New York Female Moral Reform Society transformed itself into the American Female Moral Reform Society in 1839, and again into the American Female Guardian Society in 1849. See also Hansen, *Strained Sisterhood*, 114–22.

59. *Annual Report of the Directors of the Penitent Females' Refuge* (Boston, 1830), 7; see also *Ninth Annual Report of the Penitent Females' Refuge* (Boston, 1828), 8–9; *Circular, Constitution, and By-Laws of the Boston Children's Friend Society* (Boston, 1837), 5–6. On households of organizational officials, see Porter, "Benevolent Asylum," 294; and Hansen, *Strained Sisterhood*, 151.

60. Boston Female Asylum Minutes, October 1803, May 1815; *Circular . . . of the Boston Children's Friend Society* (1837), 18; Boston Children's Friend Society, *Second Annual Report* (Boston, 1835), 5; Mathews, *Short History of the Orphan Asylum Society*, 15, 56–57; Report of the New York House of Industry, *Evening Post*, October 27, 1815; Society for the Relief of Poor Widows with Small Children Minutes, November 17, 1825; *Truth Teller* 8 (November 3, 1832); 1812 address of the Boston Female Missionary Society, quoted in Vail, *Mary Webb*, 45; Boston Female Asylum Minutes, September 1844. For a good example of early organizational rules, see *An Account of the Boston Female Asylum* (Boston, 1803), 18.

61. Norton, *Henrietta*, 62–94; Association for the Benefit of Colored Orphans Minutes, August 13, 1839, New-York Historical Society, New York City. At the second Anti-Slavery Convention of American Women in Philadelphia, Henrietta had opposed a resolution condemning churches that permitted slaveholders to take communion; she and others argued "there is still moral power sufficient in the church, if rightly applied, to purify it." *Proceedings of the Anti-Slavery Convention of American Women, Held in Philadelphia May 15, 16, 17, 18, 1838* (Philadelphia: n.p., 1838), 6. Henrietta died in 1850, a week after giving birth to her sixth child; she was thirty-five. Louise Mitchell, of the United Tailoresses' Society, employed the term "secluded lives" in 1831 to refer to the location of seamstresses' labor; she saw that seclusion as an obstacle to forming labor unions. Dolores Janiewski, "Making Common Cause: The Needlewomen of New York, 1831–1869," *Signs* 1 (1976): 780.

62. Porter, "Benevolent Asylum," 298–300; letters of Wealthy and Melinda Bryant (Providence, Rhode Island) to Boston Children's Friend Society, February 1, 14, May 20, July 23, August, November 24, 1838, Boston Children's Friend Society Collection, box 5, folder 8, University of Massachusetts, Boston; Marie de Lourdes Walsh, *Mother Elizabeth Boyle: Mother of Charity* (New York: Paulist Press, 1955), 89–93.

63. [Wales], *Reminiscences of the Boston Female Asylum*, 45–46; John Gray letter, January 20, 1845, and Eliza Lincoln resignation letter, August 27, 1811, both in Boston

Female Asylum Minutes; Porter, "Benevolent Asylum," 287–88. Eliza had been the board's secretary from 1803 until 1807; she married in 1807 and switched to the post of manager.

64. Letter of Susan Ogden, Joanna Bethune, and Eliza Saidler to Alderman Nicholas Fish, June 6, 1814, Fish Family Collection, Columbia University, New York City; *New York Evening Post*, July 5, 1814.

65. Association for the Relief of Respectable, Aged, Indigent Females Records, vol. 1, Names of Pensioners Relieved, 1813–32; vol. 2, Minutes, October 26, 1815; vol. 4, "Journal of Visits to the Asylum," 1839–43, New-York Historical Society, New York City; Association for the Relief of Respectable, Aged, Indigent Females, *Fifteenth Annual Report* (New York, 1828), 6; Widows' Society Minutes, December 3, 1817, Schlesinger Library, Cambridge, Mass.; Asylum for Lying-In Women, Board of Managers Minutes, November 11, 1823; Visiting Committee Minutes, October 21, 1834. By my calculations, twenty of the thirty-one managers of the Association for the Relief of Respectable, Aged, Indigent Females for whom religious affiliation is available (64.5 percent) were Presbyterian (including Reformed Dutch and Associate Reformed), while eight (25.8 percent) were Episcopalian. Of the 269 clients for whom religious affiliation is known, 35 percent were Presbyterian (including Reformed Dutch and Associate Reformed), and 21.6 percent were Episcopalian. Clients who shared surnames with managers included Miss Hannah Baldwin, Mrs. Mary Bingham, Mrs. DeForest, and Mrs. Sarah Innis.

66. Boston Female Asylum Minutes, October 27, December 28, 1800; March 31, 1801; October, December 1810; May 1811; Porter, "Benevolent Asylum," 92. On the larger process whereby middle-class women defined their status by distancing themselves from working-class women, see Jeanne Boydston, "The Woman Who Wasn't There: Women's Market Labor and the Transition to Capitalism in the United States," *Journal of the Early Republic* 16 (Summer 1996): 183–206; and Carol Lasser, "A 'Pleasingly Oppressive' Burden: The Transformation of Domestic Service and Female Charity in Salem, 1800–1840," *Essex Institute Historical Collections* 116 (1980): 156–75.

67. Ryan, *Cradle of the Middle Class*, 145–85. See also Elizabeth Blackmar, *Manhattan for Rent, 1785–1850* (Ithaca: Cornell University Press, 1989), 109–47. The quotations are from New York Asylum for Lying-In Women, Board of Managers Minutes, December 1, 1829, December 5, 1828, April 15, 1834, and March 7, 1831. See Visiting Committee Minutes, October 21, 1834, for an example of a manager's former employee entering the asylum; see Board of Managers Minutes, November 4, 1828, for a reference to individuals asking the matron for wet-nurses. In one instance, a kind hearted soul adopted the surviving infant of a client who had died. The adoptive mother, Margaret Barrett Allen Prior, who later worked as a missionary for the New York Female Moral Reform Society, raised Adeline Stanley Lenaw until she died of a congenital spinal injury at about eleven years of age. See Asylum for Lying in Women, Board of Managers Minutes, December 5, 1826; and Sarah R. Ingraham, *Walks of Usefulness: or, Reminiscences of Mrs. Margaret Prior* (New York: American Female Moral Reform Society, 1843), 22–26. (Ingraham erroneously writes that Adeline was adopted from the Orphan Asylum.) For a full history of the Asylum for Lying-In Women, see Virginia Metaxas Quiroga, *Poor Mothers and Babies: A Social History of Childbirth and Child Care Hospitals in Nineteenth-Century New York City* (New York: Garland, 1989).

68. See Chapter 5 for a fuller discussion of organizational finances and men's roles as financial advisers. See Boydston, *Home and Work* for an incisive analysis of the ideological separation of home from work in the nineteenth century. Both Lori Ginzberg, in *Women and the Work of Benevolence*, 127–28, and Suzanne Lebsock, in *The Free Women of Petersburg*, 229–30, see the growth of male advisory boards in the 1850s as evidence of lost autonomy.

69. Boston Female Asylum Minutes, October 27, December 28, 1800; March 31, 1801; Porter, "Benevolent Asylum," 215, 269–74. For a further discussion of clients' roles, see Chapter 5.

70. On Susannah Peterson, see E. S. Abdy, *Journal of a Residence and Tour in the United States of North America, from April 1833 to October 1834*, 2 vols. (London: J. Murray, 1835), 2:43–46. Abdy refers to the mutual aid society as the "Benevolent Daughters of Zion." On Lucia Jones Ives and Ansel W. Ives, see Stephen W. Williams, *American Medical Biography: or, Memoirs of Eminent Physicians* (1845; reprint, New York: Milford House, 1967), 304–7; *New York Evening Post*, October 16, 1818; Shepherd W. Knapp, *Personal Records of the Brick Presbyterian Church in the City of New York, 1809–1908* (New York: Trustees of the Church, 1909), 118 (the Ives children were born in 1819, 1821, 1823, and 1826); Sawyer, "Abstracts of Wills for New York County," 1838. After Ansel Ives's death, Lucia married the noted Congregationalist divine Leonard Woods in 1846; see *American National Biography*, s.v. "Woods, Leonard." On working-class white domestic ideals, see Ruth Alexander, "'We Are Engaged As a Band of Sisters': Class and Domesticity in the Washingtonian Temperance Movement, 1840–1850," *Journal of American History* 75 (December 1988): 764–85.

71. Seamen's Aid Society, *Sixth Annual Report* (Boston, 1839), 11; Leonore Davidoff, "Regarding Some 'Old Husbands' Tales': Public and Private in Feminist History," in *Feminism: The Public and the Private*, ed. Joan B. Landes (New York: Oxford University Press, 1998), 182. For later developments, see, for example, Ginzberg, *Women and the Work of Benevolence*, 193–209; Peggy Pascoe, *Relations of Rescue: The Search for Female Moral Authority in the American West, 1874–1939* (New York: Oxford University Press, 1990); Regina Kunzel, "The Professionalization of Benevolence: Evangelicals and Social Workers in the Florence Crittenton Homes, 1915 to 1945," *Journal of Social History* 22 (Fall 1988): 21–36; Sarah Deutsch, *Women and the City: Gender, Space, and Power in Boston, 1870–1940* (New York: Oxford University Press, 2000); Deborah Gray White, *Too Heavy a Load: Black Women in Defense of Themselves* (New York: W. W. Norton, 1999); Linda Gordon, ed., *Women, the State, and Welfare* (Madison: University of Wisconsin Press, 1990); and Kathryn Kish Sklar, *Florence Kelley and the Nation's Work: The Rise of Women's Political Culture, 1830–1900* (New Haven: Yale University Press, 1995).

72. Norton, *Henrietta*, 88; *Advocate of Moral Reform* 5 (February 1, 1839): 21; Ginzberg, *Women and the Work of Benevolence*, 67–97. Henrietta's comment also reflected her sense that housework was devalued, "pastoralized"; see Boydston, *Home and Work*, 142–63.

73. See Dixon, *Perfecting the Family*, 46–156; and Blanche Glassman Hersh, *The Slavery of Sex: Feminist Abolitionists in America* (Urbana: University of Illinois Press, 1978).

Chapter Three

1. *Notable American Women*, s.v. "Bethune, Joanna Graham," "Graham, Isabella Marshall," "Seton, Elizabeth Bayley"; Joanna Bethune, ed., *The Power of Faith, Exemplified in the Life and Writings of the Late Mrs. Isabella Graham*, 2d ed. (New York: American Tract Society, 1843); George Washington Bethune, *Memoirs of Mrs. Joanna Bethune* (New York: Harper & Brothers, 1863); Annabelle M. Melville, *Elizabeth Bayley Seton, 1774–1821* (New York: Charles Scribner's Sons, 1951).

2. Bethune, *Power of Faith*, 20, 40–42, 220; Joanna Graham Bethune, Autobiography, 1814, in Bethune Diaries, Clements Library, University of Michigan, Ann Arbor, Mich.; 1790 Population Census, New York City. The casual nature of the three women's references to household labor reflects their expectation that they would have servants. Graham had "two young Indian girls," slave property of John Graham, serving her in Canada and Antigua, both of whom she freed, and one of whom returned to Scotland with her. The 1790 census lists one slave at her residence, probably Pero, the "old black man" whom Joanna Bethune refers to her in autobiography. William Seton's family also owned slaves until at least 1804. Nevertheless, all three women preferred to rely on hired adult servants or indentured children for household help.

3. Bethune, *Power of Faith*, 323, 62. These friends included Willielma Campbell (Lady Glenorchy) and Mary Livingston Brown, an American married to a British officer. The daughter of Peter Van Brugh Livingston of the New York Livingstons, Brown had met Isabella Graham in New York State in 1772, then renewed the acquaintance in Scotland. Mary Brown died in 1782. See Bethune, *Power of Faith*, 21, 61; *Dictionary of National Biography*, s.v. "Campbell, Willielma"; and Edward Brockholst Livingston, *The Livingstons of Livingston Manor* (New York: Knickerbocker Press, 1910), 549–50.

4. The quotations are taken from a 1787 letter to a Scottish friend found in Bethune, *Power of Faith*, 75–76, and a 1785 letter to Joanna Bethune found in Bethune, *Mrs. Joanna Bethune*, 50. The phrase "father of the fatherless, husband of the widow" appears in several variants in Graham's correspondence and devotional exercises. See, for example, Bethune, *Power of Faith*, 79, 114, 165, 331, 374.

5. Bethune, *Power of Faith*, 11, 61, 77–78. On John Witherspoon, see *American National Biography*, s.v. "Witherspoon, John"; and Sydney Ahlstrom, *A Religious History of the American People* (New Haven: Yale University Press, 1972), 274–75. See also Mark A. Noll, *Princeton and the Nation, 1768–1822* (Princeton: Princeton University Press, 1989); John G. West, *The Politics of Revelation and Reason: Religion and Civic Life in the New Nation* (Lawrence: University Press of Kansas, 1996), 26–36; and Jon Butler, *Awash in a Sea of Faith: Christianizing the American People* (Cambridge: Harvard University Press, 1990), 282. Graham may also have had a nodding acquaintance with Elizabeth Schuyler Hamilton. In Canada in 1768 she served as baptismal sponsor for Isabella Graham Antill; a younger Antill daughter, Frances, born in 1785, was adopted at age two by Elizabeth and Alexander Hamilton. William Nelson, *Edward Antill, A New York Merchant of the Seventeenth Century, and His Descendants* (Paterson, N.J.: Press Printing and Publishing Co., 1899), 25–28; Harold C. Syrett, ed., *The Papers of Alexander Hamilton*, 27 vols. (New York: Columbia University Press, 1961–87), 4:279–80.

6. For general information on New York City during this era, see Robert Greenhalgh Albion, *The Rise of New York Port* (New York: Charles Scribner's Sons, 1939), 1–15; and Carroll Smith Rosenberg, *Religion and the Rise of the American City: The New York City Mission Movement, 1812–1870* (Ithaca: Cornell University Press, 1972), 15–29, 45–51. On the transatlantic evangelical network, see Charles I. Foster, *An Errand of Mercy: The Evangelical United Front, 1790–1860* (Chapel Hill: University of North Carolina Press, 1960); Clifford S. Griffin, *Their Brothers' Keepers* (New Brunswick: Rutgers University Press, 1960); Lois Wendland Banner, "The Protestant Crusade: Religious Missions, Benevolence, and Reform in the United States, 1790–1840" (Ph.D. diss, Columbia University, 1970), 122–40; and George Marsden, *The Evangelical Mind and the New School Presbyterian Experience* (New Haven: Yale University Press, 1970), 9–15. On the Masons, see *Dictionary of American Biography*, s.v. "Mason, John Mitchell." On the reshaping of Scottish Presbyterianism, see Leigh Eric Schmidt, *Holy Fairs: Scottish Communions and American Revivals in the Early Modern Period* (Princeton: Princeton University Press, 1989), 187–92.

7. Bethune, *Power of Faith*, 82. On Nelly Custis and the school's advertised offerings, see Alice Curtis Desmond, *Martha Washington: Our First Lady* (New York: Dodd, Mead, & Co., 1942), 234. Graham's political and social ideas are spelled out most clearly in her letters reprinted in *The Power of Faith*, 17–18, 39–40, 145–46, and in Joanna Bethune, *The Unpublished Letters and Correspondence of Mrs. Isabella Graham, from the Year 1767 to 1814; Exhibiting Her Religious Character in the Different Relations of Life* (New York: John S. Taylor, 1838), 89–93, 165–79, 222–24. On women's academies, see Ann Gordon, "The Young Ladies Academy of Philadelphia," in *Women of America: A History*, ed. Carol Berkin and Mary Beth Norton (Boston: Houghton Mifflin, 1979), 68–91; Linda K. Kerber, *Women of the Republic: Intellect and Ideology in Revolutionary America* (Chapel Hill: University of North Carolina Press, 1980), esp. 185–232; and Mary Beth Norton, *Liberty's Daughters: The Revolutionary Experience of American Women, 1750–1800* (Boston: Little, Brown, 1980). On the idea of virtue, see Ruth H. Bloch, "The Gendered Meanings of Virtue in Revolutionary America," *Signs* 13 (1987): 37–58. On Rowson's Academy, see Susanna Rowson, *A Present for Young Ladies; Containing Poems, Dialogues, Addresses, &c., &c. As Recited by the Pupils of Mrs. Rowson's Academy, at the Annual Exhibitions* (Boston: John West & Co., 1811). On Hannah More and the British evangelicals, see Nancy F. Cott, *The Bonds of Womanhood: "Woman's Sphere" In New England, 1780–1835* (New Haven: Yale University Press, 1977), 65–74.

8. Bethune, *Power of Faith*, 111, 115–27.

9. Ibid., 67–68;

10. Ibid., 143–44; Society for the Relief of Poor Widows with Small Children Minutes, April 1800, New-York Historical Society, New York City.

11. Bethune, Autobiography. See also Bethune, *Mrs. Joanna Bethune*, 40–47; and Melville, *Seton*, 2–10.

12. Bethune, Autobiography; Melville, *Seton*, 14. Note each woman's reliance on colorful novelistic language. On the use of metaphors that contrasted "the world" with "the home," see Cott, *Bonds of Womanhood*, 66. For an insightful analysis of narrative conventions in women's conversion accounts, see Virginia Lieson Brereton, *From Sin*

to Salvation: Stories of Women's Conversions, 1800 to the Present (Bloomington: Indiana University Press, 1991), 3–40. Both Catherine E. Kelly, *In the New England Fashion: Reshaping Women's Lives in the Nineteenth Century* (Ithaca: Cornell University Press, 1999), 6–7, 169–71, and Lisa Norling, *Captain Ahab Had a Wife: New England Women and the Whalefishery, 1720–1870* (Chapel Hill: University of North Carolina Press, 2000), 104–14, offer shrewd insights on how girls fashioned self-understandings through writing and reading. See also Ruth H. Bloch, "Religion, Literary Sentimentalism, and Popular Revolutionary Ideology," in *Religion in a Revolutionary Age*, ed. Ronald Hoffman and Peter J. Albert (Charlottesville: University Press of Virginia, 1994), 308–30.

13. Melville, *Seton*, 11–17. Martha Blauvelt's analysis of thirty-one women's conversion stories reveals the similarity between their experience and Bethune's. See "Society, Religion, and Revivalism: The Second Great Awakening in New Jersey, 1780–1830" (Ph.D. diss., Princeton University, 1975), 212–28. Barbara Leslie Epstein has noted the prevalence of conflict in the women's religious narratives she examined: *The Politics of Domesticity: Women, Evangelism, and Temperance in Nineteenth-Century America* (Middletown, Conn.: Wesleyan University Press, 1981), 45–65. To comprehend the importance that specific stories have for particular generations of women, one need only note the current popularity of explanatory models based on adolescent girls' "loss of self-esteem."

14. Melville, *Seton*, 25–48; Joseph Code, ed., *Letters of Mother Seton to Mrs. Julianna Scott* (Emmitsburg, Md.: Daughters of Charity of St. Vincent de Paul, 1935), 152–53. On Hobart, see Ahlstrom, *A Religious History of the American People*, 625–26. Her friend Eliza Saidler had introduced her to Rousseau's *Emile* after a trip to France in 1799.

15. Joanna Bethune, Autobiography; Bethune, *Mrs. Joanna Bethune*, 58–75; "Divie Bethune, Esq.," *American Sunday School Magazine* 1 (November 1824): 147–52; *Dictionary of American Biography*, s.v. "Mason, John Mitchell." Joanna's initial rejection of Divie (her mother's choice) reflected larger contemporary struggles over who should arrange children's marriages and how women might exercise individual choice while not displeasing parents; see Daniel Scott Smith, "Parental Power and Marriage Patterns: An Analysis of Historical Trends in Hingham, Massachusetts," *Journal of Marriage and the Family* 35 (August 1973): 419–28; and Bloch, "Religion, Sentimentalism, and Popular Revolutionary Ideology," 315–17. In her diaries, Joanna blended references to mother and husband, often in company with John Mitchell Mason; see, for example, Bethune Diaries, March 17, May 1, 1825; January 17, 1829; and September 24, 1848. Mason's theological ideas reflected the bourgeois culture of privacy and self-discipline that Joanna and Divie embraced; see Schmidt, *Holy Fairs*, 194–202. As Virginia Brereton points out, conversion narratives like Joanna's were so "highly formulaic" that writers probably "shaped their experiences" to conform to the formula; *From Sin to Salvation*, xii.

16. Martin Hoffman's first wife, Beulah Murray, had died in 1800. See William Ogden Wheeler, *The Ogden Family in America* (Philadelphia: n.p., 1897). On the Seton-Hoffman businesses, see *Longworth's American Almanac, New-York Register and City Directory* (New York: Longworth, 1800). Via Isabella Graham, the Society also had

a benefactor in Janet Livingston Montgomery, wealthy widow of General Richard Montgomery, who in addition to her yearly subscription, bestowed valuable land grants on Stanton Street in Manhattan. Janet Montgomery was a cousin of Isabella Graham's friend Mary Livingston Brown. See Cynthia A. Kierner, "Patrician Womanhood in the Early Republic: The 'Reminiscences' of Janet Livingston Montgomery," *New York History* 73 (October 1992): 389–407; note 3 above; and *Minutes of the Common Council of the City of New York, 1784–1831*, 19 vols. (New York: City of New York, 1917), February 1, 1808, 4:736.

17. On Sarah Ogden Hoffman, see Wheeler, *Ogden Family in America*, 105–6, 103, 184; T. Sharp, *The Heavenly Sisters: or, Biographical Sketches of the Lives of Thirty Eminently Pious Females* (New Haven, Conn.: N. Whiting, 1822), 116–44; John Sanford, *Composure in Death. A Discourse Delivered in the Orphan Asylum, New York, on the Death of Mrs. Sarah Hoffman* (New York: n.p., 1821), esp. 26–29; Melville, *Seton*, 20–23. On Sarah Clarke Startin, see Margherita A. Hamm, *Famous Families of New York*, 2 vols. (New York: G. P. Putnam's Sons, 1902), 1:171; Melville, *Seton*, 33, 125. On Catherine Dupleix, see Melville, *Seton*, 33, 105. On Mary Weygand Chrystie, see Bethune, *Mrs. Joanna Bethune*, 79–82; Bethune, *Power of Faith*, 351; "Thomas Witter Christie," *National Cyclopedia of American Biography*, 42: 549; *Longworth's Almanac . . . and New York City Directory* (1800); and Mary Chrystie's receipt book, 1800–1806, Chrystie Family Papers, New-York Historical Society, New York City. On the Nicholson-Few-Gallatin connections, see "The Diary of Frances Few, 1808–1809," ed. Noble E. Cunningham, Jr., *Journal of Southern History* 29 (August 1963): 345–61; and Byam K. Stevens, *Genealogical and Biographical History of the Gallatin and Nicholson Families* (New York: National Americana Society, 1911). For an example of combined family, religious, business, and political talk, see letter of Catherine Few to Hannah Gallatin, June 5, 1809, Alfred Gallatin Papers, New-York Historical Society. In the letter, Catherine, a sturdy Methodist, glides easily from denominational matters (promoting the interests of Methodist itinerants) to comments on the chaplaincy of Congress and her husband's business, to family matters, to prayers for her sister's soul. On the general context of national political life in the new capital city, see Catherine Allgor, *Parlor Politics: In Which the Ladies of Washington Help Build a City and a Government* (Charlottesville: University Press of Virginia, 2000), 4–146.

18. Bethune, *Power of Faith*, 228–34, 255–58; Richard Knill, *The Missionary's Wife: or, A Brief Account of Mrs. Loveless, of Madras* (Philadelphia: Presbyterian Board of Publication, 1839), 3–6.

19. Melville, *Seton*, 25–76; Regina Bechtle, S.C., and Judith Metz, S.C., eds., *Elizabeth Bayley Seton: Correspondence and Journals 1793–1808*, vol. 1 of *Elizabeth Bayley Seton: Collected Writings* (Hyde Park, N.Y.: New City Press, 2000), 196–305; Code, *Letters of Mother Seton*, 60, 159–61, 168 (quotation). Antonio Filicchi and his brother Filippo had business dealings with William Seton's firm. Filippo Filicchi was married to an American woman, Mary Cowper of Boston. See Melville, *Seton*, 63–69. See also Robert Seton, *Memoir, Letters, and Journal of Elizabeth Seton*, 2 vols. (New York: P. O'Shea, 1869).

20. Bechtle and Metz, *Seton: Correspondence and Journals*, 305–78 (quotation, 308); Melville, *Seton*, 82–95; Seton, *Memoir, Letters, and Journal*, 1:190–218. Amabilia Fil-

icchi was herself the mother of ten. In 1802, at age 22, Rebecca Seton became a manager of the Society for the Relief of Poor Widows; she died in June 1804. Jenny Franchot insightfully analyzes Seton's conversion story in *Roads to Rome: The Antebellum Protestant Encounter with Catholicism* (Berkeley: University of California Press, 1994), 286–301.

21. Melville, *Seton*, 103–4, 328 (n. 7); Seton, *Memoir, Letters, and Journal*, 2:271; Bechtle and Metz, *Seton: Correspondence and Journals*, 338–85, 457; Society for the Relief of Poor Widows with Small Children Minutes, November 14, 1803. On St. Peter's Church, see Leo Raymond Ryan, *Old St. Peter's: The Mother Church of Catholic New York 1785–1935* (New York: U.S. Catholic Historical Society, 1935).

22. Ryan, *Old St. Peter's*, 42–74, 210–15; Anne Hartfield, "Profile of a Pluralistic Parish: Saint Peter's Roman Catholic Church, New York City, 1785–1815," *Journal of American Ethnic History* 12 (Spring 1993): 30–59. The quotation is from Father Anthony Kohlmann, who became pastor in 1808. Quoted in James M. O'Toole, "From Advent to Easter: Catholic Preaching in New York City, 1808–1809," *Church History* 63 (1994): 367. Pierre Toussaint Papers, Rare Books and Manuscripts, New York Public Library, New York City; Arthur and Elizabeth Odell Sheehan, *Pierre Toussaint: A Citizen of Old New York* (New York: P. J. Kenedy & Sons, 1955), 10–83. Toussaint received his freedom in 1807. See also B. F. De Costa, *Three Score and Ten: The Story of St. Philip's Church of New York City* (New York: n.p., 1889), 16–17.

23. Melville, *Seton*, 85–89; Bechtle and Metz, *Seton: Correspondence and Journals* 315–17, 408, 414.

24. Melville, *Seton*, 103–83; *Notable American Women*, s.v. "Seton, Elizabeth Bayley." Successor organizations have assumed varying names, including Daughters of Charity and Sisters of Charity of St. Vincent de Paul.

25. Bethune, *Power of Faith*, 233, 166–68, 282, 260, 150. For examples of epistolary preaching, complete with biblical references, see ibid., 153–58, 260–66, 283–88.

26. Bethune, *Power of Faith*, 335; Bethune, Diary, January 9, March 18, 1825; Bethune, *Mrs. Joanna Bethune*, 79–94. On northern white women's childbearing patterns and strategies during this era, see Nancy Grey Osterud and John Fulton, "Family Limitation and Age at Marriage: Fertility Decline in Sturbridge, Massachusetts, 1730–1850," *Population Studies* 30 (1976): 481–94; and Janet Farrell Brodie, *Contraception and Abortion in Nineteenth-Century America* (Ithaca: Cornell University Press, 1994), 9–37. See also Susan Klepp, "Revolutionary Bodies: Women and the Fertility Transition in the Mid-Atlantic Region, 1760–1820," *Journal of American History* 85 (December 1998): 910–45.

27. Bethune, *Power of Faith*, 232, 250; Bethune, *Mrs. Joanna Bethune*, 94, 205.

28. Bethune, *Mrs. Joanna Bethune*, 93–104; Mrs. Jonathan Odell, et al., *Origin and History of the Orphan Asylum Society in the City of New York, 1806–1896*, 2 vols. (New York: n.p., 1896), 1:109–10; Bethune, *Power of Faith*, 249–55.

29. Bethune, *Power of Faith*, 307–48; *Minutes of the Common Council of the City of New York, 1734–1831*, 19 vols. (New York: City of New York, 1917), 7:763; *New York Evening Post*, May 31, 1814.

30. John Mitchell Mason, *Christian Mourning: A Sermon, Occasioned by the Death of Mrs. Isabella Graham: and Preached . . . 14 August 1814* (New York: Whiting and Wat-

son, 1814); Sharp, *The Heavenly Sisters*, 120–23; Bethune, Autobiography. Published in 1817, *The Power of Faith* became one of the nineteenth century's religious best-sellers; it went through a number of printings, and was revised by Joanna and republished in 1843. See also *A Memoir of Miss Eliza Van Wyck* . . . (Boston: Samuel T. Armstrong, 1812). Susan Juster's study of 225 conversion narratives from 1800 to 1830 found 135 male and 90 female examples (60 percent male, 40 percent female), but these were published accounts; by contrast, her study of earlier conversion narratives, in which women's narratives predominated, was based on manuscript records. See *Disorderly Women: Sexual Politics and Evangelicalism in Revolutionary New England* (Ithaca: Cornell University Press, 1994), 57, 184. With its emphasis on rejoining her mother's religious world, Bethune's conversion account challenges Juster's argument that postrevolutionary women's conversions encouraged them "to reduce their dependence on friends and family and enlarge their sense of self" (206). Brereton, *From Sin to Salvation*, 3–40, describes the formulaic nature of nineteenth-century women's narratives and notes the significance women attached to telling their stories, either orally or in written form.

31. Bethune, Diary, June 14, 1852. In 1843 Joanna published a completely reworked edition of *The Power of Faith*; it included new material, mostly from her mother's letters.

32. Anne M. Boylan, *Sunday School: The Formation of an American Institution, 1790–1880* (New Haven: Yale University Press, 1988), 121; New York Female Tract Society Minutes, March 22, 1822, New York City Mission Society Archives, New York City; Gardiner Spring, *A Pastor's Tribute to One of His Flock: The Memoirs of the Late Hannah Murray* (New York: Robert Carter & Brothers, 1849), 144–47; David Hosack, *Memoir of De Witt Clinton* (New York: J. Seymour, 1829), 173–76; Bethune, *Mrs. Joanna Bethune*, 146, 163; Bethune, Diary, September 18, 1828; Female Society of the City of New York for the Support of Schools in Africa, *First Annual Report* (New York, 1838).

33. Bethune, Diary, September 21, 1824, May 1, 1825, January 9, 1825, January 29, 1825, April 3, 1825, June 5, 1825, September 18, 1828, January 25, 1829. On settling the estate, see ibid., October 3, December 28, 1825 (with marginal notation dated September 18, 1830). Suzanne Lebsock, *The Free Women of Petersburg: Status and Culture in a Southern Town, 1784–1860* (New York: W. W. Norton, 1984), 39.

34. Bethune, Diary, January 18, 1846; May 7, 1848.

35. Bethune, *Power of Faith*, 375–76; Bethune, Diary, January 29, 1829. On writing Divie's biography, see Diary, June 14, 1852. Graham and the Bethunes attended Presbyterian and Associate Reformed churches, both of which were Scottish in origin, Calvinist in theology, and Presbyterian in polity. The main difference between them, from Joanna Bethune's standpoint, was whether ministers practiced open or closed communion (she favored the former). George Washington Bethune served in churches of the Associate Reformed synod throughout his career. See Bethune, Diary, May 1, 1825. The family grave had to be relocated when the Pearl Street Church closed in 1853.

36. Bethune, Diary, September 18, 1845; September 18, 1846; September 24, 1848; *Dictionary of American Biography*, s.v. "McCartee, Divie Bethune." Bethune often began a new journal book on September 18, the anniversary of Divie's death; nine of the 186 entries, most of them among the longest in the diary, are dated September 18. For comments on George Washington Bethune, see January 29, March 18, 1825; Janu-

ary 25, 1829; April 1, 1849; September 18, 1830; and March 18, 1852. On Jessie's and Isabella's pregnancies, see September 18, 1828; September 18, 1830; and April 7, 1831. On her grandchildren's conversions, see September 18, 1846; for an example of the kind of pressure she put on them, see February 1, 1847. On her ideas about the covenant, see Bethune, *Mrs. Joanna Bethune*, 195; on George's ideas, ibid., 18, 26. The comment on mother's milk is from Bethune, Diary, November 2, 1845 (she was visiting George in Philadelphia and had just heard him preach). On nineteenth-century correspondences between human milk and human blood, see Adrienne Berney, "Reforming the Maternal Breast: Infant Feeding and American Culture, 1870–1940" (Ph.D. diss., University of Delaware, 1998), esp. chapter 4. See also Lewis Schenck, *The Presbyterian Doctrine of Children in the Covenant* (New Haven: Yale University Press, 1940). In his own memoirs, her grandson, Divie Bethune McCartee, attributed his interest in missionary work to the family legacy, and to his mother's interests: *A Missionary Pioneer in the Far East: A Memorial of Divie Bethune McCartee*, ed. Robert E. Speer (New York: Fleming H. Revell Co., 1922), 27–29, 41–43.

37. Bethune, *Mrs. Joanna Bethune*, vi; Bethune, Diary, January 9, 1825; William Henry Boyd, *Boyd's New York City Tax Book; Being a List of Persons, Corporations and Co-Partnerships . . . Who Were Taxed According to the Assessors' Books, 1856 and '57* (New York: W. H. Boyd, 1857). On New York merchants in general and Bethune's business in particular, see Robert Greenhalgh Albion, *The Rise of New York Port, [1815–1860]* (New York: Charles Scribner's Sons, 1939), 260–86, and advertisement on 277. On the real estate market, see Elizabeth Blackmar, *Manhattan for Rent, 1785–1850* (Ithaca: Cornell University Press, 1989), esp. 76–105, 113–14, 128–31, and table 1. On very wealthy New Yorkers of the Bethunes' era, see Edward Pessen, *Riches, Class, and Power before the Civil War* (Lexington, Mass.: D. C. Heath, 1973), 31–35, 46–71. My analysis here has benefited greatly from Leonore Davidoff and Catherine Hall's insightful study of the British middle class, *Family Fortunes: Men and Women of the English Middle Class, 1780–1850* (Chicago: University of Chicago Press, 1987).

38. Bertram Wyatt-Brown, *Lewis Tappan and the Evangelical War against Slavery* (Cleveland: Case Western Reserve University Press, 1969), 43–52; Divie Bethune to Isabella Graham, October 8, 1801, in *Unpublished Letters of Isabella Graham*, ed. Joanna Bethune, 263; Bethune, Diary, March 18, February 6, 1825. See also George Duffield's 1834 temperance sermon, "On the Traffic in Ardent Spirits" (New York: American Tract Society, 1834); *Dictionary of American Biography*, s.v. "Bethune, George Washington," "Duffield, George," "McCartee, Divie Bethune"; Abraham Van Nest, *A Memoir of Rev. George W. Bethune, D.D.* (New York: Sheldon, 1867); Donald Scott, *From Office to Profession: The New England Ministry, 1750–1850* (Philadelphia: Temple University Press, 1978); Leonard Sweet, *The Minister's Wife: Her Role in Nineteenth-Century American Evangelicalism* (Philadelphia: Temple University Press, 1983).

39. Davidoff and Hall, *Family Fortunes*, 51; Mary P. Ryan, *Cradle of the Middle Class: The Family in Oneida County, New York, 1790–1860* (Cambridge: Cambridge University Press, 1981), 200–202; Jeanne Boydston, *Home and Work: Housework, Wages, and the Ideology of Labor in the Early Republic* (New York: Oxford University Press, 1990), 142–63.

40. Melville, *Seton*, 105–20, 336 (n. 127); Code, *Letters of Mother Seton*, 204–13; Bechtle and Metz, *Seton: Correspondence and Journals*, 403–24.

41. Melville, *Seton*, 143–49, 160, 194–95, 340 (n. 40). The Emmitsburg school's curriculum is reprinted in Barbara Misner, "A Comparative Social Study of the Members of Apostolates of the First Eight Permanent Communities of Women Religious within the Original Boundaries of the United States, 1790–1850" (Ph.D. diss, Catholic University, 1980), 273. See also Joseph G. Mannard, "Maternity . . . of the Spirit: Nuns and Domesticity in Antebellum America," *U.S. Catholic Historian* 5 (1986): 305–24.

42. Thomas F. Meehan, "A Self-Effaced Philanthropist: Cornelius Heeney, 1754–1848," *Catholic Historical Review* 4 (April 1918): 3–17; C. J. Juesse, *The Social Thought of American Catholics, 1634–1829* (Westminster, Md.: Newman Book Shop, 1945), 270–71.

43. Melville, *Seton*, 194–95, 255–57. The Roman Catholic Asylum for the Children of Widows and Widowers, formed in 1829 by Seton's friend and former coworker Catherine Dupleix (who had also converted to Catholicism), constitutes a partial exception to this generalization. When it incorporated in 1835, however, male trustees held all corporate power. See *Truth Teller* 5 (October 24, 1829): 342, and Chapter 5 below.

44. Lee Chambers-Schiller, *Liberty, A Better Husband: Single Women in America, the Generations of 1780–1840* (New Haven: Yale University Press, 1984); Mannard, "Maternity . . . of the Spirit," 318–22. Daniel A. Cohen comments similarly on the contradictions between submission and pride that Boston's Ursuline nuns experienced; I find his argument that convents attracted "ambitious" women problematic, however. Most convent entrants were young women, and convent rules were extremely restrictive. See "Miss Reed and the Superiors: The Contradictions of Convent Life in Antebellum America," *Journal of Social History* 30 (Fall 1996): 149–84.

45. The Sisters of Charity of St. Joseph's were incorporated in Maryland in 1817, and in Washington, D.C., in 1828. See Misner, "A Comparative Social Study," 71–72.

46. Melville, *Seton*, 158–72, 182, 192, 343 (n. 106), Code, *Letters of Mother Seton*, 302; Jay P. Dolan, *The American Catholic Experience: A History from Colonial Times to the Present* (Garden City, N.Y.: Doubleday, 1985), 121. Dubois later became bishop of New York diocese; Dubourg became bishop of New Orleans in 1815, and returned to his native France in 1826. Conflicts between nuns and bishops over convent rules seem to have been common during this era, in part because of the need to adopt European rules to American conditions. See Mary Ewens, *The Role of the Nun in Nineteenth Century America* (1971; reprint, New York: Arno Press, 1978), 32–64.

47. Melville, *Seton*, 151, 262. By contrast, the order's membership drew heavily from farm families; see Misner, "A Comparative Social Study," 107–21.

48. Melville, *Seton*, 197–98, 212.

49. Leo R. Ryan, "Pierre Toussaint: 'God's Image Carved in Ebony,'" *Historical Records and Studies* 25 (1935): 39–58; John Gilmary Shea, *Catholic Churches of New York City* (New York: Lawrence G. Goulding & Co., 1878), 732–37; Mary Agnes McCann, *The History of Mother Seton's Daughters*, 3 vols. (New York: Longman's Green, 1917), 1:90–103; Melville, *Seton*, 255–57; Marie de Lourdes Walsh, *Mother Elizabeth Boyle: Mother of Charity* (New York: Paulist Press, 1955), 33–47.

50. Melville, *Seton*, 186–7, 246, 260–65, 371 (n. 45).

51. Melville, *Seton*, 311 (n. 53), 206. In "Bronx Miracle," *American Quarterly* 52 (Oc-

tober 2000): 405–43, John T. McGreevy notes the continuing importance of an international consciousness within American Catholicism.

52. See Shane White, *Somewhat More Independent: The End of Slavery in New York City, 1770–1810* (Athens: University of Georgia Press, 1991), 3–55. As White shows (table 4), the proportion of black New Yorkers who were enslaved declined from 66.5 percent in 1790 to 16.2 percent in 1818.

53. Elizabeth Mason North, *Consecrated Talents; or, The Life of Mrs. Mary W. Mason* (New York: Carlton & Lanahan, 1870), 142; "Rules for the Schools of the Female Association and Minutes of the Trustees," Female Association Records, July 20, 1810; May 29, 1811; May 2, 1818, New York Female Association Records, Friends Historical Society, Swarthmore College, Swarthmore, Pa.

54. Samuel Cornish wrote an obituary for Henrietta Regulus Ray; it appeared in *The Emancipator* 1 (November 24, 1836): 119, and *The Colored American* 1 (March 4, 1837): 3. Other information can be found in the following sources: Ray C. Sawyer, comp., "Abstracts of Wills for New York County, 1801–1855," 20 vols., typescript, New York Public Library, 2:90; death record of Lawrence D. Regulus, November 5, 1828, Register of Deaths, 1798–1865, New York City Department of Health, microfilm, New York Public Library, New York City; letter of administration for Lawrence D. Regulus, November 11, 1828, Surrogate's Court, New York City; *Freedom's Journal*, November 7, 1828; and *Longworth's . . . New York City Directory* (New York, 1827, 1828). On the Orange Street brothels, see Timothy J. Gilfoyle, *City of Eros: New York City, Prostitution, and the Commercialization of Sex, 1790–1920* (New York: W. W. Norton, 1992), 319. On French Caribbean immigrants in New York, and on free blacks' economic situation, see White, *Somewhat More Independent*, 31–32, 157–66; and Rhoda Freeman, *The Free Negro in New York City in the Era before the Civil War* (New York: Garland, 1973), 219–311.

55. *Emancipator* 1 (November 24, 1836): 119; Register of Deaths, New York City Department of Health, 1836; letter of administration for Henrietta D. Ray, October 25, 1836, Surrogate's Court, New York City (oddly, the letter of administration is dated two days before Henrietta Ray's recorded death); "Charles B. Ray," *Dictionary of American Negro Biography*, ed. Rayford W. Logan and Michael R. Winston (New York: W. W. Norton, 1982), 515–16; Florence T. Ray and Henrietta Cordelia Ray, *A Sketch of the Life of Rev. Charles B. Ray* (New York: Press of J. J. Little & Co., 1887), 6–57; *Freedom's Journal*, March 16, 1827; *Colored American* 1 (April 1, 1837); Boyd, *Boyd's New York City Tax Book*; Freeman, "Free Negro in New York City," 228–30, 279; Clara Merritt DeBoer, *Be Jubilant My Feet: African American Abolitionists in the American Missionary Association, 1839–1861* (New York: Garland, 1994), 207–10. On the health status of New York's free African Americans, see John B. Duffy, *History of Public Health in New York, 1625–1866* (New York: Russell Sage Foundation, 1968). On the economic and familial status of northern free blacks in general, see Gary B. Nash, "Forging Freedom: The Emancipation Experience in the Northern Seaport Cities, 1775–1820," in *Slavery and Freedom in the Age of the American Revolution*, ed. Ira Berlin and Ronald Hoffman (Charlottesville: University Press of Virginia, 1983), 3–48; and Leon Litwack, *North of Slavery: The Negro in the Free North, 1790–1860* (Chicago: University of Chicago Press, 1961), 153–86.

56. North, *Consecrated Talents*, 14–91; John Wigger, *Taking Heaven by Storm: Methodism and the Rise of Popular Christianity in America* (New York: Oxford University Press, 1998), 151–72; Dee Andrews, *The Methodists and Revolutionary America: The Shaping of an Evangelical Culture* (Princeton: Princeton University Press, 2000). As Virginia Brereton has pointed out, conversion narratives like Mason's often possessed a "submerged plot" whereby the female convert was unwillingly propelled into public activism in the name of doing God's will. Such narratives "both affirmed women's role in a patriarchal society and subverted some of the assumptions of that society" by permitting individuals "if need be, boldly to flout the wills of their fathers and husbands." See *From Sin to Salvation*, 28–32. Susan Juster makes a similar point about the "empowering" nature of women's conversion experiences despite church polities "where power was reserved for men"; *Disorderly Women*, 200–207. In *Strangers and Pilgrims: Female Preaching in America, 1740–1845* (Chapel Hill: University of North Carolina Press, 1998), 185, Catherine A. Brekus found that women who prayed and exhorted in small Protestant sects always described their "calls to preach as . . . beyond their control."

57. *Emancipator* 1 (November 24, 1836): 119; *The Articles of Faith, Church Discipline, and By-Laws of the Abyssinian Baptist Church in the City of New York, April 3, 1833* (New York: n.p., 1833). On gender conventions among free African Americans, see James Oliver Horton, *Free People of Color: Inside the African American Community* (Washington, D.C.: Smithsonian Institution, 1993), 98–121; on church practices, see Freeman, *Free Negro in New York City*, 376–420, and Litwack, *North of Slavery*, 187–213. As Susan Juster points out, in the eighteenth century, Baptist church covenants routinely enjoined church members against disorderly speech because tattling and slander undercut the community of believers; see *Disorderly Women*, 88–96.

58. *Freedom's Journal*, January 25, 1828, 175; February 1, 1828, 179.

59. *Freedom's Journal*, March 7, 1828, 197; February 7, 1829, 355. See ibid., January 9, 1829, 319, for an editorial (probably written by Cornish) praising the African Dorcas Society's manner of doing business. On literary societies in general, see Dorothy B. Porter, "The Organized Educational Activities of Negro Literary Societies, 1828–1846," *Journal of Negro Education* 5 (October 1936): 555–76. On New York and the Female Literary Society, see Daniel M. Perlman, "Organizations of the Free Negro in New York, 1800–1860," *Journal of Negro History* 56 (July 1971): 187; *Colored American* 1 (March 4, 1837): 3; and Dorothy Sterling, ed., *Turning the World Upside Down: The Anti-Slavery Convention of American Women, Held in New York City, May 9–12, 1837* (New York: Feminist Press, 1987), 22.

60. North, *Consecrated Talents*, 87, 180–90, 207–15, 229–34.

61. See Emma Jones Lapsansky, "Friends, Wives, and Strivings: Networks and Community Values among Nineteenth-Century Philadelphia Afroamerican Elites," *Pennsylvania Magazine of History and Biography* 104 (January 1984): 8–9.

62. Lori D. Ginzberg, *Women and the Work of Benevolence: Morality, Politics, and Class in the 19th-Century United States* (New Haven: Yale University Press, 1990), 220.

63. North, *Consecrated Talents*, 239; Sterling, *We Are Your Sisters*, 118–19; *Weekly Anglo-African* 1 (April 7, June 23, 1860); Ray, *Charles B. Ray*, 45–47.

Chapter Four

1. For excellent overviews of women's political history, see Paula Baker, "The Domestication of Politics: Women and American Political Society, 1780–1920," *American Historical Review* 89 (June 1984): 620–48; and Louise M. Young, "Women's Place in American Politics: The Historical Perspective,"*Journal of Politics* 38 (1976): 295–335. On individual women political thinkers, such as Judith Sargent Murray, and on the revolutionary-era Ladies Association, see Linda Kerber, *Women of the Republic: Intellect and Ideology in Revolutionary America* (Chapel Hill: University of North Carolina Press, 1980); and Mary Beth Norton, *Liberty's Daughters: The Revolutionary Experience of American Women, 1750–1800* (Boston: Little, Brown, 1980). The quotation is from Leonore Davidoff, "Regarding Some 'Old Husbands' Tales': Public and Private in Feminist History," in *Feminism, the Public and the Private*, ed. Joan Landes (New York: Oxford University Press, 1998), 164–87. For an overview of political change during the 1790–1830 era, see Richard Hofstadter, *The Idea of a Party System: The Rise of Legitimate Opposition in the United States, 1780–1840* (Berkeley: University of California Press, 1969).

2. Lori Ginzberg and Mary Ryan have examined these issues insightfully. The quotation is from Ginzberg, *Women and the Work of Benevolence: Morality, Politics, and Class in the 19th-Century United States* (New Haven: Yale University Press, 1991), 18. See also Ryan, *Women in Public: Between Banners and Ballots, 1825–1880* (Baltimore: Johns Hopkins University Press, 1990).

3. *An Account of the Boston Female Asylum* . . . (Boston, 1803), 4; Female Auxiliary Bible Society of Boston and Its Vicinity, *Ninth Annual Report* (Boston, 1823), 10.

4. New York Orphan Asylum Society Petition to the City Corporation, 1809, reprinted in *A Short History of the Orphan Asylum Society in the City of New York*, comp., Joanna H. Mathews (New York: Anson D. F. Randolph, 1893), 28. Linda Kerber has been the foremost and most incisive analyst of these issues, beginning with *Women of the Republic*, esp. 110–13, 269–88, and continuing through "A Constitutional Right to Be Treated like American Ladies: Women and the Obligations of Citizenship," in *U.S. History as Women's History* (Chapel Hill: University of North Carolina Press, 1995), 17–35, and *No Constitutional Right to Be Ladies: Women and the Obligations of Citizenship* (New York: Hill and Wang, 1998). See also Stephanie McCurry, "The Two Faces of Republicanism: Gender and Proslavery Politics in Antebellum South Carolina," *Journal of American History* 79 (March 1992): 1245–64. McCurry's argument that republicanism wore "two faces," an egalitarian public and an inegalitarian private one, is highly suggestive and helps explain the relationship between men's republican independence and their control of dependents in the home. For a different approach, see Rosemary Zagarri, "The Rights of Man and Woman in Post-Revolutionary America," *William and Mary Quarterly* 55 (April 1998): 203–30.

5. Boston Fatherless and Widows Society, *Seventeenth Annual Report* (Boston, 1834), 8. Here I agree fully with Jeanne Boydston on the effect that the gendering of politics had on "female assertiveness"; I would emphasize more than Boydston does, though, the importance of women's organizations in shaping the process. See Jeanne Boydston, "The Woman Who Wasn't There: Women's Market Labor and the Transition to Cap-

italism in the United States," *Journal of the Early Republic* 16 (Summer 1996): 183–206. See also Ginzberg, *Women and the Work of Benevolence*, 36–97.

6. Pastoral Letter of 1837, printed in *Up from the Pedestal: Selected Writings in the History of American Feminism*, ed. Aileen Kraditor (Chicago: Quadrangle, 1968), 50–52. For general background on the issues raised in this paragraph, see Baker, "Domestication of Politics"; Ginzberg, *Women and the Work of Benevolence*; Linda K. Kerber, "Separate Spheres, Female Worlds, Woman's Place: The Rhetoric of Women's History," *Journal of American History* 75 (June 1988): 9–39; Elizabeth Varon, "*We Mean to Be Counted": White Women and Party Politics in Antebellum Virginia* (Chapel Hill: University of North Carolina Press, 1998); Michael McGerr, "Political Style and Women's Power, 1830–1930," *Journal of American History* 77 (December 1990): 864–85; Ryan, *Women in Public*, and *Civic Wars: Democracy and Public Life in the American City during the Nineteenth Century* (Berkeley: University of California Press, 1997); Catherine Allgor, *Parlor Politics: In Which the Ladies of Washington Help Build a City and a Government* (Charlottesville: University Press of Virginia, 2000); and Leonore Davidoff, *Worlds Between: Historical Perspectives on Gender and Class* (London: Polity Press, 1995), chapter 8.

7. Jürgen Habermas's concept of "the public sphere" has proven both useful and problematic for historians. For a cogent review of the debates, see *Habermas and the Public Sphere*, ed. Craig Calhoun (Cambridge: MIT Press, 1992), especially the essays by Calhoun, Nancy Fraser, Mary P. Ryan, and Michael Schudson. I find helpful Ryan's distinction between the formation of public opinion and public policy. On the notion of "publicity" as created by print capitalism in the early modern era, see Benedict Anderson, *Imagined Communities: Reflections on the Origin and Spread of Nationalism* (London: Verso, 1983). For a general discussion of "public life" and its relation to private life, see Sara M. Evans, "Women's History and Political Theory: Toward a Feminist Approach to Public Life," in *Visible Women: New Essays on American Activism*, ed. Nancy A. Hewitt and Suzanne Lebsock (Urbana: University of Illinois Press, 1993), 119–39.

8. On Samuel Stillman, see *Dictionary of American Biography*, s.v. "Stillman, Samuel"; and Clifford K. Shipton, *Sibley's Harvard Graduates*, 17 vols. (Boston: Massachusetts Historical Society, 1942–75), 14: 216–27. On the Boston Female Asylum's founding, see Susan Lynne Porter, "Benevolent Asylum—Image and Reality: The Care and Training of Female Orphans in Boston, 1800–1840" (Ph.D. diss., Boston University, 1984), 70–76. On Mary Webb, see Albert L. Vail, *Mary Webb and the Mother Society* (Philadelphia: American Baptist Publication Society, 1914), 1–3, 16–36; and *Stimpson's Boston Directory* (Boston, 1800, 1805, 1813, 1837). On Hannah Caldwell, see Anne Van Wyck, *Descendants of Cornelius Barentse Van Wyck and Anna Polhemus* (New York: Tobias A. Wright, 1912), 134–35; and William Armstrong, *The Kerr Clan of New Jersey* (Morrison, Ill.: Shawver Publishing Co., 1931), 13. Hannah's first husband, Theodorus Van Wyck, in partnership with his brother-in-law Isaac Sebring, had accumulated a substantial fortune at his death in 1803. Her second husband, John E. Caldwell, a successful merchant, was a great-grandson of Jonathan Edwards, and an orphan who had been raised for a time by the Marquis de Lafayette. At the time of his death in 1819, he had embraced the business of benevolence and was working as the American

Bible Society's agent. See also Ginzberg, *Women and the Work of Benevolence*, 44–45; and Nancy Hewitt, *Women's Activism and Social Change: Rochester, New York, 1822–1872* (Ithaca: Cornell University Press, 1984), 52–55.

9. Vail, *Mary Webb*, 28–49; *A Brief Account of the Boston Female Missionary Society . . .* (Boston, 1818); *A Short Account of the Penitent Females' Refuge* (Boston, 1825), 9. Patricia Cline Cohen subtly explores the dilemmas that later moral reformers faced when they publicized their antiprostitution campaigns in the 1830s; see *The Murder of Helen Jewett: The Life and Death of a Prostitute in Nineteenth-Century New York* (New York: Random House, 1998), 274–76.

10. Corban Society Minutes, 1811–48, September 1825, Congregational Library, Boston, Mass.; Graham Society Minutes, 1817–31, Congregational Library, Boston, Mass.; Widows' Society Minutes, December 12, 1821; December 11, 1822; January 3, 1827; June 4, 1828; December 8, 1830, Schlesinger Library, Cambridge, Mass. *An Account of the Widows' Society* (Boston, 1823), 6; *Constitution and By-Laws and Address of the Female Bethel Association* (New York, 1836), 7; *The Third Annual Report of the New York Female Bethel Union* (New York, 1838), 3.

11. Vail, *Mary Webb*, 49; Boston Female Asylum Minutes, October 27, 1800, Massachusetts State Library, Boston, Mass.; Fragment Society Minutes, December 12, 1814, Fragment Society Collection, Schlesinger Library, Cambridge, Mass.; Asylum for Lying-In Women, Board of Managers Minutes, November 1, 1824, New York Weill Cornell Medical Center Archives, New York City; Society for the Relief of Poor Widows with Small Children Minutes, January 10, 1803, New-York Historical Society, New York City; Widows' Society Minutes, June 14, 1822.

12. *Religious Intelligencer* 2 (May 2, 1818): 780; *Boston Recorder* 14 (June 18, 1829): 98; Boston Female Asylum Minutes, November 1810. See also David Paul Nord, "The Evangelical Origins of Mass Media in America, 1815–1835," *Journalism Monographs* 88 (1984): 1–31.

13. *New York Evening Post*, May 31, 1814; Association for the Benefit of Colored Orphans Minutes, April 7, November 24, 1837, New-York Historical Society, New York City; Hetty Low King was also from a well-connected family; her father, Nicholas Low, had been a wealthy merchant and land speculator, an associate of Alexander Hamilton, and a delegate to the New York State ratification convention in 1787; see *American National Biography*, s.v. "King, Charles"; "Low, Nicholas." At the same time, Sarah Beach Hall promised six weeks of free advertising, courtesy of her husband, Francis, editor of the *Commercial Advertiser*. On the "print revolution," see Cathy Davidson, *Revolution and the Word: The Rise of the Novel in America* (New York: Oxford University Press, 1986); Nord, "Evangelical Origins of the Mass Media"; Michael Schudson, *Discovering the News: A Social History of American Newspapers* (New York: Basic Books, 1978); and David M. Henkin, *City Reading: Written Words and Public Spaces in Antebellum New York* (New York: Columbia University Press, 1998), 106–9.

14. Mrs. Jonathan Odell, comp., *Origin and History of the Orphan Asylum Society in the City of New York, 1806–1896*, 2 vols. (New York: n.p., 1896), 1:36; *The First and Second Annual Reports of the Female Society for Promoting Christianity among the Jews* (Boston, 1818), 3; Boston Female Asylum Minutes, April 1821.

15. On the existence of "multiple publics," see Nancy Fraser, "Rethinking the Pub-

lic Sphere: A Contribution to the Critique of Actually Existing Democracy," in Cal-houn, *Habermas and the Public Sphere*, 121–28. On Sarah Hall, see *Christian Advocate and Journal*, September 30, 1846. On Henrietta Regulus Ray, see Chapter 3 above.

16. *Truth Teller* 15 (April 13, 1839): 119; *Weekly Advocate*, January 7, 1837, 1–2. On the *Weekly Advocate's* history, see Rhoda Golden Freeman, *The Free Negro in New York City in the Era before the Civil War* (New York: Garland, 1994), 175–76. In her 1831 speech to the United Tailoresses' Society, printed in the *New York Daily Sentinel*, Louise Mitchell called upon her sisters to renounce the "helplessness" that had ren-dered them "silent and submissive" and to seek "publicity" for their cause. Dolores Janiewski, "Making Common Cause: The Needlewomen of New York, 1831–1869," *Signs* 1 (1976): 779–81.

17. See David Waldstreicher, *In the Midst of Perpetual Fetes: The Making of Ameri-can Nationalism, 1776–1820* (Chapel Hill: University of North Carolina Press, 1997), 337. For fairly typical examples of how insulting many newspapers were in depicting African American women reformers, see *New York Herald*, May 2, 1842, [1], and May 13, 1853, [7].

18. *Freedom's Journal*, August 15, 1828; January 9, 1829; *Weekly Advocate*, January 7, 1837, 1–2; *Emancipator*, November 24, 1836, 119; Constitution of the Afric-American Female Intelligence Society, in *Black Women in White America*, ed. Gerda Lerner (New York: Vintage, 1973), 437–39. See also James Oliver Horton, "Freedom's Yoke: Gender Conventions among Antebellum Free Blacks," *Feminist Studies* 12 (Spring 1986): 55–59; and Shane White, "'It Was a Proud Day': African Americans, Festivals, and Parades in the North, 1741–1834," *Journal of American History* 81 (1995): 13–50.

19. *Right and Wrong in Boston, in 1836. Annual Report of the Boston Female Anti-Slavery Society* . . . (Boston, 1836), 6n, 24. Lori Ginzberg astutely notes Chapman's crit-icisms of benevolent women's privileges; see *Women and the Work of Benevolence*, 33, 65, 72.

20. Female Benevolent Society Minutes, January 12, 1841, Inwood House, New York City; on the controversy between the Female Benevolent Society and Rev. John Mc-Dowall, see *Charges Preferred against the New-York Female Benevolent Society and the Auditing Committee, in 1835 and 1836* (New York: n.p., 1836); and Larry Howard Whiteaker, "Moral Reform and Prostitution in New York City, 1830–1860" (Ph.D. diss, Princeton University, 1977), 123–38. See also Cohen, *The Murder of Helen Jewett*, 274–76.

21. "N.Y. Female Benevolent Society," *Advocate of Moral Reform* 1 (August 1835): 64; circulation figures from ibid., 2 (May 15, 1836): 65; Ginzberg, *Women and the Work of Benevolence*; Barbara Miel Hobson, *Uneasy Virtue: The Politics of Prostitution and the American Reform Tradition* (New York: Basic Books, 1987). By the 1830s, of course, women like Sarah Josepha Hale were editing popular women's magazine; the owners and publishers were usually men.

22. Sarah J. Hale's byline first appeared on the Seamen's Aid Society, *Third Annual Report* (Boston, 1836), her last on the *Eighth Annual Report* (Boston, 1841). Hale had begun editing the *Ladies Magazine* in 1828. *The Constitution and Circular of the New York Female Moral Reform Society, with the Addresses Delivered at its Organization* (New York: J. N. Bolles, 1834); New York Female Moral Reform Society, *An Appeal to*

the Wives, Mothers, and Daughters of our Land, in the City and the Country . . . (New York: H. R. Piercy, 1836). On abolitionists and moral reformers, see Ginzberg, *Women and the Work of Benevolence*, 71–78. On anonymity in print, see Michael Warner, *The Letters of the Republic: Publication and the Public Sphere in Eighteenth Century America* (Cambridge: Harvard University Press, 1990), x. See also Nancy Isenberg, *Sex and Citizenship in Antebellum America* (Chapel Hill: University of North Carolina Press, 1998), 55–63.

23. Dorothy Sterling, ed., *Turning the World Upside Down: The Anti-Slavery Convention of American Women Held in New York City May 9–12, 1837* (New York: Feminist Press, 1987), 10, 20, 27–32.

24. Stillman quoted in Porter, "Benevolent Asylum," 69–70; Boston Female Asylum Minutes, September 26, 1800.

25. Seamen's Aid Society, *Third Annual Report* (Boston, 1836), 15–17; David Hosack, *Memoir of DeWitt Clinton* (New York: J. Seymour, 1829), 173–76; *Second Annual Report of the Female Missionary Society of the City of New York and Its Vicinity* (New York, 1818), 5–6; *Advocate of Moral Reform* 3 (July 15, 1837): 293–94; Association for the Benefit of Colored Orphans Minutes, December 9, 1836.

26. Orphan Asylum Society in the City of New York, "Twelfth Annual Report," in Odell, *Origin and History of the Orphan Asylum Society*, 1:85; Association for the Relief of Respectable, Aged, Indigent Females, *Twenty-First Annual Report* (New York, 1834), 6; Widows' Society Minutes, December 1, 1819; [Mary W. Mason], "New York Asylum for Lying-In Women: An Account of the Organization and Growth of the Society" [1823], Asylum for Lying-In Women Minutes, New York Weill Cornell Medical Center Archives, New York City; *Proceedings of the Board of Aldermen of the City of New York*, 228 vols. (New York, n.p, 1831–97), 6:112. Roman Catholics were also critical of the almshouse for its treatment of orphans; see *Truth Teller* 2 (February 11, 1826): 45–46. Comments about respectable women "reduced to penury" by the death of a male breadwinner, of course, also reflected the benefactors' own sense of economic vulnerability.

27. *A Brief Account of the Origin and Progress of the Boston Female Society for Missionary Purposes. With Extracts from the Reports of the Society, in May 1817 and 1818 . . .* (Boston, 1818), 4–5; *Second Annual Report of the Female Missionary Society of the City of New York and Its Vicinity*, 7–9.

28. The quotation is from a petition of New York House of Industry's managers to the Mayor and Common Council; see *New York Evening Post*, July 5, 1814. On the $15,000 lottery, see Society for the Relief of Poor Widows with Small Children Minutes, March 21, 1803, New-York Historical Society, New York City; and *Minutes of the Common Council of the City of New York, 1784–1831*, 19 vols. (New York: City of New York, 1917), May 9, 1803, 3:276; May 23, 1803, 3:287; November 28, 1803, 3:403; January 3, 1804, 3:437. On the Orphan Asylum Society, see Joanna H. Mathews, *A Short History of the Orphan Asylum Society in the City of New York, Founded 1806* (New York: Anson D. F. Randolph, 1893), 23–32; Odell, *Orphan Asylum Society*, 1:56–57, 75–78, 133, 196; and *Minutes of the Common Council of the City of New York*, October 11, 1824, 14:100–101; December 1, 1828, 17:478. On land grants to individual societies, see ibid., January 20, 1817, 7:771 (grant to Association for the Relief of Respectable, Aged, Indigent Females); December 18, 1815, 8:371 (grant to Female Assistance Society); and February 16, 1818,

9:494–95 (grant to House of Industry). On the lamp and the guard, see ibid., December 1, 1817, 9:372; and Female Benevolent Society Minutes, August 9, 1842. On storage rights at the Almshouse, see *Minutes of the Common Council of the City of New York*, April 1, 1805, 3:716; July 30, 1810, 6:297. On the grant of manure, see ibid., March 28, 1808, 5:67; and May 30, 1808, 5:141.

29. Society for the Relief of Poor Widows with Small Children Minutes, January 6, 1812; *New York Evening Post*, November 29, 1819; Seamen's Aid Society, *Eleventh Annual Report* (Boston, 1844), 7–12; *Eighteenth Annual Report* (Boston, 1851). See Chapter 5 for additional discussion of the contract.

30. Ryan, *Civic Wars*, 104; Hobson, *Uneasy Virtue*, 119 (Hobson's figures for Penitent Females' Refuge residents cover the years 1822–50); *A Short Account of the Penitent Females' Refuge* (Boston: n.p., 1825), 14; *Proceedings of the Board of Aldermen of the City of New York*, January 5, 1835, 8:115–17; Female Benevolent Society Minutes, July 14, 1840; *The Third Annual Report of the Association for the Benefit of Colored Orphans* (New York, 1839), 10; Leslie Maria Harris, "Creating the African American Working Class: Black and White Workers, Abolitionists and Reformers in New York City, 1785–1863" (Ph.D. diss., Stanford University, 1994), 126–27. As Harris notes, the managers stopped returning children to the almshouse after 1843, when a new building permitted them to maintain an infirmary. In 1847 alone, claimed the managers of New York's Society for the Relief of Respectable, Aged, Indigent Colored Persons, their asylum transferred a "large proportion" of its thousand clients from the almshouse. See Mary W. Thompson, *"Broken Gloom": Sketches of the History, Character, and Dying Testimony, of the Beneficiaries of the Colored Home, in the City of New York* (New York: n.p., 1851), 77. I am grateful to Lori Beth Finkelstein for this reference.

31. *Minutes of the Common Council of the City of New York*, May 30, 1814, 7:764; December 28, 1828, 10:164; November 6, 1815, 7:333–34; December 4, 1815, 7:359; October 11, 1824, 14:100–101; *Proceedings of the Board of Aldermen*, January 5, 1835, 8:154. On the House of Industry generally, see Christine Stansell, *City of Women: Sex and Class in New York, 1789–1860* (New York: Knopf, 1986), 16. On the practice of giving public money to charitable groups, see Raymond Mohl, *Poverty in New York, 1783–1825* (New York: Oxford University Press, 1971), 147–51.

32. David M. Schneider, *The History of Public Welfare in New York State, 1609–1866* (Chicago: University of Chicago Press, 1938), 321–39; Ronald P. Formisano, "Boston, 1800–1840: From Deferential-Participant to Party Politics," in *Boston, 1700–1980: The Evolution of Urban Politics*, ed. Ronald P. Formisano and Constance K. Burns (Westport, Conn.: Greenwood Press, 1984), 29–57; Joseph Hawes, *Children in Urban Society: Juvenile Delinquency in Nineteenth-Century America* (New York: Oxford University Press, 1971), 28–45. Like the House of Refuge, New York's Humane Society (founded 1787) enjoyed the patronage of city and state leaders; the group occasionally met at City Hall. See Mohl, *Poverty in New York*, 121–35.

33. Boston Female Asylum Minutes, January 1806. In *We Mean to Be Counted*, 72–84, Elizabeth R. Varon suggests that the 1840 election marked a turning point for southern white women, as the Whig party enlisted them as partisans for the Whig cause. My reading of the evidence is somewhat different. It seems to me important to distinguish between enlisting individual women and women collectively in partisan

causes, and between ascribing partisanship to womanhood and to actual women. Nancy Isenberg makes a similar point in *Sex and Citizenship*, 19.

34. On Sarah Bowdoin, see Boston Female Asylum Minutes, September 1803; and Robert L. Volz, *Governor Bowdoin and His Family: A Guide to an Exhibition and a Catalogue* (Brunswick, Maine: Colby College Press, 1969), 27–33. On the Act of Incorporation, see Boston Female Asylum Minutes, April 1802; May 29, 1802; January 1803. On Maria Theresa Gold Appleton, see Widows' Society Minutes, June 4, 1828; and Louise Hall Tharp, *The Appletons of Beacon Hill* (Boston: Little, Brown, 1973). On DeWitt and Maria Franklin Clinton, see William W. Campbell, *The Life and Writings of DeWitt Clinton* (New York: Baker and Scribner, 1849), xxv–xxxix, 32, 173; Edward A. Fitzpatrick, *The Educational Views and Influence of DeWitt Clinton* (New York: Teachers College, 1911), 78–120; Evan Cornog, *The Birth of Empire: DeWitt Clinton and the American Experience, 1769–1828* (New York: Oxford University Press, 1998), 30, 65–72; and Mathews, *History of the Orphan Asylum Society*, 23.

35. New York Asylum for Lying-In Women Minutes, December 19, 1829; January 5, 1830; March 14, 1833; *Minutes of the Common Council of the City of New York*, January 12, 1818, 9:433; February 16, 1818, 9:494–95; November 23, 1818, 10:111; December 28, 1818, 10:164–65. New Yorker John Pintard was present on one occasion when a committee of alderman visited the House of Industry; see *Letters of John Pintard to his Daughter, Eliza Noel Pintard Servoss, 1816–1833*, ed. Dorothy C. Barck, 4 vols. (New York: New-York Historical Society, 1940), 1:104.

36. See Kathryn Kish Sklar, *Catharine Beecher: A Study in Domesticity* (New Haven: Yale University Press, 1973), 158–67; Jeanne Boydston, Mary Kelley, and Anne Margolis, *The Limits of Sisterhood: The Beecher Sisters on Women's Rights and Woman's Sphere* (Chapel Hill: University of North Carolina Press, 1988), 228–29; and Ginzberg, *Women and the Work of Benevolence*, 67–69.

37. On the Female Assistance Society, see *Minutes of the Common Council of the City of New York*, December 18, 1815, 8:371; December 9, 1816, 8:71; January 13, 1817, 8:758. On the Orphan Asylum Society, see ibid., 1809–17. On the House of Industry request, see *New York Evening Post*, November 29, 1819. Public debates about the causes of poverty also shaped city fathers' spending decisions; see Chapter 5 for a fuller discussion of this issue. See also Mohl, *Poverty in New York*, 152; and Robert W. Kelso, *The History of Public Poor Relief in Massachusetts, 1620–1920* (1922; reprint, Montclair, N.J.: Patterson Smith, 1969).

38. *Minutes of the Common Council of the City of New York*, October 9, 1815, 8:319; May 30, 1814, 7:763–64 ("respectible characters"); January 6, 1817, 8:749; December 28, 1818, 10:164–65; *New York Evening Post*, May 31, 1814. As Bertram Wyatt-Brown points out, discussing the role of deference in the antebellum South, reputation and respectability were central to the possession of honor; *Southern Honor: Ethics and Behavior in the Old South* (New York: Oxford University Press, 1982), 63–64.

39. *Minutes of the Common Council of the City of New York*, January 7, 1822, 12:174; January 21, 1822, 12:196; *Proceedings of the Board of Aldermen*, March 7, 1836, 10:309 (on the Association for the Relief of Respectable, Aged, Indigent Females); *Minutes of the Common Council of the City of New York*, March 23, 1829, 17:652; *Proceedings of the Board of Aldermen*, March 7, 1836, 10:305 (on the Female Assistance Society). John F.

Richmond, *New York and Its Institutions, 1609–1872* (New York: E. B. Treat, 1872), 423–25, mentions grants to the Association for the Relief of Respectable, Aged, Indigent Females but omits two given in the 1830s.

40. On men's societies and incorporation, see Craig Steven Wilder, "The Rise and Influence of the New York African Society for Mutual Relief, 1808–1865," *Afro-Americans in New York Life and History* 22 (July 1998): 7–18. On women's groups in general, see Linda Perkins, "Black Women and Racial 'Uplift' Prior to Emancipation," in *The Black Woman Cross-Culturally,* ed. Filomina Chioma Steady (Cambridge, Mass.: Schenkman Publishers Co., 1981), 317–34; Dorothy Sterling, ed., *We Are Your Sisters: Black Women in the Nineteenth Century* (New York: W. W. Norton, 1984), 107–16; Gerda Lerner, ed., *Black Women in White America: A Documentary History* (New York: Vintage, 1973), 437–40; and the essays in Jean Fagan Yellin and John Van Horne, eds., *The Abolitionist Sisterhood: Women's Political Culture in Antebellum America* (Ithaca: Cornell University Press, 1994).

41. *Truth Teller* 5 (November 28, 1829): 382–83. On Catherine Dupleix, see Annabelle Melville, *Elizabeth Bayley Seton, 1774–1821* (New York: Charles Scribner's Sons, 1951), 105–9.

42. Hannah Gallatin to Frances Gallatin, March 11, 1825, Gallatin Papers, New-York Historical Society, New York City. On political change, see Formisano, "Boston, 1800–1840: From Deferential-Participant to Party Politics," 28–57; Formisano, *The Transformation of Political Culture: Massachusetts Parties, 1790s–1840s* (New York: Oxford University Press, 1983); Richard P. McCormick, *The Second American Party System: Party Formation in the Jacksonian Era* (Chapel Hill: University of North Carolina Press, 1966), 36–50, 104–24; and Amy Bridges, *A City in the Republic: Ante-Bellum New York and the Origins of Machine Politics* (Cambridge: Cambridge University Press, 1984), 1–7, 70–72. See also Harlow W. Sheidley, "The Politics of Honor: The Massachusetts Conservative Elite and the Trials of Amalgamation, 1824–1829," in *Entrepreneurs: The Boston Business Community, 1700–1850* (Boston: Massachusetts Historical Society, 1997), 297–323.

43. Leo Raymond Ryan, *Old St. Peter's: The Mother Church of Catholic New York (1785–1935),* (New York: U.S. Catholic Historical Society, 1935), 236–60; percentages calculated from statistics on 242. St. Peter's received a share in 1806, nothing between 1807 and 1813, then yearly shares between 1814 and 1824. The St. Patrick's Cathedral School received shares covering 82 percent of its budget between its establishment in 1817 and 1824. See ibid., 243. On the Orphan Asylum Society, see *Minutes of the Common Council of the City of New York,* December 1, 1828, 17:478. Carl F. Kaestle provides the best analysis of the Public School Society and the controversy over the school fund; see *The Evolution of an Urban School System: New York City, 1750–1850* (Cambridge: Harvard University Press, 1973), 86–88, 159–70.

44. Mathews, *A Short History of the Orphan Asylum Society,* 29; Schneider, *History of Public Welfare in New York State;* Barck, *Letters of John Pintard,* June 11, 1830, 3:152; Marie De Lourdes Walsh, *The Sisters of Charity of New York, 1809–1959* (New York: Fordham University Press, 1960), 65–71.

45. See *Minutes of the Common Council of the City of New York,* November 20, 1826, 15:690, for an (accepted) invitation to a Catholic orphanage event. On the Ladies' As-

sociation's events, see *Truth Teller* 3 (August 13, 1827): 254; 4 (November 1, 1828): 351; and 7 (January 8, 1831): 15. On Dominick Lynch, see Mathews, *Short History of the Orphan Asylum Society*, 30. On Protestant benefactors, see *Letters of John Pintard*, June 11, 1830, 3:152–53; June 14, 1830, 3:155; December 2, 1830, 3:199; and Walsh, *Sisters of Charity*, 65.

46. *Minutes of the Common Council of the City of New York*, March 7, 1831, 19:533; *Truth Teller* 7 (May 7, 1831): 150. See also Henry J. Browne, "Public Support of Catholic Education in New York, 1825–1842: Some New Aspects," *Catholic Historical Review* 39 (April 1953): 8.

47. *Truth Teller* 7 (August 6, 1831): 255; for Rhinelander's November 7, 1831, speech, see ibid. 8 (April 21, 1832): 132–33. The Sixth Ward became even more Irish and Catholic in the 1840s with the famine immigrants' arrival; see Carol Groneman Pernicone, "The 'Bloody Ould Sixth': A Social Analysis of a New York City Working Class Community in the Mid-Nineteenth Century" (Ph.D. diss., University of Rochester, 1973). For the School Fund donation, see *Truth Teller* 8 (November 10, 1832): 365. For the state legislature's donations, see ibid., 13 (December 16, 1837): 397. The newspaper acknowledged its own transformation into "the organ of the Roman Catholics of this City" in 1832; see the issue of July 28, 247. See also Thomas F. Moriarty, "The *Truth Teller* and Irish Americana of the 1820s," *Records of the American Catholic Historical Society of Philadelphia* 75 (March 1964): 39–52. John Rhinelander, a physician, was one of a handful of well-to-do New Yorkers supporting the Democratic Party. See Anthony Gronowicz, *Race and Class Politics in New York City before the Civil War* (Boston: Northeastern University Press, 1998), 63.

48. Boston Female Asylum Minutes, September 1840; Society for the Relief of Poor Widows with Small Children Minutes, November 28, 1839; Kaestle, *Evolution of an Urban School System*, 148–51; Bridges, *A City in the Republic*, 70–77. On postbellum battles over funding for Catholic charities, see Maureen Fitzgerald, "Irish-Catholic Nuns and the Development of New York City's Welfare System, 1840–1900" (Ph.D. diss., University of Wisconsin, 1992), 445–64, 590–92.

49. *Advocate of Moral Reform* 5 (June 1, 1839): 84; 5 (October 15, 1839): 155.

50. *The Liberator* 6 (August 13, 1836): 130. On antislavery petitions, see especially Gerda Lerner, "The Political Activities of Antislavery Women," in *The Majority Finds Its Past* (New York: Oxford University Press, 1973), 112–28; Julie Roy Jeffrey, *The Great Silent Army of Abolitionism: Ordinary Women in the Antislavery Movement* (Chapel Hill: University of North Carolina Press, 1998), 86–93; Isenberg, *Sex and Citizenship*, 64–68; and Susan Marie Zaeske, "Petitioning, Antislavery, and the Emergence of Women's Political Consciousness" (Ph.D. diss., University of Wisconsin, 1997). On women's petitioning in general, see Kerber, *Women of the Republic*, 85–99; Ginzberg, *Women and the Work of Benevolence*, 80–95; Ginzberg, *Women in Antebellum Reform* (Wheeling, Ill.: Harlan Davidson, 2000), 53–56, 99–110; and Cynthia Kierner, ed., *Southern Women in Revolution, 1776–1800: Personal and Political Narratives* (Columbia: University of South Carolina Press, 1998), xix–xxviii. As both Suzan Zaeske and Mary Hershberger have pointed out, the petition campaign against Indian removal, using printed petition blanks as well as private mailings, provided a significant prece-

dent to these larger, mass-oriented drives. See Zaeske, "Petitioning, Antislavery and the Emergence of Women's Political Consciousness," 60–65; and Hershberger, "Mobilizing Women, Anticipating Abolition: The Struggle against Indian Removal in the 1830s," *Journal of American History* 86 (June 1999): 15–40.

51. Lerner, "Political Activities of Antislavery Women," 116–17; *Advocate of Moral Reform* 4 (October 1, 1838): 152; Ginzberg, *Women and the Work of Benevolence*, 77–79; *Advocate of Moral Reform* 5 (January 15, 1839): 13; 5 (March 15, 1839): 55; Whiteaker, "Moral Reform and Prostitution in New York City," 255–60. Reed's reference was to Kings 19:12, Revised Standard Version. Susan Zaeske has superbly delineated the evolution of abolitionist women's petitioning from an incidental to a central tactic, identified the key significance of the congressional "gag rule" (1836) in shifting the nature of antislavery women's petitions, and demonstrated the importance of their switch from lengthy statements filled with "palaverous prose" to short-form printed petitions. See Zaeske, "Petitioning, Antislavery, and the Emergence of Women's Political Consciousness," 106–211.

52. Zaeske, "Petitioning, Antislavery, and the Emergence of Women's Political Consciousness," 175–94; Dorothy Sterling, ed. *Turning the World Upside Down: The Anti-Slavery Convention of American Women, Held in New York City, May 9–12, 1837* (New York: Feminist Press, 1987), 12, 27; *Advocate of Moral Reform* 4 (June 1, 1838): 85–86; *Proceedings of the Anti-Slavery Convention of American Women, Held in Philadelphia, May 15, 16, 17, 18, 1838* (Philadelphia, 1838), 3–5; *Liberator* 8 (September 28, 1838): 156; *Advocate of Moral Reform* 5 (June 1, 1839): 84; *Proceedings of the Third Anti-Slavery Convention of American Women, Held in Philadelphia, May 1, 2, and 3rd, 1839* (Philadelphia, 1839), 5. Sarah Grimké considered the first Antislavery Convention to be "a step of great importance" for abolitionist women; see Larry Ceplair, ed., *The Public Years of Sarah and Angelina Grimké: Selected Writings, 1835–1839* (New York: Columbia University Press, 1989), 128. On class-based political deference, see Kathryn Kish Sklar, "The Historical Foundations of Women's Power in the Creation of the American Welfare State, 1830–1930," in *Mothers of a New World: Maternalist Politics and the Origins of Welfare States*, ed. Seth Koven and Sonya Michel (New York: Routledge, 1993), 52.

53. On Martha Hooper Adams (1802–48), see *Dictionary of American Biography*, s.v. "Adams, Nehemiah"; and *Vital Records of Marblehead, Massachusetts to the End of the Year 1849*, 2 vols. (Salem: Essex Institute, 1903), 1: 273. The text of the statement can be found in Kraditor, *Up from the Pedestal*, 50–52. On Catharine Beecher, see "Essay on Slavery and Abolitionism," in Boydston, Kelley, and Margolis, *The Limits of Sisterhood*, 127–28; Sklar, *Catharine Beecher*, 135–37; and Ginzberg, *Women and the Work of Benevolence*, 67. See also Hansen, *Strained Sisterhood*, 83. Jeanie Attie argues that Beecher's position was a compromise or "gender bargain" that many antebellum women found very appealing. See *Patriotic Toil: Northern Women and the American Civil War* (Ithaca: Cornell University Press, 1998).

54. Ginzberg, *Women and the Work of Benevolence*, 67–97; Seamen's Aid Society, *Seventh Annual Report* (Boston, 1840), 9, 12.

55. "A Word in Season: Who is Circulating Petitions?" *Advocate of Moral Reform* 4 (November 15, 1838): 173; *Right and Wrong in Boston, in 1836. Annual Report of the*

Boston Female Anti-Slavery Society . . . (Boston, 1836), 24, 47. Lori Ginzberg insightfully explores the complex issue of women's partisanship in *Women and the Work of Benevolence*, 67–114.

56. *Advocate of Moral Reform* 5 (March 15, 1839): 55; 4 (November 15, 1838): 171; 5 (February 1, 1839): 21. See Chapter 5 for a fuller analysis of the wage question.

57. *Right and Wrong in Boston . . . in 1836*, 47–48, 52, 91; *Colored American* 1 (September 9, 1837): 3; Ladies' New York City Anti-Slavery Society, *First Annual Report* (New York, 1837), 9. See also Amy Swerdlow, "Abolition's Conservative Sisters: The Ladies' New York City Anti-Slavery Societies, 1834–1840," in Yellin and Van Horne, *The Abolitionist Sisterhood*, 31–44.

58. Boston Female Moral Reform Society, *Second Annual Report* (Boston, 1837), 11; *Third Annual Report* (Boston, 1838), 7. "The Province of Woman," *Advocate of Moral Reform* 3 (September 15, 1837): 325; "Clerical Objections," ibid. 3 (October 15, 1837): 340–41; Sarah M. Grimké, "What Are the Duties of Woman at the Present Time?," ibid. 4 (January 1, 1838): 3–5. See also Zaeske, "Petitioning, Antislavery, and the Emergence of Women's Political Consciousness," 187–260.

59. *Advocate of Moral Reform* 3 (December 15, 1837): 372–73. By the 1850s, as Lori Ginzberg has documented, Sarah Towne Smith (now Martyn) had become an advocate for women's voting. Ginzberg, *Women and the Work of Benevolence*, 113–14.

60. Debra Gold Hansen, *Strained Sisterhood: Gender and Class in the Boston Female Anti-Slavery Society* (Amherst: University of Massachusetts Press, 1993), 93–156; *Proceedings of the Anti-Slavery Convention of American Women . . . 1838*, 5–6. See also Ginzberg, "The Hearts of Your Readers Will Shudder: Fanny Wright, Infidelity, and American Free Thought," *American Quarterly* 46 (June 1994): 195–227.

61. Compare *Advocate of Moral Reform* 2 (February 15, 1836) and 4 (November 1, 1838): 164–65, with Boston Female Moral Reform Society, *Second Annual Report* (Boston, 1838), 9–11, and *Advocate of Moral Reform* 5 (June 1, 1839): 84. Sterling, *Turning the World Upside Down*, 13. On this issue in general, see Ginzberg, *Women and the Work of Benevolence*, 28–32. On the response of New York male abolitionists to charges of "amalgamation," see Leslie M. Harris, "From Abolitionist Amalgamation to 'Rulers of the Five Points': The Discourse of Interracial Sex in Antebellum New York City," in *Sex, Love, Race: Crossing Boundaries in North American History*, ed. Martha Hodes (New York: New York University Press, 1999), 191–212.

62. Ginzberg, *Women and the Work of Benevolence*, 84, 98–132; Judith Wellman, "The Seneca Falls Women's Rights Convention: A Study of Social Networks," *Journal of Women's History* 3 (1991): 9–37; Isenberg, *Sex and Citizenship*, 21–28. The "corrupt customs" phrase, used in the 1837 Convention report, reappeared in the "Declaration of Sentiments" of the 1848 Seneca Falls Women's Rights Convention; for the text, see Kraditor, *Up from the Pedestal*, 187.

63. Allen Nevins and Milton Halsey Thomas, eds., *The Diary of George Templeton Strong*, vol. 1, *A Young Man in New York, 1835–1849* (New York: Macmillan, 1952), 98. Nine years later, "old Mrs. Hamilton" was still visiting the office; Strong considered her a "specimen of juvenile ante diluvianism" such as he had "never encountered." *Diary*, 1:334. See also U.S. Congress, *Report of the Committee of Claims on Petition of Eliza-*

beth Hamilton (Washington, D.C., 1810); Elizabeth did not actually receive the pension until 1837; see *American National Biography*, s.v. "Hamilton, Elizabeth Schuyler." On Female Moral Reform Societies' political activities, see Mary P. Ryan, "The Power of Women's Networks: A Case Study of Female Moral Reform in Antebellum America," *Feminist Studies* 5 (Spring 1979): 78–83.

64. Of the Orphan Asylum Society's leaders whose religious affiliation is known (nineteen of forty-three), twelve were Episcopalian, six Presbyterian, one Methodist (see Table A.1). Hamilton's adopted daughter, Frances Antill, married Arthur Tappan in 1810; while living in New York City in the 1820s and early 1830s and mothering eight children of her own (born between 1812 and 1827), Frances Tappan had served as an officer of four societies (the Female Bible Society, Female Tract Society, Association for the Relief of Respectable, Aged Indigent Females, and Asylum for Lying-In Women). See William Nelson, *Edward Antill . . . and His Descendants* (Paterson, N.J.: n.p., 1899), 27–28; and Daniel Langdon Tappan, *Tappan-Toppan Genealogy: Ancestors and Descendants of Abraham Tappan of Newbury, Massachusetts, 1606–1672* (Arlington, Mass.: n.p., 1915), 37–38.

65. See *Notable American Women*, s.v. "Hamilton, Elizabeth Schuyler"; and Mathews, *Orphan Asylum Society*, 51–52; the quotations are from "Journal of Visits to the Asylum," January 5, 1839, vol. 4, Association for the Relief of Respectable, Aged, Indigent Females Records, New-York Historical Society, New York City, and Boston Female Asylum Minutes, September 1840. For the importance of publicly visible buildings in a later era, see Sarah Deutsch, *Women and the City: Gender, Space, and Power in Boston, 1870–1940* (New York: Oxford University Press, 2000), 78–114.

66. Association for the Benefit of Colored Orphans Minutes, March 17, 1837; Association for the Benefit of Colored Orphans, *First Annual Report* (New York, 1837), 5; *Liberator* 8 (September 28, 1838): 156; *Proceedings of the Anti-Slavery Convention of American Women . . . 1838*, 7–8. See also Dorothy Sterling, *Ahead of Her Time: Abby Kelley and the Politics of Antislavery* (New York: W. W. Norton, 1991), 41–66.

67. Janet Coryell, "The Woman Politico: Women and Partisan Politics in Mid-Nineteenth-Century America," in *Women and the Unstable State in Nineteenth-Century America*, ed. Alison M. Parker and Stephanie Cole (College Station: Texas A & M Press, 2000); Varon, "*We Mean to Be Counted*," 71–102; Allgor, *Parlor Politics*, 116–17; Young, "Women's Place in American Politics," 294–317; Zaeske, "Petitioning, Antislavery, and the Emergence of Women's Political Consciousness," 311–66; Boston Female Asylum Minutes, January 1806; Nancy F. Cott, *The Grounding of Modern Feminism* (New Haven: Yale University Press, 1987), 109.

Chapter Five

1. Eleanor Davis served from 1807 until her death in 1821; Frances Erving served from 1816 to 1824, then switched to a manager's position in 1825, leaving the society in 1833 when she married Rev. Benjamin Parker of Vermont (his mother was a coworker in another society); Deborah Torrey served from 1835 until 1850; Elizabeth Seton for one

year, 1803; Sarah Bane in 1828 and 1829; and Julia Lockwood in 1836 and 1837. At the time of service, Davis and Startin were widows and Erving unmarried; Torrey, Seton, Bane, and Lockwood were married.

2. My thinking about these issues has been influenced especially by Jeanne Boydston, *Home and Work: Housework, Wages, and the Ideology of Labor in the Early Republic* (New York: Oxford University Press, 1990); Boydston, "The Woman Who Wasn't There: Women's Market Labor and the Transition to Capitalism in the United States," *Journal of the Early Republic* 16 (Summer 1996): 183–206; Mary P. Ryan, *Cradle of the Middle Class: The Family in Oneida County, New York, 1790–1860* (Cambridge: Cambridge University Press, 1981), 210–25; Amy Dru Stanley, "Home Life and the Morality of the Market," in *The Market Revolution in America*, ed. Melvyn Stokes and Stephen Conway (Charlottesville: University Press of Virginia, 1996), 74–96; and Leonore Davidoff and Catherine Hall, *Family Fortunes: Men and Women of the English Middle Class, 1780–1850* (Chicago: University of Chicago Press, 1987), 149–92.

3. On economic trends in this era, the secondary works are innumerable, but see especially Robert Greenhalgh Albion, *The Rise of New York Port (1815–1860)* (New York: Charles Scribner's Sons, 1939); Christine Stansell, *City of Women: Sex and Class in New York, 1790–1860* (New York: Knopf, 1986); Sean Wilentz, *Chants Democratic: New York City and the Rise of the American Working Class, 1788–1850* (New York: Oxford University Press, 1984); Richard B. Stott, *Workers in the Metropolis: Class, Ethnicity, and Youth in Antebellum New York City* (Ithaca: Cornell University Press, 1990), esp. 87–122, 162–90; Elizabeth Blackmar, *Manhattan for Rent, 1785–1850* (Ithaca: Cornell University Press, 1989); Robert F. Dalzell, Jr., *Enterprising Elite: The Boston Associates and the World They Made* (Cambridge: Harvard University Press, 1987), esp. 75–163; and Stokes and Conway, *The Market Revolution*. As many historians have demonstrated, the transition to a market economy characterized by new social relations of production occurred in countryside as well as city. See Christopher Clark, *The Roots of Rural Capitalism: Western Massachusetts, 1780–1860* (Ithaca: Cornell University Press, 1990); and Catherine E. Kelly, *In the New England Fashion: Reshaping Women's Lives in the Nineteenth Century* (Ithaca: Cornell University Press, 1999), 3–18.

4. On Protestant donations to New York's Roman Catholic Orphan Asylum, see Marie de Lourdes Walsh, *The Sisters of Charity of New York, 1809–1959*, 3 vols. (New York: Fordham University Press, 1960), 1:65; on Protestant donations in Boston, see Donna Merwick, *Boston Priests, 1848–1910: A Study of Social and Intellectual Change* (Cambridge: Harvard University Press, 1973), 3–5. On Father Francis Matignon's "beneficent" donations, see Fragment Society Minutes, October 1818, Fragment Society Collection, Schlesinger Library, Cambridge, Mass. On Bishop Jean Cheverus's and Bishop Benedict Fenwick's donations to Protestant enterprises, see Boston Female Asylum Minutes, June 1813, Boston Female Asylum Records, Massachusetts State Library, Boston; and Seamen's Aid Society, *Second Annual Report* (Boston, 1835), 21. For Strong's comment, see Allan Nevins and Milton Halsey Thomas, eds., *The Diary of George Templeton Strong: Young Man in New York, 1835–1849* (New York: Macmillan, 1952), entry of December 16, 1836, 44. Bishop Dubois had instituted the Christmastime collection for the Roman Catholic Orphan Asylum in 1833; in 1838, Easter collections

were earmarked for the Roman Catholic Asylum for the Children of Widows and Widowers (or Catholic Half-Orphan Asylum); see Walsh, *Sisters of Charity*, 1:71, 88.

5. Female Auxiliary Bible Society of Boston and Its Vicinity, *Ninth Annual Report* (Boston, 1823), 3; *Twenty-Second Annual Report* (Boston, 1836), 2–3; Female Union Society for the Promotion of Sabbath Schools, *Second Annual Report* (New York, 1818), 31, and Minutes, December 18, 1827, Brooklyn Historical Society, Brooklyn, New York.

6. *First and Second Annual Reports of the Female Society for Promoting Christianity among the Jews* (Boston, 1818), 3–10; *Eleventh Annual Report* (Boston, 1827), 2; *Seventeenth Annual Report* (Boston, 1832), 2–4; *Twentieth Annual Report* (Boston, 1835), 3–5.

7. *Second Annual Report of the Ladies' New-York City Anti-Slavery Society* (New York, 1837), 12. On abolitionist fund-raising in general, see Julie Roy Jeffrey, *The Great Silent Army of Abolitionism: Ordinary Women in the Antislavery Movement* (Chapel Hill: University of North Carolina Press, 1998), 85–93.

8. Corban Society Records, September 26, 1820, Congregational Library, Boston; Society for the Relief of Poor Widows with Small Children Minutes, April 8, 1807, New-York Historical Society, New York City. For similar comments, see Boston Widows Society Minutes, December 13, 1826, December 12, 1832, Schlesinger Library, Cambridge, Mass.

9. For examples of men being hired, see Boston Female Asylum Minutes, May 1805, July 1809; Fragment Society Minutes, October 1817.

10. Boston Female Asylum, *Thirty-Fourth Annual Report* (Boston, 1834); Orphan Asylum Society in the City of New York, *Twenty-Second Annual Report* (New York, 1828), 6; [A. F. Wales], *Reminiscences of the Boston Female Asylum* (Boston, 1844), 77–78; Corban Society Records, September 28, 1812; September 26, 1831; November 13, 1848; Female Association, Treasurer's Book, 1824–54; Female Association Accounts and Minutes, 1855–1905, Friends Historical Library, Swarthmore College, Swarthmore, Pa.

11. Boston Female Asylum Minutes, May 1833, September 1840.

12. Joanna Graham Bethune Diary, January 9, 1825, Bentley Library, University of Michigan; [Caroline Wells Healey Dall], *Alongside: Being Notes Suggested by "A New England Boyhood" of Doctor Edward Everett Hale* (Boston: Privately Printed, 1900), 87. Caroline collected for a North End child care center set up by evangelical Congregationalist women in the late 1830s; her donors were personal friends, members of Boston's wealthy mercantile and professional families.

13. The records of Philadelphia's Daughters of Africa (1821–29) present rare evidence of an African American women's mutual aid society at work. See Dorothy Sterling, ed., *We Are Your Sisters: Black Women in the Nineteenth Century* (New York: W. W. Norton, 1984), 105–7. Comparable records from New York and Boston have not survived.

14. Roman Catholic Female Charitable Society, Records, 1832–37, RG v. 3.1, Archives, Archdiocese of Boston. An annual subscription cost $2, but only 89 (28.6 percent) of the 311 subscribers paid the fee at one time. My thanks to Robert Johnson-Lally of the Archdiocesan Archives for making the subscription list available to me.

15. Mary Morgan Mason's description of the Female Assistance Society provides a good example of this process; see Elizabeth Mason North, *Consecrated Talents: or, The Life of Mrs. Mary W. Mason* (New York: Carleton and Lanahan, 1870), 59–60, 118–20. Teaching a school for the Quaker Female Association may have provided Mary Morgan

with a model to emulate; see Female Association Records, and *Annual Report of the Female Association for the Relief of the Sick Poor* . . . (New York, 1816), 3–6.

16. Fragment Society Minutes, October 10, 1870; Margery Drake Ross, "A Brief History of the Fragment Society, 1812–1862," and *Boston Sunday Herald* clipping, December 6, 1953, 2:2, Fragment Society Collection, Schlesinger Library, Cambridge, Mass.; Anne Firor Scott, *Natural Allies: Women's Associations in American History* (Urbana: University of Illinois Press, 1993), 27–36.

17. Dorothy C. Barck, ed., *Letters of John Pintard to His Daughter, Eliza Noel Pintard Servoss*, 4 vols. (New York: New-York Historical Society, 1936); Nevins and Thomas, *Diary of George Templeton Strong*, 102, 171, 252. On African American concerts, see the report on Boston teacher Susan Paul's "Juvenile Concert of Colored Children," *New York Evangelist*, February 25, 1837; and *The Liberator* 6 (August 27, 1836): 139. For examples of both male- and female-sponsored sermons and concerts designed to benefit New York's Roman Catholic Orphan Asylum, see *Truth Teller* 2 (June 24, 1826): 198; 3 (January 13, 1827): 14; 3 (August 4, 1827): 246; 4 (November 1, 1828): 351; 5 (June 27, 1829): 206; 8 (December 28, 1832): 422; 13 (January 14, 1837): 15; and *A Sermon, Preached in St. Patrick's Cathedral New-York, on Sunday, September 2, 1827, in Aid of the Friends of the Ladies' Roman Catholic Benevolent Society, by the Rev. Hatton Walsh, Pastor of St. Mary's Church* (New York: n.p., 1827). For Boston examples, benefiting the Roman Catholic Ladies Charitable Clothing Society of Holy Cross Cathedral, see *Jesuit, or Catholic Sentinel* 1 (February 27, 1830): 212; 1 (March 6, 1830): 215; 3 (December 16, 1831): 94. Robert R. Grimes provides information on sacred concert music during this era: *How Shall We Sing in a Foreign Land?: Music of Irish Catholic Immigrants in the Antebellum United States* (Notre Dame, Ind.: University of Notre Dame Press, 1996).

18. *Truth Teller* 10 (December 13, 1834): 399; 13 (December 16, 1837): 399; 15 (April 13, 1839): 119; 15 (September 31, 1838): 301; 15 (November 23, 1839): 372; Susan Hayes Ward, *The History of the Broadway Tabernacle Church from its Organization in 1840 to the Close of 1900* (New York: n.p., 1901); *The Colored American*, n.s., 1 (December 26, 1840; February 13, 1841).

19. Lee Chambers-Schiller, "'A Good Work among the People': The Political Culture of the Boston Antislavery Fair," in *The Abolitionist Sisterhood: Women's Political Culture in Antebellum America*, ed. Jean Fagan Yellin and John Van Horne (Ithaca: Cornell University Press, 1994), 249–74; Debra Gold Hansen, *Strained Sisterhood: Gender and Class in the Boston Female Anti-Slavery Society* (Amherst: University of Massachusetts Press, 1993), 124–39; Deborah Bingham Van Broekhoven, "The Political Economy of Massachusetts Women's Benevolent Fairs during the 1840s" (paper presented at the annual meeting of the Society for the History of the Early American Republic [SHEAR], Boston, 1994); Jeffrey, *Great Silent Army of Abolitionism*, 108–26; Jean Fagan Yellin, *Women and Sisters: Antislavery Women in American Culture* (New Haven: Yale University Press, 1989), 3–26; *Truth Teller* 15 (April 13, 1839): 119; (September 31, 1839): 301. See also *Truth Teller* 10 (December 20, 1834): 406.

20. Female Auxiliary Bible Society of Boston and Its Vicinity Minutes and Reports, March 26, 1828, Schlesinger Library, Cambridge, Mass.; Justin Edwards, *Joy in Heaven over the Penitent. A Sermon Delivered before the Penitent Females' Refuge Society*

(Boston, 1825), 24; *Report of the Committee of Advice for the Society for Employing the Female Poor* (Boston, 1824), 6; *New York Evening Post*, November 29, 1819. Many historians have contributed to our understanding of the developing consumer marketplace in the antebellum years, and the questions moralists raised about spending and gentility. See especially Richard Bushman, *The Refinement of America: Persons, Houses, Cities* (New York: Random House, 1992), 262–79; Daniel Horowitz, *The Morality of Spending: Attitudes toward the Consumer Society in America, 1875–1940* (Baltimore: Johns Hopkins University Press, 1985), 1–12; Karen Halttunen, *Confidence Men and Painted Women* (New Haven: Yale University Press, 1982), 56–65; and Kelly, *In the New England Fashion*, 214–41.

21. Hansen, *Strained Sisterhood*, 129, 133; *Truth Teller* 15 (April 13, 1839): 119. Recall also (from Chapter 3) the 1860 fair at which "some of the colored friends" of the New York Colored Orphan Asylum, including Charlotte Burroughs Ray, raised $1,100, donating it to the white women who ran the asylum; *Weekly Anglo-African* 1 (June 23, 1860).

22. Recall from Chapter 3 Joanna Bethune's belief in plain living in order to give money to benevolent causes. Describing Joanna's home décor, her grandson, Divie Bethune McCartee, emphasized prints depicting missionaries arriving in Tahiti, Africa, and India, and bookshelves filled with missionaries' memoirs and religious pamphlets. Robert E. Speer, ed., *A Missionary Pioneer in the Far East: A Memorial of Divie Bethune McCartee* (New York: Fleming H. Revell Co., 1922), 27–29. See also Daniel Walker Howe, "Protestantism, Voluntarism, and Personal Identity in Antebellum America," in *New Directions in American Religious History*, ed. Harry Stout and D. G. Hart (New York: Oxford University Press, 1997), 206–35.

23. Boston Female Moral Reform Society, *Third Annual Report* (Boston, 1838), 12; Hansen, *Strained Sisterhood*, 126–36; Jeffrey, *Great Silent Army of Abolitionism*, 108–26; *Weekly Anglo-African* 1 (June 23, 1860); Boydston, *Home and Work*, 142–63. The members of a middle-class sewing circle in Worcester, Massachusetts, calculating the market value of their labors, found that hundreds of hours of labor had yielded them a mere thirteen dollars in profits. It did not occur to them, however, that their donations of time might undermine the earning potential of local seamstresses. Carolyn J. Lawes, *Women and Reform in a New England Community, 1815–1860* (Lexington: University of Kentucky Press, 2000), 64–65.

24. Orphan Asylum Society, *Thirtieth Annual Report*, quoted in Mrs. Jonathan Odell, *Origin and History of the Orphan Asylum Society in the City of New York, 1806–1896*, 2 vols. (New York: n.p., 1896), 1:191; *Minutes of the Common Council of the City of New York, 1784–1831*, 19 vols. (New York: City of New York, 1917), May 1814, 7:763–64. For another calculation of average benefits, see Widows' Society Minutes, December 17, 1836. On Beecher's ideas and influence, see Kathryn Kish Sklar, *Catharine Beecher: A Study in American Domesticity* (New Haven: Yale University Press, 1973), 156–63.

25. On paying male but not female collectors, see Boston Female Asylum Minutes, October, November 1802, July 1809; and Fragment Society Minutes, 1817. Male voluntary organization leaders collected subscriptions and donations gratis, too, but seldom by going from house to house; unlike collectors for women's groups, they could dun contributors at workplaces, churches, or organizational meetings. On occasion, men also hired male collectors; see *Truth Teller* 11 (March 21, 1835): 96.

26. For a precise description of financial practices, see *Constitution of the Widows' Society: Together with Some Account of the Institution . . .* (Boston, 1823), 7. For specific investment decisions, see Orphan Asylum Society, *Twelfth Annual Report* (New York, 1818), 6, and Association for the Relief of Respectable, Aged, Indigent Females, *Second Annual Report* (New York, 1815), 16. For an example of internal auditing, see New York Female Union Society for the Promotion of Sabbath Schools, *Third Annual Report* (New York, 1819), 31. See also Lori D. Ginzberg, *Women and the Work of Benevolence: Morality, Politics and Class in Nineteenth-Century America* (New Haven: Yale University Press, 1990), 36–66.

27. On Elizabeth Peck Perkins, see *Notable American Women* s.v. "Perkins, Elizabeth Peck"; and Carl Seaburg and Stanley Paterson, *Merchant Prince of Boston: Colonel T. H. Perkins, 1764–1854* (Cambridge: Harvard University Press, 1971), 16–19, 22–29. On Mary Chrystie, see Mary Chrystie Receipt Book, 1800–1806, New-York Historical Society, New York City; George Washington Bethune, *Memoirs of Mrs. Joanna Bethune* (New York: Harper and Brothers, 1863), 79–80; and *Longworth's . . . City Directory* (New York, 1800–1810). On Sarah Bane, see *Freedom's Journal*, March 7, 1829, and an abstract of her 1840 will in Ray C. Sawyer, comp., "Abstracts of Wills for New York County, New York, 1801–1856," 20 vols., typescript, New York Public Library, New York City. On Mary Bowers, see Louise Hall Tharp, *The Appletons of Beacon Hill* (Boston: Little, Brown, 1973), 66; Bowers was vice-president of the Female Auxiliary Bible Society, collector for the Society for Promoting Christianity among the Jews, president of the Female Tract Society, and president of the Corban Society; she died in 1832 at age 82. On Sarah Startin, see Odell, *Orphan Asylum Society*, 1:109–10; Regina Bechtle, S.C., and Judith Metz, S.C., eds., *Elizabeth Bayley Seton: Correspondence and Journals, 1793–1808*, vol. 1 of *Collected Writings* (Hyde Park, N.Y.: New City Press, 2000), 24, 437–38, and Sawyer, "Abstracts of Wills for New York County," 4:90. Startin helped support Elizabeth Seton financially, even after her conversion to Catholicism, though she cut her out of her will. On Eleanor Davis, see letters from Eleanor Davis to Benjamin West and others regarding financial affairs, 1798–1828, and Eleanor Davis Account Book, 1812–23, Caleb Davis Papers, Massachusetts Historical Society, Boston; and Susan Porter, "Benevolent Asylum—Image and Reality: The Care and Training of Female Orphans in Boston, 1800–1840" (Ph.D. diss., Boston University, 1984), 98. On women merchants of the 1760–1800 era, see Patricia Cleary, "'She Merchants' of Colonial America: Women and Commerce on the Eve of the American Revolution" (Ph.D. diss., Northwestern University, 1989). On Hannah Adams's famous and successful battle with Jedidiah Morse for textbook sales, see Richard J. Moss, "Republicanism, Liberalism, and Identity: The Case of Jedidiah Morse," *Essex Institute Historical Collections* 126 (October 1990): 224–26. On Susanna Rowson, see *Notable American Women* s.v. "Rowson, Susanna Haswell"; and Eve Kornfeld, "Women in Post-Revolutionary American Culture: Susanna Haswell Rowson's American Career, 1793–1824," *Journal of American Culture* 6 (Winter 1983–84): 56–62.

28. On Mary Webb, see Albert L. Vail, *Mary Webb and the Mother Society* (Philadelphia: American Baptist Publication Society, 1914). The Ball sisters ran a school for African American girls; their co-worker in the Boston Female Anti-Slavery Society,

Susan Paul, earned her salary at the African (or Smith) School; see Hansen, *Strained Sisterhood*, 76–77. On Mary Perry, see *The Articles of Faith and the Covenant of Park Street Church, Boston* (Boston, 1825), 16; and Widows' Society Minutes, March 3, 1819. New Yorker Mary Morgan Mason taught in several schools during her long benevolent career, beginning with the Quaker Female Association school in 1811; see North, *Consecrated Talents*, 37–38. On Elizabeth Jackson Riley (who was also a member of the Boston Female Anti-Slavery Society), see Carol Buchhalter Stapp, *Afro-Americans in Antebellum Boston: An Analysis of Probate Records* (New York: Garland, 1993), 350–64; and *Frederick Douglass's Paper* 8 (February 2, 1855): 2. On Mary Irena Treadwell Hubbard, see *New York Tribune*, January 12, 1883, 2. Catherine E. Kelly chronicles comparable shifts in rural women's earning patterns: *In the New England Fashion*, 35–47.

29. Starting in 1817, Boston's Widows' Society appointed an official auditor, the 30-year-old treasurer's brother; later auditors were managers' husbands: Widows' Society Minutes, 1817–23. Seamen's Aid Society, *Fourth Annual Report* (Boston, 1837), 17; Eleanor Davis Account Book, Caleb Davis Papers; Bethune Diary, October 3, December 28, 1824; January 9, 1825 (Divie Bethune died on September 18, 1824). Elizabeth Bayley Seton served as her husband's amanuensis in the 1790s; see Annabelle M. Melville, *Elizabeth Bayley Seton, 1774–1821* (New York: Charles Scribner's Sons, 1951), 28–30; and Bechtle and Metz, *Seton: Correspondence and Journals*, 195. Similarly, Hannah Murray, treasurer of the New York Infant School Society between 1827 and her death in 1836, and of the Female Bible Society between 1816 and 1834, was a skilled manager of her family inheritance; see Gardiner Spring, *A Pastor's Tribute to One of His Flock: The Memoirs of the Late Hannah L. Murray* (New York: Robert Carter & Brothers, 1849), 135–38. My argument here differs from that of Susan Branson, who sees women's "social and cultural activities" as "unconnected to the marketplace": "Women and the Family Economy in the Early Republic: The Case of Elizabeth Meredith," *Journal of the Early Republic* 16 (Spring 1996): 71; Kelly, *In the New England Fashion*, 15–17, refutes that position convincingly.

30. Gerald T. White, *A History of the Massachusetts Hospital Life Insurance Company* (Cambridge: Harvard University Press, 1955), 23–62; in 1838, the Fragment Society had a permanent fund of $2,442, most of it in Massachusetts Hospital Life stock (*Annual Report*, 6); the same held true for the Widows' Society's $6,000 permanent fund (Widows' Society Minutes, 1839), and the Female Asylum's $65,000+ permanent fund; Boston Female Asylum, *Thirty-Fourth Annual Report* (Boston, 1834).

31. Peter Dobkin Hall, "What the Merchants Did with Their Money: Charitable and Testamentary Trusts in Massachusetts, 1780–1880," in *Entrepreneurs: The Boston Business Community, 1700–1850*, ed. Conrad Edick Wright and Katheryn P. Viens (Boston: Massachusetts Historical Society, 1997), 384; Larry Ceplair, ed., *The Public Years of Sarah and Angelina Grimké: Selected Writings, 1835–1839* (New York: Columbia University Press, 1989), 117; Alan L. Olmstead, *New York City Mutual Savings Banks, 1819–1861* (Chapel Hill: University of North Carolina Press, 1976), 99; Howard Bodenhorn, *A History of Banking in Antebellum America: Financial Markets and Economic Development in an Era of Nation-Building* (New York: Cambridge University Press, 2000), 84–118. On New Yorkers' ties to the cotton economy, see Albion, *The Rise of*

New York Port, 95–121. On the rental market and the rise of manufacturing, see Stansell, *City of Women*, 46–52; and Blackmar, *Manhattan for Rent*, 104–6. See also Dalzell, *Enterprising Elite*, 113–63.

32. Hall, "What the Merchants Did with Their Money," 365; Hall, *The Organization of American Society, 1700–1900: Private Institutions, Elites, and American Nationality* (New York: New York University Press, 1982), 122–24; William H. Pease and Jane Pease, *The Web of Progress: Private Values and Public Styles in Boston and Charleston, 1828–1843* (New York: Oxford University Press, 1985), 20–22, 121–23. It is perhaps worth noting that although John Jacob Astor donated generous amounts to certain women's charities, neither his wife nor his daughters gave any time to women's organizations.

33. Jane H. Pease and William H. Pease, *Ladies, Women, and Wenches: Choice and Constraint in Antebellum Charleston and Boston* (Chapel Hill: University of North Carolina Press, 1990), 127–29; Gertrude Meredith, *The Descendants of Hugh Amory, 1605–1805* (London: n.p., 1901), genealogical chart; Cora Codman Wolcott, *The Codmans of Charlestown and Boston* (Brookline, Mass.: n.p., 1930), 21. Ann McLean remarried in 1830, to William Lee, and died in 1834; Catherine Amory Codman, widowed in 1803, derived "$3000 per annum" from John Codman's $100,000 estate; Catherine's daughters, Catherine M. and Mary Ann, married the wealthy merchants, John R. Hurd and William C. Ropes. Jane Austen, *Sense and Sensibility* (1811; reprint, Toronto: Ryerson Press, 1965), 13. Spring, *A Pastor's Tribute to One of His Flock*, 138. Well-off Catholic women who took the veil at Elizabeth Seton's Maryland convent were similarly knowledgeable about family inheritances; they retained "the right of disposing of their patrimony, or of any legacy that may fall to them in favor of their family." See *Jesuit, or Catholic Sentinel* 1 (November 28, 1829): 100. See also Hall, "What the Merchants Did with Their Money," 380–83; Ronald H. Story, *The Forging of an Aristocracy: Harvard and the Boston Upper Class, 1800–1870* (Middletown, Conn.: Wesleyan University Press, 1980), 10–14; and Edward Pessen, *Riches, Class, and Power before the Civil War* (Lexington, Mass.: D. C. Heath, 1973), 251–80.

34. Pease and Pease, *Web of Progress*, 123–24; Spring, *Pastor's Tribute to One of His Flock*, 138–40, 147; [Wales], *Reminiscences of the Boston Female Asylum*, 77–78; Joanna H. Mathews, *A Short History of the Orphan Asylum Society in the City of New York* (New York: Anson D. F. Randolph, 1893), 21–61; Orphan Asylum Society Sixth Annual Report, quoted in Odell, *Orphan Asylum Society*, 1:56–57; Fifteenth Report, 1822, 1:109–10; Sawyer, "Abstracts of Wills for New York County," 4:90; Barck, *Letters of John Pintard to His Daughter*, 2:126–28.

35. See Chapter 2 for a discussion of the move to advisory committees; see Table A.9 for a list of advisory boards. *Freedom's Journal*, February 1, 1828; Walsh, *Sisters of Charity*, 82; *Report of the Committee of Advice of the Society for Employing the Female Poor* (Boston, 1823), 1; [John Gallison, Esq.], *Explanation of the Views of the Society for Employing the Female Poor* (Boston, 1824), 2; Nathan M. Kaganoff, "Organized Jewish Welfare Activity in New York City (1848–1860)," *American Jewish Historical Quarterly* 56 (1966): 33; Boston Children's Friend Society, *First Annual Report* (Boston, 1834), 2, 9; *Circular of the Boston Children's Friend Society* (Boston, 1837), 5–11; *Annual Report of the Bethesda Society, November 15, 1854* (Boston, 1854), 3; Mrs. S. R. I. Bennett, *Woman's Work among the Lowly: Memorial Volume of the First Forty Years of the Amer-*

ican Female Guardian Society and Home for the Friendless (New York: American Female Guardian Society, 1877), xi–xii. The Bethesda Society was the new name for the Penitent Females' Refuge, Ladies Auxiliary, chosen when the women incorporated the society in 1854. On married women's property acts, see Norma Basch, *In The Eyes of the Law: Women, Marriage, and Property in Nineteenth Century New York* (Ithaca: Cornell University Press, 1982).

36. Olmstead, *New York City Mutual Savings Banks*, 21–27; Susan Yohn, "They Hated Me on Spec: Women and Investment" (paper presented at History Workshop in Technology, Society, and Culture, University of Delaware, April 4, 2000). Bank directors were unpaid volunteers, but one of their number generally served as cashier, a paid position; see Henry W. Domett, *A History of the Bank of New York, 1784–1884* (New York: n.p., 1884), 12. Gerda Lerner's 1969 article on how professionalization affected women's economic opportunities remains trenchant: "The Lady and the Mill Girl: Changes in the Status of Women in the Age of Jackson," in *The Majority Finds Its Past: Placing Women in History* (New York: Oxford University Press, 1979), 15–30.

37. See Ginzberg, *Women and the Work of Benevolence*, 53–58. Bostonians Mary and Isaac Bowers, who ran a shop on Cornhill, provided goods and services to several local organizations, including those that Mary helped lead. While she was president of the Corban Society from 1811 until 1835, for example, Mary's shop was the source for much of the cloth the women needed. Similarly, while she was its vice-president from 1814 until 1837, the Female Bible Society found it convenient to have Mary receive Bibles mailed from New York at her store. During these years, Mary also collected subscriptions for the Female Society for Promoting Christianity among the Jews, and the Fragment Society. She died in 1839 at age 82. Information on Mary Bowers can be found in organizational reports, Boston city directories, and Tharp, *Appleton*, 66.

38. Association for the Relief of Respectable, Aged, Indigent Females Minutes, September 29, 1814, February 23, December 5, 1815, New-York Historical Society, New York City; Fragment Society Minutes, October 1815, October 1819; *Circular, Act of Incorporation, Constitution, Government, and By-Laws of the Boston Children's Friend Society. Organized December 4, 1833* (Boston, 1837), 13–15; "Constitution of the Afric-American Female Intelligence Society," *The Liberator* 2 (January 7, 1832): 2.

39. *Constitution of the Boston Fatherless and Widows Society, Instituted 1817, Including the Report for 1827* (Boston, 1827), 6; Society for the Relief of Poor Widows with Small Children Minutes, November 8, 1809; November 18, 1819; November 16, 1820, New-York Historical Society, New York City; Fragment Society Minutes, October 11, 1824. See also *Ninth Annual Report of the Boston Female Auxiliary Bible Society* (Boston, 1823), 4.

40. Association for the Relief of Respectable, Aged, Indigent Females, *Constitution* (New York, 1814), 4; Society for the Relief of Poor Widows with Small Children Minutes, February 14, 1806, February 3, March 4, 1812, November 21, 1822, November 23, 1823; *An Account of the Boston Female Asylum* (Boston, 1803), 19; Porter, "Benevolent Asylum," 108–9; *The Constitution of the Fragment Society* . . . (Boston, 1816), 6; *The Liberator*, 2 (January 7, 1832): 2; Constitution of the Abyssinian Benevolent Daughters of Esther Association, quoted in Daniel Perlman, "Organizations of the Free Negro in New York City, 1800–1860," *Journal of Negro History* 56 (July 1971): 187; Asylum for

Lying-In Women, Visiting Committee Minutes, May 13, 1824, New York Weill Cornell Medical Center Archives, New York City; Widows' Society Minutes, December 17, 1836, Schlesinger Library, Cambridge, Mass. See also Stansell, *City of Women*, 71–74.

41. Association for the Relief of Respectable, Aged, Indigent Females, *Fifteenth Annual Report* (New York, 1828), 6; Female Missionary Society for the Poor of the City of New York and Its Vicinity, *Second Anniversary Report* (New York, 1818), 6; Dorothy Sterling, ed., *Turning the World Upside Down: The First Anti-Slavery Convention of American Women, 1837* (New York: Feminist Press, 1987), 14; and *Proceedings of the Third Anti-Slavery Convention of American Women, Held in Philadelphia, May 1, 2 and 3rd, 1839* (Philadelphia, 1839), 10. For an example of managers canvassing themselves to help out in a financial squeeze, see New York Female Benevolent Society Minutes, June 9, 1840, Inwood House, New York City. On the phenomenon of "retrenchment" and its connections to evangelical zeal in the 1820s, see Paul Johnson and Sean Wilentz, *The Kingdom of Matthias* (New York: Oxford University Press, 1994).

42. Orphan Asylum Society, *First Annual Report* (New York, 1807), 8.

43. Raymond Mohl, *Poverty in New York, 1780–1825* (New York: Oxford University Press, 1971), 162–87, 241–48; Robert E. Cray, Jr., *Paupers and Poor Relief in New York City and Its Rural Environs, 1700–1830* (Philadelphia: Temple University Press, 1988), 168–94; Carroll Smith Rosenberg, *Religion and the Rise of the American City: The New York City Mission Movement, 1812–1870* (Ithaca: Cornell University Press, 1972), 51–64.

44. Mohl, *Poverty in New York*, 241–47; David M. Schneider, *The History of Public Welfare in New York State, 1609–1866* (Chicago: University of Chicago Press, 1938), 211–30; Josiah Quincy, *Municipal History of the Town and City of Boston . . .* (Boston: Charles C. Little and James Brown, 1852), 88–120; Quincy, Report on the Subject of Pauperism, *A Volume of Records relating to the Early History of Boston* (Boston: n.p., 1900), 184–93. See also Robert A. McCaughey, *Josiah Quincy, 1772–1864: The Last Federalist* (Cambridge: Harvard University Press, 1974), 89–95; and, for a similar trend in Philadelphia, Priscilla Ferguson Clement, *Welfare and the Poor in the Nineteenth-Century City: Philadelphia, 1800–1854* (Cranbury, N.J.: Associated University Presses, 1985), 50–80.

45. Society for the Relief of Poor Widows Minutes, November 18, 1819; November 27, 1823; November 17, 1825; November 18, 1821; March 23, 1840; November 27, 1834; November 22, 1824; December 31, 1827.

46. Fragment Society Minutes, October 11, 1819; October 10, 1825; October 8, 1827; *Report of the Committee of Advice of the Society for Employing the Female Poor*, 3; Boston Children's Friend Society, *Second Annual Report* (Boston, 1835), 4–5.

47. *Liberator* 2 (December 29, 1832): 207; *Colored American* 1 (September 23, 1837): 3; *Liberator* 2 (November 17, 1832): 183; *Truth Teller* 6 (April 3, 1830): 108–9; 15 (June 23, 1839): 196. See also Ronald D. Patkus, "A Community in Transition: Boston Catholics, 1815–1845" (Ph.D. diss., Boston College, 1997), 144–45.

48. Association for the Relief of Respectable, Aged, Indigent Females, *Twenty-First Annual Report* (New York, 1834), 3–4, and *Twenty-Second Annual Report* (New York, 1835), 7–8; "Journal of Visits to the Asylum, 1839–1843," Records of the Association for the Relief of Respectable, Aged, Indigent Females; J. F. Richmond, *New York and Its Institutions, 1607–1872* (New York: E. B. Treat, 1872), 321–23, 439–40; *Circular, Act of*

Incorporation, Constitution, Government, and By-Laws of the Boston Children's Friend Society . . . (Boston, 1834); Barbara Miel Hobson, *Uneasy Virtue: The Politics of Prostitution and the American Reform Tradition* (New York: Basic Books, 1987), 54–61. Although Lori Ginzberg dates institution-building to the 1840s and 1850s, I believe the shift began in the late 1830s in New York and Boston. See Ginzberg, *Women and the Work of Benevolence*, 119–126; and Anne M. Boylan, "Women in Groups: An Analysis of Women's Benevolent Organizations in New York and Boston, 1797–1840," *Journal of American History* 71 (December 1984): 508–9.

49. Fragment Society Minutes, October 1814, October, 1822; Society for the Relief of Poor Widows with Small Children Minutes, December 26, 1837; November 21, 28, 1814; January 28, 1828; November 17, 1825; Boston Female Auxiliary Bible Society, *Ninth Annual Report* (Boston, 1823), 7; Association for the Relief of Respectable, Aged, Indigent Females, *Twenty-Second Annual Report* (New York, 1835), 7–8, and *Seventeenth Annual Report* (New York, 1830), 5; Stansell, *City of Women*, 69–71. Sarah Deutsch's insightful discussion of changing urban geography in the post–Civil War era is relevant here, too; see *Women and the City: Gender, Space, and Power in Boston, 1870–1940* (New York: Oxford University Press, 2000), 76–77.

50. Association for the Relief of Respectable, Aged, Indigent Females Minutes, September 23, 1815; Association for the Relief of Respectable, Aged, Indigent Females, *Sixth Annual Report* (New York, 1819), 3; Society for the Relief of Poor Widows with Small Children Minutes, November 20, 1828; Fragment Society Minutes, October 13, 1845. On the Committee of Delegates, see Fragment Society Minutes, October 18, 1834; Widows' Society Minutes, February 7, March 5, September 3, December 1834; and *Report of the Committee of Delegates from the Benevolent Societies of Boston* (Boston, 1834); *Constitution and By-Laws of the Society for the Relief of Poor Widows with Small Children* (New York, 1857), 11.

51. *Third Annual Report of the Seamen's Aid Society* (Boston, 1836), 15. See also "The Economy of Charity," *Advocate of Moral Reform* 5 (August 15, 1839): 125. In this editorial, Sarah Towne Smith lifted the phrase "charity of wages" from Hale's Seamen's Aid Society reports. Elsewhere in the issue, she reprinted much of the society's annual report.

52. Society for the Relief of Poor Widows with Small Children Minutes, January 10, 1803; *Second Annual Report of the Seamen's Aid Society* (Boston, 1835), 5; *New York Evening Post*, October 27, 1814; July 5, 1815; November 29, 1819; *Report of the Committee of Advice for the Society for Employing the Female Poor* (Boston, 1824), 3, 5; *Third Annual Report of the Seamen's Aid Society* (Boston, 1836), 6; *First Annual Report of the Seamen's Aid Society* (Boston, 1834), 9; *Explanation of the Views of the Society for Employing the Female Poor* . . . (Boston, 1825), 2. The 1837 depression ended the earlier society's existence. See also Stansell, *City of Women*, 16–19.

53. Society for the Relief of Poor Widows with Small Children Minutes, November 10, 1813; November 16, 1837; *New York Evening Post*, November 29, 1819; *Minutes of the Common Council of the City of New York*, March 13, 1820, 11:22.

54. Society for the Relief of Poor Widows with Small Children Minutes, November 16, 1826; November 19, 1829; January 6, 1812. For good examples of how economic instability could directly affect middle-class women, see Hewitt, *Women's Activism and Social Change*, 4–30; and Lawes, *Women and Reform in a New England Community*, 83–112.

55. *Minutes of the Common Council of the City of New York*, October 20, 1817, 9:324; *Explanation of the Views of the Society for Employing the Female Poor . . . ,* 3; *Report of the Committee of Advice of the Society for Employing the Female Poor . . . ,* 3–4, 7; Dolores Janiewski, "Making Common Cause: The Needlewomen of New York, 1831–1869," *Signs* 1 (1976): 779–81; Stansell, *City of Women,* 130–37.

56. Seamen's Aid Society, *First Annual Report* (Boston, 1834), 9; *Third Annual Report* (Boston, 1836), 15; and *Seventh Annual Report* (Boston, 1840), 10–11; Peter Holloran, *Boston's Wayward Children: Social Services for Homeless Children, 1830–1930* (Boston: Northeastern University Press, 1989), 73; *Advocate of Moral Reform* 2 (September 15, 1836): 136; 2 (December 1, 1836): 171–72; 5 (August 15, 1839): 125; *Friend of Virtue* 7 (April 1844): 121–22, as cited in Hobson, *Uneasy Virtue,* 63; Boston Fatherless and Widows Society, *Twenty-Second Annual Report* (Boston, 1839), 2; Fragment Society Minutes, October 18, 1834.

57. Association for the Relief of Respectable, Aged, Indigent Females, *Twenty-Second Annual Report* (New York, 1835), 7; Society for the Relief of Poor Widows with Small Children Minutes, November 15, 1838; Boston Fatherless and Widows' Society, *Nineteenth Annual Report* (Boston, 1836), 8–10; *Fourth Annual Report of the Seamen's Aid Society* (Boston, 1837), 13.

58. Boston Fatherless and Widows Society, *Nineteenth Annual Report* (Boston, 1836), 8–10; Boston Widows Society Minutes, December 9, 1835; *Sixth Annual Report of the Seamen's Aid Society* (Boston, 1839), 8–10; *Seventh Annual Report* (1840), 9–13; *Eleventh Annual Report* (1844), 14; *Eighteenth Annual Report* (1851).

59. *Notable American Women,* s.v. "Hale, Sarah Josepha Buell." Hale's support for changes in married women's property rights were consistent with these positions. Indeed, in the *Fourth Annual Report of the Seamen's Aid Society* (Boston, 1837), 15–18, in discussing the plight of poor women, Hale expanded her remarks to denounce "the law which gives to the husband uncontrolled power over the personal property of his wife," and included the comment about wives having to "beg money" for charitable donations from husbands. As Norma Basch has astutely pointed out, Hale's main concern was individual women's personal and domestic influence, not the full political participation of women as a group. See "Equity vs. Equality: Emerging Concepts of Women's Political Status in the Age of Jackson," *Journal of the Early Republic* 3 (1983): 297–318.

60. Janiewski, "Needlewomen of New York," 781; Stansell, *City of Women,* 131–37, 144–49; Mari Jo Buhle, "Needlewomen and the Vicissitudes of Modern Life: A Study of Middle-Class Construction in the Antebellum Northeast," in *Visible Women: New Essays on American Activism* (Urbana: University of Illinois Press, 1993), 145–66; Rosalyn Baxandall, Linda Gordon, and Susan Reverby, "Boston Working Women Protest, 1869," *Signs* 1 (Spring 1976): 806.

61. Peter Mandler, "Poverty and Charity in the Nineteenth-Century Metropolis: An Introduction," in *The Uses of Charity: The Poor on Relief in the Nineteenth-Century Metropolis,* ed. Peter Mandler (Philadelphia: University of Pennsylvania Press, 1990), 1–37; Boston Female Asylum Minutes, September, October 1841, March 1842; Porter, "Benevolent Asylum," 269–74; Carol Lasser, "A 'Pleasingly Oppressive' Burden: The Transformation of Domestic Service and Female Charity in Salem, 1800–1840," *Essex Institute Historical Collections* 116 (1980): 156–75, and "The Domestic Balance of

Power: Relations between Mistress and Maid in Nineteenth-Century New England," *Labor History* 28 (Spring 1987): 5–22. See also Linda Gordon, "New Feminist Scholarship on the Welfare State," in *Women, The State, and Welfare*, ed. Linda Gordon (Madison: University of Wisconsin Press, 1990), 9–35.

62. Boston Female Asylum Minutes, September, October 1841; John J. McCusker, "How Much Is That in Real Money?: A Historical Price Index for Use as a Deflator of Money Values in the Economy of the United States," *Proceedings of the American Antiquarian Society* 101 (1992): 297–333. I am grateful to my colleague Farley Grubb for his advice on using historical price indexes.

Conclusion

1. Elizabeth Duncan Putnam, "Diary of Mrs. Joseph Duncan (Elizabeth Caldwell Smith)," *Journal of the Illinois State Historical Society* 21 (1928): 1–91. Elizabeth's mother was Hannah Caldwell Smith (later Rodgers); her aunts were Hannah Ker Van Wyck Caldwell and Maria Caldwell Robertson; her husband Joseph was first a member of the House of Representatives from Illinois (she met him in Washington, D.C.), then governor of Illinois. On Serena Downing, see *The North Star* (Rochester), April 26, 1850; and Henry B. Hoff, "Frans Abramse Van Salee and His Descendants: A Colonial Black Family in New York and New Jersey," *New York Genealogical and Biographical Record* 121 (October 1990): 209–10.

2. On these points, see especially Linda K. Kerber, "Separate Spheres, Female Worlds, Woman's Place: The Rhetoric of Women's History," *Journal of American History* 75 (June 1988): 9–39; and Amy Dru Stanley, "Home Life and the Morality of the Market," in *The Market Revolution in America: Social, Political, and Religious Expressions*, ed. Melvyn Stokes and Stephen Conway (Charlottesville: University of Virginia Press, 1996), 78–83.

3. Nancy A. Hewitt, *Women's Activism and Social Change: Rochester, New York, 1822–1872* (Ithaca: Cornell University Press, 1984), 96; Mary P. Ryan, *Cradle of the Middle Class: The Family in Utica, New York, 1790–1860* (New York: Cambridge University Press, 1981), 105–45; Carolyn Lawes, *Women and Reform in a New England Community, 1815–1860* (Lexington: University of Kentucky Press, 2000).

4. Barbara Bellows, *Benevolence among Slaveholders: Assisting the Poor in Charleston, 1670–1860* (Baton Rouge: Louisiana State University Press, 1993), 40–45; William H. Pease and Jane H. Pease, *Ladies, Women, and Wenches: Choice and Constraint in Antebellum Charleston and Boston* (Chapel Hill: University of North Carolina Press, 1990), 125–29; Suzanne Lebsock, *The Free Women of Petersburg: Status and Culture in a Southern Town, 1784–1860* (New York: W. W. Norton, 1984), 195–235; Elizabeth R. Varon, *We Mean to Be Counted: White Women and Politics in Antebellum Virginia* (Chapel Hill: University of North Carolina Press, 1998), 10–70, 120–23.

5. Carolyn Williams, "The Female Antislavery Movement: Fighting against Racial Prejudice and Promoting Women's Rights in Antebellum America," in *The Abolitionist Sisterhood: Women's Political Culture in Antebellum America*, ed. Jean Fagan Yellin and John Van Horne (Ithaca: Cornell University Press, 1994), 159–78; Nancy Isenberg, *Sex*

and Citizenship in Antebellum America (Chapel Hill: University of North Carolina Press, 1998), 88–95; David Brion Davis, *The Problem of Slavery in the Era of the American Revolution, 1770–1823* (Ithaca: Cornell University Press, 1975), 213–54.

6. Maureen Fitzgerald, "Irish-Catholic Nuns and the Development of New York City's Welfare System, 1840–1900" (Ph.D. diss., University of Wisconsin, 1992), 374–92; Carol K. Coburn and Martha Smith, *Spirited Lives: How Nuns Shaped Catholic Culture and American Life, 1836–1920* (Chapel Hill: University of North Carolina Press, 1999), 215–18. Catholic laywomen in Ireland had very similar experiences; not only were most laywomen's charities "given over to the care of nuns" after 1830, but even though Catholics were in the majority, "lay Catholic women . . . function[ed] in the charitable sphere . . . in a much less public fashion than women of other denominations." See Maria Luddy, *Women and Philanthropy in Nineteenth-Century Ireland* (Cambridge: Cambridge University Press, 1995), 34–35.

7. Debra Gold Hansen, *Strained Sisterhood: Gender and Class in the Boston Female Anti-Slavery Society* (Amherst: University of Massachusetts Press, 1993), 108–9, 140–56; Martha Violet Ball Will, January 8, 1895, Suffolk County Probate Court, 696:88, Boston, Mass. Nancy Hewitt has traced these changes in Rochester with great precision; see *Women's Activism and Social Change*, 122–91. See also Lawes, *Women and Reform*, 161–79.

8. Frances Willard and Mary Livermore, *A Woman of the Century* (New York: Charles Wills Moulton, 1893), 50; Barbara Leslie Epstein, *The Politics of Domesticity: Women, Evangelism, and Temperance in Nineteenth Century America* (Middletown, Conn.: Wesleyan University Press, 1981), 115–46; Evelyn Brooks Higginbotham, *Righteous Discontent: The Women's Movement in the Black Baptist Church, 1880–1920* (Cambridge: Harvard University Press, 1993), 69–73, 101–7; "Address of the Massachusetts Female Emancipation Society, to the Women of Massachusetts," April 1, 1840, Antislavery Collection, Boston Public Library.

9. Adelaide M. Cromwell, *The Other Brahmins* (Fayetteville: University of Arkansas Press, 1994), 224–25; Franklin A. Dorman, *Twenty Families of Color in Massachusetts, 1742–1998* (Boston: New England Historic Genealogical Society, 1998), 117–23; Paula Giddings, *When and Where I Enter: The Impact of Black Women on Race and Sex in America* (New York: Morrow, 1984).

10. Peggy Pascoe, *Relations of Rescue: The Search for Female Moral Authority in the American West, 1874–1939* (New York: Oxford University Press, 1990), 177–207; Sarah Deutsch, *Women and the City: Gender, Space, and Power in Boston, 1870–1940* (New York: Oxford University Press, 2000), 24; Regina Kunzel, "The Professionalization of Benevolence: Evangelicals and Social Workers in the Florence Crittenton Homes, 1915 to 1945," *Journal of Social History* 22 (Fall 1988): 21–43; Linda Gordon, "Black and White Visions of Welfare: Women's Welfare Activism, 1890–1945," *Journal of American History* 78 (September 1991): 559–90. See also Joanne J. Meyerowitz, *Women Adrift: Independent Wage Earners in Chicago, 1880–1930* (Chicago: University of Chicago Press, 1988), 43–55; Elizabeth Hayes Turner, *Women, Culture, and Community: Religion and Reform in Galveston, 1880–1920* (New York: Oxford University Press, 1997); Anastasia Sims, *The Power of Femininity in the New South: Women's Organizations and Politics in North Carolina, 1880–1930* (Columbia: University of South Carolina Press, 1997).

11. Robert Putnam, although conceding that community organizations are often "exclusionary along racial and gender lines" and wield a power that "may well widen class differences," nevertheless concludes that "the have-nots" in American society can wield influence through community associations of their own. Left unanalyzed is the question of how much influence an organization of "have-nots" can possibly wield. *Bowling Alone: The Collapse and Revival of American Community* (New York: Simon & Schuster, 2000), 358.

193, 218, 282 (n. 67). *See also* New York Female Moral Reform Society

American Female Moral Reform Society, 80, 161, 180. *See also* New York Female Moral Reform Society

American Revolution, 6, 15, 18, 21, 216

Anthon, Judith Hone, 70, 288 (n. 37)

Anti-Slavery Conventions of American Women, 36, 39, 46–47, 73, 83, 145, 161–63, 165, 169, 197

Antislavery societies: men's, 44; mixed-sex, 88; women's, 4, 36–37, 44, 45, 143, 163–64, 214–15, 282 (n. 4)

Appleton, Maria Theresa Gold, 151

Appleton, Nathan, 151

Associate Reformed Church, 299 (n. 35)

Association for the Benefit of Colored Orphans (New York), 32, 40, 58, 83, 130–32, 146, 149, 168–69, 175, 190

Association for the Relief of Respectable, Aged, Indigent Females (New York), 24, 26, 29, 57, 86, 153–54, 190, 195, 200

Astor, John Jacob, 108, 191, 322 (n. 32)

Asylum for Lying-In Women (New York), 33, 40, 45, 50, 55, 65, 68, 70, 76, 80, 86, 88, 147, 152, 200, 205

Bacon, Susannah, 27, 273 (n. 20)

Badger, Sophia Thompson Cross, 69

Ball, Lucy, 49, 185, 188, 215, 216

Ball, Martha, 49, 185, 188, 215–16, 218

Bane, Sarah, 171–72, 187

Baptists, 6, 7, 10, 18, 41, 50, 129

Beecher, Catharine, 162, 186

Bennett, Sarah R. Ingraham. *See* Ingraham, Sarah R.

Bethesda Society (Boston), 217. *See also* Penitent Females' Refuge Ladies Auxiliary

Bethune, Divie, 100, 103, 110–15 passim, 117–18

Bethune, George Washington, 110, 114, 115–18

Bethune, Isabella Graham. *See* Duffield, Isabella Graham Bethune

Bethune, Jessie. *See* McCartee, Jessie Bethune

Bethune, Joanna Graham, 38, 48, 71, 128, 130, 152, 179, 185, 189; biography of, 101–4, 110–18; conversion narrative of, 102–3, 112–13; marriage and child-bearing, 103, 110, 114; as organization leader, 101, 110–14; widowhood, 114–17, 130–31

Bird, Lucy Pico, 65

Bloch, Ruth, 7

Boston: changes in, 9–11, 32–33, 190–91, 198–99, 201, 202; churches in, 50–51

Boston Children's Friend Society, 33, 40, 58, 63, 64–65, 67, 82, 84, 171, 191–200 passim, 217

Boston Female Anti-Slavery Society, 32, 65; African American women in, 41, 74, 165, 216; and benevolent organizations, 46–47, 143, 215–16; class composition of, 49; and evangelical ideals of womanhood, 36–37, 165; fund-raising fairs of, 182–85; leaders' age and marital status, 56–58 passim, 72; and petitioning, 159–60; and split in 1840, 47, 51, 76, 165, 215

Boston Female Asylum, 24; beginnings of, 18–21; early history rewritten, 31, 84–85; finances of, 177–82, 189–96; incorporation of, 21; indenturing by, 84; later history of, 217; leaders' age and marital status, 52, 63–69 passim; leadership of, 39, 47–48, 53; leaders' religious leanings, 27, 273 (n. 20); leaders' use of orphanage, 85–87; meeting places of, 217 (n. 12); political activities of, 151, 155, 158; and publicity, 140–41; and public policy, 145–46; records of, 266 (n. 6); rules for clients, 83, 89, 209; use of familial imagery by, 78, 83

Boston Female Moral Reform Society, 49, 56, 63, 72, 75, 80, 165, 200, 205, 215–16, 218

Boston Female Society for Missionary

Purposes, 18, 19, 26, 39, 40, 41, 48, 58, 138, 140

Boston Infant School Society, 28, 32, 63, 66, 67

Bowdoin, Sarah, 48, 151

Bowers, Mary, 187–88, 323 (n. 37)

Brekus, Catherine, 303 (n. 56)

Brereton, Virginia, 303 (n. 56)

Brick Presbyterian Church (New York), 204

Budgets, organizational. *See* Economies; Fairs, fund-raising; Income of women's organizations; Investing by women's organizations

Caldwell, Hannah Ker Van Wyck, 25, 112, 138, 198, 305 (n. 8)

Caldwell, John E., 112

Campbell, Williamina (Lady Glenorchy), 102

Carey, Matthew, 204–5

Carney, Andrew, 205, 208

Carroll, Archbishop John, 108–9

Chapman, Maria Weston, 49, 74, 143, 163, 183, 185, 215

Charity, 18, 105, 110, 119–22; collective as opposed to individual, 1–2, 17–18, 20, 104, 135, 145, 151, 159–61, 172–73, 195–97, 212, 309 (n. 33); criticisms of, 198–99, 208; debates about, 146–48, 198–200, 202–9; purposes of, 208; uses of, 208–9

Charleston Female Domestic Missionary Society, 213

Chatham Street Chapel (New York), 44, 45, 50

Cheverus, Jean, 120

Childbearing: and organizational leadership, 70–71, 110

Chrystie, Adden Nicholson, 104

Chrystie, Frances Few, 104

Chrystie, Mary Weygand, 19, 104, 187

Churches: in Boston, 10; in New York, 10, 44–45. *See also* names of specific denominations

Civil society, 12–13, 269 (nn. 15, 16)

Clients, 24, 25, 82–89, 180, 183–84, 194–209, 292 (n. 65)

Clinton, DeWitt, 152, 154

Clinton, Maria Franklin, 152

Clouston, Lois, 48

Codman, Catherine Amory, 67, 191, 322 (n. 33)

Codman, Catherine M., 67–68, 69, 76, 322 (n. 33)

Codman, Mary Ann, 67–68, 322 (n. 33)

Codwise, Martha Livingston, 59

Coit, Lydia Howland, 40

Colonization societies, 114, 211, 213

Colored Female Charitable Society (Boston), 142

Colored Female Union Society (Boston), 39, 73, 188

Colored Ladies Literary Society (New York), 36, 41, 130

Colored Orphan Asylum (New York). *See* Association for the Benefit of Colored Orphans (New York)

Committee of Delegates from Benevolent Societies (Boston), 201

Common School Fund (New York), 155

Concerts, fund-raising, 182–83

Congregationalists, 10, 18, 25, 27, 32, 41, 50, 126, 162

Consumer goods: attitudes toward, 183–85, 195–97

Conventions, women's, 161–62

Conversion narratives, women's, 102–3, 124, 128, 296 (nn. 13, 15), 299 (n. 30), 303 (n. 56)

Cooper, Anna Paul, 51

Cooper, Margaret Phillips, 48

Cooper, Samuel Sutherland, 108, 118, 120

Corban Society (Boston), 25, 40, 65, 69, 139, 177, 188, 272 (n. 17)

Cornish, Samuel E., 126, 129, 133, 141, 142

Cott, Nancy, 3

Cox, Abby Ann Newbold, 44, 45–46, 50, 74

Cox, Abiah Cleveland, 46

Hamilton, Elizabeth Schuyler, 48, 104–5, 166–69, 314 (n. 63)
Hansen, Debra Gold, 47, 76, 165
Hearn, Catherine and Brissenta, 87
Hebrew Female Benevolent Society (New York), 24, 42
Heeney, Cornelius, 42, 108, 122
Hersh, Blanche Glassman, 3
Hewitt, Nancy, 3
Hilton, Lavinia Ames, 41, 216
Hobart, John Henry, 103–4, 105, 107, 192
Hoffman, Sarah Ogden, 48, 104, 109, 110–11
Holy Cross Church (Boston), 175
Home/work distinctions, 78, 85–90 passim, 193
House of Industry (New York), 24, 27, 33, 38, 43, 85, 112, 113, 140, 148, 149, 152, 155, 202–4
House of Refuge (New York), 150, 152
Huntington, Susan Mansfield, 63, 71–72, 288 (n. 40)
Hurd, Catherine Codman. *See* Codman, Catherine M.
Hyde, Julia Ely, 45, 70, 77

Income of women's organizations: from bequests, 192; from interest, 178; from sale of clients' work, 24, 183–84; from subscriptions, 177–79
Incorporation, 21, 43, 58, 151, 193, 272 (n. 14)
Indenture, 33, 81, 82–83, 84, 209
Infant schools, 32–33, 113–14, 146, 182
Infant School Society (Boston). *See* Boston Infant School Society
Infant School Society (New York), 32, 60, 66, 113–14, 152, 192
Influence, women's: ideas about, 136, 151, 152, 158, 162
Ingraham, Sarah R., 75, 76, 289 (n. 47)
Institutions: founding of, 1, 20, 33, 37, 85–88 passim, 111–12, 200
Investing by women's organizations, 19, 187–93

Ireland, 124, 328 (n. 6)
Irish: in Boston, 10, 180; in New York, 11, 108, 154, 156, 157–58
Isaacs, Magdalen Sidell, 278 (n. 46)
Ives, Lucia Jones, 90, 293 (n. 70)

Jackson, Betsey Lane, 58, 69
Jackson, Harriet, 72
Jews, 10–11, 24, 213; Jewish women's organizations, 34, 42, 193
John Street Methodist Episcopal Church (New York), 40, 128
Juster, Susan, 7, 299 (n. 30), 303 (n. 56)
"Juvenile" societies, 29, 44, 274 (n. 26)

Kerber, Linda K., 6
King, Hetty Low, 141, 306 (n. 13)
Kohlmann, Anthony, 120

Labor, women's: in family economies, 19, 50–51, 74, 75–76, 117–18, 172, 179, 187–88; in institutions, 19, 24, 175, 183–84, 202–3; payment for, 20, 179, 202–3; sex differential in payment for, 203–6; unpaid, 185–86, 187–89, 197–98, 319 (n. 23); value of, 206–7, 208. *See also* Economies; Working women
Ladies Association of the Roman Catholic Orphan Asylum (New York), 25, 42, 50, 61, 62, 119, 156, 215
Ladies Charitable Society, St. Mary's Church (New York), 61
Ladies Clothing Society, Transfiguration Church (New York), 61
Ladies Depository Association (New York), 275 (n. 31)
Ladies' New York City Anti-Slavery Society, 39, 46, 63, 73, 83, 131, 164–65, 171, 175–76
Lane, Betsey. *See* Jackson, Betsey Lane
Lang, Abigail ("Nabby"), 85, 87
Lasala, Ann Louisa Lametti, 50
Lasala, Charlotte Crone, 50, 122
Lasala family, 50–51

Law and legal system, 57–58, 59, 190–91. *See also* Incorporation

Leadership: and life-course stage, 63–76; and marital status, 55–64; patterns of, 38–42, 95–96; and transition to marriage, 68–70

Lebsock, Suzanne, 3, 114

Lee, Ann Amory McLean, 38, 65, 66–67, 76, 191–92, 322 (n. 33)

Lerow, Deborah Torrey, 171

Life course: and organizational leadership, 54–55, 63–76, 109–14, 125, 130, 133

Lincoln, Eliza Frothingham, 85, 292 (n. 63)

Lincoln, Sarah Cushing, 48

Lindsay, Sarah, 111

Literacy, women's, 126

Literary societies, 35–36

Livingston family, 51

Lobbying by women, 161–62, 169. *See also* Politics

Lockwood, Julia Gouge, 171

Lowell, Rebecca Amory, 67, 191

Ludlow, Abby Welles (Wills), 46

Ludlow, Henry G., 46

Lynch, Dominick, 108, 156

Magdalen Society (New York), 112

Malcom, Lydia Morris Shields, 28

Mandler, Peter, 208

Mannard, Joseph, 61

Marital titles: use of, by women leaders, 72–73

Marriage: African American women and, 55, 73–74, 89–90, 130–31; legal constraints of, 57–59; organizational leadership and, 55–64, 68–73, 125, 130; remarriage, 130–31; Roman Catholic women and, 60–62, 119–20, 123–24

Martha Washington Temperance Societies, 34

Martyn, Sarah Towne Smith. *See* Smith, Sarah Towne

Marvin, Augusta Willcox, 84

Mason, John, 99

Mason, John Mitchell, 99, 103, 112

Mason, Mary Morgan: biography of, 124–33; memorial to, 133; as organization leader, 128, 130, 132, 147; teaching career of, 125, 128, 130, 317 (n. 15), 321 (n. 28)

Mason, Mary Vans, 48

Massachusetts Female Emancipation Society, 51

Massachusetts General Hospital, 191–92

Massachusetts Hospital Life Insurance Company, 189–90, 191

Maternal associations, 25, 29, 55, 66, 77, 211, 213

May, Abigail, 87

McCartee, Divie Bethune, 117, 319 (n. 22)

McCartee, Jessie Bethune, 110, 114, 115–18 passim

McCartee, Robert, 114, 115, 118

McDowall, John, 45

McLean, Ann Amory. *See* Lee, Ann Amory McLean

McLean, John, 191

Men: as advisers to women's organizations, 88–89, 129, 151, 188–89, 192–93; as collectors, 319 (n. 25); as donors, 191–92; as treasurers, 192; as trustees, 193

Men's organizations, 12, 18, 42, 150, 272 (n. 13)

Meriam, Eliza Jackson, 46–47, 280 (n. 53)

Methodists, 6, 10, 24, 40, 50, 124, 128–29, 175

Mitchell, Louise, 204, 208, 276 (n. 33), 291 (n. 61), 307 (n. 16)

Montgomery, Janet Livingston, 297 (n. 16)

Montgomery, Maria Nicholson, 104

Mooney, Maria Theresa, 51

Moore, Harriet, 69

Moral reform societies, 47, 50, 72–76,

159; criticism of, 162; individual, 159, 166–68; women's organizations and, 145, 151, 152–55, 159–61, 166, 213. *See also* Lobbying by women; Politics

Phillis Wheatley Homes, 90

Politics: and partisanship, 162–63, 169; and political change, 135–37, 156–58; women's political culture and, 136–37, 145–46, 150–55, 158–62. *See also* Lobbying by women; Petitions and petitioning

Poor relief, 27, 195–96, 198–99

Porter, Susan, 273 (n. 20)

Post, Mary Bayley, 107

Post, Theodosia Steele, 38

Poverty: beliefs about, 146–48, 197–206; remedies for, 194–96, 202–6; "respectable" poverty vs. indigence, 146–47, 194, 196–98, 200, 202–3. *See also* Poor relief; Wages, women's; Working women

Presbyterians, 10, 44–45, 50, 86, 99, 114, 117, 175

Prescott, Catherine Hickling, 53–54, 282 (n. 1)

Prices: as subject of public discussion, 205–8

Printing and print culture, 18, 19, 21, 112, 118, 138–42, 144–45

Print revolution, 140–41

Prior, Margaret Barrett Allen, 75, 76, 289 (n. 47), 292 (n. 67)

Prostitution and prostitution reformers, 26, 36, 45, 55–56, 61, 75, 81, 126, 146, 149

Protestant Episcopal Tract Society (New York), 26

Protestant Half-Orphan Asylum (New York), 33, 40, 193, 200

Public funds: controversies over, 155–58

Publicity: women's organizations and, 36, 138–45

Public policy: women's organizations and, 145–52, 158–66

Public/private distinction, 5, 12, 78, 83–84, 87–88, 91–93, 136–37, 147–48, 151, 158, 162–64, 214–15

Public School Fund (New York), 111, 155–58

Public School Society (New York), 113, 152, 155–57

Public services: women's organizations providing, 147–51

Public sphere: women's organizations and, 137–55

Publishing. *See* Printing and print culture

Putnam, Jane Clark, 41

Putnam, Robert, 269 (n. 16), 329 (n. 11)

Quakers and Quakerism, 10, 18, 19, 26, 41, 46, 50, 72, 128, 175, 214, 283 (nn. 7, 9)

Quincy, Josiah, 198

Race and racism, 35, 41, 43–44, 49, 71, 73, 90, 131–33, 141–43, 216. *See also* African American women; Women's organizations: African American; Women's organizations: white

Ray, Charles B., 126, 132

Ray, Charlotte Burroughs, 132, 319 (n. 21)

Ray, Henrietta Green Regulus: biography of, 124–33; memorial to, 133; as organization leader, 4, 129–30, 141; religious views of, 129

Reed, Esther DeBerdt, 21, 274 (n. 28)

Reed, Julia, 161

Regulus, Henrietta Green. *See* Ray, Henrietta Green Regulus

Regulus, Laurent (Lawrence), 125

Religion: and abolitionism, 47–49; and ideals of womanhood, 16, 52, 123–24, 142; and organizational profiles, 47, 49–51; and women's rights, 164–65, 199–201. *See also names of individual denominations*

Rents: as subject of public discussion, 205–6

Republican motherhood, ideology of, 6–8, 16, 27, 29–30, 48, 136, 166–68
"Retrenchment," 197
Reynolds, Elizabeth Carter, 66
Rhinelander, John T., 157–58
Riley, Elizabeth Jackson, 38–39, 73–74, 188, 289 (n. 44)
Robertson, Elizabeth, 70–71, 288 (n. 38)
Robinson, Catherine, 29
Robinson, Frances Duer, 29
Rodgers, Helen Robertson, 70, 77
Rogers, Augusta Temple Winthrop, 68–69, 287 (n. 33)
Roman Catholic Asylum for the Children of Widows and Widowers (New York), 33, 42, 43, 50, 61, 80, 154–55, 157, 182, 193, 215, 301 (n. 43)
Roman Catholic Female Charitable Society (Boston), 42, 62, 180, 317 (n. 14)
Roman Catholic Female Clothing Society (Boston), 57
Roman Catholic Orphan Asylum (New York), 42, 84, 119, 156–58, 175. *See also* Ladies Association of the Roman Catholic Orphan Asylum (New York)
Roman Catholics, 6, 11, 62, 86, 106–7; attitudes toward marriage and singleness, 60–62, 63–64, 119–21; fund-raising, 179–80, 182–83; ideals of womanhood, 123–24; laywomen's benevolent organizations, 25, 34, 42–43, 50–51, 61, 119–20, 154–55, 179–80, 182, 188, 213, 215, 278 (n. 47); nuns, 42, 43, 60–61, 63–64, 80, 119–22, 215, 217, 279 (n. 48), 285 (n. 18), 286 (n. 25), 301 (nn. 44, 46); Protestants' assistance to, 156–67, 175, 182, 199–200; Protestants' hostility to, 60–61, 107, 199
Romeyn, John B., 114
Rowson, Susanna Haswell, 59, 100, 145, 187–88
Ryan, Mary P., 4, 149

Safford, Ann Eliza Bigelow Turner, 40, 277 (n. 43)

Saidler, Eliza Craig, 107, 111
St. James's Roman Catholic Church (New York), 182
St. Joseph's Industrial Home (New York), 215
St. Mary's Church (New York), 161
St. Patrick's Cathedral (New York), 156, 175, 182, 311 (n. 43)
St. Peter's Roman Catholic Church (New York), 107–8, 156, 182–85, 311 (n. 43)
St. Philip's Episcopal Church (New York), 10, 108
St. Vincent de Paul Society (Boston), 61
Samaritan Asylum for Colored Children (Boston), 32, 37, 168, 175
Scarlett, Margaret, 41, 49
Schools, 56, 98, 119; funding of, 155–58
Scotch Presbyterian Church (New York), 103–4, 114
Scotland and Scots, 97–99, 101, 104; Scotch-Irish, 10
Scott, Julia Sitgreaves, 120
Seamen's Aid Society (Boston), 33, 144, 146, 149, 162, 182, 205–8. *See also* Hale, Sarah Josepha
Second Great Awakening, 6
Seton, Anna Maria, 106
Seton, Catherine, 121, 122
Seton, Cecilia, 108, 119
Seton, Elizabeth Bayley, 111, 171, 188; biography of, 101–9, 118–24; as Episcopalian, 105–7; memorials to, 122–24; as organization leader, 104, 106–7; as Roman Catholic, 106–9, 118–22; Sisters of Charity and, 108–9, 119–24
Seton, Harriet, 108
Seton, Rebecca (1780–1804), 103, 106
Seton, William, 122, 124
Seton, William Magee, 102–4, 106
Settlement houses, 90, 216
Sewing, 57, 146, 206; as young women's occupation, 57
Sewing societies, women's, 29, 129–30, 139, 211

Shearith Israel Congregation (New York), 10, 42
Shotwell, Anna, 58, 186
Shotwell, Mary, 58
Singleness: and organizational leadership, 55–64, 119–20, 163, 286 (n. 26); Roman Catholic laywomen and, 61–62
Sisterhood, ideal of, 80, 90, 131
Sisters of Charity of St. Joseph, 109, 120–22
Sisters of Mercy (New York), 215
Slavery, 35, 36, 45, 62, 80, 161, 294 (n. 2), 302 (n. 52)
Smith, Isabella Graham, 103
Smith, Mary Lynde, 48
Smith, Sarah Towne, 75, 80, 163, 164, 289 (n. 47)
Social class: and organizational membership, 17, 37–38, 41, 47–50, 104–5, 117–18, 121, 133, 185; process of defining, 88, 136
Social work, 90, 217
Society for Employing the Female Poor (Boston), 24, 27, 33, 183, 193, 202–4 passim
Society for the Promotion of Christianity among the Jews (Boston), 25, 29, 40, 56, 59, 69, 141, 176
Society for the Relief of Half-Orphan and Destitute Children (New York). *See* Protestant Half-Orphan Asylum (New York)
Society for the Relief of Poor Widows with Small Children (New York), 62, 109–10, 120, 121, 171; beginnings of, 18–20, 96–97, 100–101; bequests to, 192; clients of, 24, 198–99; criticism of, 21; early history rewritten, 31; and evangelical "turn," 25–26; fund-raising by, 148, 177; later history of, 217; leaders' age and marital status, 60, 70–71; leaders' class backgrounds, 104–5, 187; leadership networks in, 38–40, 43; meeting places of, 271 (n. 12); political activities of, 150, 152, 155, 158; and pub-lic policy, 195, 201–2, 205; rules for clients, 81, 196
Society for the Relief of Worthy, Aged, Indigent Colored Persons (New York), 200
Society of Friends. *See* Quakers and Quakerism
South, the: women's organizations in, 213–14
Southwick, Sarah, 72
Spending: attitudes toward, 184–85; by women's organizations, 194–98
Spheres, ideology of, 6–7, 16–17, 59, 142; and beginnings of women's organizations, 5, 19–20, 31, 54, 59, 71–72, 187, 212, 214–15; debates over, in 1830s, 37, 163–64, 214–15; dissemination of, 51–52; and financial management, 192–93; and political influence, 152, 212; and race, 142–43; and religion, 16, 41–42, 60–61, 119–20; and social class, 17; and womanhood, 15, 37
Spring, Gardiner, 60
Stansell, Christine, 201
Startin, Sarah Clarke, 48, 104, 107, 111, 171, 187–88, 192, 193
Stewart, Maria W., 199
Stillman, Hannah Morgan, 20, 29, 47, 79, 87, 138, 145
Storrs, Harriet Moore. *See* Moore, Harriet
Strong, Ann Bradley, 153
Strong, George Templeton, 166–68, 175, 182
Strong, Roger, 153

Tappan, Arthur, 44, 117
Tappan, Frances Antill, 294 (n. 5), 315 (n. 64)
Tappan, Lewis, 44, 117
Tappan Female Benevolent Society (New York), 182
Temperance, 34, 41, 214, 216
Temporary Home for Fallen Women (Boston), 200

religious divisions among, 38–39, 43–44, 47, 72–76; reform-oriented, 17, 36–37, 39, 44–47, 49, 72–76, 137; Roman Catholic, 33, 34, 188; social class and, 47–50, 72–75, 104–5, 136, 142–43; southern white women's, 213–14; waves of founding, 17–21, 24–28, 32–37; white, 4, 13, 39, 55, 146, 212; working-class white, 4
"Workfare," 194, 202
Working women: and women's organizations, 33–35, 59, 62, 75, 76, 86, 90, 130, 187–88, 194, 206–9

Work programs: workrooms and houses of industry, 33, 85–86, 147–50, 194, 202–4
Wright, Frances, and "Fanny Wrightism," 9, 45, 46, 164
Wyckoff, Mary Robertson, 70

Young Women's Christian Association, 2, 90

Zaeske, Susan, 313 (n. 51)